MODERN MATERIAL CULTURE
The Archaeology of Us

This is a volume in

Studies in Archaeology

A complete list of titles in this series appears at the end of this volume.

ODERN MATERIAL CULTURE
The Archaeology of Us

Edited by

Richard A. Gould
Department of Anthropology
University of Hawaii at Manoa
Honolulu, Hawaii

Michael B. Schiffer
Department of Anthropology
University of Arizona
Tucson, Arizona

ACADEMIC PRESS
A Subsidiary of Harcourt Brace Jovanovich, Publishers
New York   London   Toronto   Sydney   San Francisco

ACADEMIC PRESS, INC.
111 Fifth Avenue, New York, New York 10003

United Kingdom Edition published by
ACADEMIC PRESS, INC. (LONDON) LTD.
24/28 Oval Road, London NW1 7DX

Library of Congress Cataloging in Publication Data
Main entry under title:

Modern material culture: The Archaeology of Us.

Studies in archaeology
Bibliography: p.
Includes index.
1. United States--Antiquities--Addresses, essays,
lectures. 2. Archaeology--Philosophy--Addresses,
essays, lectures. 3. Archaeology--Methodology--
Addresses, essays, lectures. I. Gould, Richard A.
II. Schiffer, Michael B. III. Series.
E159.5.A72   930.1'028   80-2332
ISBN 0-12-293580-2

PRINTED IN THE UNITED STATES OF AMERICA

81 82 83 84   9 8 7 6 5 4 3 2 1

Contents

3

The Use of Material Culture
in Diachronic Anthropology   31
Jeffrey L. Eighmy

4

A Manifesto for Modern Material-Culture Studies   51
William L. Rathje

EARLY AND LATE AMERICANA

5

Waste Not, Want Not: An Ethnoarchaeological
Study of Reuse in Tucson, Arizona   67
Michael B. Schiffer, Theodore E. Downing,
and Michael McCarthy

6

Graffiti and Racial Insults: The Archaeology
of Ethnic Relations in Hawaii   87
C. Fred Blake

7
A Herbalist's Shop in Honolulu:
Traditional Merchandising in a Modern Setting   101
Jane Allen-Wheeler

8
Ideology and Material Culture   113
David J. Meltzer

9
Don't Fence Me In   127
Patricia Price-Beggerly

10
The Cemetery and Culture Change:
Archaeological Focus
and Ethnographic Perspective   137
Edwin S. Dethlefsen

11
Pennies from Denver   161
Nan A. Rothschild

12
The Raw and the Cooked:
The Material Culture of a Modern Supermarket   183
Joyce E. Bath

13
The Community Store: A Dispersal Center
for Material Goods in Rural America   197
Paul L. Cleghorn

EXPERIMENTAL APPROACHES

List of Contributors

Numbers in parentheses indicate the pages on which the authors' contributions begin.

Jane Allen-Wheeler (101), Department of Anthropology, University at Hawaii at Manoa, Honolulu, Hawaii 96822

Charles M. Baker (247),[1] Department of Sociology and Anthropology, Western Carolina University, Cullowhee, North Carolina 28723

Joyce E. Bath (183), Department of Anthropology, University of Hawaii at Manoa, Honolulu, Hawaii 96822

C. Fred Blake (87), Department of Anthropology, University of Hawaii at Manoa, Honolulu, Hawaii 96822

Cheryl P. Claassen (239), Department of Anthropology, Peabody Museum, Harvard University, Cambridge, Massachusetts 02138

J. Desmond Clark (303), Department of Anthropology, University of California, Berkeley, California 94720

Paul L. Cleghorn (197), Department of Anthropology, University of Hawaii at Manoa, Honolulu, Hawaii 96822

Edwin S. Dethlefsen (137), Department of Anthropology, College of William and Mary, Williamsburg, Virginia 23185

Theodore E. Downing (67), Department of Anthropology, University of Arizona, Tucson, Arizona 85721

---

[1] Present address: Archaeological Research Consultants, P. O. Box 3296, Chapel Hill, North Carolina 27514.

Jeffrey L. Eighmy (31, 225),[2] Department of Anthropology, Colorado State University, Fort Collins, Colorado 80523

Richard A. Gould (269), Department of Anthropology, University of Hawaii at Manoa, Honolulu, Hawaii 96822

Robert F. Heizer (283),[*] Department of Anthropology, University of California at Berkeley, Berkeley, California 94720

Thomas R. Hester (283), Center for Archaeological Research, University of Texas at San Antonio, San Antonio, Texas 78285

Daniel W. Ingersoll, Jr. (255), Department of Anthropology, St. Mary's College of Maryland, St. Mary's City, Maryland 20686

Hiro Kurashina (303), Department of Anthropology/Geography, University of Guam, UOG Station Mangilao, Guam 96313

Mark P. Leone (5), Department of Anthropology, University of Maryland, College Park, Maryland 20742

Michael McCarthy (67), Department of Anthropology, University of Arizona, Tucson, Arizona 85721

David J. Meltzer (113), Department of Anthropology, University of Washington, Seattle, Washington 98195

Alice W. Portnoy (213), Department of Anthropology, Texas Tech University, Lubbock, Texas 79409

Patricia Price-Beggerly (127), Department of Anthropology, University of Hawaii at Manoa, Honolulu, Hawaii 96822

William L. Rathje (51), Department of Anthropology, University of Arizona, Tucson, Arizona 85721

Nan A. Rothschild (161), Department of Anthropology, Hunter College, City University of New York, New York, New York 10021

Michael B. Schiffer (15, 67), Department of Anthropology, University of Arizona, Tucson, Arizona 85721

Richard Wilk (15), Department of Anthropology, University of Arizona, Tucson, Arizona 85721

---

[2] Present address: Institute of Meteorology and Arid Land Studies, King Abdulaziz University, Jeddah, Saudi Arabia.
[*] Deceased.

Preface

"Never underestimate the importance of serendipity in science." This book is proof of that truism. In 1978 Pierre Morenon and Michael Schiffer organized a symposium entitled "The Archaeology of Us" for the annual meeting of the American Anthropological Association in Los Angeles. That symposium represented the culmination of a series of research and pedagogical efforts—centered mainly at the University of Arizona at Tucson—directed toward exploring the relationships between human behavior and materials to contemporary societies. Meanwhile, and since 1971, at the University of Hawaii in Honolulu, Richard Gould had been giving a seminar on ethnoarchaeology that was heavily involved with similar themes. Like the Arizona efforts, the Hawaii seminar involved students in organized "field expeditions" on and around the campus and in the local community to observe human behavior from a modern material culture perspective. In 1978 Gould attended the AAA symposium. The discussions there led us all to recognize the mutuality of our interests in this field. From there, it was a short step to our joint approach to Academic Press, the publisher of this volume.

In some instances the approaches we had been pursuing independently were so similar as to encourage one to believe in that hoary old anthropological idea of independent invention. The visits to on-campus parking lots and off-campus auto wrecking yards in Honolulu were closely paralleled by on-campus observations of sidewalks and architectural details and off-campus studies of campgrounds in the Tucson area. In each case, our principal concern was with the discovery and extension of general principles of human behavior vis-à-vis materials. By making observations of contemporary behavior, could we posit general relationships that could be tested cross-culturally and might eventually achieve the status of behavioral laws? In some cases these studies were primarily oriented toward material residues, with the emphasis on processes of discard and the final, physical context in which such discards come to rest. In other cases the emphasis was on the flow of materials through the contemporary cultural system, from procurement to ultimate discard, and including stages in this flow, such as manufacture, use, and reuse of these materials. Chapters representing both kinds of emphasis will be found in this volume.

But one can still ask what kind of archaeology this is. For many, if not most, scholars, archaeology refers to the past rather than to the present. Anyone looking for *direct* applications of the research findings to past human behavior presented by the chapters in this book will be disappointed. The archaeological payoff of this book can only be realized *indirectly*, first by positing relationships of a general nature and then by deriving predictions or tests of each relationship with respect to particular prehistoric- or historic-archaeological cases.

So, although this book is not about archaeology in the conventional sense, it is vitally concerned with the nature of archaeological reasoning. This is consistent with the way in which archaeologists have sought, over the last decade or so, to make their reasoning more explicit and susceptible to scientific validation. So when we address the theme of "the archaeology of us," we are looking for as many ways as possible to observe contemporary human behavior as a theoretically self-conscious archaeologist might do, with the aim of testing and extending whatever generalizations we can derive from our data in a way that encompasses both past and present human activities. Thus this book will be of interest to anyone interested in human behavior in relation to materials. We view these efforts as a kind of intellectual elixir being pumped into the mainstream of archaeology in particular and social science in general. As the reader will note, many of the contributions in this book are by young scholars whose enthusiasm and willingness to innovate and generalize may at times exceed their evidence. But the whole point of this book and the teaching and research that led to it is to open doors and reveal new and exciting possibilities in the "archaeological" study of familiar or even commonplace aspects of material behavior in our own and other contemporary human societies. This book is not the last word on the subject; it is the first word. And it must be viewed in that way. Each chapter presents ideas that are capable of further expansion and testing, and they are meant to stimulate rather than to demonstrate.

This is especially important to keep in mind when comparing the essays in this volume with earlier, descriptive studies of material culture by anthropologists. The ethnographic literature abounds with studies of potterymaking, weaving, carving, house construction, canoe-building, stone toolmaking, and other arts and crafts which are essentially atheoretical and particularistic. Often, these studies involve exotic or unfamiliar societies. Such studies are useful—for example, to museum curators in researching and planning exhibits—but that usefulness has little to do with the goals of social science. This is not a "how-to" book about different kinds of human technology, nor will it appeal to collectors or others interested in material objects for their own sake. Instead, it is a book that is intended for people who wish to begin to explore the general nature of human behavior vis-à-vis materials.

The first section of the book consists of chapters that explicitly address both the theory and teaching of the modern material culture approach. These basically discursive chapters are followed by the second section that represents the core of the book—a sampling of a wide range of behavior involving materials in contemporary and historic American society. These are ethnographic case studies that posit different general statements about human behavior in relation to materials as varied as coins, herbs, graffiti, fences, and domestic architecture and topics ranging from mortuary practices and beliefs to the reuse and recycling of goods in America. More than in any other part of the book, we can recognize "Us"—that is, ourselves—while at the same time we can often see how different we are from what we thought we were. A special section is included on experimental approaches to modern material culture studies, since this has proven to be one of the most effective ways of doing this kind of research. And, finally, there is a section containing chapters that attempt to provide a bridge between traditional areas of interest in archaeology—such as stone toolmaking, Egyptology, and Paleolithic technology—and the modern material culture approach. These papers do not exhaust the possibilities for useful research of this kind. On the contrary: In the aggregate they demonstrate that any aspect of human behavior in relation to materials provides an opportunity for making useful discoveries and positing cross-cultural generalizations.

Acknowledgments

We wish to thank William Rathje (University of Arizona) and Pierre Morenon (Rhode Island College) for their ideas and timely advice at the beginning of this project.

METHOD AND THEORY IN MODERN MATERIAL-CULTURE STUDIES

As the pages of this book will disclose, the archaeology of modern societies does not boast a unified body of theory nor a suite of widely accepted methods. The present volume, when taken together with other recent works (e.g., Ascher 1974; Deetz 1977b; Ferguson 1977; Gould 1978a; Quimby 1978; Richardson 1974; South 1977), documents the diverse theoretical stances and methodological approaches now undergoing trials in this nascent field. *Modern Material Culture: The Archaeology of Us* presents a sampling—by no means representative—of current positions. Some are by now quite familiar to the archaeologist and even lay persons, while a number of others explore new territory. Although these general viewpoints are aired throughout the book, in this part we have assembled papers that are particularly devoted to theoretical or methodological issues.

Mark Leone begins with a provocative essay that represents an attempt to reconcile or at least moderate divergent views on how the past and present are related. Archaeologists will feel at home with Leone's rejection of Bloch's extreme relativism—that the past is simply a creation of the present. Our conceptions of the past, Leone contends, are surely constrained by the past that survives—material culture. Though not all stories or images of the past are compatible with the material record, there is still ample room for the influence of the present to be felt in the perceived past. Social systems exploit the inherent ambiguities of historical evidence by interjecting sociological and ideological messages that serve to reproduce and reinforce the existing order.

1

MODERN MATERIAL CULTURE
The Archaeology of Us

(Meltzer, in a later chapter, also drives home this point.) Leone draws illustrative material from Colonial Williamsburg, an outdoor historical museum in Virginia. His analysis suggests that present social structure (and perhaps past) is manifest in the behavior acted out in a bakery demonstration, but the rifle exercise by a single individual lacks this level of meaning. Leone concludes his essay with a discourse on boredom. He suggests that reconstructions like Colonial Williamsburg are essentially static and require a temporal dimension that can show how, as the present changes, so does the ritually presented past. Not all readers will agree with Leone's analysis or advice, but few can ignore the profound issues he raises.

In the next chapter Richard Wilk and Michael B. Schiffer argue that the principles of fieldwork are the last frontier in using modern material culture to teach archaeology. They critically compare a number of conventional and experimental approaches to fieldwork instruction, and conclude that modern material culture offers some important advantages. In addition to convenience and lack of expense, a major benefit is that emphasis is placed squarely on learning archaeology's most general principles, those which can be applied later by the student in any specific setting. That all principles of fieldwork can be illustrated with modern material culture is a claim that some investigators will consider to be quite preposterous. Nevertheless, Wilk and Schiffer support this position with a detailed discussion of their "modern material-culture" field school. The course they describe consists of a mix of lectures, demonstrations, readings and, above all, a series of library and practical exercises. The latter, which make use of modern material culture on and near the university campus, strive to train the student in important facets of fieldwork, particularly stressing that fieldwork is as much an intellectual as physical activity.

Jeffrey L. Eighmy examines the potential of material culture to contribute to diachronic studies in anthropology. Because material culture is durable, he points out, it can yield information on past behavior that is unavailable from the verbal sources customarily relied on by ethnographers and sociologists. Eighmy's ethnoarchaeological researches among two Mennonite communities in Chihuahua, Mexico, elegantly demonstrate how this diachronic potential of artifact studies may be achieved. In a classic use of the comparative method, Eighmy attempts to resolve a paradox in change studies: While theoretical assumptions support the view that behavioral change in small-scale, isolated agricultural communities is slow, a number of empirical works indicate that just the opposite is true. Altkolonier and Sommerfelder, where Eighmy did his fieldwork, are two communities matched in nearly all characteristics except social isolation. Data on over 50 years of architectural modifications show that in the more conservative and isolated Altkolonier, architectural innovations catch on later than in Sommerfelder but the actual adoption rate is higer. Eighmy then offers a general explanation to account for these patterns. Ironically, the same forces of conformity that promote conservatism eventually bring about the speedy and whole-hearted adoption of innovations. The arguments and case material presented by Eighmy raise the hope that diachronic ethnoarchaeology can provide a long-needed methodological breakthrough in the study of behavioral change.

William L. Rathje concludes the first part with an overview of modern material-culture studies. He suggests that their contributions to archaeology fall into four principal areas. Contribution 1 is the teaching of archaeological principles. Modern artifacts are said to offer the teacher of archaeology many advantages, not the least of which is student interest. In addition, many investigations, including the Garbage Project, began as student exercises or drew inspiration from them. Contribution 2 of modern material-culture studies is the testing of archaeological principles. Classic investigations such as those carried out by Dethlefsen and Deetz (1966), and more recent efforts, illustrate the expanding role that modern artifacts are playing in refurbishing archaeology's methodological toolkit. Several later chapters provide evidence for the vitality of this approach. Contribution 3 is in effect "salvage" ethnoarchaeology, recording the archaeology of today. Rathje underscores how imperfect are the traditional methods of record-keeping and conservation of material culture, even in an industrial society. All modern material-culture studies, by recording present-day human behavior and material culture, contribute to salvage ethnoarchaeology (for especially good examples, see the fourth part of this volume). And, finally, Contribution 4 is that of relating our society to past societies. Here Rathje's discussion shifts from outlining accomplishments to indicating the possibilities for using material-culture studies to develop context-free yardsticks for comparing varied societies—those long dead and those we live in. Rathje's neat scheme seems to accommodate the goals vis-à-vis archaeology of most modern material-culture studies.

At the present time, the diversity of modern material-culture studies is a decided strength. As archaeologists grapple with new-found applications for their unique perspective on human behavior, a premature orthodoxy or normal science would be stultifying. The freedom to experiment without paradigmatic shackles, to identify wholly novel questions and creatively devise ways to answer them, are among the undeniable attractions of modern material-culture studies. We should enjoy this exhilarating period of theoretical and methodological anarchy, for it is likely to be short-lived. Already the elements for synthesizing a new science of society, focused through archaeological principles on human behavior and material culture, seem tantalizingly close at hand.

M.B.S.

1

Archaeology's Relationship to the Present and the Past

Mark P. Leone

Once archaeological materials are put on display there are two messages. The obvious one is what the past was like. The other one is the meaning the present imposes on data from another time and which the present thus feeds back to itself. The first message is one we help create as archaeologists. The second is one we can help understand as anthropologists.

This second message, one that is essentially ideological (Althusser 1971), occurs when artifacts and historical information are interpreted and put on display in any of the settings that we associate with the interpretation of archaeology like natural history museums, outdoor history museums, or picture books. This excludes communication within academic or scholarly archaeology. Once the material dug up is presented to the public, the entire presentation, not just the actual facts about the past, or excavation, or analytical techniques, becomes an entirely new artifact, a piece of modern material culture, one to be analyzed for what it tells about the culture creating it, not about the past per se.

The insight that people speaking of the past are both the speakers and the listeners and that the subject matter is other than what it seems to be is widely shared. Among social anthropologists the most current form of the debate begun by Edmund Leach (1961) occurs in Maurice Bloch's articles (1977, 1979). Among scholars of American studies. operating independently of social anthropology and within the context of outdoor history museums, this insight is articulated by Thomas Schlereth (1978).

5

MODERN MATERIAL CULTURE
The Archaeology of Us

For Bloch, in particular, discussions of the past among most peoples are "static and organic imaginary models of their society which gain a shadowy phenomenological reality in ritual communication [1977:287]." Discussions of the past have little or nothing to do with the facts or processes described in the conversations; they are entirely about the present and they are a highly specialized part of the present: A model of how society ought to work. Bloch is careful to say that most peoples have ways of piercing this imaginary model and that, despite the model, virtually every group that has as much as discovered agriculture also has a chronological, linear notion of time that is independent of the idea of the past communicated in ritual, and capable of a revealing commentary on that imaginary model. For him the "presence of the past in the present" is an artifact of particular circumstances in the present and is basically there to mystify. The mystification is overcome by another source of concepts, everyday life, "which can lead to the realization of exploitation and its challenge."

Thomas Schlereth, commenting on the proliferation of outdoor history museums in the United States, is concerned that they should develop a sense of their own history and communicate it to their visitors. Without a public commentary within these museums, such as a preface, statement of authorship, methodological problems, or evidential gaps in an exhibition, a historical museum seems self-generating (1978:42). Schlereth urges museum curators to explain to the public "epistemological questions of chronology, causation, periodization and generalization [1978:43]." This will enhance the public's understanding of how the past is known.

Schlereth's concern is for the quality of interpretation in historical villages. He is convinced that if such places communicated the most basic assumption Bloch uses, which is that discussions of the past are specialized messages about the present, such explorations would be comprehensible to the average visitor. Schlereth does not go beyond this, does not suggest what the present may actually be learning from its immersion in history, and thus his suggestions about increasing sophistication, while concrete enough, are not tied to any aim, let alone one as specific as Bloch, that is, the past is an imaginary model of social structure mystifying those involved in discussing it. However, Schlereth does avoid the error of arguing that increasingly sophisticated interpretations will lead to a fuller and more accurate understanding of the past. He understands that the accuracy of use of the past is not an issue but that the present's relationship to it is.

With this understanding, Schlereth is at odds with the whole of the new archaeology and with one of the two aims of modern material-culture studies. The new archaeology immersed itself in philosophy of science, statistics, and other ways of evaluating data to create more accurate models of the past. Ethnoarchaeology, which is one form of modern material-culture studies, also was concerned, fundamentally, with improvements in our comprehension of the past. Both activities within archaeology made important contributions but were unaware of the growing school of thought within anthropology that refused to separate objective and subjective knowledge. Bloch's work is part of this body of thought in British social anthropology as is symbolic analysis within American cultural anthropology.

A second aim of modern material-culture studies is not concerned with the past per se but with analyzing objects made in the present for what they can tell of the present. A good example of this second aim is the Tucson Garbage Project which is based on the assumption that material culture may provide information about an aspect of culture unavailable from those who create and use the objects. That Project shares two of Bloch's assumptions: People are not always aware of what they mean when they discuss themselves, and there are structured clues, daily life for Bloch, artifacts for Rathje, that pierce the ritualized and mystifying discussions of social organization.

This chapter builds on these two assumptions to understand the relationship between past and present and uses a context from the past for the exploration. Bloch virtually dismisses history as myth, and Rathje, in using archaeological methods on modern subject matter, makes useful discoveries that are untied in any way to the past. Here I use ethnographic data from Colonial Williamsburg to attempt to disentangle the past and present without dismissing either. Colonial Williamsburg is a modern setting involving tens of thousands of eighteenth- and twentieth-century artifacts. It is a place to observe the behavior and concepts modern Americans use to understand a particular problem: the relationship between past and present. By observing people in the context of a particular kind of material culture, antiques and reproductions assembled in an outdoor history museum, my problems are: What do Americans think the past is, and what do they make it into while actively engaged with objects true to another time? These questions mean that archaeological contexts can have a special use in exploring specific pieces of modern behavior which we do not yet understand, that is, how the past is given meaning. The answer can be informative for the ethnography of the United States. It is also informative for archaeology because it explores the basis for the public use of archaeology. This in turn is important because it explores the unresolved relationship between archaeology and anthropology, namely, the contribution the past makes to understanding human nature. These are problems common to Bloch and Schlereth and, in a different way, to Rathje. For Bloch the actual past is irrelevant and discussions of it filled with illusion; for Schlereth the past is real enough but fully impregnated with the present, though in a way he cannot specify; for Rathje archaeological methods used on modern data produce conclusions untied to the past and so contribute nothing to archaeology. All three are concerned with the symmetry between past and present within a discipline deeply, if unclearly, committed to the existence of a relationship between the two. This chapter tries to clarify the symmetry.

To discuss these related problems, (a) the vernacular relationships between past and present and (b) the relationship between archaeology and the concept of culture, two episodes are reported. Both are from Colonial Williamsburg, Virginia. Beginning in 1926 John D. Rockefeller, Jr., provided financial backing for the reconstruction and restoration of Williamsburg, Virginia. This eighteenth-century town was bought up by the Colonial Williamsburg Foundation ans was gradually made the most famous outdoor history museum in the United States. Built around the motto "That the future may learn from the past," Williamsburg was refurbished and rebuilt with all the care, skill, documentation, and authenticity that dedication could provide using America's greatest fortune. Archaeology played a central role in establishing much of Williamsburg's accuracy and is one of the keys to the authenticity of the reconstruction. Archaeology provided some otherwise unavailable details thus giving it a status, along with written records, as one of the foundations for accuracy.

As a counterpoint to the achievement of accuracy John Cotter (1970) has written about the disputes between the archaeologists at Williamsburg and the officials who frequently disregarded the findings from excavations in favor of some other presentation. Ivor Noël Hume, the chief archaeologist at Williamsburg, has also pointed out (1976) how notions of authenticity have shifted as well as how impossible it is to recapture the past. He too is aware as an archaeologist that whatever Williamsburg is, there is some question about just how separate the eighteenth century is from the present it is supposed to instruct.

That there is an as yet unspecified relationship between the archaeology and the public presentation based on it has been commented on frankly and lucidly before. To explore the tie I relate the following episode observed in the Bakery of Raleigh's Tavern on September 11, 1978. It is a straightforward case of the replication of current social structure through discussion of the past, just as might be predicted from Maurice Bloch. The bakery is a large room with the work area separated from tourists by a series of struts which were once a solid wall. A baker in period dress mixes dough with a wooden paddle in a large wooden trough. Speaking to six to eight tourists at a time he explains that he mixes 50 pounds of dough at once which, when finished, yields about 1000 gingerbread cookies. He said these were for sale—$.22 a piece, $1.25 the half dozen, $2.50 the baker's dozen—down the hall. While he talked, he mixed, spread flour on his work table, spilled out the dough, kneaded it, floured it, kneaded it, floured the table, dipped flour from a bag to a tray, explained the flour was stone ground, and finished work with a large white mound of ready dough. Tourists continued to pass by in small groups every few minutes and he repeated his explanation and mentioned the price four or five times in 15 or 20 minutes. Sometimes he made comments to someone in the room that were not clearly audible to tourists but which amounted to a commentary on the dcugh, the day, the afternoon—comments that made one wonder to whom he was talking. When the dough was done, which he said was a matter of feel, he stood back, and from a corner not visible to tourists came a much younger man, in fact, a teenager, who took a rolling pin, and began to roll out the dough spreading flour as he went. Then the young man began cutting cookies with a metal cutter in a manner so deft and quick the audience gasped. The cutting was virtually manual choreography with rows of cookies dancing out of the dough. The cookies were just as deftly picked up in piles. This process went on until the dough was used up. The whole gingerbread cookie operation was done two or three times a day depending on how fast tourists bought up the cookies.

With an authentically dressed baker and his helper turning out quite nice cookies from a genuine recipe, where is the present in the past? To begin with, the baker was white, his helper black, and half the time hidden in a corner, never speaking to tourists even when visible. The baker answered all the questions. The baker worked with the whole dough, the helper cut it into pieces; the helper did the mechanical, repetitive work, work not dependent on subjective feel for ready dough, the helper was told explicitly when the dough was ready. Gingerbread dough is dark brown. It was kept white with flour when the baker worked with it; it became dark brown as the helper rolled it out and prepared it for cutting, a process which wipes the flour away making the dough's color apparent.

In this setting, the details of which we take safely to be true to another time, tourists see the following relationships acted out, relationships true also to his time: master, helper; one who creates a whole product, one who fragments it through repetitive acts; one who orders, one who is ordered; one who can have several audiences and can change roles, one who is tied to one role and one audience. White and black are structurally related this way both historically and ethnographically in Virginia. The symmetry of the relationship is so complete it is reflected in the change that took place in the very product to match the color of the hands working it.

The social structural duplication seen in the gingerbread cookie illustration verifies Bloch's idea that discussions of the past are models of society which gain reality in ritual communication. (A visitor's journey through Williamsburg is certainly a secular ritual as described in Robert Bellah's American civil religion [1970:168]). But Bloch also says that such models are static and imaginary. Static, certainly we can agree with from this episode; there is no concern with change, or conflict, or contradiction which could produce the tension leading to change. Imaginary? Bloch means unreal and here is, I believe, either incorrect or using the wrong word. The viewers are indeed imagining things. They are imagining that what they see was reality and in seeing that it was so and is so all at the same time, they can believe that the past can be had again. Once they believe this, they reproduce within themselves the modern social structure portrayed so plausibly. They duplicate within themselves present conditions through being actively absorbed in the vignette which is itself taken to be from the past. When people participate in it, ask questions, buy and eat cookies, and take the whole seriously in its own terms they have reproduced the present within themselves. I prefer to depart from Bloch on the characteristic "imaginary" and rely on Althusser whose analysis credits history and ritual with more power than Bloch. Althusser suggests that the mystification provided by history and ritual permits people to operate smoothly in the everyday world, as opposed to Bloch who would provide believers with the everyday world as a commentary to pierce the mystification of history. Bloch would build a continuing revolution or at least revelation. Althusser has spun a web that people do not escape. However, using either Bloch or Althusser the presence of the past in the present is clear in this illustration. Clear too is the fact that the presence is a structured, not a happenstance, matter, and that the past, contrary to Bloch's implication, is not a pure manufacture. We can see, through modern material-culture studies used in a context of the past, the social structural tie between past and present.

A second episode will expand this point and show that the tie between past and present is not made arbitrarily. First, the tie is structured and structural as just seen. Second, the tie is not a mere invention of the present imposed on the past; the tie is effective because it is accurately representative of conditions past as well as present. The past cannot and is not molded any which way. Since the past did indeed occur, since it is well recorded, well excavated, well interpreted, and preserved with full scholarly integrity, there is no way the presentations can be called fictional or infinitely plastic. Bloch implies such a radical position. The inaccuracy stemming from such ignorance of history becomes clear in the following episode.

Several times every day in Colonial Williamsburg there is a demonstration of loading and firing a flintlock rifle near the magazine in the center of the historic site. The scene before the magazine involves a man costumed in eighteenth-century layman's clothes who primes, loads, aims, and fires a weapon true to the times while explaining all his procedures to watching visitors—usually a couple dozen in good weather. The scene is in the open before the magazine, itself an original building, not a reproduction. The costumed worker, as he is called in Williamsburg, deals comfortably with his audience of adults and youngsters. He shows them the long-barreled gun, small cylindrical paper tube of powder, tears off a corner of the tube with his teeth, pours in the powder, drops in the ball, uses a ramrod to press all together. It is all done knowledgeably. Then the watching folks are prepared for the firing, prepared several times, then, with a count of 1, 2, 3, there is a loud bang and it's over. "Any questions?" the man asks. There are several as men and boys engage the costumed worker in conversation. Meanwhile most of the crowd walks off in various directions to other attractions.

There are two qualities to the demonstration. The first can be gained by listening to the conversations between costumed worker and visitors. "Is the gun real or a reproduction?" "No, it's a reproduction, but all those in the magazine for people to look at are authentic. But you know, even though we use these modern guns made in Italy and Japan, the originals are better. We were using one of these new ones and noticed it had a hairline crack all the way down the barrel just after a few months. Now, that never happened to the originals when we used them." To another question, the costumed worker made comments on care, cost, and frequency of use of the guns. There were almost no questions about the eighteenth century, very few facts were offered, no information was given on social or economic context of eighteenth-century gun use. Plenty of information is available; the costumed worker was routinely taught a good deal and probably went out of his way to learn even more of eighteenth-century practice. But usually nothing is asked and little is offered. But despite the site's motto about the future learning from the past, very few facts, no social context, and nothing we would think of as historical interpretation are normally taken away. Everything is accurate and responsible, but the content one might expect about eighteenth-century life and custom are virtually absent. There are two likely reasons for this. There was no structure in the vignette. That is, while there is interaction between present and present, the past can not be represented in lifelike fashion with only one person in the demonstration representing another time. This means there could not be any conversation between past and past. Thus it was impossible to replicate modern social structure by recreating the dead structure because there was no conversation of the past with itself as there was between the two bakers. Second, unlike the gingerbread cookie episode, there is nothing for the visitor, having bought the past intellectually or cognitively, to buy thus expressing and possessing conviction through individual, voluntary action. Visitors are not invited to go down the fence and buy a piece of shot or march in a passing militia for a quarter.

This leads to a final observation. Visitors to Colonial Williamsburg are frequently bored. This is a neutral observation and not meant to be critical. People at Williamsburg begin to wear a glazed look, children tire, husbands and wives squabble, older people begin to pat their clothes, and everybody starts to pick on the workers. They argue with guides, bully the waitresses, comment on high prices to salespeople, and doubt the reality of what they are being told. Boredom is not particular to Colonial Williamsburg; Teotihuacan can be tedious; if you have never been there, the most boring place in Rome is the world's most important archaeological site, the Roman Forum. They can all be tedious.

These observations would not normally be noted by archaeologists concerned with the objective integrity and accuracy of archaeological or historical interpretations. But they are useful clues to the more basic concepts which archaeology as an endeavor is built on. Initially, of course, we know artifacts never speak for themselves; we have to give them meaning. But we are primarily concerned with accurate meaning and feel no obligation to notice the boredom our own interpretations communicate when made public. The message of the rifle demonstration, or rather messages, consisted of a bang which is a meaningless noise, the fact that the gun was Japanese or Italian and not likely to be as good as an original whose country of origin was neither asked for nor volunteered, and the quick dispersal of the on-lookers when the show concluded. In other words, instead of seeking buried social structure to explain this event, the message is its meaninglessness; it had nothing to say because it did not use the social structural tie between past and present.

Our search for objective accuracy is responsible for the boredom as is our refusal to use self-reflection, or modern material-culture studies as a way of understanding the relationship between objective and subjective knowledge. Accuracy itself is a culture-specific effort to resolve the paradox between an unenterable past and a past thought essential for our self-definition. The puzzle Williamsburg presents and the reason it and virtually all other archaeological settings can produce the glaze of boredom is summed up in the common and the archaeological notion of the past: We assume it must be instructive and we say we need instruction because we assume the world is always changing, yet we hold the past still and will not allow it to change. We cannot let it change because it is supposed to be separate from our direct experience and we will not let it change because we need a comparison with ourselves, one which would be compromised if we saw the social structural tie between the past and ourselves.

A modern material-culture study on a setting of the past shows the problem with the flat or uninteresting nature of what archaeologists have to say to the public. Such a study shows that the problem can be understood through the paradox formed by the public's and the archaeological professions's twin basic assumptions: The past cannot be relived but knowledge of it is believed essential for our identity as a society. To resolve this puzzle some understanding of the social functions of archaeology and of history is essential. What messages do our professional creations give to our society? My earlier illustrations use Bloch's and Schlereth's concerns about the tie between past and present as a way of showing one specific relationship between archaeology and its society. Second, and rather more important, such a study is not supposed to produce better knowledge of the past, but to dispose of the twin fears of professional archaeologists. Archaeologists are afraid, on the one hand, to say too much lest they be wrong; this sometimes produces intellectual conservatism and boring interpretations. And, second, archaeologists fear they are unable to say anything new or innovative. (If you have ever been a new archaeologist searching for a hypothesis or a culture process—let alone several—you know the problem.)

Archaeological assumptions hobble the profession in its public practice. The past, just like foreign cultures, for ethnographers, is entered through the imagination—the agreed on source of all hypotheses. This process includes, inevitably, the replication of the scientist's social structure when his or her work is presented to the public. Such knowledge could allow archaeologists involved in creating public settings based on their interpretations to let the settings change, show them changing, and teach how they are changed and what they change in response to, just as Thomas Schlereth would have it. The settings could be signed with names of archaeologists and designers and show the dates when last changed. Basically we could make of the past the changing society we are trying hard to make a success living in. This is a simple conclusion drawn from my illustrations of Bloch's hypothesis of the social structural tie between past and present.

How does this affect professional work: writing, teaching, paper giving? Since we dig and write up for publication as our two main activities, does this work make a difference? Not until the interpretations are given public performance. But then once one realizes a specific piece of archaeology is tedious, the realization can be used to advantage because it will be clear that meaning is missing. Boredom and hysteria are opposite ends of the flow of information. Too little produces boredom; too much, hysteria. Hysteria is not one of our problems, I admit, but when boredom accompanies archaeology, it is because the facts and data are not tied to the present the way they may be. That way is to allow the past to be the image of the present it must be by its very nature in a ritual setting. For our culture and the archaeological profession the problem is not as we all suppose, how did we get from past to present, the problem is what is communicated by going from present to past. That is where the news is. It is the locale where modern material-culture studies, a form of applied anthropolgy on archaeological sites, have an impact. Such studies can examine how we go back in time to describe the "presence of the past in the present." It is in examining how we get back, not forward, that we will learn about ourselves.

Acknowledgments

I am grateful for help in this research provided by Gary Carson, Director of Research, and Ivor Noël Home, Director of Archaeology, of the Colonial Williamsburg Foundation.

I am indebted to Ellen Pader for pointing out Bloch's articles.

2

The Modern Material-Culture Field School: Teaching Archaeology on the University Campus[1]

Richard Wilk and Michael B. Schiffer

There is a certain kind of learning which comes from handling objects which is not supplied by any amount of reading or listening to lectures or even looking at pictures. I think our archaeological teaching tends to be significant in proportion to the extent to which the student has this kind of experience

Clyde Kluckhohn, quoted in Woodbury [1963:228]

Introduction

Considering the vastness of the archaeological literature, it is surprising to find that so little of it concerns teaching (McHugh 1977: iii). Apparently, new approaches to doing archaeology have not been matched by new approaches to teaching archaeology. Perhaps this is due to a general reluctance among archaeologists to systematize their science and translate their findings into terms that can be understood by a wider audience.

Several trends in archaeology lead us to believe that this situation is changing. Contract work has increased demand for archaeologists, thus favoring more efficient and streamlined training methods. Also, archaeologists have become more introspective about their own goals, procedures, and principles, making it easier to identify and teach those parts of archaeology that are in some sense fundamental. The greatly expanded

[1] An earlier version of this chapter was read at the 78th Annual Meeting of the American Anthropological Association, Los Angeles, 1978.

MODERN MATERIAL CULTURE
The Archaeology of Us

topical scope of modern archaeology is another factor that may promote improved teaching. The discipline is now defined to embrace the full range of human behavior and material culture, wherever and whenever it occurs (Deetz 1970; Rathje 1979; Reid, Schiffer, and Rathje 1975; Schiffer 1976). Now that ethnoarchaeology, experimental archaeology, historical archaeology, and modern material-culture studies have achieved a certain respectability, the problems and challenges of archaeology can be related to our everyday material surroundings. Therefore it is legitimate to investigate archaeological problems and to teach the principles of archaeology in one's own community. This new relevance and involvement for archaeology can make the teaching of even the most traditional and uninspiring topics easier, more interesting, and less expensive.

Rathje and others have successfully used modern material culture to introduce archaeology to undergraduates. It is not surprising that modern material culture can be used to illustrate basic principles of material culture and archaeological inference, such as seriation, typology, and relationships between social status and possessions. These principles are certainly manifest in our material culture no less than in that of any other society. It seems to us, however, that the next challenge lies in employing modern material culture to teach the more advanced method and theory of archaeological fieldwork, usually taught in other ways. On the basis of our experience we believe that the "modern material-culture field school" has advantages over conventional methods. To highlight these advantages we briefly review the strengths and weaknesses of other approaches for teaching the principles of fieldwork.

Teaching Archaeological Fieldwork

The summer field school or weekend dig has been the traditional means for providing hands-on experience in excavation and giving students limited accreditation as fieldworkers. Recently, field schools have begun to place more emphasis on survey methods.

Our critical evaluation should not be interpreted as a blanket indictment of field schools, nor of any one in particular. Rather, our view is that field schools are a valid way of teaching *some* aspects of field archaeology. The fault lies not in field schools themselves but in the expectation that they will somehow turn naive students into competent, all-around fieldworkers in a 10-week period. This expectation, unfortunately held by far too many employers these days, is unrealistic.

Let us consider what field schools do well, what they do poorly, and what they do not do at all.

Unquestionably, field schools succeed in acquainting students with the tools and techniques traditionally employed at a specific site in a specific area. Sometimes they also demonstrate or discuss a wider variety of techniques than those immediately needed. In some field schools visiting scholars lecture on their specialties, broadening the student's exposure to recovery, analytical, and interpretive techniques (e.g., see Longacre and Reid 1974). Often field schools are the scene of complex and innovative research, as at the well known site of Koster (Struever and Holton 1979). Depending on the specific site and setting, students can gain considerable experience with diverse excavation problems, site features and sediments—although this is more the exception than the rule. Finally, field schools do a valuable service by introducing the social tenor of the profession and the uniqueness of the field situation; field schools also help in the establishment of social ties that provide opportunities for advancement later in a student's career.

If good fieldwork is an interaction between theory and technique and is also a process of forming and testing hypotheses, then field school students are only trained to do half the job in a profession where half a job is worse than none at all. In most cases, training in interpretation or in making informed choices *between* techniques is sporadic or entirely lacking. Part of the problem is that field school activities alternate between hard manual labor, the numbing tedium of labwork, and listening to the most abstract lectures on theory. Missing are the conceptual bridges between coating bones with PVA and hypotheses for the rise of food production in the Near East. Lacking the ability to apply theoretical knowledge to unique, specific problems, the usual field-school graduate tends to be an overly narrow technical specialist.

Another major problem for field schools, one receiving considerable attention recently, is their dubious ethical position (Judge 1977; Meighan 1977). By current professional standards in American archaeology, a site cannot be excavated merely as a student exercise; a genuine research goal also must be kept in view. This can lead to conflict between research and training objectives and often to unsatisfying compromises. A proposed solution to this dilemma is to excavate "more common" and "less fragile" historic remains which are to be found on many university campuses (Turnbaugh 1976:209). Although such exercises may sometimes be feasible, we doubt that many historical archaeologists would enthusiastically endorse this as a general strategy.

The financial picture for field schools, especially those dependent on grant support, has changed drastically in recent years. They must now compete for students with contract projects that offer attractive salaries. While an accomodation is to create contract-funded field schools, a solution would be to offer training which is intrinsically more valuable than a summer's wages.

Archaeologists have shown creativity in proposing alternatives to the field school. Artificial sites, both full-scale and miniature, have long been heralded as the ideal adjunct to classroom instruction (Adams and Eddy 1977; Ascher 1968a; Chilcott and Deetz 1964; Jennings 1950). An artificial site can be very effective in teaching some basic techniques of recovery, recording, and cataloging and the archaeologist's "respect for detail and minutiae [Jennings 1963:25]." They can also be used simultaneously for carrying out experiments in decay and disturbance processes (Ascher 1970) and recovery biases (Chilcott and Deetz 1964). In addition, full-scale models furnish experience in problems of visualizing three-dimensional relationships, and they facilitate instruction in the selection of recovery units to suit various situations.

Despite their many advantages, artificial sites have a number of practical and conceptual drawbacks. Sites are time-consuming and sometimes expensive to assemble, and often they can be used only once. The most serious shortcoming, however, is the oversimplification and distortions introduced when they are built. Archaeologists make these sites, not innumerable cultural and noncultural formation processes; the sites are therefore peculiar artifacts that embody the ideas and prejudices of the archaeologist. The student cannot discover anything more than what the teacher put into the site. There is little room for genuine dispute and disagreement, which is so much a part of fieldwork. Inevitably, the frustrating complexity of archaeological deposits and the problems of interpreting them are lost.

A recent addition to the arsenal of teaching techniques is the excavation of sites by computer simulation (Robert Fry, personal communication to Schiffer, 1978). As these programs become more widely available they should help students to learn sampling theory, multistage decision-making, and the rationales behind various recovery strategies. In our view, the major difficulties with computer teaching are boredom for the student, oversimplification of complex problems, and lack of hands-on experience with material culture. Nevertheless, computers may well form one component of future teaching approaches.

Above we mentioned the interaction between theory and practice as the major nexus of learning in archaeology. While field schools often fail on the theory side of the equation, traditional classroom instruction, on which there is a fair amount of literature (e.g., Baerreis 1963; Braidwood 1963; Fagan 1977; Jennings 1963; Kidder 1963; Woodbury 1963), fails on the practical. Supervisors are familiar with students who talk a good line on sampling theory and the ethnoarchaeology of hunter-gatherer camps, but who are unable to level a plane table or comprehend the need to straighten sections or clip roots. The overall situation in teaching seems to overdose the student alternatively with theory or technique with no attempt at mediation or linkage between the two.

We believe there is an effective alternative to the traditional approaches used to teach field archaeology. Once the view is accepted that archaeology includes all the material culture around us, the scope of what to teach and where to teach it expands dramatically. Students can be shown that the principles of archaeological inference and recovery operate everywhere, even in the classroom and the university. Indeed, we believe that all the principles needed to conduct archaeological fieldwork can be taught in modern settings. We do not mean that every specific formation and disturbance process can be observed on any university campus (we have seen few examples of cryoturbation in Tucson), but the *principles* that enable archaeologists to interpret ancient phenomena such as alluviation and trash dumping are more general, and are therefore more generally teachable.

Moreover, a modern material-culture approach avoids the ethical pitfalls of field-school excavations, and the toil of creating artificial sites. A modern material-culture field school is also cheaper, more convenient and can involve the student in archaeological problems as challenging as those encountered in most excavations. Surprisingly, the excitement of "discovery," so much a part of the fieldwork experience for both student and professional, is not lost. Indeed this experience can be heightened when discoveries are made in familiar places.

Throughout our course, the emphasis is on learning fundamental principles that will allow the student to quickly acquire the competence needed to deal with specifics of each site and area. To be sure, one cannot teach everything needed to excavate anywhere in the world, but it is possible to instill basic concepts, fundamental questions, and modes of thought so that the novice fieldworker will know what must yet be learned to cope with each new field situation. In particular, emphasis is placed on how to make decisions about when to employ each recovery, recording, and preservation technique. We also teach a core of general techniques for recovery and interpretation that can be applied almost anywhere.

This view of fieldwork training dovetails neatly with the realities of modern conservation archaeology. The fieldworker, who may spend spring in the Ozarks and summer in the Yukon, is constantly confronting new practical and theoretical problems. To their consternation, employers have discovered that crew members, even those with many seasons behind them, do not have the flexibility and knowledge of general principles needed to cope with unfamiliar archaeological situations.

With these optimistic intentions we proceeded to teach an experimental course in the spring semester of 1978 on the Method and Theory of Archaeological Fieldwork, using 20 unsuspecting University of Arizona students as subjects. Those enrolled for credit were primarily upper-division undergraduates and graduate students. Their positive reactions and our own satisfaction with the results have prompted us to bring our ideas and course design to a wider audience.

Course Design

The course called for a full complement of reading assignments, three library projects, laboratory sessions, and four field projects, in addition to two, 50-minute lectures per week.

The laboratory sessions, 2 hours in duration, covered traditional techniques and tools. Laboratory subjects included (a) instruments and techniques of survey, (b) interpretation and use of maps and aerial photographs, (c) recognition and identification of prehistoric material culture (using objects from the Arizona State Museum), (d) excavation tools and equipment (all the tools needed to conduct a small excavation were brought to class), and (e) techniques of sediment analysis. Although use of the transit was not demonstrated, plane table and alidade, and tape and compass survey were explicated by mapping the outlines of the classroom and plotting its major features. It would be a simple matter to have future students construct a rudimentary alidade and plot for themselves various landmarks in the classroom.

There were three library assignments, each requiring a writeup. The first was a critique of a published survey report, focusing on details of the design and implementation. The second required the students to design their own survey, given a problem and area supplied by the instructors. Finally, students were asked to critically evaluate an excavation report in the same way they had previously tackled a survey.

A major intention of the field assignments was to heighten students' powers of observation. They learned, like detectives, to attribute significance to otherwise mundane or trivial phenomena. Students literally began to perceive their surroundings in a new way, involving them in a learning process that extended far outside the bounds of the classroom. They found themselves sitting in gutters, poking around in flowerbeds, feeling stairways and sidewalks, and then having to account for their strange behavior to interested passersby.

To promote this reorientation students were guided through a modern material-culture tour of the campus during the first class session. Throughout the tour, they were sensitized to archaeological ways of looking at material culture and the environment.

The first stop on the tour, less than 10 m from the classroom, was the most frequently used pair of restrooms in the Anthropology Building. Close examination of the restroom doors served to illustrate several archaeological concepts. Students were shown a discolored patch on the mens' room door, and were then asked to posit, drawing upon their own experience, a process that might be responsible for its formation. They guessed correctly that countless hands pushing open the door had produced a wear pattern. From this starting point we introduced major approaches that archaeologists use to support their inferences: ethnoarchaeological observations, and the gathering of independent evidence. The ethnoarchaeological data materialized almost immediately when an innocent party, going about his normal business, demonstrated the genesis of the use wear quite convincingly. An independent test was performed by examining the door of the neighboring womens' room. We proposed that if our hypothesis were correct, we would find a similar wear mark, but lower on the door. This prediction was promptly verified.

We pointed out that the use wear in both cases was concentrated several inches from a metal push-plate that, if properly positioned, could easily have prevented the wear. The gap between design and use processes which this demonstrates is potentially present in every artifact. As archaeologists begin to think about this sort of problem more systematically, perhaps they can play a role in establishing the nature of relationships between design and use in the modern world, relationships which also interest the architect, engineer, and urban planner.

We moved on to the second stop of the tour after several curious and apparently anxious persons had assembled in the hallway behind us.

In the stairwell at the end of the hallway, we introduced the distinction between events and processes, and the ways they can be identified in the archaeological record. The events had left traces in the form of streaks and holes in the wall plaster, while a process was revealed in the rounded and eroded surfaces of the concrete steps. We then suggested that patterns in the attrition of the steps could disclose variation in the use of the building. By comparing the wear on different flights of steps we were able to show a correlation between the amount of use and the amount of wear. The higher we went in the building, the less wear was found, mainly because the lower floors are devoted to classrooms, while the upper floors house faculty offices and laboratories. Again, design and subsequent use intersected to produce an archaeologically visible result.

From the stairwell we moved on to several scenes of recent construction on the third floor of the Anthropology Building. The first was a doorway that had been installed in a previously existing wall. Traces of the alteration could be seen in the pattern of wall tiles, the fresh grouting, and irregularities in plastering around the door frame. These characteristics contrast markedly with nearby door frames that were contemporary with the walls. We called attention to similar examples from archaeological sites (e.g., Wilcox 1975).

Just down the hall were found additional traces of new construction. Wear on the linoleum continued beneath a wall, and wall plaster visibly overlapped the acoustic ceiling tiles; these subtle imperfections neatly illustrated the basic concepts of bonding and abutment. Everyone quickly appreciated that the wall was a recent addition, in this case to create a new office (for Schiffer, incidentally). We discussed the ways archaeologists use the relationships of bonding and abutment to build sequences of construction events.

Next, we paused in the exhibition hall of the Arizona State Museum to examine the indentations left by previous exhibits in the linoleum floor. Students offered ideas about the variables that could affect the depth of these traces, including the weight of the exhibit, length of time the exhibit was in place, or the time elapsed since its removal. This example introduced the ideas that archaeologically visible traces often result from a complex interplay of independent forces and that different combinations of processes can produce the same material outcome.

While in the museum we also briefly mentioned that the modifications we observed could be used as indirect measures of the behavior of museum visitors. Students were encouraged to think of ways to infer the popularity of exhibits, some of which have been proposed elsewhere (Webb, Campbell, Schwartz, and Sechrist 1966).

As we departed the Anthropology-Museum complex, the effects of erosion and fluvial deposition were noticed in several unvegetated areas of the campus. We urged students to visualize the kinds of changes that would result if these processes continued over long periods of time without the intervention of campus groundspeople.

After walking about 200 m we arrived at Old Main, the oldest building on campus, dating to 1891. From this vantage point we compared a series of buildings, erected between the late nineteenth century and the 1960s, with reference to the problem of seriation. Regular stylistic and technological trends over time were easily identified, and students were asked to analyze their own native perception of why old buildings look old. As students identified visible changes in ratios of glass to brick, iron to aluminum, and wood to concrete, and noted shifts in the use of other basic building materials, they began to appreciate the difficulties in differentiating stylistic from utilitarian variation, especially with reference to features like roof overhang and window design. We mentioned that availability of materials and costs of electricity for cooling have affected building design over the years. This discussion led students to recognize that the quaint "stylistic" features of Old Main effectively reduced direct sunlight on interiors, and kept the building cool in the pre-air-conditioning era. In the future, students could be sent back to Old Main in order to describe the long sequence of additions and modifications to the basic structure; a sequence which could then be compared with university records.

In the final stop of the tour we presented a problem requiring the students to apply their newly acquired knowledge. In a nearby lecture hall we called attention to a peculiar asymmetrical pattern of use wear on the seats of wooden desk-chairs. Viewed from the front, the right side of each seat displayed a small oval patch where the varnish was completely worn.

In response to our queries about the possible causes, students offered several hypotheses, including clothing studs, fasteners, wallets, and postural aberrations, that were easily ruled out by the abrasive nature of the wear. When asked to feel the seats, some students discovered sand grains concentrated in the worn oval. From this observation they conjectured that sand was deposited by seated students when resting their foot on the seat in front of them. The sand was then ground in by the posterior of the next occupant of the seat. The observed asymmetry is due to the construction and placement of the desk-chairs, which are bolted to the floor. The occupant's movements are restricted so that feet can only be placed on one side of the back of the chair, resulting in the observed asymmetrical wear. Our point here was that archaeological hypotheses are easy to generate, but are harder to confirm or disconfirm without additional observation and the use of as many lines of evidence as possible. To underscore this point we asked students to develop an independent test of the posited mechanism of use wear. With a little prompting they soon suggested that the last row of seats in the classroom should not display any abrasive wear at all, a prediction that was quickly confirmed.

Stimulated by the success of this prediction, and the realization that there was, after all, something interesting to look at in the average classroom, students began to generate more hypotheses and applications. One suggested that the amount and distribution of seat wear could be used to study classroom proxemics, while another recommended that wear on the podium might disclose the nervous habits of professors.

This concluded our orientation session for the students and primed them for the first few weeks of lectures.

The Projects

It is one thing to memorize archaeological principles for the next exam, or to read a textbook, but it is a very different thing to apply that knowledge while excavating. Fieldwork has little use for rote learning. The key to training students to be good fieldworkers, then, is to give them practice in applying their knowledge in situations that require creative thought and analytical skills. Students are much more willing to commit to memory concepts and data when they can be convinced of the practical importance of retaining such knowledge. Using this approach, we also find that students become more critical of what they are taught, and tend to ask better and harder questions. Because of these considerations, we assigned a number of practical projects which students completed independently as "take-home" labs.

Project 1

Project 1 was the self-guided modern material-culture tour, which dealt in more depth with concepts and principles introduced previously. Students were supplied a list of instructions directing them to a series of locations, and requiring them to answer specific questions.

The first stop was the main stairway of the building that was once the University library. Here a complex wear pattern was observed on the steps of the main lobby. Students were directed to examine and describe the wear, assess how the design of the building had affected the wear process, and hypothesize the specific behaviors and mechanical causes responsible for the wear.

The students displayed considerable sophistication in this exercise. Some observed traffic on the stairs to lend weight to their hypotheses, while others delved into the past functions of the building that might have affected traffic flow. All became interested in the curiously narrow paths which people seem to follow even on broad expanses of steps. Several pointed out that variability in wear was the product of complex interactions between the intensity of foot traffic and the quantity of abrasive particles present, confounding the initial commonsense assumption that less wear is a direct product of less traffic.

The second stop acquainted students with some basic principles of stratigraphy and to the peculiar interpretive problems posed by complex structures. They examined a series of bricked-up windows in the Arizona State Museum building, and were asked to explore the logic and assumptions which enabled them to identify these features as alterations. Students discovered that decay processes can play an important role in temporal reconstruction; additions were less weathered than the rest of the wall, though the relationship was complicated by changes in quality of building material over time.

At the base of the wall students were confronted with a typically knotty problem in the interaction of style and function. What looked like large stone blocks turned out, on closer examination, to be concrete cast in plywood molds; students noted many traces of the molds, including lines of junction and the grain of the plywood.

A few meters away, in front of the Anthropology Building, there is an inconspicuous asphalt ramp rising from street to sidewalk. By looking closely at this feature, students could discern a complex sequence of construction, painting and modification. They identified several asphalt layers with different textures, a buried drain pipe, and the overlapping and eroding vestiges of numerous repaintings of both ramp and curb. From these details, they built a construction sequence and proposed an excavation strategy to confirm and expand it.

A retaining wall of basalt rubble construction was the next observation station. Here students were shown how noncultural processes can effect the decay of structures. They compared two segments on the wall, one of which was more deteriorated than the other, and were asked to offer some hypotheses to account for the difference. It turned out that the area sheltered by vegetation was better preserved, though quite discolored by leaf decay. On the exposed segment of the wall they noted areas where water was dissolving mortar along small fissures and cracks, and spots where decay had led to repairs. Mortar casts of plaques and vanished railings were also visible. We asked students to predict what would happen to the wall in the distant future if presently acting noncultural processes continued to operate unchecked by the maintenance staff. Surprisingly few students realized that the weight of earth would make the retaining wall slump outward as it deteriorated. Few also appreciated that parts of the wall protected by vegetation would remain standing longer. These weaknesses could be corrected by more discussion in class of basic engineering and construction principles.

A short walk down the street, opposite a university dormitory, students were given their first problem in interpreting refuse disposal patterns. This project required the description and recording of 20 different objects lying in the gutter along a short segment of the street. Our intention was to pique the student's curiosity and show them some of the formidable difficulties in pinpointing specific processes or events responsible for artifact deposition. Students were asked to speculate about the interaction between deposition and disturbance processes, but more sophisticated treatment of these subjects was delayed until later in the semester.

Students had no difficulty identifying traces of beer drinking, automobile repair, and consumption of prepackaged foods. Other items, notably pieces of clothing, were more difficult to interpret. (Long after the project ended a student observed that residents leaving the dormitory to go to the laundromat were the main source of this refuse.) We made it clear that archaeologists usually have to operate without a participant's intimate knowledge of artifact use and disposal. Further, we demonstrated that even with a participant's knowledge, archaeological techniques often have the power to confound commonsense explanations, and to lift our ignorance of our own material environment. This observation point allowed us to stress the difference between discard at location of use, and discard elsewhere, and the archaeological problem of telling the two apart.

After this project was completed, we made an inspection of the gutter and found that our novice surveyors had uniformly overlooked several common artifact types, as do many experienced archaeologists. They tended to miss inconspicuous but informative items such as paint flecks, match sticks, hair, small glass fragments, and oil spots. While pointing out in class the shortcomings of the students' surveys, we admitted that archaeologists' counts from sites are similarly biased and that specialized recovery techniques are needed to deal with small and unobtrusive—though often abundant—artifacts.

The remaining three projects developed further some of the issues introduced in the first assignment.

Vacant Lot Archaeology

The next project became the instructors' favorite, and has since provided the raw material for a publication on the archaeology of Tucson's vacant lots (Wilk and Schiffer 1979). This assignment required students to carry out a rudimentary archaeological survey in one of the ubiquitous vacant lots of Tucson.

This project furnished experience in interpreting a variety of cultural and noncultural formation processes. After choosing a lot, preferably one with paths, students were asked (a) to construct a pace map of the area, including all major features, paths, sidewalks, artifact concentrations, and vegetation patterns, (b) to describe in general terms the distribution and variety of material culture, (c) to record the artifact inventory in five standard-sized sample units, (d) to formulate hypotheses about past and ongoing formation processes, and (e) to make whatever additional observations were needed for hypothesis testing. A total of 17 lots were surveyed, in a variety of locations clustered around the university area.

This assignment was not ethnoarchaeological; it dealt instead with the archaeology of the recent past. Although students could draw upon general knowledge of their own society, they were not asked to make any systematic observation of behavior in vacant lots.

Students located and mapped a great number of features and artifact concentrations, including play areas, parking and car repair zones, middens, storage piles, borrow pits, house foundations, fences, hearths, a nomadic encampment, and even a filled-in swimming pool. In two locations the actual ruins of historic dwellings were found.

From their map of features and artifact concentrations, students inferred a variety of activities that recurred throughout the sample of vacant lots. Many of the activities are only marginally legal, and the remains they leave are often unique to the vacant lot. This has led us to further thought about the role of open areas within the modern and ancient urban landscape and their archaeological potential (Wilk and Schiffer 1979).

Students faced many interpretive problems during their surveys, and often found surface remains which rivaled the complexity of any prehistoric site. However, by the time of this assignment, students had been exposed to enough lecture and laboratory material to approach these problems with some sophistication. Many got involved in trying to unravel the complex and subtle interactions of deposition, disturbance, and reclamation processes, in some cases even proposing experimental and ethnoarchaeological projects in order to verify their hypotheses. In retrospect, the most important lesson of this project is that patterns of artifact distribution result from both patterned deposition *and* patterned disturbance. This is a potent antidote to the student's first assumption that human behavior is directly reflected in the distribution of artifacts on the ground. They learned that hypotheses about specific interactions of deposition and disturbance must constantly be proposed, tested, and often discarded in the course of fieldwork.

Sidewalk Stratigraphy

Most practical excavation problems concern the perception and interpretation of stratification. Unfortunately, the university campus rarely offers deep, complex exposures which can give students experience in stratigraphic analysis. We believed, however, that such an important part of field archaeology could not be dismissed with a lecture and an invocation of the law of superpositioning. We dealt with this problem by breaking up stratigraphic interpretation into two parts: the perception of archaeological units of stratification, and the ordering of those strata into a sequence. Each part became the subject of a field project.

The first project used the concrete sidewalks which encircle the Anthropology-Museum complex to teach students methods of building stratigraphic units into a relative chronology that could be tied to absolute dates and displayed in a standardized and intelligible format (Harris 1975, 1977). Students began by distinguishing the minimal construction unit or "sidewalk segment." Then criteria were developed, such as color, texture and molding patterns, for tying adjacent segments into construction events. The latter were related to each other by junction patterns, functional, technological, and stylistic characteristics, differential wear and weathering, associated stamped dates, intruded features, and historic research. Students' Harris diagrams reveal the complexity as well as the uncertainties of stratigraphic analysis. Although this exercise was carried out on concrete, a material rarely encountered in the archaeological record, it provided a challenging test in stratigraphy and chronology building, even to the professionals who undertook it at our goading. We recommend this assignment for all desk-bound archaeologists who would like to exercise their wits.

Campus Dirt

The final project was aimed at developing students' perceptions of the differences between stratigraphic units using soils and sediments similar to those found in excavations. The fieldwork was preceded by a laboratory session which demonstrated manual methods of soil-texture analysis and summarized common modes of soil description.

A series of eight observation points was visited by each student. The sample stations included slopes with active erosion, gutters with ongoing deposition, a building dripline, and mulched flower beds. The gutters in particular provided interesting examples of the interaction between fluvial, eolian, and cultural deposition in the genesis of sediments. At each observation point soil color and texture were described as well as constituent cultural materials. We solicited hypotheses about the cultural and noncultural processes that were responsible for the differences between stations. One student performed a standardized laboratory texture analysis on samples he collected during this project. This served as a means of assessing the accuracy of the various pinch, roll, and blow tests which are advocated by Limbrey (1975) and Shackley (1975). Surprisingly, though the results of the manual tests are fairly consistent, they are sometimes at variance with results of USGS laboratory screening tests. A following lab period was devoted to demonstrating a simple sedimentation method for texture analysis that renders the manual methods unnecessary.

Together, campus dirt and sidewalk stratigraphy teach students how to apply general principles and expose them to most of the problems encountered in stratigraphic analysis at any site.

Discussion and Conclusions

We believe that the most accurate way in which these assignments correspond to real fieldwork problems is in their open-endedness. Often, there was no single correct answer and ambitious students could go far beyond the project requirements. In fact, some developed plausible arguments and solutions that were completely unanticipated by the project designers. While this open-endedness promoted creativity and independence, as well as heightened anxiety, it also made the assignments very difficult to grade. The problem was to avoid equating the time spent on the project with the grade earned. Instead, we strived, sometimes unsuccessfully, to assess the quality of the student's logic and the structure of argument and evidence.

We also found that the classroom sessions sometimes did not provide adequate preparation in the procedures of hypothesis verification. In particular, we often failed to appreciate the problems created when a single bit of evidence can support a number of quite different hypotheses. In the vacant lot project, for example, most students came across scatters of small glass fragments. Although dozens of possible processes could have been responsible for these deposits, students generally chose a pet explanation, without attempting to formulate and test the alternatives. This emphasized both to students and instructors the practical importance of abstract conceptions, such as the method of multiple working hypotheses. We are still trying to devise better ways of teaching adequate standards of explanation.

Another general deficiency of the course was the lack of systematic instruction on procedures and methods of artifact analysis. Because we believe that considerable time should be devoted to such instruction, a new semester-long course on artifact analysis was begun in the spring of 1979.

Other revisions of the course seem to be warranted, particularly in the scheduling of projects. For instance, the vacant lot project should be assigned later in the semester, so that students will have an even greater background on formation processes and field methods before tackling such a difficult job. It might also be advisable to reorder some of the later projects, with campus dirt preceding sidewalk stratigraphy. If this course were to be adapted to undergraduate students, it would be necessary to reduce the number of projects and library assignments or give greater credit for the course.

Because of the interesting results generated by the vacant lot project, we would like in the future to gather more data on the situational factors which affect variability in the material culture deposited on these lots. It should not be too much additional work to determine the location of surrounding stores and schools, the population density and average income of the neighborhood, and the flow of traffic on nearby streets.

The projects undertaken by our students in Tucson scarcely probe the wealth of archaeologically interesting settings from which students can gain valuable field experience. Abandoned structures, back alleys, drive-in theaters, swap meets, parks, and other public or semi-public activity areas also furnish opportunities for teaching the basic principles of fieldwork. In these respects, Tucson and the University of Arizona are hardly unique. Any modern community, rural or urban, young or old, east or west, contains the raw archaeological materials out of which an instructor can fashion provocative field exercises.

In the eyes of some archaeologists, the modern material-culture field school will never be a substitute for "real" fieldwork. Marian White (1977:146), for example, argued that the one kind of experience that is difficult to replicate outside of an actual excavation is "the unpredictable element." We concede the difficulty of simulating the frustration that is felt when a tree-ring sample crumbles upon removal for lack of paraffin-gasoline solution, or the utter desperation met on the last day of the field season when, during subflooring, a Paleo-Indian component is found as three pothunters observe the proceedings with utmost interest, or the total exasperation caused by moving for the fourth time, the same 17 tons of backdirt. We suggest, however, that the greater familiarity that our students achieve with archaeological principles can improve their planning and decision making so that the number of unpleasant surprises encountered in the field is reduced. If we meet our teaching goals, then perhaps our students will be capable of approaching each new field project, not as merely manual labor, but as a learning experience requiring the use of their highest mental faculties. In the final analysis, what distinguishes archaeological fieldwork from mining and looting are the records we keep and the quality of the decisions made in the field as we attempt to understand the past before the evidence of it is destroyed by our own hands.

The Use of Material Culture in Diachronic Anthropology

Jeffrey L. Eighmy

Among those archaeologists interested in human social behavior there has been a growing awareness of the potential offered by material culture to understanding human behavior. This awareness has been reinforced by the current popularity of ecology and behavioral analysis and cultural materialism. For example, in response to arguments for units of observation that measure behavior directly (Barker 1968; Harris 1964), various social scientists (Webb, Campbell, Schwartz, and Sechrest 1966; Wagner 1972) have pointed out the utility of material culture in behavioral research. Wagner (1972:x) expresses the point in these terms:

> Evidence derived from verbal statements of people under study has traditionally served as basis for the ethnological analysis of culture. But a discipline that draws its evidence for culture from the concrete artifacts, material activities, and transformations of environment produced by man, instead of taking its material from such linguistic sources, may possess its own advantages.

The recent trends within the social sciences converge to underscore the assertion that material culture can aid in the solution of many social research problems. As a result several archaeologists have revived the claim of Hutton (1944) that material culture has been needlessly neglected in anthropological research (Deetz 1970; Ferguson 1975; Reid, Rathje, and Schiffer 1974).

31

MODERN MATERIAL CULTURE
The Archaeology of Us

We do not advocate the use of material culture just because we are familiar with material-culture analysis. Too much of the recent work in ethnoarchaeology seems to have little justification beyond showing the facility with which archaeologists can manipulate modern, as well as ancient material culture. Rather, we advocated material culture because it is oftentimes the best data source for the research at hand. The criteria for selecting data in any scientific enquiry is its appropriateness and effectiveness for solving particular problems. The use of material culture in one instance must still be justified on the basis of its potential to solve a particular research problem. It is an unfortunate fact, however, that material culture is more often than not overlooked as a potential data source. It is overlooked because it is assumed that material culture is inferior as a behavioral data source. We feel that if anthropologists were more than casually aware of the qualities that give material culture a problem-solving potential, then the full exploitation of artifactual data would follow.

The question becomes: Given a particular problem, what are the characteristics which give material culture a research potential? Rathje (1978:51-52) provides a brief review of some of these characteristics. He points out that material culture is nonreactive, quantifiable, and a data source independent of traditional interview techniques. Rathje's Tucson Garbage Project illustrates the advantages well.

The Use of Material Culture in Diachronic Anthropology

To Rathje's list can be added a fourth characteristic, a characteristic well known to archaeology but often forgotten in the historical and ethnographic contexts. The durability of material artifacts can provide researchers with a crucial temporal dimension in social change research. Time series observation of social change is not a common feature of anthropological literature on social change, but it should be obvious that a clear understanding of social change requires observation at various points in time. However, much social change research in anthropology fails to provide the basic diachronic information necessary for even the initial description of change. Typical anthropological data are collected in a 1- to 2-year field session, but this provides only an extremely shallow temporal dimension from which to describe and understand change. Anthropologists have frequently tried other methods, such as generational studies, restudies, and longitudinal field studies, but none of these methodologies is satisfactory for efficient diachronic analysis (Plog 1977:30-42) or to obtain diachronic records.

Although conceptual schemes for operationalizing the direct observation and measurement of behavior have been developed (Barker 1968: Harris 1964), they have done little to relieve the problem of obtaining temporal data. It is hoped that anthropology realizes the elementary points made by Plog and Bates (1976:209) in their introductory text:

> Anthropologists cannot continue to be satisfied with simply attempting to reconstruct patterns of culture change. Instead, they must try to find ways of conducting studies of change that stretch over many years, yielding precise records of what has transpired over the long run.

Material culture provides a significant opportunity for meeting the requirements of over-time observations. First, artifacts, as products of past human behavior, can be particularly useful in reconstructing the past adaptive context of social change (Cook 1973; Longacre 1970). Geertz (1963:8-9) points out that material culture is an important element in human adaptation. Given its durability, material culture holds considerable potential for the development of a temporal parameter in studies of ecological and technical change. Second, durable material artifacts as records of past behavior can be important in behavior-trend analysis. Glassie (1968) has argued that historic records seldom record the behavior of a majority of the people in any society. When questions involve the change trends of a population, research may have to turn to the material products of this behavior (Richardson and Kroeber 1940). Material culture may also be of crucial importance in the diachronic study of the fundamental processes of social change (Hodgen 1974).

From the preceding arguments it should not be surprising to find dated material culture as a common data source in social change research. Richardson and Kroeber (1940) and Hodgen (1945, 1950) provide the first anthropological demonstration of the utility of material culture in social change research, but by and large material culture has not been exploited. For those anthropologists who find a tangible example more convincing than an argument in the abstract, the remainder of this chapter attempts to supplement the theoretical case for the value of material culture with an example of how material culture can be used in social change research.

Social Change within Isolated Agricultural Communities

A good argument can be made that, given the enormous temporal potential of archaeological data, a central concern of archaeology should be the general question of social change. How is change measured? What are the important independent variables? What are the underlying processes in change? To deal with such questions, an anthropological archaeology should be very familiar with general theories and models of change. These theories and models should in turn provide some of the questions which stimulate research activity. For example, of particular interest to archaeologists will be social change in small isolated agricultural communities because change in these communities will relate most directly to the enormous body of post-neolithic archaeological data. Theoretically, what sort of change patterns are expected under these circumstances?

Current theory concerning isolated agricultural communities conceives of the rate of social change there as extremely slow. Hagen (1962:57) in a discussion of the "traditional" society argues, in fact, that most of them never achieve any significant and permanent departure from "traditionalism:"

> In some cases the society preserved its new techniques but became traditional in their use; in many others, the society lapsed into its old ways. . . . Traditional peasant society, in short, has been a stable institution from which departures have occurred, departures that in the long run were temporary.

While few social scientists hold to this extreme position or see little value in the restricted concept of traditional peasant society offered by Hagen, most still hold to the idea that agrarian communities modernize slowly. Concerning peasants, Mendras (1970:33) writes, "Thus the historian and the anthropologist show us that in normal times, in a peasant society, the mechanisms of change are very slow." Redfield (1950:4) argues that among folk people, "the career of one generation repeats that of the preceding. So understood, homogeneous is equivalent to slow changing."

A serious problem arises with this characterization, however, because empirical evidence does not agree with theoretical prediction. In several recent data sets, when behavioral innovations are studied, their diffusion through isolated agricultural communities appears rapid. For example, Mendez D. (1968) found some Guatemalan villages in which a majority of the villagers adopted a brand-name analgesic in a relatively short period of time. Data reported by Rogers and Svenning (1969:293) indicate that the adoption of fertilizers and weed spray was occurring more rapidly in traditional villages than they were in more modern villages (Figure 3.1). In the restudy of an Indian village, Epstein (1973:79-86) shows that in the case of a number of specific parameters, Indian folk communities had changed with extreme rapidity.

Currently, the inconsistency between theoretical expectation and actual rates of internal diffusion are ignored, and despite evidence to the contrary internal diffusion is assumed to proceed at a slow rate. For example, after

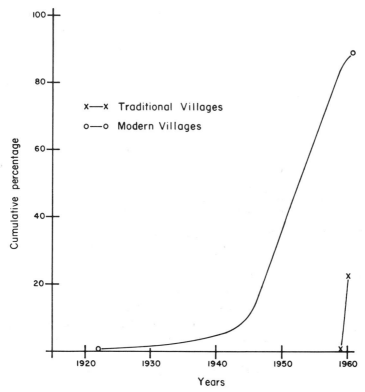

Figure 3.1 *Adoption of fertilizer in modern and traditional Colombian villages (Rogers and Svenning 1969:293).*

describing the rapid diffusion of the automobile through an Amish community, Hostetler (1968: 332) feels compelled to add that the example is more dramatic than is the usual pattern in Amish social change. It is at once Hostetler's only detailed description of Amish social change and at the same time, according to Hostetler, uncharacteristic of them. In the preceding example drawn from Roger's study of adoption-diffusion among Colombian peasants, traditional villages are characterized as changing at a "slower rate" than modern villages despite the fact the data reveal a precisely opposite pattern. Rogers and Svenning present the graphical summary reproduced in Figure 3.1. Obviously, the rate of adoption among the traditional Colombian villages is faster than among the modern villages. Further, evidence such as Amish automobile adoption and Colombian peasant weed spray adoption call into question fundamental assumptions about change in these communities. Available evidence suggests that accurate description of change in these communities awaits further empirical demonstration and that it is time to reevaluate the theory of agrarian community social change. To provide a structure to this reevaluation the following hypothesis needs to be tested.

The closer a community conforms to the qualities of an isolated agricultural community, the slower will be the internal diffusion of innovations— all other factors being equal.

The obvious and most efficient step in testing this hypothesis is to review the literature. Unfortunately, most attention to change in rural society has concerned the general-level modernization process. Little attention has been paid to change in specific behavior through time. As a result the few examples presented here nearly exhaust the quantitative (non-Western) data dealing with the adoption of specific behavioral innovations through time and illustrate the general poor quality of the existing data of testing this hypothesis.

An immediate problem for anthropologists is then further documenting diffusion in these communities. To show exactly how diffusion proceeds in isolated agricultural communities, it will be necessary to obtain as much control as possible over other variables which influence the rate of diffusion. A productive approach used to achieve experimental control in studying social change is the historical-comparative method (Bennett 1969; Eggan 1950; Hodgen 1974; Spicer 1962). In controlled comparisons, two or more societies from among the world's ethnographic population are as similar as possible while varying in the one parameter of research interest. As expected, anthropologists (Bennett 1969; Eggan 1950; Spicer 1962) have been largely interested in the impact of the culture contact situation on cultural patterns and form, but the method of using a sample of the existing social experiments to investigate the operation of a naturally manipulated independent variable has proved a promising tool for social research. In an attempt to obtain this type control for the study of diffusion within isolated agricultural communities, two groups of Mennonites living in Mexico, the Sommerfelders and the Altkolonier, were selected for investigation to see if they exhibited different diffusion patterns.

Comparative Mennonite Architectural Change

The Sommerfelder and Altkolonier Mennonites used in this study live in large colonies around but mostly north of Cuauhtemoc, Chihuahua, Mexico. These Mennonites came to Mexico between 1922 and 1926, from Canada for a poorly understood combination of reasons, primarily population pressure, refusal to assimilate, and opportunism. (See Eighmy 1977; Redekop 1969; Sawatzky 1971). The Sommerfelder and Altkolonier Mennonites were chosen for study because they are so similar in most respects but different in the one character of interest—degree of isolation.

Altkolonier Mennonites resemble Sommerfelder Mennonites in terms of historical background, farming practices, land distribution, mechanization, village form and structure, diet, health, patterns of social interaction, and the importance of kinship relations. However, the Altkolonier are socially more isolated than the Sommerfelders. This isolation is manifested in more behavioral distinctiveness and internal homogeneity and can be quantitively measured in patterns of clothing, architecture, transportation, and domestic furnishing. For example, in the study of clothing, not only do the Altkolonier wear more stylistically distinctive clothing, they also display less variability. In the study sample, Altkolonier dresses were invariably monochromatic with 1 of 6 basic dark colors, while those of the Sommerfelders were of 17 colors and color combinations. In 12 of 16 comparisons the Altkolonier show considerably more homogeneity (see Eighmy 1977:Chap. 3) and are consistently more distinctive in style, color, and form. The Chihuahua Mennonites are ideal for the study except for the problem of diachronic records of social change. While the Mennonites are literate and keep good census data, they have never been interested in written records of community behavior patterns. It is in Mennonite material culture that a behavioral record of over 50 years of adoption diffusion patterns are readily available for study.

Mexican Mennonite architecture has been changing continually over the last 50 years. Despite the fact that conservative Mennonite groups resist change and appear "behind the times" the architecture of Mexican Mennonites has experienced continual alteration and innovation in form. Sawatzky (1971:272–279) mentions numerous recent changes. Among these changes are a decline in the *wohnstallhaus* house plan, increase in adobe walls and earth roofs, and a reduction in roof pitch. But in general he gave little indication of how the adoption of architectural innovations among the Altkolonier compared with the Sommerfelders.

In order to prepare a comparative picture of Mennonite architectural change, the time between 1922 and 1976 was grouped into nine time periods and nine housing samples per group created. The samples were opportunistic rather than randomly selected, but it is felt that the size of the samples (approximately 12 to 42% per time period per group)[1] are large

---

[1] These estimates are based on a reconstruction of the history of housing growth derived from dating a 10% random sample of all Altkolonier houses. See "The Archeological Significance of Counting Houses: Ethnoarcheological Evidence," Chapter 15 of this volume.

enough to avoid any major sampling errors since the populations did not exhibit great variability. The period samples were created as we went through selected Mennonite villages making observations on all available houses in the village. When certain time periods became underrepresented, a village established just prior to these periods was selected for inclusion in the survey. This intensive survey comprised 98% of the houses in the Altkolonier village of Klefeld (Campo 1A), Silberfeld (Campo 26), Waldheim (Campo 23), Osterwick (Campo 18), and Lowenfarm (Campo 6 1/2A and 6 1/2B) and the Sommerfelder villages of Halbstadt (Campo 55), Bergthal (Campo 40), Neuanlage (Campo 53A), and Schoenthal (Campo 51). By doing all houses within a particular village the suspicion which would have been created by the random selection of a fraction of all houses was avoided.

Strictly speaking, the unit of observation was a farmstead. A farmstead was defined as a complex of farm buildings from which a single farming operation was directed. This complex may include more than one house and household. A discrete farmstead was indicated by the existence of a driveway and gate opening to the main street. Observations were made on barns as well as houses. An attempt was made to date houses, barns, and all major modifications. When two or more houses existed on a farmstead the earliest house available was chosen for treatment. A total of 236 houses and 201 barns were observed for the Altkolonier and 118 houses and 95 barns for the Sommerfelders (Table 3.1). Barns were not always present nor as easily dated since many of the early barns had been rebuilt; so, the sample of barn architecture is less adequate. One Sommerfelder time period for barns is omitted altogether because only one barn was recorded. Due to an uneven distribution of houses through time, the period lengths were varied from 4 to 6 years in an attempt to more evenly distribute houses and barns through the periods.

Three hundred sixty six architectural observations could be made on houses and 15 could be made on barns. A number of these were observations of the same type variable taken several times for each farmstead. For example, it was possible to observe different types of window variables for 20 different windows. The number of different variable types was actually 71 per house and 14 per barns. In the analysis each period sample is treated separately, and the results reported for each period refer to the products of behavior actually performed during that period. Observations on later additions and modifications were avoided so that period observations refer to period behavior.

These results show considerable period to period variability. This variability is probably a result of sample size, dating error, and actual behavioral variability resulting from fluctuating short-term influences. Since we are interested in longer-term trends, short-term variations have been sup-

Table 3.1

Size of House and Barn Samples by Time Period

		Altkolonier		Sommerfelder	
Time periods		Houses	Barns	Houses	Barns
First	1922-1926	42	19	10	7
Second	1927-1932	19	15	9	5
Third	1933-1939	27	24	10	1
Fourth	1940-1945	28	28	18	10
Fifth	1946-1951	18	13	15	10
Sixth	1952-1958	18	22	13	13
Seventh	1959-1964	22	22	14	16
Eighth	1965-1970	26	26	17	13
Ninth	1971-1976	36	32	12	20
Total		236	201	118	95

pressed by transforming the period observations into three-period moving averages. This transformation helped express the longer-term change trends.

Some of the variables turned out unreliable as temporal information because of an inability to maintain detailed dating control. For example, doors cannot be assumed to date to the house construction because they are so easily changed. Porches are often added later. House and trim color can be easily changed as well as such items as shutters and screens. As a result, these observations should have been dated separately to provide good diachronic information.

Several of the reliably dated variables showed no significant change over the last 50 years. House shape, chimney position, raking and eave trim material, door and window frame material, and barn roof shape showed no major changes. House perimeter shape (without later additions) was mostly rectangular, chimneys almost always passed through the roof ridge at a point interior to the wall. Raking trim, eave trim, door frame, and window frame material was nearly always wood (metal has very recently been used as frame material). Other variables change in one group and not in the other, like dormers and Mexican style roofs among the Sommerfelders.

In other cases observations reveal erratic and dissimilar records in the adoption of architectural innovations. The orientation of Altkolonier houses became increasingly perpendicular to the main street through 1958, while the Sommerfelder houses were tending to be built parallel. The trend in both groups reversed after 1958. Average window width, floor area, wall area, and house volume show numerous trend reversals during the history of their use. The irregularity and numerous trend reversals make it difficult to com-

pare change rates between the Altkolonier and Sommerfelder, and they
have been excluded from further analysis. Comparable change trends were
found for 21 innovations. The three-period running average of these trends
are summarized in Tables 3.2 through 3.5.

Social versus Chronological Time

In order to further clarify the comparison of Altkolonier-Sommerfelder
architectural change, a distinction has been made between chronological
time and social time. From Tables 3.2 through 3.5 it appears that an
Altkolonier change trend may not start at the same time as it does among the
Sommerfelder. For example, the decline in gabled earth roofs or Type C
houses began prior to the 1922-1926 period for the Sommerfelder but did
not begin until 1933-1939 for the Altkolonier. Since we are interested in comparing the Altkolonier rate of social change with that of the Sommerfelders, it
will be helpful to compare these trends from the same point in social time,
that is, the point at which the change begins. By moving the beginning of the
Altkolonier change trends to coincide, so to speak, with the beginning of the
Sommerfelder trends relative rates of change are more obvious.

An interesting pattern is revealed in the conversion from chronological
to social time. The Sommerfelder almost always start the adoption of an innovation years before the Altkolonier. In 13 cases the Altkolonier appear to
begin their internal diffusion trend later than the Sommerfelder, in 6 cases
the groups begin at the same time, while in only 1 instance do the Altkolonier
adopt an innovation before the Sommerfelders.

Results: Quantitative Comparison of Change Trends

A linear-regression model was used to convert the social change trends
into quantitative indices to average rates of change for each of the 21 useful
cases. Although a linear model may not be appropriate for describing adoption of innovation under ideal conditions (Hamblin, Jacobson, and Miller
1973), it is a means of comparing the relative rates of social change under
less than ideal circumstances. The more the slope of the regression analysis
deviates from zero, the greater is the rate of change (Table 3.6). Often the
rate of change between the two groups is similar, but it should be remembered that the two Mennonite groups are themselves similar so that any
significant difference in rates of change is remarkable.

In only 6 cases is there any indication that the Sommerfelder change at a

Table 3.2
Three-Period Running Averages of Altkolonier Housing Variables

Period	Percentage house type C	Percentage roofs with commercial material	Percentage wall vents	Percentage concrete door sills	Percentage modern type windows	Non-earth roof pitch (degrees)	Percentage concrete and brick walls	Percentage trimmed eaves	Percentage metal chimneys	Percentage molded and shaped window and door heads	Percentage concrete foundations	Percentage "ornate" chimneys	Percentage oriented east or west
1 (1922–1926)	48	38	73	6	0	36	0	32	20	72	6	0	44
2 (1927–1932)	56	32	77	10	0	35	0	31	19	68	11	0	41
3 (1933–1939)	62	30	77	10	0	34	0	24	19	71	20	0	45
4 (1940–1945)	61	34	79	8	0	34	0	23	26	62	40	14	46
5 (1946–1951)	48	44	79	25	0	31	2	24	30	73	52	14	53
6 (1952–1958)	35	63	83	42	0	28	4	32	39	82	68	24	51
7 (1959–1964)	24	79	74	62	4	24	19	42	53	85	77	26	56
8 (1965–1970)	17	94	59	62	17	19	44	49	73	80	91	47	56
9 (1971–1976)	14	96	47	62	26	17	64	56	86	74	92	56	64

42

Table 3.3

Three-Period Running Averages of Sommerfelder Housing Variables

Period	Percentage house type C	Percentage roofs with commercial material	Percentage wall vents	Percentage concrete door sills	Percentage modern type windows	Non-earth roof pitch (degrees)	Percentage concrete and brick walls	Percentage trimmed eaves	Percentage metal chimneys	Percentage molded and shaped window and door heads	Percentage concrete foundations	Percentage "ornate" chimneys	Percentage oriented east or west
1 (1922–1926)	44	38	76	12	6	26	0	42	16	52	6	0	67
2 (1927–1932)	36	35	80	8	4	26	0	50	19	51	7	17	68
3 (1933–1939)	29	32	81	8	12	25	0	54	27	49	12	39	67
4 (1940–1945)	16	35	77	17	8	25	2	61	38	52	22	56	71
5 (1946–1951)	12	43	68	33	13	23	5	68	39	66	46	72	69
6 (1952–1958)	5	57	63	42	12	23	4	86	39	75	70	67	75
7 (1959–1964)	3	70	66	38	21	21	5	95	40	85	87	74	78
8 (1965–1970)	3	77	58	38	21	21	13	97	48	88	93	46	88
9 (1971–1976)	4	78	56	45	22	19	20	96	52	90	97	44	90

Table 3.4
Three-Period Running Averages of Altkolonier Barn Variables

Period	Percentage sheet metal and carton roof material	Percentage concrete and metal walls	Total floor area (m²)	Percentage barns attached to houses	Percentage two-story barns	Barns to house distance (m)	Percentage metal doors	Percentage concrete foundations
1 (1922-1926)	16	0	107	32	9	12.1	4	6
2 (1927-1932)	17	0	107	37	7	11.7	7	9
3 (1933-1939)	26	0	113	50	9	8.7	11	15
4 (1940-1945)	49	0	128	45	13	10.1	21	32
5 (1946-1951)	70	0	133	35	23	10.9	30	40
6 (1952-1958)	87	0	130	24	28	14.1	33	60
7 (1959-1964)	91	16	109	22	22	15.2	41	72
8 (1965-1970)	97	38	89	19	14	18.7	46	90
9 (1971-1976)	97	57	74	16	8	19.6	58	90

Table 3.5
Three-Period Running Averages of Sommerfelder Barn Variables

Period	Percentage sheet metal and carton roof material	Percentage concrete and metal walls	Total floor area (m²)	Percentage barns attached to houses	Percentage two-story barns	Barns to house distance (m)	Percentage metal doors	Percentage concrete foundations
1 (1922-1926)	34	0	102	17	20	17.6	0	12
2 (1927-1932)	—	—	—	—	—	—	—	—
3 (1933-1939)	50	0	101	15	15	16.6	0	34
4 (1940-1945)	—	—	—	—	—	—	—	—
5 (1946-1951)	64	0	88	9	10	25.5	14	46
6 (1952-1958)	81	4	80	6	8	30.1	16	58
7 (1959-1964)	92	8	79	3	5	29.4	36	67
8 (1965-1970)	100	18	81	2	2	30.2	48	90
9 (1971-1976)	100	22	79	2	0	29.4	62	96

Table 3.6

Comparison of Average Annual Rates of Architectural Change [a]

Variable	Altkolonier	Sommerfelder	Satisfied significance of difference in slope
Roofing material			
House	2.01	1.42	.001
Barn	2.16	1.59	
Wall material			
House	2.10	.48	.20
Barn	3.13	.94	.10
Chimney material	1.81	.69	.10
Foundation material			
House	1.94	2.19	
Barn	1.99	1.68	
Barn door material	1.08	1.67	
Door still material	2.33	1.87	
Modern windows	1.47	.36	.025
Wall vents	−2.00	.65	
Non-earth roof pitch	.40	− .14	
Molded and shaped heads	1.22	1.22	
Trimmed eaves	1.14	1.35	
"Ornate" chimneys	1.40	2.01	
Orientation	.40	.57	
Barn size			
Total floor area	−2.54	− .70	.05
Two stories	−1.10	−. 40	.05
Barn and house			
Attached	− .95	− .38	.10
Distance	.31	.71	.025
House type C	−1.46	−1.14	

[a] All are in the percentages except barn floor area and barn-house distance which are in square meters and meters.

faster rate than the Altkolonier (Table 3.6), and in only one of these instances, barn to house distance, has the change occurred at a statistically
significant faster rate. On the other hand, 15 cases indicate that the
Altkolonier change at an average faster rate than the Sommerfelder with the
difference being statistically significant in 7 of these cases. The data, then,
lend very little support to the hypothesis that change occurs more slowly in
more isolated agricultural communities. In only one case did the Altkolonier
change at a statistically significant slower rate. The Altkolonier change trends
start later but proceeded more rapidly.

An Explanation and Discussion of Rapid Internal
Diffusion in Isolated Agricultural Communities

Mennonite architectural change trends, then, add further evidence con-
tradicting the notion that isolated agricultural rural communities can be
characterized as slow changing. The paradox of change in these societies
becomes more glaring. How can the diffusion process be rapid when the
communities always appear "behind-the-times" and to modernize slowly?
Would it not make more sense if the diffusion process, too, were slow? On
the surface it seems so obvious that isolated agricultural communities should
have slow diffusion rates that current assumptions have become deeply en-
trenched. At a deeper level, however, slower diffusion rates do not make
more sense, and in fact, the nature of rural community social structure provides a highly reasonable explanation for rapid internal diffusion and for the
initial adoption lag of isolated rural communities behind more modern ones.
The explanation leads to a model of social change in isolated agricultural communities which begins to resolve the paradox of rapid internal
diffusion and the slow modernizing transition of isolated agricultural communities.

Two factors are crucial in explaining how innovations can diffuse more
rapidly through Altkolonier society. One of these factors is a higher level of
behavioral conformity. The extreme conformity of isolated agricultural communities is probably the most important factor in creating rapid internal diffusion. Conformity, itself, is a prerequisite to membership in any group
(Homans 1961:114-119), but in many agrarian communities conformity is
carried to an extreme. Several of the characteristics of these communities,
stable group membership, isolation, homogeneity, distinctiveness, and the
dominance of primary relations combine to produce extreme conformity
(Berelson and Steiner 1964:327-339). The desire for group acceptance and

lack of easy alternatives for group affiliation invest isolated agricultural communities with substantial power over an individual's behavior. These communities often mobilize this power when innovations are involved.

Innovations not adherent to local norms undergo maximum resistance due to extreme social pressure for conformity (Burt 1973:126). As a result of the community's attempt to arrive at a consensus concerning the new practice, the adoption of innovations is often postponed. Since conformity apparently tends to retard the introduction of innovations, it is not surprising to find that of the 21 architectural innovations considered, 13 were adopted later by Altkolonier. With a delayed date of introduction the second factor, indirect experience, becomes significant. Because isolated social systems take more time to acquire innovations, they tend to accumulate more information regarding such innovations. By watching and learning what happens with the introduction of the innovation among more adventuresome groups, isolated groups can base their decision to adopt on a broader range of information. They accumulate more indirect or vicarious experience with the innovation (Erasmus 1961:22).

Going one step further, it can be argued that with more (vicarious) experience isolated systems can adopt innovations with more assurance. In an interesting set of observations concerning the adoption of hybrid seed corn, Rogers (1962:115) shows that those individuals who adopt an innovation relatively late tend to adopt wholeheartedly and with much more assurance than those who adopt early. He broke the adoption process down into two periods: the awareness-to-trial period and the trial-to-adoption period and measured the length of time involved in each. Rogers observed that the length of the trial-to-adoption period decreased regularly and significantly from early adopters to laggards. Rogers also observed that early adopters try innovations on a smaller scale than later adopters. He suggests that the laggards use less time in switching to the new behavior because they are more sure of the utility of the innovation. Rogers' data on individual adoption illustrate what appears to occur at the community level. Retarding innovation introduction may allow communities to accumulate more information about an innovation which in turn permits the innovation, once accepted, to be adopted with more assurance by community members.

The relationship between isolation, behavioral conformity and social change is now clearer. Conformity contributes to rapid internal diffusion in two ways. First, with greater assurance that an innovation will be useful, individual group members will adopt immediately creating a very rapid rate of internal diffusion. Second, it must not be forgotten that even though an innovation has been introduced, the stringent normative structure remains. The same normative structure that retarded introduction will tend to speed diffusion once an innovation is adopted because conformity is important regardless of the specific norm.

Summary and Discussion

Recently Schiffer (1978:239-242) has rightfully criticized ethnoarchaeology for an insufficient emphasis on behavioral laws and a narrow range of interests. These criticisms are particularly serious because they speak to the very relevance of ethnoarchaeology to the social sciences, and to overcome them a major reorientation is necessary. First, it must be recognized that the object of ethnoarchaeology is not to study material culture as an end unto itself. The problem is not explaining material culture. Rather, ethnoarchaeology is a body of techniques and methods for material-culture research performed by any social scientist interested in the study of human social behavior and finding material culture a useful body of data. There are, in fact, no ethnoarchaeologists, just social scientists, and their range of interests is theoretically unlimited. Second, the object of ethnoarchaeology is not just to help archaeologists interpret the behavioral significance of their prehistoric material culture. The research findings of nomothetic ethnoarchaeology are of general interest to all social sciences. It seems particularly parochial for achaeologist interested in the lawful relationship between social behavior and material culture to think these relationships, if discovered and confirmed, are of use only to archaeology. Discovering and confirming the laws relating material culture and human social behavior is no mean feat and, as a result, are a significant contribution to all social sciences.

Given their significance, Schiffer's points can serve as a standard by which to evaluate the case of Mennonite architectural change as ethnoarchaeological social science. In terms of an emphasis on a generalizing approach to the study of social behavior, this study's position is self evident. A new behavioral hypothesis concerning diffusion innovation in isolated agricultural communities is proposed for future testing:

The closer a community conforms to the qualities of an isolated agricultural community, the faster will be the internal diffusion of innovations—all other factors being equal.

In addition, a superior conceptualization of the change problem was developed. Since adoption usually occurs *chronologically later* in isolated agricultural communities then in less isolated communities, it became apparent that it is crucial, when studying diffusion rates, to distinguish between the dates of introduction for each community. To understand and explain rates of diffusion, while essentially a temporal phenomenon, the trends should be considered in social rather than chronological time.

With regard to Schiffer's second point, it can be noted that the study uses material culture data in areas outside the more common synchronic studies. Through both an abstract argument and an empirical demonstration it has been shown that dated material culture provides a useful diachronic record of behavior change, and the results of the study of Mennonite architectural change recommend consideration of material culture in future social change research. Lacking diachronic records, questions requiring over-time observations like those concerning rates of change, have been inadequately handled in anthropology. As the durable products of past behavior, however, material culture offers a real opportunity for more detailed social change analysis. If the basis for selecting a given body of data rests with its efficient solution to problems, then material culture should be used more. Data gathering is nonreactive, quantifiable, inexpensive, and replicable; it preserves an important and easily tapped record of changing human behavior.

4

A Manifesto for Modern
Material-Culture Studies

William L. Rathje

"Every time I run across an article relating how archaeologists are interpreting a new dig, I can't help but wonder what would happen should our civilization be abruptly extinguished." Thus wrote Nancy Stahl in a newspaper article which concluded that archaeologists in the year 3000 would reconstruct our society "based on the contents of our basements." Upon finding empty cardboard boxes "archaeologists would undoubtedly jump to the conclusion that we were a race of box worshippers." And if Disneyland were "inadvertently" chosen as an excavation site, archaeologists would conclude we were a "race of giant three-fingered mice" (Stahl 1975). This genre of popular archaeology asks the question—what if archaeologists studied us? The answer is always the same—they would be unabashedly dumb. This is a dismal prospect. Luckily it has not robbed archaeologists of their sense of humor nor repressed their curiosity.

Most of us have played the game "what will an archaeologist learn about us in 1000 years?" A few archaeologists have decided not to wait for the answer, and are doing the archaeology of us now.

This development is part of a general trend in the discipline. During the last decade, a number of archaeologists have independently rejected two traditional parts of the definition of archaeology—that we must dig for our data, and that archaeological data must be old (cf. Ascher 1974; Deetz 1970, 1977a,b; Ferguson 1977; Fontana 1970; Leone 1973; Reid, Rathje, and Schiffer 1974; Salwen 1973; and others). This action left archaeology

MODERN MATERIAL CULTURE
The Archaeology of Us

with a single defining characteristic: a focus on the interaction between material culture and human behavior, regardless of time or space.

It is this focus on the social context of technology which is the organizing principle of archaeology. It is this focus which has led to "historic sites," "industrial," "ethno," and "experimental archaeology." Studies of modern material culture by archaeologists are a part of this development. These studies are not designed to replace the work of other disciplines, but to supplement them by providing the insights into our society and our relation to past societies which are unique to an archaeological perspective (cf. Rathje 1979a).

The archaeological exploitation of modern data does have precedents. The most legendary is A. V. Kidder's excavation of a town dump in Massachusetts, in the 1920s. Since then enough studies have been formally and informally reported to outline the general research avenues they are pioneering in (1) teaching archaeological principles, (2) testing archaeological principles, (3) doing the archaeology of today, (4) relating our society to those of the past.

The most obvious contribution of modern material-culture studies is *teaching archaeological principles.* The main advantage of these studies is that students can do their own. Involving undergraduates as archaeological investigators of their society has a variety of unique benefits: *(a)* Studying an ongoing society makes students aware of the systematic relation between material culture and behavior; *(b)* students can easily learn the strengths and weaknesses of archaeological methods by applying them in a familiar setting; and *(c)* data for study are available locally in an unending supply and there is no destruction of older, scarcer sites.

Archaeological studies at a number of universities have benefited from these advantages (Ascher 1974; Kavanaugh 1978; McVicker 1972, 1973; Morenon 1978; Rathje 1974; Salwen 1973). The University of Arizona is an example. Archaeology students began doing studies of modern material culture there in 1971. At the time the majority of projects were straight-forward tests of archaeology's basic premise—that behavior and material culture are related in a systematic manner. John Hohman (1975), for example, selected behaviors at isolated road ends as his topic and carefully recorded the surface remains at the ends of dirt roads. The resulting maps showed two concentric rings of materials. The ring closest to the road was composed of broken beer bottles; the larger ring consisted of beer cans. In areas secluded from the lights of approaching cars, a number of sex-related items were encountered. Thus, the patterns of material remains at road ends conformed to the activities that were assumed to occur at road ends.

Over the past 7 years, the direction of student projects has expanded. At present, undergraduates participate in modern material-culture field school exercises that involve them in seriation, chronology building, soil analysis, usewear analysis, and identification of the factors which affect site formation (Wilk and Schiffer, this volume). Students fresh from their own modern material culture projects are likely to approach traditional data from productive new directions. In this sense, students are themselves a much more important reservoir than their papers. Nevertheless, modern material-culture studies can do more than train students. They can also develop the method and theory components of the discipline of archaeology—enter Contribution 2, *testing archaeological principles*.

Developing archaeological techniques is the rationale for ethnoarchaeology of small communities in nonindustrial societies. While these studies are useful in interpreting hunter-gatherer campsites and farming villages, archaeologists excavate large urban centers as well. Bert Salwen (1973) has proposed several research areas where studies of modern cities could make contributions to the archaeology of ancient urban sites. In a recent paper focusing on one of Salwen's suggestions, Wilk and Schiffer (1979) have identified several patterns in behavior and material remains associated with vacant lots in Tucson. Testing these patterns in traditional archaeological sites may lead to new interpretations of the functions of the "vacant" portions of ancient cities.

The techniques and principles that can be tested in modern settings are not limited in application to urban sites. Seriation, for example, is based on general propositions about behavior patterns and material culture that can be applied and tested in any society, including our own. Feldman and Hughes (1972) selected a sample of 100 cars from a used car lot for a seriation experiment. A set of 10 stylistic and 10 functional attributes were recorded for each. First the cars were seriated on the basis of style alone, then just on the basis of function. The results were surprising. Archaeologists usually assume that stylistic attributes are the best for seriations. Modern cars, however, show considerable stylistic variability at any one time. In contrast, functional attributes such as ignition locks and seat belts, are usually adopted by all manufacturers at the same time. Thus, in this one test case, functional attributes produced a more accurate seriation than stylistic attributes.

The more we use our society as a place to apply archaeological techniques, the more information we will retrieve about our own society from archaeology's unique perspective—enter Contribution 3, *recording the archaeology of today*.

Continual change is one of the defining characteristics of modern civilization, but somehow we are too egotistical to believe it. We seem to feel that things will stay the same as they are today. Otherwise we would realize that what future archeologists will say about us is not really a game. Decades from now archaeologists will be trying to reconstruct lifeways of the 1970s. Decades from now relevant archaeological data will not be easy to find.

One of the classic folktales of archaeology is "Tell-el-New York III"

(Greenberg 1953), an account of an archaeologist's attempt in A.D. 2000 to interpret the ruins of Ebbets Field, the home stadium of the Brooklyn Dodgers. It is more than ironic that the Dodgers are now in Los Angeles and that in the mid 1960s Ebbets Field was completely torn down and replaced by an apartment complex. As this example shows, contextual analysis of our material products will be extremely difficult for future archaeologists. The flow of goods and materials from context to context has become increasingly rapid through recycling, second-hand organizations, garage sales, swap meets, other forms of reuse, and the mixing of garbage at landfills. Based on these patterns of preservation, or lack of preservation, several archaeologists have argued for a contemporary study of the material culture in use in our everyday lives (cf. Glassie 1977).

Many of the studies which intentionally make a contribution to recording our culture history focus on material culture as an important component in our belief systems. Leone has carried this aspect to its most sophisticated form in (a) analyzing the role of fences in Mormon life (1973) and (b) discussing the implications of the differences between the Mormon Temple in Washington and the Catholic and the Episcopal National Cathedrals (1977).

Another type of study which records our current lifestyles and culture history does so in a context of "relevance." The Garbage Project is an example. Begun in 1972 as a training exercise for archaeology students, the Project soon found that its record of the contents of modern household garbage cans was useful to a variety of scholars and government policy makers concerned with consumer behavior in the acquisition, use and disposal of food and other resources at the household level (Harrison, Rathje, and Hughes 1975; Rathje 1978; Rathje and Harrison 1978; Rathje and McCarthy 1977).

Every archaeological study of modern material culture, whether done in the name of teaching or testing or relevance or cognitive studies, preserves data on the current conditions of our society. These behavior-material descriptions are important for understanding ourselves today and, in addition, our relation to the past—enter Contribution 4, *relating our society to past societies*.

For us to really understand how we are similar to, or different from, our ancestors, we must be able to look at ourselves in ways which are comparable to the way we look at past societies. Archaeological remains reach in an unbroken line from the first discarded tool to the contents of our garbage cans and archaeology's perspective seems uniquely capable of examining the evolution of human societies.

Archaeologists digging sites in modern cities have already found that "many of our current problems have considerable historical depth, with clear manifestations in the archaeological record [Dickens and Bowen 1978]." This record can be used as a bridge connecting past and present. One example of an attempt to relate historic sites to the present is Daniel Ingersoll's investigations at Puddle Dock, a filled waterway and wharf structure built between 1830 and 1840 in New Hampshire. The problems investigated all related to the genesis of modern cities: solid waste disposal, land-use patterns, immigration, and slum development (Ingersoll 1971 and this volume). Perhaps the most significant bridge to the present resulted from the dock fill data which showed that the age of the throw-away world began not in the twentieth century but during the nineteenth.

This and similar studies all point toward erasing the dividing line between past and present (see Richardson and Kroeber 1940; Adams 1973, 1975). As yet, however, archaeologists have failed to explore questions raised by historic sites in modern society. Ingersoll says that the "throw away age" began in the nineteenth century. But what are the actual differences between modern solid wastes and those discarded in the mid 1800s? For this comparison, Ingersoll seems to rely on his stereotype of modern refuse. In this and other cases, archaeologists draw a line between the material commodities that are the traditional domain of their discipline and the material culture that shapes every day of their lives.

We are always in the process of becoming the past. In fact, we can often catch ourselves in the act of continuing the long-term trends that archaeologists identify in their studies of change. The linking of past to present in an archaeological perspective is a natural by-product of doing modern material-culture studies. When this link is forged, archaeological data change from "historical curiosities" to an empirical foundation for understanding our current society. Archaeologists like Ingersoll see the value of making statements which directly relate the past to the present; we now need the quantitative archaeological studies of modern societies which will give such statements validity.

The potential is clear for modern material-culture studies in archaeology, but what about the realities. Few comprehensive archaeological studies of modern material culture have yet to be undertaken and published. In fact, their contribution to traditional archaeological interests has yet to be demonstrated, perhaps because of the tempting sirens archaeologists find waiting in modern settings to lure them into other pursuits.

The first bait that subverts archaeologists is encountering living informants. With the potential to talk to people comes an interest in what people say, in "meaning" and "values." This view can separate the archaeologists of modern society from his colleagues, dusting sand from broken pots. Often, archaeologists in modern settings produce "mentalist archaeology," using material culture as one key to belief systems. But even these interests have relevance to traditional dirt archaeologists.

The first value of mentalist archaeology is in documenting the importance of belief systems in human behavior. Archaeologists, might find this stress on ideas and attitudes depressing if not for the studies which try to identify the cognitive correlates of material culture. For example, in a study of folk houses in Middle Virginia, Henry Glassie attempted to understand the relation between house forms and mental systems. He concluded, among other things, that the architectural designs seemed to "accurately reflect the conflict in a society that is schizophrenically attracted at once to hierarchical social classification and to equalitarian activity [Glassie 1975:181]." Heady stuff for an archaeologist to attempt, but it speaks of a potential to identify systems of attitudes and beliefs from material culture.

The other element of modern material culture that can subvert archaeologists is relevance (see Rathje 1979a, 1979b:17-28, for a discussion of archaeology's role as an applied behavioral science in modern society). The Garbage Project, for example, has made relatively few direct contributions to dirt archaeology. Again, however, there are indirect benefits. The most important aspect of "relevant" studies is that an archaeological perspective and methodology are making contributions to useful knowledge about our present, underscoring the ability of archaeologists to learn about our past.

These indirect benefits aside, the ideal "archaeological" study of modern material culture contributes not only to the present, but also directly to knowledge of the past. The first real modern material-culture breakthrough in archaeology awaits those purists who will shun the temptations of mental systems and relevance and walk the straight and narrow of testing archaeological principles for the past in the present.

The traditions of modern material culture studies in archaeology are only beginning to be set. This challenge offers an exciting opportunity; if well done, every study in a modern setting can contribute at one time to: (a) teaching archaeological principles, (b) testing archaeological principles, (c) recording culture history, and (d) recording data for quantitative cross-cultural comparisons. Any good dirt archaeology project performs these functions. The challenge of studying modern material culture is translating the potential of good archaeology into action in our own society.

Doing the archaeology of our own constantly changing civilization may be a little frightening to archaeologists used to carefully exhuming the remnants of dead civilizations. But we need not worry. At the very worst, we are bound to do better than finding a race of giant three-fingered mice worshipping boxes in our basements.

EARLY AND LATE AMERICANA

Who are we? One way we can begin to answer that question is to infer our identity from observations of how we Americans manipulate and discard materials. Materials and material residues provide circumstantial evidence of how Americans behave and adapt. Sometimes they provide a truer "signature" of ideational processes than the rhetoric normally associated with beliefs and ideology. Critics often decry American society as materialistic, which they equate with crassness of spirit and neglect of human values. On the basis of the chapters which follow, one can argue that, indeed, Americans are intensely materialistic, but in unexpected ways that might prompt us to revise our notions of materialism and reconsider our assumptions about how Americans really behave when dealing with materials. What I wish to do here is to offer a series of provisional inferences about the real nature of American materialism based upon the papers in this section of Modern Material Culture: The Archaeology of Us.

This effort involves both the debunking of commonly accepted ideas about American behavior as well as discoveries, sometimes of an unexpected nature, of how Americans really behave. When, for example, James Deetz tells us that:

In the cellars of the seventeenth-century Pilgrims of Plymouth Colony large quantities of pig bones have been found. The remains of pigs so outnumber those of other food animals, that we are almost tempted to suggest that the first Thanksgiving may have consisted of roast pork rather than turkey [1967:71],

57

our cherished assumptions about this quintessentially American holiday are bound to be affected. Material evidence like this demands an explanation, and in this case, as Deetz points out, pigs would have been a good basic food source for the early colonists, since they could be let run in the forest and since the meat can be preserved readily by salting and smoking. Similarly, contemporary American behavior can be subjected to the same sort of "archaeological" scrutiny, with similar effects upon our perception of life as it is really lived in America.

By using a combination of interviews and direct observations, Schiffer, Downing, and McCarthy demonstrate that present-day Tucsonans do not conform to the widely accepted stereotype of Americans as "wastemakers." Such familiar marketing techniques as planned obsolescence and aggressive salesmanship to encourage people to buy things they do not really need are effectively counterbalanced by strong tendencies to reuse objects and materials. Nonmarket transactions, often between relatives and friends, play a crucial role in American life, just as they do among people like the Trobriand Islanders, Australian Aborigines, and other classic, so-called primitive societies that have been studied in detail by anthropologists. Household stability (what Schiffer, Downing, and McCarthy refer to as the "at rest effect") is also decisive in determining both the number and variety of material items present as well as the percentage of reused items. Household stability in this case is a function of "time since last move" combined with regular changes in composition of household personnel due to aging and reproduction and to factors such as income.

According to the results of this study, reuse is widespread and is most prevalent in immature, early-stage households characterized by young adult age, low "time since last move," and low income. These households characteristically acquire their used furniture, appliances, and other items through nonmarket exchanges which escape formal bookkeeping or other records. With increased length and stability of residence there is a marked tendency to pass on used items to other households, with a resulting increase in the frequency of new items in the total inventory. Such relationships, if borne out by further testing, can radically modify our stereotyped perceptions of American society as a market-dominated economy and one which is essentially wasteful of the material products of that economy.

Ethnicity is another topic of current interest in American life, and nowhere do questions of ethnicity become more apparent than in Hawaii. Two of the papers in this section deal with the material by-products of ethnicity; Blake's study of graffiti as a mechanism for expressing ethnic slurs and Wheeler's account of *materia medica* in a Chinese herbalist's shop in Honolulu. While avoiding melting pot fantasies about ethnicity in Hawaii, the local media tend to deemphasize racial or ethnic conflicts. Yet such conflict does occur, most notably in the public schools, in campgrounds and on beaches, and in bars (especially those adjacent to military bases). The occurrence of such conflict leads one to ask: How can we identify and explain the attitudes that lead to ethnic conflict, especially in a place where efforts are made to deny that such conflict exists? The graffiti one finds in certain kinds of places in Hawaii, especially in public school toilets, reveal attitudes that cannot be expressed openly without leading to some form of censure or retaliation. Just how violent that retaliation can be is revealed by a much-publicized episode at the Hawaii State Legislature in 1978 that is described in Blake's paper along with another, even more violent case. Graffiti, when presented in specific physical contexts, represent a sensitive material indicator of tensions between ethnic groups and, as such, constitute a valuable source of circumstantial evidence about race relations in Hawaii. Or, all is not aloha in Hawaii!

The subject of ethnicity has always been difficult for social scientists to deal with effectively. How does one measure ethnicity? So much of what we refer to as ethnicity is subjective in nature and has to do with internalized values that are self-expressed or self-identified. Wheeler's study of a Chinese herbalist's shop in Honolulu demonstrates, among other things, how a modern material culture approach permits us to observe behavior and draw reliable inferences about ethnicity from that behavior. When, for example, we find that 75.9% of the bulk materia medica contained in this shop derive from China, Hong Kong, or Taiwan, despite the fact that many of these substances are available locally in Hawaii, we are confronted with an anomaly that requires more than a simple utilitarian explanation. After all, if simple utilitarian considerations were all that mattered, we would expect locally derived materia medica to dominate the assemblage in the shop. The proprietor's perceived advantages of Chinese as opposed to local medicines may or may not explain this anomaly, but there is no escaping the degree to which this measures the attraction of *things Chinese* in this particular domain. The resulting measurement may not be exactly repeatable in all such situations, but it is certainly a more objective and reliable indicator of the "Chinese connection" and its importance to people who identify themselves as Chinese than total reliance upon statements of ethnic self-identification.

If ethnicity is difficult to objectify in social science, ideology is even more intractable. Once again, a modern material culture approach affords us a look at overt behavior upon which to base reasonable inferences. Anyone who has ever visited the National Air and Space Museum in Washington, D.C., as David Meltzer did, can testify to the outstanding collections and elegant displays there. What Meltzer is suggesting, however, is that these exhibits constitute a statement about social values that goes beyond merely chronicling the history of aviation and space exploration. This is not so much an explicit, stated message as it is an expression based upon the kinds of materials which are displayed—and, of equal importance, the ones that are not. When we encounter Julia Child mixing primordial soup in her "kitchen," this is not merely a literal message about how life can begin anywhere in the universe, but it also embodies an unstated point of view or ideology concerning America's technological and organizational abilities to face a future in space. Similarly, the conspicuous omission of aircraft and events from both the Korean War and Vietnam (while, at the same time, making much of World War I and II aircraft) implies that, for whatever reasons, Americans are uncomfortable enough about these two wars to prefer not to be reminded about them. The materials chosen for display thus can be viewed, as Meltzer proposes, as a sensitive indicator of ideological positions that we, as Americans, can test against our own experiences. What would our reactions today be to a fully developed exhibit on the use of air power in Vietnam, commensurate in scope and detail with the World War I and II displays?

Relationships between material culture and beliefs, values, and other ideational components of the total cultural system are not simple or easy to get at, as is demonstrated by Price-Beggerly in her paper on the use of fences in Mormon communities in Nevada and Hawaii. In a pioneering effort to apply the modern material-culture approach, Leone argued in 1973 that there were connections between Mormon cognitive and religious categories and fencing behavior. The principal value of Leone's original paper was not so much the essential truth of this particular set of relations as the fact that it was posited in a manner susceptible to further testing. What Price-Beggerly has done here is to apply the test. All scientific hypotheses must specify what it would take to *disprove* them, and in this case, it was Price-Beggerly's discovery that fencing behavior among orthodox Mormons in Nevada and Hawaii differed significantly from that of the Mormons of eastern and central Arizona described by Leone that disproved this relationship. This is a revealing example of how science lurches on. Each step in this process of positing, testing, and disproving this set of relations is a positive step toward our understanding both of Mormon material and religious behavior and a more general knowledge of such relationships.

Thanks to Leone's original efforts and Price-Beggerly's test, we are now in a position to ask a new order of question, which is: How can we account for the variability in fencing behavior in these different Mormon communities? Without the process of hypothesis building and testing, we would not have known enough to ask this question. If Price-Beggerly is correct in her assertion that Mormon religious beliefs in these three areas do not differ significantly, we may find that the answer to this question is more circumstantial than ideational. Regardless of how the question is finally answered, this case serves as a useful example of how the modern material culture approach can be applied in a scientifically acceptable manner to discovering the essential relationships between material behavior and beliefs in a cultural system.

In his classic study of the Indians of California, A. L. Kroeber (1925:841-843) noted that geographic and tribal distribution of the practices of cremating versus burying the dead varied considerably from one area to another, with no apparent relationship either to ecological variables or to cultural traditions. While Kroeber did not pursue this idea, one might ask whether or not such practices associated with the disposal of the dead vary independently of other aspects of the cultural system, somewhat in the manner of fashions in European women's dresses described in a couple of important papers that can clearly be regarded as early forerunners of the modern material-culture approach in anthropology (Kroeber 1919, 1940). Dethlefsen's study of cemeteries in north central Florida examines how this approach can be used to identify those elements of American mortuary behavior that do show consistent relationships with other components of the cultural system, especially in the areas of religious belief and social relations.

As Dethlefsen points out, cemeteries provide a remarkable array of material data that are expressive of community values and beliefs, especially when one is considering the rates at which changes in these values and beliefs take place through time. For example, the material, locational, and stylistic uniformities of Federal period graves give way to greater variety during the Civil War period. Relatives are grouped in dispersed locations rather than together, and motifs and epitaphs also begin to vary to a greater degree. The Federal period graves reveal more community uniformity than do later periods, and one needs to inquire about the factors that would have produced such changes. Perhaps the answer lies in the realm of cultural or ideational behavior, such as the values placed on community solidarity, or possibly it has to do with circumstantial factors like population size and composition. One can also see shifts in the size of grave markers that may be indicative of greater emphasis on sexual or status distinctions, especially when the potential for sculptability of marble was being exploited most fully from about the 1890s to the 1920s. And why do wedding dates appear for the first time on gravestone inscriptions in the 1940s and 1950s along with the more usual information about years of birth and death? In addressing questions like this, Dethlefsen's study represents an effort to identify material attributes of cemeteries that will serve as sensitive indicators of changes in community beliefs and attitudes, and his initial results here demonstrate the potential for discovery afforded by application of the modern material-culture approach to this unique body of data.

Coins are for spending, right? Not entirely. According to Rothschild's study of pennies from the Denver Mint, American behavior in relation to coins extends considerably beyond their use as currency. Looked at as materials circulating in a contemporary society, this class of items is affected by various kinds of behavior on the part of the American public that has sometimes been overlooked—occasionally with costly results. Her study reveals processes at work that account for such events as the failure of the Susan B. Anthony dollar and the recent shortages of pennies being experienced by banks in different parts of the United States.

What are Americans doing with these coins besides spending them? One important kind of behavior is hoarding (that is, retention of coins for the value of their component metals), especially when the price of copper rises to such an extent that pennies cost more than 1 cent each to produce. Another is collecting, especially whenever a market develops for rare and unusual coins. And there is always casual (but, nevertheless significant) withdrawal from circulation of pennies in pickle jars and piggie banks. Why, for example, did the Mint decide to falsify the dates of pennies made in 1965 to read "1964"? Rothschild explains this unusual behavior as an effort by the Mint to anticipate the behavior of collectors, who would otherwise have scooped up the "rare" 1964 pennies to the point of taking a significant number of coins out of circulation. Rothschild also explores the use of Central Place Theory and symbolic anthropology as possible ways of explaining how Americans behave in relation to pennies in particular and money in general, noting that many aspects of this behavior do not conform to expectations based on the profit motive or other purely rational, "economic" incentives. By looking at pennies as *objects* rather than as currency, the modern material-culture approach applied by Rothschild draws attention to processes of behavior in American society that might otherwise go unnoticed.

The studies by Cleghorn and Bath explore opposite ends of the spectrum represented by markets in contemporary Hawaii. On the one hand, there is the Friendly Market in Maunaloa, on the rural island of Molokai. On the other hand, we have a modern supermarket in urban Honolulu. Neither is simple or easy to deal with. Each study, by applying a modern material-culture perspective to the materials occurring in these situations, is able to infer order amid apparent chaos. Cleghorn's study represents an unformalized but orderly approach to the problem that includes activities familiar to most anthropologists, relying as it does on direct observations of behavior as well as the contents of the store, and using limited interviews where appropriate. Bath's study applies a more formalized, linguistic methodology that examines the contrastive categories underlying the physical arrangement and presentation of goods in the store.

What accounts for the association of different categories of goods in a store? Bath argues that such associations reveal basic organizing principles.

The linguistic metaphor is an important part of her analysis, with dichotomies of categories represented on the shelves being akin to the phonology (i.e., sound system) of a language and the arrangement and manipulation of these categories resembling a grammar. Given the complexities of American consumerism, there are many goods which might appear to defy neat categorization in such a scheme, and anomalies do appear. Yet, what sometimes appear to be inconsistencies with respect to the "language" or structure of categories in use turn out upon closer examination to be explainable in terms of behavior. Note, for example, the occurrence of dried or powdered soft drinks on the same shelves as the category of "drinkables" (i.e., consumable as is, rather than as a class of "delayed consumption" items). Kool-Aid and Jello products certainly require processing before they can be consumed—or do they? Bath notes that teen-age competitors at swimming meets will consume these products straight from the package between events. It turns out there is even a powdered product called Pixie Stix that is marketed for precisely this kind of instant consumption! Thus the discovery of the categories of goods in the supermarket is not simply an end in itself but also serves to direct our attention to the extraordinary flexibility of American product marketing. Some pundit once said that in America one can merchandise anything, and Bath's study reveals how true this can be.

The same can be said for the Friendly Market of Maunaloa, although sometimes there may be evidence for miscalculations in the marketing operation. Cleghorn points out, for example, that a substantial number of goods and facilities in the store are subject to a "persistence effect"—that is, they have remained in place long beyond either their normal use-life or the time one would normally expect for them to be consumed. The Chinese cookhouse (no longer functional), the butchering appliances (meat is not butchered at the store), and the presence of unsold decorative items (vases and figurines) and electrical goods reveal this effect in various ways. For a community that is anything but cosmopolitan in nature, the wide range and variety of goods for sale at the Friendly Market is remarkable and probably represents a greater degree of risk for the merchant than would be true of a Honolulu supermarket, especially at a time when the members of the local community are undergoing a loss of purchasing power. The fate of the Friendly Market is more immediately tied to the economic fortunes of the small community it serves than is the case for a supermarket in urban Honolulu, where economic changes affect the community more unevenly and where the risk is spread more widely. By applying a modern material-culture analysis to the data at the Friendly Market, Cleghorn offers a first step toward showing how the goods in such a store can serve as a sensitive indicator of economic conditions in the community.

Physical structures, especially as they relate to domestic architecture, and spatial arrangements have traditionally been an important category of data used by archaeologists in their studies of prehistoric human behavior. Portnoy uses a classic distinction between "front" and "back" regions proposed by the sociologist, Irving Goffman, and applied by other social scientists to explain uses of materials in the residential and domestic behavior in a small Texas city, and she goes on to test her findings against the recent ethnoarchaeological studies made by Yellen among the !Kung Bushmen. The use of this distinction reveals aspects of behavior in relation to materials that are sometimes unexpected. Take the case of study desks in childrens' bedrooms. In no case in her sample did Portnoy find a child who actually used this desk for studying or for doing homework. Here is an example of dissonance between intended or designed use and actual use which Portnoy explains as a by-product of the ambiguity engendered by parental definitions of homework as a back region activity and child definition of it as a front region activity. That is, parents expected the children to do their homework in a relatively secluded and private part of the home rather than in a more formal or public area like a dining room or living room (which is, of course, where the children actually do their homework). Whether or not one accepts Portnoy's redefinition of Goffmann's distinction and her adaptation of Yellen's ring-shaped model for human settlements, it is clear that the modern material-culture approach can be usefully applied to residential and spatial behavior in contemporary societies.

Eighmy's study of Manitoba Colony Mennonites who migrated to Mexico in the 1920s examines another aspect of domestic architecture and spatial arrangements—the relationship between family composition and household size. Is mean household size constant through time, as has been assumed by many archaeologists? This assumption has served as a basis for estimating prehistoric population size from architectural remains, especially in areas like the American Southwest, where ancient architecture is abundant and well preserved. In fact, Eighmy finds that among the Mexican Mennonites mean household size (that is, people per house) has increased by about 50% since the founding of the colony in 1922. Mean roofed area per person increased as well during this period, due mainly to remodeling of existing houses and to abandonment of some already roofed space (as, for example, when families grew and left their senior generation in the old house while they established their own households). What emerges is a valuable and positive observation that, while the house site itself is not a good indicator of household size or composition, it does offer a reliable signature of the existence of the household as a social and economic unit. Such an identification is important to any archaeologist who wishes to analyze the ecological relationships in a prehistoric community, and house numbers emerge in this study as good indicators of changes in subsistence behavior.

To return to our earlier question: Who are we? More than anything else, these modern material-culture studies show us that we are not always what we seem, even to ourselves. We rely more upon kinship and friendship in our economic dealings than we may have realized, and our economic relations are more often based upon nonmarket and even perhaps nonrational behavior than we were aware. Factors like ethnicity and a willingness to reuse manufactured goods can be more decisive in our patterns of consumerism than media advertising and published economic indicators would suggest. Americans have a historic commitment to civil rights and racial equality, yet that commitment does not mean that different ethnic groups have achieved the sort of "love feast" that is sometimes popularly attributed to a place like Hawaii. Perhaps one could go even further and suggest that greater racial or ethnic equality means increased conflict (with appropriate social controls), and graffiti in Hawaii are one expression of that conflict. Americans are just as prone to rewrite history as anyone else, as shown by the omission of selected wars from the public exhibits at the National Air and Space Museum. We hoard, collect or lose pennies almost as much as we spend them, yet our marketing and merchandising system is remarkably flexible and able to respond to unusual and unlikely demands (who else would have thought of a product like Pixie Stix?). One could go on in this vein, generating and testing observations about the realities of American life, and, indeed, that is exactly what this collection of chapters is intended to do.

R.A.G

5

Waste Not, Want Not: An Ethnoarchaeological Study of Reuse in Tucson, Arizona

Michael B. Schiffer, Theodore E. Downing,
and Michael McCarthy

Americans are stereotyped as wasteful consumers. Two decades ago, Vance Packard (1959, 1960) argued that Americans discard a prodigious amount of usable material goods for the sake of having newer, less tarnished status symbols. As we now face energy shortages, inflation, and demands for recycling, "wastemaking" has become a respectable topic for scientific investigation and social action. Surprisingly, little is known about what happens to material goods after their original owners no longer find them useful. Jacoby, Berning, and Dietvorst (1977:22) remark that "virtually no conceptual or empirical work has been addressed to the general issue of disposition by consumers." In this chapter we attempt to formally organize the scientific study of one part of "disposition" processes, that having to do with the reuse of material goods. We contend that reuse substantially prolongs the life of material goods in the United States. Although Americans continually discard usable items, many goods are also circulated to other individuals and social units for further use. Using data collected by a pilot study of reuse patterns in Tucson, Arizona, we examine empirically the proposition that contemporary Americans conserve more material culture than the "wastemaker" image portrays. We document the prevalence of reuse processes and suggest some of the general factors that promote reuse in all societies.

MODERN MATERIAL CULTURE
The Archaeology of Us

Preliminary Definitions

All societies practice to some degree conservation of material resources. By prolonging the life of material culture, reuse processes are among the simplest and most widespread conservation practices. Reuse processes occur when an object, after some period of use, undergoes a change in the user (a person or social unit) or the activity of use (Schiffer 1977:17). We will follow Schiffer's (1976a, 1977) provisional classification of reuse processes. *Recycling*, a familiar process in our society, occurs when a used item is remanufactured into a new item (adapted from Darnay and Franklin 1972:3). For example, after cutting and filing, a leaf from an automobile spring becomes a machete. *Secondary use* takes place when an unmodified item is employed in a different activity (Darnay and Franklin 1972:3). A common example is the use of a peanut butter jar for storing nuts and bolts. Recycling and secondary use may or may not involve a change in the user. *Lateral cycling* occurs when an object is transferred, without change in form or use, from one user to another (Schiffer 1972:159, 1977:32-33). For example, a sofa is sold to a new owner who uses it as a sofa. *Conservatory processes* or collecting behavior bring about a change in the use (but not form) of an object such that preservation is intended (Schiffer 1976a:39, 1977:33-34). (In effect, it is a specialized variety of secondary use.) American individuals as well as public and private institutions collect everything from Mickey Mouse memorabilia to light bulbs. Among conservatory processes we also include less goal-directed "accumulating" or "hoarding" behavior, the incongruous results of which can be found in attics, basements, garages, and closets.

A *reuse mechanism* is an activity that transfers objects from person to person, thus facilitating recycling, secondary use, lateral cycling and conservatory processes (Schiffer 1977:32). Societies have developed a bewildering array of reuse mechanisms, including inheritance, gifts, dowries, brideprice, pawn shops, markets, theft, black markets, swap meets, yard sales, auctions, junkyards, and thrift shops. Reuse mechanisms vary along a number of important dimensions. First of all, we note that the transfer need not involve the use of either money or a market system. Inheritance, gift, theft, dowries, and brideprice are cases in point. Secondly, reuse mechanisms vary greatly as to whether the social or economic aspect of reuse is dominant. Clearly, gift giving, swap meets, rummage sales, yard sales, and probably auctions have an impressive social component; on the other extreme are theft and many retail stores. Third, and especially in modern America, reuse mechanisms differ in the extent that transactions are recorded. Most retail stores and auctions document their transactions in detail for tax purposes. In many societies dowries, brideprice, and inheritance are a matter of public knowledge. On the other hand, gifts, yard sales, and swap meets entirely escape the record keeping of our society, which is noted for its persistence in monitoring economic activities.

The data and analyses presented in the following show that, to a surprising degree, Americans employ reuse mechanisms having a large social component that involve neither record keeping nor money. Thus, techniques for determining the popularity of reuse based on established economic statistics will produce consistent underestimates. On the basis of these preliminary findings, we conclude that reuse in modern America is a widespread and important means of material conservation.

Background to the Reuse Project

Since 1972 the senior author has intermittently studied reuse processes in Tucson, Arizona. Tucson is the largest city in Pima county, located in the Sonoran desert of southern Arizona. Its 350,000 people account for about two-thirds of this highly urbanized county's population. Tucson is an old but rapidly growing multiethnic city, having a mixed economic base consisting of mining, tourism, light industry, commerce, an Air Force base, and the University of Arizona.

Our investigations of reuse in Tucson have followed two complementary research strategies. First, we have studied a number of particular reuse mechanisms by drawing upon casual observations, questionnaires, and participant observation. The field studies, a few of which have been conducted in other cities, include thrift shops, antique stores (Claassen 1975), garage sales (Linton 1977), antique car clubs (Poor 1978), swap meets (Brown and Johnson 1973; Kassander 1973; Wood 1973), gifts (Young 1973), and second-hand stores (Brown and Johnson 1973; Kassander 1973). Schiffer (1976a,b) has partially summarized the results of these investigations. The second strategy, begun in 1976, focused on reuse patterns of households. It had become apparent by then that many of our hypotheses, involving relationships between socioeconomic variables and reuse patterns (Schiffer 1976a,b), could be most efficiently tested on a household level. To set the stage for presenting the results of the household interviews, we discuss briefly some findings from the background studies of reuse mechanisms.

Participant observation has been concentrated in recent years on two of the more colorful reuse mechanisms: yard sales and swap meets. In yard sales, one or more households offer for sale a motley assortment of "junk" and treasures, usually in a front yard, patio, or carport. These are generally weekend events, occurring mostly in middle class neighborhoods. Yard sales, which appear to have begun in Southern California in the early 1960s, are now prevalent throughout the United States. Indeed, the classified section of newspapers often contains a "yard sale" entry. A handful of trade books have appeared advising potential buyers and sellers on appropriate strategies (Copeland 1977; Young and Young 1973). According to the participants, yard sales are held for a number of reasons, including securing extra cash and "getting rid of excess items," especially before a move (Linton 1977). During late spring and early summer—the heavy moving seasons—eager bargain hunters, and a handful of dealers, can be seen driving from sale to sale.

Quite clearly, yard sales are becoming an important means for American households to dispose of unwanted material goods, particularly at certain points in their history. We immediately grasped the possibility that other reuse mechanisms arose for similar reasons: to promote the transfer of used goods, when an individual or household undergoes a change in status, such as loss or gain of a member, rise or fall in income, or a move. We shall return in the following to these ideas.

Swap meets are periodic markets consisting of independent vendors. Like yard sales, the greatest amount of swap-meet activity occurs on weekends. In contrast to yard sales, which take place at private residences, swap-meet vendors congregate in a central location, usually in public facilities, such as parking lots and drive-in theaters, used primarily for other purposes. However, Tuscon's most viable swap meets, Oracle Road and Tanque Verde, have their own exclusive facilities, including snack bars, restrooms, and entertainment for children.

There are three major kinds of swap-meet vendors. One-timers come occasionally, usually to dispose of a great variety of household items. In many ways, one-timers are similar to yard-salers in their reasons for engaging in reuse. Part-timers are likely to be hobbyists attempting to pick up extra dollars by specializing in a few types of items such as antique tools, coins, or clothing. Some part-timers, especially jewelers, have permanent shops in town but "moonlight" at swap meets. Professionals make most of their living at swap meets by selling a limited variety of new and used items. At the Oracle Road and Tanque Verde swap meets, a stable core of professionals can be found year round. During weekdays or at particular times of the year they attend auctions and engage in other reuse activities to secure their inventories. Professionals tend to make a relatively large investment in facilities, including elaborate display cases, awnings, lounge chairs, and other creature comforts.

Swap meets sometimes have an unsavory reputation, owing to the occasional discovery of stolen items and the attention drawn to these disclosures by more established merchants. Yet, with the many attractions swap meets offer, especially in times of economic difficulty, they are gaining ever-greater numbers of participants. They are also becoming much more institutionalized and "accepted." In addition to the staple assortment of tires, guns, and tools offered by the professionals, one can also find displays by a real estate company and the National Guard. Tanque Verde swap meet even advertises on television with its own catchy jingle.

Our research into swap meets has suggested much about the nature of periodic markets (Schiffer and Schaefer n.d.), as well as informing us about certain characteristics of reuse processes. Specifically, we have formulated hypotheses about the socioeconomic correlates of reuse. For example, swap meets seem to involve the movement of items between members of the lower middle and upper lower classes (defined by income), as well as within these classes. Upper class individuals take part in swap meets as buyers, often searching for particular kinds of antiques or collectables. These tentative findings led us to hypothesize that many reuse mechanisms are class-specific, at least in terms of the kind and amount of participation.

The Reuse Project

These first-hand glimpses into particular reuse mechanisms served to document some of the more public varieties of reuse in Tucson and furnished a series of testable hypotheses (Schiffer 1976b). However, it was apparent that to progress beyond vague impressions and gross concepts, we would have to examine reuse from the standpoint of households. If the hypotheses had any merits, household studies would disclose them.

With great trepidation and no funding, Schiffer and Downing launched a project in the spring of 1976 to investigate household reuse. With the assistance of a dozen, enthusiastic undergraduate students, we devised a questionnaire and pretested it in 20 households. The 17-page questionnaire was exploratory, with the directly administered questions reflecting the many hypotheses under consideration. Specifically, we obtained data on: (a) type and size of dwelling, (b) length of residence, (c) number of times the household moved in the previous 5 years, (d) household composition, including a kinship chart; and, for each individual, occupation, age, sex and level of education, (e) ethnicity and race for the household unit, (f) income, (g) rates of replacement and disposition of replaced items for a sample of furniture and appliances, (h) kinds of collections, (i) whether household members acquire or dispose of material culture by using various reuse mechanisms, (j) participation in swap meets and yard sales, and (k) an inventory of furniture and major appliances. For each inventoried item, we recorded its formal category (couch, TV), present use, how long it had been in the household's possession, whether it was obtained new or used, whether it was considered to be an antique, and, if it was obtained used, the specific mechanism of acquisition.

The questionnaire was administered to 184 households during the spring semesters of 1976 and 1977. Interviewers were undergraduate student volunteers enrolled in several upper-division archaeology courses taught by the senior author and William L. Rathje at the University of Arizona.

Many factors influenced our sampling design; of these, statistical purity had the lowest weighting. First of all, because many of the interviewers lacked automobiles, the sample households had to be accessible by foot or bus. Second, because few of the students were bilingual, Mexican-American neighborhoods had to be excluded. Third, we wished to include an adequate representation of diverse socioeconomic classes, although not necessarily in proportion to their relative frequency in the population. Even with these constraints, a satisfactory sampling design was easily devised. Since U.S. census data indicated a general gradient of household income along the east-west midline of the city, it was possible to construct a simple east-west transect that cross-cut income groups and paralleled major bus lines, while avoiding predominantly Spanish-speaking neighborhoods. The transect, averaging 1 mile in width, consisted of 12 units—each approximating 1 square mile. Five additional square-mile units were purposely placed in other parts of the city to increase the number of low- and high-income households. Within each unit, 5 streets were randomly selected and letters of introduction that announced the possibility of an interview were distributed to a sample of the residences—houses as well as individual apartments and mobile homes. Skeptical or worried residents were encouraged to call the university to verify the legitimacy of the interviewer who might, we feared, be mistakenly accused of "casing" the premises. In the next step, the students attempted to conduct interviews in five households on each street. When no one was home or no adults were present, the interviewers either returned later or picked another residence. Quite frequently the interviewer was turned away. In that case as well additional households were selected. Overall, turndown rates were high, but varied in a predictable manner. They were lowest (ca. 20%) for teams of two, neatly dressed females. For a lone male, the rate went as high as 90%. As a result of various factors, including students who dropped the courses, incompatible teams, variable turndown rates, and the reluctance of students to venture into low-income neighborhoods, the actual number of interviews varied considerably among the sample units, ranging from 7 to 25.

Once permission was granted for the interview, few problems were encountered. Indeed, students complained that their greatest difficulty was in concluding the interview. Most questions, even of a personal nature, were answered cheerfully. The exception was income. Twenty households, or 10.7% of the sample, refused to divulge their income or claimed ignorance. On the average, interviews lasted about 1.5 hours, with a range of 20 minutes to 2 hours. This length of time is correlated with the number of rooms occupied by the household, since the latter closely determines the number of items that must be inventoried.

In view of the many problems inherent in our procedures of household selection, we anticipated that the sample would be biased with respect to one or more important parameters. We have identified some of the biases by comparing selected variables with the results of a much larger interview survey (N = 1300) done by the Valley National Bank and the *Tucson Daily Citizen* in 1976 (Table 5.1). In the Reuse Project sample, higher-income households are overrepresented relative to lower-income households. This

Table 5.1
Biases in the Reuse Project Household Sample[a]

	a. Annual income (dollars)		
	0-9999	10,000-19,999	20,000+
VNB/TDC	40%	39%	21%
Reuse Project	32%	36%	32%

	b. Time in present dwelling (as a percentage)	
	0-5 years	more than 5 years
VNB/TDC	64	36
Reuse Project	55	45

	c. Ethnicity (as a percentage)			
	Anglo	Mexican-American	Black	Indian	Other
VNB/TDC	70	24	3	2	1
Reuse Project	94	6	0	1	0

	d. Home ownership (as a percentage)	
	Own	Rent
VNB/TDC	71	29
Reuse Project	69	31

[a] Comparison of selected variables in the reuse sample with results of the Valley National Bank/*Tucson Daily Citizen* Survey (Tucson Newspapers 1976).

bias was predictable, given our deliberate effort to increase the absolute number of the rarer, high-income households. The sample is also biased against various ethnic groups, a serious limitation given the prevalence (24%) of Mexican–American households in Tucson. In addition, sample households tend to be more sedentary than those in the entire population. This bias is also to be expected because of the positive relationship of income to stability of residence (see following). Fortunately, the sample does accurately reflect the ratio of renters to owners of dwellings. It is evident that the high turndown rate may have introduced more subtle biases into the sample. Presently, however, we are unable to specify the characteristics of those households willing to cooperate versus those that would not.

Despite the biases in the Reuse Project sample and the relatively small number of interviews, we are confident that the data are adequate for a pilot study of major reuse patterns at the household level.

Reuse Project Findings

Contrary to the "wastemaker" stereotype, the data indicate that reuse is widespread. All households admit to employing one or more reuse mechanisms for acquiring material culture. All households dispose of at least some unwanted material culture through reuse processes, as opposed to discard. In addition our results demonstrate a rather impressive involvement of social ties in reuse behavior. Let us examine these patterns more closely.

In order to evaluate directly the proposition that items replaced by a household are more likely to be reused than thrown away, the Reuse Project sought data on a sample of replaced items. Interviewers asked the following question:

> One of the problems we all have is replacing furniture that is worn out, broken, or items that we are simply tired of. Now I will read you a short list of things, and I would like to know which ones, if any, you or any member of the household have replaced in the last 5 years (or the period since establishment of the household) and what you did with the old one?

The list contained 13 items: bed, couch, dining chair, easy chair, dresser, bookcase, stereo, TV, washer, dryer, dining table, range, and refrigerator. The results present a picture of consistent household reuse.

Respondents in our 184 households reported replacing 743 items, an average of 4 each. Of the total, 30.5% were retained by the household, the majority being recycled (12.8%), secondarily used (5.4%), or stored (6.0%); the remainder were abandoned (4.3%) or sold with the dwelling (2.0%). Another large segment of the replaced items (34.1%) was sold or given to strangers or stores. The most popular of such disposal methods was gift to a thrift shop or charitable foundation (12.7%), sale to a stranger (5.0%) and sale to a new-used specialty store (3.6%). The latter includes trade-ins. Relatives (outside of the household) and friends were the recipients, by gift, sale, and loan of 29.9% of the replaced items. The most interesting finding of all is that only 46 items (6.2%) were thrown away.

Although the 6.2% figure should not be taken at face value, it does indicate overall that replaced items are seldom discarded. At least two factors influence the true discard rate. First of all, some of the items abandoned with a dwelling may be discarded eventually. However, even if all abandoned items are tossed out the total discard percentage would rise to just 10.5%. Second, objects that are thrown out may not reach archaeological context or stay there very long. Items of furniture and appliances are routinely scavenged from alleys in residential neighborhoods as well as vacant lots and the landfill (Schiffer 1976b). Indeed, large items are not collected by the city in their biweekly pickups. Thus, it appears that few pieces of furniture and appliances reach the Tucson archaeological record intact. Taking into account abandoned items and scavenging, we can conclude that the true percentage of items that enters archaeological context (and stays there) is probably below 10.5%. In any event, it appears that the vast majority of replaced items are indeed retained within the system and reused.

The Reuse Project also obtained some data on conservatory processes. Respondents were asked to identify the kinds of objects collected by members of the household, and to enumerate the acquisition mechanisms usually employed. Unfortunately, the respondent in most instances was not the principal collector. This problem raises considerable doubts about the reliability of the collection data, but we shall attempt to discern patterns in it nonetheless.

As might be expected, a majority of the households engage in conservatory processes: 62.5% collect one or more kind of item. This amounts to 296 collections, with a mean of 2.6 per collecting household. Although there were 61 different types of collection, 7 items account for 54% of the total. From most to least popular they are: books-magazines, records, plants, coins, stamps, rocks, and bottles. Curiously, 38 types of collection were unique. Among the unique items are music boxes, insulators, kitchen utensils, doilies, ashtrays, cigar boxes, cameras, and Hummel figurines. Collectors obtain objects from a bewildering variety of sources—virtually every conceivable mechanism is employed, although for any given collection only 1.3 reuse mechanisms are cited by the respondents. Because the respondents are not likely to know the entire range of mechanisms resorted to by all collectors in the household, we can surmise that the latter figure is probably a sizable underestimate.

Consistent with our earlier findings, we discovered that conservatory processes depend heavily upon transfer of objects, both new and used, among friends and relatives. Of the 392 acquisition mechanisms listed 101 or 25.5% are *gifts*, mostly from friends and family. Purchase from a friend or relative accounts for another 7.9%, bringing to one-third the fraction of acquisition mechanisms dependent upon close social ties. The actual percentage of collected *items* may even be higher than the one-third figure. Perhaps it would be useful to view collections, particularly those of a hobby as opposed to an investment nature, as primarily a by-product of gift giving in a social context. Exploration of this idea can make use of information on the age and sex of collectors of varying items. We would expect type of collection to be dependent upon the sorts of relationships established between the collector and his or her social field and these are likely to be influenced strongly by age and sex. Harrington (1976), using only the 1976 Reuse Project questionnaires ($N = 57$), discerned some patterning of collections by age and sex. She found, for example, that record collectors tend to be males, aged 26 to 35. We have not further analyzed the data with this question in mind, but we suspect that such patterns will be found in the larger sample. Based on the present slim evidence, it would appear that gift giving to supply collectors is an important process for cementing social ties, kin and nonkin, in our society.

Data from the furniture-appliance inventory also hold some gratifying surprises about the prevalence of reuse in Tucson. In over one-third of the households (37%), more than half of the furniture and major appliances were received in used condition (Figure 5.1). Only 8% claim to own no used items. In addition, 32.2% of the entire furniture-appliance inventory of 7499 items was obtained used. This high estimate of reuse nevertheless is

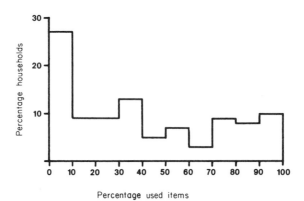

Percentage used items

Figure 5.1. *The occurrence of used items in a sample of 184 Tucson households.*

probably an *underestimate*, because the sample bias favors high-income households which, as we shall see below, engage less frequently in reuse.

Interesting results emerge when we examine which reuse mechanisms supplied the 2412 used items in the furniture-appliance inventories. The eight most popular mechanisms are displayed in Table 5.2. These can be grouped into three general categories that account for 86.5% of the acquisition events:

1. Obtained from a relative or friend (41.2%).
2. Acquired with the dwelling (28.4%).
3. Purchased in a store (16.9%).

Quite clearly, there is a remarkably high reliance on unrecorded, nonmarket transactions. Apparently, kinship and social networks provide households with access to material goods. Purchase from a store is a last resort that contributes only a small fraction of the reused items. In fact, all retail sales combined (new-used specialty stores, auctions, junk shops, and thrift stores), supplied only 16.9% of the used items. Apparently, a monumental amount of economic activity (i.e., transactions in material goods) escapes formal record keeping entirely. A large number of households have obtained some of their furniture and appliances without participating in the marketing system! It would seem that our industrial society has some characteristics usually considered to typify "primitive" economies. Although market mechanisms are employed, a substantial amount of household reuse is facilitated entirely by social ties—not unlike other societies.

Before reuse processes are considered further, it is useful to explore basic patterns of material goods in Tucson households. In this way, reuse processes can be viewed against a backdrop of more general household pro-

Table 5.2
The Eight Most Popular Mechanisms for Acquisition Based on 2412 Used Items

Mechanism	Percentage of items
Gift from a relative	19.9
Rented with a dwelling	19.5
Purchased at a new-used specialty store	11.9
Inheritance	9.5
Gift from a friend	5.8
Purchased with dwelling	5.6
Found with dwelling	3.3
Purchased from a friend	3.3
All others	18.0

cesses. These analyses are based on the Spearman rank correlation coefficient, a nonparametric test that is well suited to the abnormalities of behavioral data (Nie, Hull, Jenkins, Steinbrenner, and Bent 1975).

The first hypothesis treats the relationship between residential stability and the size of a household's inventory of material goods. Some economists, social anthropologists, and archaeologists believe that as social units become more sedentary, the number of their possessions increases. At the most general level, this hypothesis is already well supported (Spier 1973). Highly mobile hunter-gatherers accumulate few material items compared to more sedentary village agriculturalists. The material culture of the latter is dwarfed by totally sedentary industrial cities. We seek to examine this relationship on an intrasocietal level. In the Tucson study, residential stability is indicated by the number of household moves in the previous 5 years. The fewer the moves, the more stable the household. The total number of items in the furniture-appliance inventory is taken as an index of the household's material culture burden. The variables are somewhat related, with a coefficient of .37. Although our test furnishes slight support for the hypothesis, other variables are also involved, as we shall see. Interestingly, the data suggest a not very surprising *at rest effect:* The longer a household remains at a residence (measured as "time since last move") the more items it accumulates.

Another common assumption is that the number of people in a household is closely reflected in the number of household items and the size of the dwelling. Our analyses partially support this assumption. Household size and the total inventory of items are weakly correlated (rho = .34); household size is a bit more strongly related to dwelling size (rho = .48). Dwelling size, however, was measured by the number of rooms rather than total floor area—though both must be highly covariant. Interestingly, the number of rooms and inventory size are related more closely to household income than to household size. Clearly, household income is a strong determinant of material goods and dwelling size.

This series of bivariate relationships is summarized in Figure 5.2. The graphic model portrayed should not be confused with a path analysis; it is merely our impressionistic causal model based solely on theory and supported by the Spearman's rank correlation coefficients. Had a path analysis been undertaken, the model probably could have been streamlined somewhat. Nevertheless, we believe it is a good starting point for discussing the most general relationships between household dynamics and material culture.

Given this model as background, we can now probe reuse processes in more detail. Four composite variables were used in the analysis:

1. The number of used items in the furniture-appliance inventory.
2. The percentage of used items in the furniture-appliance inventory.

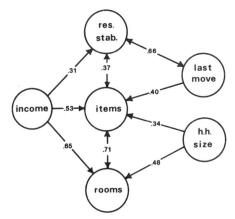

Figure 5.2. *A model of basic material-culture dynamics at the household level. Numbers refer to values of Spearman's rank correlation coefficient.*

   3. The number of different mechanisms employed by the household for acquiring used items.
   4. The number of different mechanisms employed by the household for disposing of items.

With respect to these reuse variables, several patterns are found. We must point out, however, that most of the rank correlation coefficients are rather low, between .2 and .6, indicating minor trends rather than dominant regularities. It should also be noted that the highest correlation, .72, was obtained between the variety of reuse processes employed for both disposal and acquisition. The results are as follows:

   1. More mobile households tend to have a greater number and larger percentage of used items and to employ more varied reuse mechanisms for disposal and acquisition.
   2. Lower-income households, and those with smaller dwellings, tend to have a larger number and percentage of used items and to utilize a greater variety of reuse mechanisms for disposal and acquisition.
   3. As the "time since last move" increases, households tend to have fewer used objects and to utilize a more limited range of reuse mechanisms for disposal and acquisition.
   4. Higher-income households tend slightly to replace basic furniture–appliance items (couch, washer, etc.) at a higher rate than lower-income households, thus creating considerable opportunities for reuse.

The most interesting finding of all, however, is that neither income nor residential stability are related as strongly with the number of used items as either the age of the household's principal adult male or female. As the people grow older, the number of used items they own declines. This finding raises questions about the completeness of the preceding analyses; for it indicates that an additional causal process underlies the bivariate relationships. The major independent, underlying variable that seems to be at work is the stage of household development. In all areas of material culture and reuse processes, immature, early-stage households should contrast sharply with more developed ones. We hypothesize that as household development proceeds, residential stability, income, household and dwelling size and the inventory of material items should all increase. At the same time, the number of used items should decline, as will participation in reuse processes for acquisition. As the most advanced stages are reached, these trends may reverse, as household income drops and they become more mobile. In order to evaluate these hypotheses and to learn if the household developmental cycle is an important variable underlying the patterns, we turned to other analytical tools.

It was first necessary to scale households according to developmental stage. A classification devised by an urban geographer served our purposes (McCarthy 1976), although its cross-cultural applicability is certainly limited (Table 5.3). This scheme contains eight stages, beginning with a young, single head of household and progressing through a predictable sequence of aging and children. The system breaks down slightly in the last three stages, for they do not necessarily fall along the same household trajectory. In addition, many anomalous households were forced into the latter three categories—households which probably follow analogous but very different developmental cycles. Given these problems, the first five stages should be the most reliable for testing the hypotheses. The results are displayed in Figure 5.3, while the basic data are contained in Table 5.4.

Table 5.3
The Stages of the Developmental Cycle of the Household. Adapted from McCarthy (1976:58).

Stage	Composition
1	Young, single head; no children
2	Young couple; no children
3	Young couple; young children
4	Young couple; adolescent children
5	Older couple; older children
6	Older couple; no children
7	Older single head, no children
8	Single head; with children

Table 5.4
Reuse Project Data Showing the Relationship between Developmental Stage of the Household and Selected Material-Culture, Socioeconomic, and Reuse Variables[a]

House-hold stage	Sample size	Income[b]	House-hold size	Dwelling size[c]	Years in dwelling	Percentage of home ownership	Total items	Percentage of rented items	Age of oldest item	Percentage of used items
1	35	9.1	1.77 (.84)	2.9	1.77 (1.47)	17.1	25.48 (11.83)	23.7	5.88 (5.82)	74.9
2	19	27.8	2.36 (.68)	5.3	2.21 (2.41)	21.1	30.52 (11.63)	24.1	9.11 (13.87)	55.0
3	22	60.0	4.09 (1.01)	40.0	3.22 (2.04)	72.7	38.09 (16.10)	2.0	12.48 (6.36)	39.8
4	15	80.0	4.60 (.82)	50.0	4.93 (3.41)	86.7	49.00 (10.30)	1.9	18.80 (11.75)	26.0
5	16	57.1	4.43 (1.31)	9.4	12.81 (7.4)	100.0	67.00 (17.86)	.5	30.41 (17.10)	16.6
6	42	75.7	2.44 (.73)	25.1	13.95 (10.79)	95.2	51.65 (31.80)	.9	30.90 (14.29)	22.5
7	21	33.4	1.13 (.35)	12.9	17.00 (13.00)	95.2	65.72 (122.21)	.8	38.40 (20.17)	26.9
8	8	42.9	2.37 (.51)	—[d]	9.74 (2.58)	75.0	33.12 (8.00)	.5	23.13 (23.81)	30.9

[a] Note that most variables are recorded as mean values for each stage. These data are the basis for Figure 5.3. Where appropriate standard deviations are provided in parentheses.
[b] Recorded as the percentage of households having an annual income greater than $14,999.
[c] Recorded as the percentage of households having greater than five rooms in their dwelling.
[d] Lost data.

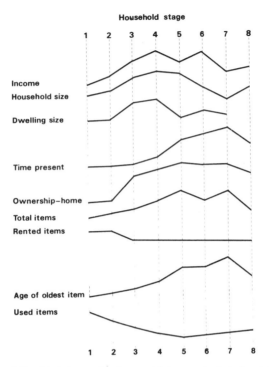

Figure 5.3. *The relationship between developmental stage and selected variables of households in the Reuse Project sample.*

As we would expect, income and household size go up regularly until Stage 5 is reached, when both decline. Consistent with our earlier findings, dwelling size behaves in a fashion quite similar to income; it, too, experiences the most precipitous drop as the founding couple and their children grow older (Stage 5). The remaining general patterns also conform closely to the predictions. The number of years present at the dwelling gradually increases through the developmental cycle (until Stage 8); this is paralleled by a rise in the number of homeowners.

Material goods and reuse practices keep pace with household development. The total number of items grows regularly as the household matures; after Stage 5, it fluctuates. The percentage of rented items, which never exceeds one quarter of the household inventory, plummets quickly to near zero when couples begin having children (Stage 2). As we expect, the age of the oldest item in the household rises, all the way to the household's greatest maturity. And, finally, the percentage of used items falls briskly at a fairly constant rate, until it begins a slow rise at Stage 6. These graphs, it should be emphasized, are based on *mean* values for each stage, and, in many cases, the standard deviations are high. Despite our small and biased sample, the vagaries of Tucson households, and the use of means, the regularities in material-culture dynamics of households seem clearcut and consistent.

Given the limitations of our data and consequent lack of more fine-grained causal analyses, we cannot state that the developmental stage of the household, per se, is the most influential variable in determining material-culture and reuse patterns. We have clearly demonstrated that it is important. We are inclined to believe that income, residential stability, and time since last move may go a long way toward explaining much of the residual variability.

Examination of a subset of our sample illustrates how the variables working together influence material culture and reuse behavior. Forty-two households were composed of an older couple without children (Stage 6). In this stage are retired people as well as those who still work, and both groups contain high- and low-income households. Some have not moved for a long time (in one case more than 50 years) and retain a fairly large house with many furnishings. Those which have recently moved, however, usually have many fewer items. If they migrated to Tucson from a distant state, most of their furniture and appliances were purchased on their arrival, and are likely to have been bought new. Presumably, they disposed of their previous furniture and appliances just before moving. Clearly, these statements cannot be statistically validated because of small sample size, yet we believe the patterns are fairly robust.

Cross-Cultural Implications

Studies of specific reuse mechanisms and the results of the household interviews enable us now to frame a number of specific, potentially cross-cultural hypotheses regarding household material culture and reuse.

In any society, the kinds and quantities of household material items, including dwellings, should be related to four principal factors:

1. Stage in the developmental cycle of the household (i.e., size and composition).
2. Residential stability.
3. Time since last move.
4. Wealth or income.

These, we believe, are fairly strong determinants and should account for much of the gross variability in household material culture within a society.

Insofar as reuse is concerned, it is suggested that the major factors promoting household *acquisition* through reuse processes are:

1. Early stages of the developmental cycle.
2. Low status or income.
3. High residential mobility.

Ethnicity may also influence the relative importance of certain reuse processes, but the Reuse Project's sampling bias has prevented systematic exploration of this variable.

We also can begin to specify the kinds of recurrent, general situations where in all societies opportunities are created for the disposal of material culture. As in Tucson, these situations may produce items that are reused rather than discarded.

Whenever there is a change in the social status of an individual various items of a household's inventory will no longer be appropriate and may be reused by others. Status changes are categorized as follows:

1. *Age-dependent.* Clothing is outgrown; items of enculturation and recreation change; and, of course, cosmetics and medicines vary.
2. *Rites of passage.* Socially recognized stages often require the addition or deletion of material items, either as symbols or for performance of new roles. Rites of passage can create substantial reuse opportunities. Death obviously is the most far-reaching of these events, and may lead to much reuse through the mechanism of inheritance.
3. *Achieved status positions.* When individuals attain new positions in the social order, primarily during adulthood, they acquire new material symbols and may dispose of old ones. Some of the latter may be reused.

Just as changes in an individual's status have consequences for material culture and reuse, so also do changes in the developmental cycle of social units. As social units vary in size or composition, alter their activities or move from one dwelling to another, reuse opportunities arise. For example, when households enter an expansion phase they may occupy more or larger dwellings. A smaller one left behind may be reused. Households in a contraction phase, particularly when they move, may dispose of a considerable amount of material culture. Similarly, as communities age, more material simply becomes available for reuse processes.

The extraordinarily high rates of household formation and dissolution that currently characterize the United States are contributing to the growth in importance of reuse mechanisms such as yard sales and swap meets. Avoidance of sales taxes and the reduction in disposable income may also help to account for the increased popularity of these reuse mechanisms.

Another factor at work is the high rate of residential mobility. Fewer children are living in the same town as their parents or other family members, thus creating a situation that has greatly reduced the opportunity to pass along items to relatives. As a result, items which would once have been stored for future use by family members are increasingly being sold to friends or strangers. These factors together, in the context of general economic uncertainty, are making reuse processes an increasingly visible economic activity.

Together, the preceding statements form a network of hypotheses that can orient cross-cultural investigations of reuse. Our studies have isolated certain factors that seem relevant to explaining variability in reuse. In addition, a series of recurrent situations has been identified that provide a potential for the occurrence of reuse processes. As these are examined in a variety of sociocultural settings, more refined hypotheses will certainly replace our provisional formulations.

Conclusions

On the basis of Reuse Project findings, tentative though they may be, we anticipate that reuse processes are widespread and constitute an important set of strategies for households to obtain and dispose of material goods. These results clearly call into question the view that Americans irrationally waste resources by throwing away perfectly usable items. On the contrary, it appears that the high rates of acquisition and disposal of goods in more mature, affluent households—admittedly generated by status needs—make available a flow of serviceable items to early stage and poorer households. Our data suggest that relatively few intact items of furniture and appliances ever enter the sanitary landfills of a modern city. One or more reuse mechanisms would have intervened to make this an unlikely occurrence.

At the present time, planners and policy makers at various levels of government are trying to come to grips with the world of scarce energy and resources that mankind faces in the last 2 decades of the twentieth century. Before any of the measures for energy and material conservation are adopted, we should be able to predict how they will affect on-going reuse processes. After all, reuse processes are a means of material conservation already employed by a majority of households. Unfortunately, the prevailing opinion that reuse processes are insignificant has hindered investigations of the topic. In the long run, Americans may pay dearly for this ignorance, particularly if government-imposed programs inadvertently disturb current reuse practices, causing less, not more, conservation of our resources. In order to prevent this, we need to obtain additional ethnoarchaeological information on present-day reuse behavior so that disruptions can be minimized by careful planning. It would appear that ethnoarchaeology's unique perspective, a concern with the behavioral context of material culture, is indispensable for properly managing complex societies.

Acknowledgments

Michael McCarthy was responsible for the basic numerical analyses, while Schiffer and Downing supplied the interpretations. The Reuse Project was supported entirely by the Department of Anthropology, University of Arizona. We thank Raymond H. Thompson for making available computer time and departmental resources. Barbara Curran assisted in the formulation of the Reuse Project questionnaire. We extend our warm thanks to the University of Arizona students who participated in the Reuse Project: M. Barnes, M. Bartlett, S. Bernheim, J. Bramhall, G. Bruno, R. Chandler, H. Deluga, K. Downing, L. Eure, F. Harrington, K. Keller, S. Kelly, K. Kreutzer, P. Larich, G. Lemmler, M. Lichter, K. McCluskey, G. Miller, P. Morris, L. Olander, J. Peters, J. Quinn, L. Richards, and J. Wyant. Randall H. McGuire, George Teague, Nat de Gennaro, and William L. Rathje provided helpful comments on the manuscript. Earlier versions of this chapter were read by Schiffer at the Annual Meeting of the American Anthropological Association, Los Angeles, 1978, and the 49th Congress of the Australian and New Zealand Association for the Advancement of Science, Auckland, 1979.

6

Graffiti and Racial Insults: The Archaeology of Ethnic Relations in Hawaii

C. Fred Blake

When asked for his impressions of America after an absence of some 35 years, Professor Fei Xiaotong, a leading anthropologist in the People's Republic of China, replied: "Jogging and writing on subway walls—what do you call it?" Graffiti," I responded. Dr. Fei qualified his remarks by stating that his impressions of America may be superficial since he only had 1 month, and that, he said with a note of frustration, was spent mostly in the company of other professors!

Professor Fei's remarks struck a familiar chord. Only several months before, I had occasion to speak on my impressions of China—I had traveled there for 2 weeks during the summer of 1978. As with professor Fei, I caught only fleeting glimpses of the common people's daily lives. My tour included many public parks and ancient temples. Here I encountered an unexpected phenomenon, one which had a lasting impression on me. It was the *cu ke* (or "graffiti"), especially the poetry scrawled all over the Liu Ho Pagoda in storied Hangchow.

This uncanny coincidence of impressions (I with Chinese *cu ke* and Fei with American graffiti) is possibly explained by the frustration we each felt at not having anthropological access to the common people during our respective tours. To encounter the thoughts of common people on walls was bound to leave vivid and lasting impressions on the minds of two frustrated anthropologists. In fact as I toured China I sometimes felt like an archaeologist barred from the voices of the living and having to rely on such residues of bygone behaviors as graffiti.

87

MODERN MATERIAL CULTURE
The Archaeology of Us

When I returned from China, I could hardly help but notice some of the graffiti which I daily encounter. I gave considerable thought to ways that graffiti might be significant to ethnological research. In the few pages that follow I examine graffiti as a hitherto underexploited source of data, data which is essentially archaeological in nature, for the ethnologist. I focus on a corpus of graffiti which has particular interest to ethnologists working in Hawaii, namely racial or ethnic remarks. I argue that by classifying variations in the content of graffiti and by observing variations in their spatial distribution, we can posit specific rules of ethnic group relationships in Hawaii. In the course of positing these rules we might also posit some general principles which explain the production of graffiti in society.

The Artifacts

Since graffiti are artifacts of anonymous behavior fixed in time and space, I find it useful to treat them as an archaeologist treats potsherds from the shell middens of an archaeological community. The first task is to classify the artifacts (that is the graffiti) that I collected over a period of several months in 1979 from a number of men's rooms around the University of Hawaii. I am not prepared to render a rigorous, much less a complete, taxonomy of graffiti. The taxonomy I derive is based on a set of rough and ready attributes aimed at elucidating the contexts in which ethnic signatures can be apprehended.

There are at least three sets of attributes that may be brought to bear on a collection of graffiti. The first consists of materials and techniques used in the production of the message. These include available writing and etching instruments, surface textures, and color combinations which may facilitate or hinder the production of graffiti. Although these material aspects are intrinsically interesting, a detailed description of them would take us beyond the scope of this paper. In other studies where a comparison of frequencies between two sites constitutes the main variable these material attributes are methodologically significant.

The second set of attributes defines the form of the message. Discursive messages can be classified on the basis of grammatical or poetical structures. A prosodic classification might be relevant to a study of the Liu Ho Pagoda graffiti in Hangchow or to the graffiti which Shakespeare's Orlando carved on every tree as a testament of his love for Rosalind. However, any such classification of my corpus of ethnic graffiti would lend unnecessary elegance to the messages, which as the reader is about to witness possess little or no redeeming literary value. In fact all of the ethnic graffiti in my collection are simple exclamatory statements, interrogatives, comparatives, and superlatives. Few involve extended discourse or attempt to rhyme; none are traditional in the sense of what Alan Dundes (1966) means by "latrinalia"; and few are even trite in the sense that they are repeated in time and space.

The third set of attributes defines the content of the message. Here there seems to be several relevant categories. First is what I call the immortalizing "Kilroy was here" variety. It includes names of persons, native places, schools, and dates. They are most prevalent on public mouments and natural objects. Second is the romanticizing "Orlando loves Rosalind" variety. These include testimonies and revelations of romantic love carved in tree trunks and park benches or scrawled all over rear bus seats and bus shelters in Honolulu. Both the "Kilroy" and the "Orlando" varieties contain ethnic signatures. However, ethnic identities are revealed only inadvertently in the names. For instance "Kilroy" reveals the presence of American GIs. Or in the case of "Orlando-n-Rosalind" the names, especially surnames of the lovers may reveal their ethnic identities. Neither of these two types contain overt statements identifying specific ethnic groups.

This brings me to the third variety of message, namely vulgar statements utilizing sexual, scatological, and phenotypical terms. Most of these terms are abusive. They are found in most sites where graffiti are found, although their frequency increases markedly in the vicinity of toilets and schools for reasons to be examined later. It is also within this broad category of vulgarity that ethnic signatures are most apparent. Indeed, ethnic boundaries are consciously phrased in phenotypical, sexual, and scatological idioms. Ethnic graffiti thus constitute a subset of the vulgar graffiti.

The range of vulgarity extends from a few tantalizing fantasies to many grotesquely abusive slurs. A rare example of the first comes from the inside door of a University elevator in a remote corner of the campus:

> 1. Japanese girls taste very good
>   nice and salty like *ume*

Ume is the tart red plum Japanese wrap in rice balls for picnic lunches. Unfortunately few graffiti attain even this level of subtlety. The vast majority are explicit:

> 2. Japanese cunt taste mo betta!

"Mo betta" is local creole for "better." However, most of the explicit graffiti is abrasive or downright hostile:

> 3. Getting a Jap bitch to come
>   is like squeezing water out of a rock!!!!

Many graffiti contrast the alleged sexual characteristics of different groups. Among the most invidious comparisons are those which allege sexual and mental inferiority:

> 4. Japs have small cocks
>   Hawaiians have small brains

A number of graffiti explain alleged phenotypes by reducing them to scatological habits:

> 5. Why are the Jap chicks bowlegged?
>   From squatting to piss in the gutter!

Alleged national characteristics are reduced to sexual traits. In a number of graffiti possession of mental aptitude is inversely related to sexual magnitude:

> 6. Japs do good in school cause they respond
>   to authority and have small dicks!! (They
>   don't know what to do with them.)

In fact the relative excellence of Japanese scholastic achievement in local schools is a point of animosity and sometimes open hostilities among various ethnic groupings (see, e.g., Ong 1978:A-1). Other alleged character traits are reduced to patterns of child rearing:

> 7. Local boys are latent homosexuals to a great
>   extent cuddled and coddled by 'mama' and
>   spoiled fucking rotten

From these examples it appears that Japanese and other local groups are generally depicted in effeminate images.

By contrast, whites tend to be caricaturized as "dumb." The abusive epithet for whites is "dumb" *haole.*" *Haole* is a Hawaiian word that means "stranger" but which now applies to whites exclusively. *Haole* is often used by whites to distinguish themselves from other local groups since by itself the term carries no necessary stigmata other than having roots on the U.S. mainland. The epithet "dumb" applied to *"haole"* does not refer to the inability of whites to use their mouths as we can see in the following exchange. The first author, perhaps feeling the loss of white political power during the last 2 decades to local groups, asserts:

> 8. Haole Power

A second writer responds:

> 9. All your power stay in your mouth

Local people allege that whites use their mouths too much and for all the wrong things. Whites tend to talk in abstractions—they use words that nobody understands (see Phrase 14, for example). Whites as representatives of the nationally dominant group allegedly sweet talk their way into the hearts of local girls with empty promises; indeed, the white ability to woo local girls is a point of long standing conflict between the two groupings. In this vein one graffito (presumably written by a white) boasts:

> 10. I fuck all Jap chicks!

The local response is:

> 11. Get a haole chick!

On the other hand, among some there is an equally strong rejection of white girls:

> 12. Fuck what you can
>   mom, sis, even your hand
>   Beats fucking haoles

As we see from these examples, most of the ethnic graffiti take forms ranging from provocative to openly hostile remarks. There are others which take the form of requests for the sexual services of certain groups. They are evenly divided among requests for ethnically endogamous and exogamous homosexual and heterosexual services. They range from desperate pleadings to simple advertisements replete with phone numbers. Summarizing thus far, we can say that the graffiti found in Hawaii express fundamental conflicts among Hawaii's various ethnic groupings.

Before proceeding to my analysis I should point out that a number of authors censor the ethnic slurs especially ones presumably written by their ethnic cohorts. In many cases the ethnic label is erased or scratched out leaving the abusive message minus an ethnic identity. Other authors advise the slur-maker to have more Christian tolerance; while still others refer to the slur-maker as a "problem child," "pregidous [sic] asshole," "racist," "fucking naieve," "unhappy," "forlorn of friends." One graffitist comments on a slur against local people by pointing out that:

> 13. People like him give us haoles a bad name

And another graffitist responding (only as a white would be expected to respond) to an especially reprehensible attack on Japanese says:

> 14. We must remember that
>   assertion is the hallmark
>   of homo-sapiens [sic] while
>   longanimous placasibility
>   and condonation are the
>   indicia of supermundane
>   aminisciences.

It is signed: "—a dumb haole."

Some graffiti provoke extremely passionate responses. The assertion that "local boys are spoiled by their mothers" (Phrase 7) received the angriest response:

> 15. I spoil you fucking ass punk

And this provoked yet a third person to advise the second in terse local creole:

> 16. Cool head bra—cool head main thing!

Analysis of Content

As I stated at the outset, graffiti may provide the ethnologist with an archaeological avenue into a particular social organization. While the prehistorian does not work directly with the expressive content of his artifacts much less with discursive data, still, as an ethnologist I can hardly pass up the opportunity to draw some obvious conclusions, especially those which can be drawn on the basis of simple quantification. In this section I want to examine briefly some of the information which ethnologists may extract from the nominal content of ethnic graffiti. In fact the nominal content of my corpus tells us a great deal about ethnic group relations in Hawaii.

The ethnic signatures in these graffiti, that is the explicit terms which are written on the walls, tell us which ethnic groups in Hawaii are socially salient. The question as to what degree this or that ethnic grouping actually exists is a perrenial problem for scholars and administrators in Hawaii and in other societies where ethnic groups do not constitute part of the corporate order. The standard instruments used to identify the ethnic complexion of Hawaiian society are state and federal census categories. However, there is no way to know if these categories constitute real groups or to what degree they are merely the arbitrary conventions of census makers. Here is where graffiti might prove most relevant. Graffiti may provide a less arbitrary method for determining the socially based ethnic groups in Hawaii. Figure 6.1 illustrates the number of terms I collected in each ethnic category from my sample of sites around the university. The figure provides a visual representation of the viable ethnic groupings. The most viable groupings are obviously the whites in contention with the Japanese. Now, if we look at Table 6.1, we see that the numbers of whites and Japanese represented in the graffiti are roughly proportional to their demographic representation in the population at large as reported in the state census (State of Hawaii 1972:4-5). (I believe that the overrepresentation of white terms in the graffiti is due in part to whites writing about themselves [Phrase 8], censoring themselves [Phrase 13], or signing their remarks [Phrase 14].) On the other hand, there are two significant census categories, namely, the Chinese and the Filipinos, that are significantly

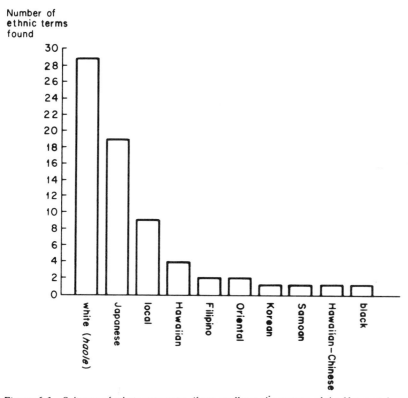

Figure 6.1. *Saliency of ethnic categories (from graffiti in the vicinity of the University).*

C. Fred Blake

Table 6.1

Number of Ethnic Graffiti Compared to Census Data

Ethnic category	Number of terms found in graffiti	Percentage of terms found in graffiti	Percentage of population by "race" (see State of Hawaii 1972:4-5)
White *(haole)*	29	42	38.8
Japanese	19	28	28.3
Local	9	13	—
Hawaiian	4	6	9.3
Filipino	2	3	12.2
Oriental	2	3	—
Korean	1	1.25	1.1
Samoan (and others)	1	1.25	2.4
Hawaiian-Chinese	1	1.25	—
Black	1	1.25	1
Chinese	—	—	6.8
American Indian	—	—	.1
Total	69	100.	100.

underrepresented in the graffiti. An even more significant disparity between what the census tells us and what the graffiti tell us is the saliency of the category "local" in the graffiti and its absence as an ethnic category in the census.

I would conclude this discussion with two main points. One is that the groupings represented in the graffiti constitute the socially relevant and politically viable ethnic groupings in Hawaii, and these facts cannot be derived from the census. The groupings derived from graffiti also represent the complexity of ethnic realities in so far as different taxonomic levels of the ethnic order (for example, "Japanese" and "local") are recognized. The second point is that in keeping with the spatial interpretation I am developing, the present results are relative to the university community. However, insofar as the university is an important state institution its graffiti may reflect the larger state of affairs in the State of Hawaii.

There are other questions which my corpus of graffiti raises. The reader may wonder why, for instance, the grossest slurs seem to be aimed at local groups? There is even the more fundamental question: Why are there ethnic graffiti in the first place? I think that answers to these questions can be found in a closer examination of the spatial distribution of graffiti and of the variant nature of social space itself. Let us consider each of these in turn.

Distribution of Sites

My corpus of graffiti reveals many interesting facets in the cultural content of ethnic group relations in Hawaii. However, when we examine their spatial contexts, the graffiti tell us even more about ethnic group relations in Hawaii and something about the nature of graffiti in general. The first thing to note is that the graffiti occur on public properties. Graffiti are part of the public domain; they are private assertions aimed at public consumption; or to put it in the words of one graffitist: People write on walls "because it seems the best way to really put yourself across in the world!" The vast majority of graffiti is found in bars, theatres, parks, playgrounds, bus shelters, back seats of buses, schools, and similar areas of *diversion*. Indeed, schools ranging from secondary through post-secondary provide the bulk of graffiti in Hawaii. As we move away from the peripheries of diversion toward the centers of commerce and administration, the incidence of graffiti diminishes.

The second thing to note is that within the public domain of diversion, particular types of graffiti tend to exhibit different distribution patterns. Scatological and sexual remarks tend to occur in the direction of increased diversion; while those with ethnic labels attached are increasingly restricted to the walls of toilets, especially school toilets. Finally, let us ask why this is so and what this can lead us to infer about ethnic group relations in Hawaii?

Graffiti Are Products of Liminal Spaces

These spatial patterns suggest that the frequency of graffiti in general, and of certain types in particular, increase as space becomes more diverse, unstructured, or liminal. Space becomes liminal where it is used for transitory and expressive purposes rather than for instrumental, discreet, and specialized purposes. People behaving in liminal spaces do not "put on acts." Rather they tend to "play around." This is distinct from areas where people are constrained to perform roles, put on acts, and standardize their messages as they do in commercial and bureaucratic settings. This distinction between performance and play has been treated variously in the sociological and anthropological literatures (Goffman 1959; Turner 1969). Victor Turner distinguishes liminal behavior settings as transitional areas where social boundaries are blurred and normal rules of conduct and role expectations are held in abeyance or even in opposition. In liminal settings persons shed their roles and statuses and emerge as whole persons, warts and all, behaving in ways that are unusually pleasureful, painful, shameful, nonsensical, or downright grotesque. As I pointed out, such liminal behavior settings include parks, playgrounds, bus stops, back seats of buses, elevators, restrooms, and schools—these are all places where people *move* through time and space interacting as whole human beings (or for that very reason failing to interact at all) and giving more or less free reign to their impulses.

If we place liminal and normative behavior settings at opposite ends of a continuum, we can see that liminality is a matter of degree. Then if we place the various categories of space along this continuum, we find that the most liminal space in American culture is the public toilet. The toilet stall is designed to maximize the individual's privacy right in the smack of the public domain. It offers individuals a moment of solitude shut away from the public glare. Given certain technological considerations mentioned earlier, the walls around the toilet offer a public forum while they also guarantee the author's anonymity, as one defender of the art points out, by the latch on the door (McGlynn 1972:353).

There is a more profound sense in which the toilet is a liminal, indeed a structurally inverted behavior setting. Defacation is not a social act; it is quite the contrary a crucial *biological movement*—it is a diurnal life crisis, which as all life crises provokes a three stage rite de passage à la Van Gennep (1961) and Turner (1969). In the first phase one experiences increased tension, anxiety, and physical exertion. During the second phase one is secluded and defiled. In the third phase one undergoes purification and reentry into the mundane world of order and discernment. In this particular passage, which we call "going to the toilet" or to which we refer by other polite euphemisms, the period of seclusion involves the release of cloacal residues. There is a concomitant tendency to release mental residues in the form of fantasy every bit as defiling. The normal boundaries which society rigorously maintains between the anus and the brain collapse in the liminal area of the toilet, and for a few brief moments the whole body is mobilized and unified in one of its most vital struggles for survival.

It would seem then, given the degree of spatial restriction observed, that the most defiling mental residues in Hawaii are ethnic slurs. Whereas a person may feel some constraint in writing a scatological or sexual remark on a bus shelter, it seems that one needs the added security and sense of liminal removal provided by the latched door of a public toilet before he attaches an ethnic label to it.

Finally, schools have important liminal properties which are magnified in school restrooms. Schools are where young people undergo traumatic passage from childhood to adulthood. The modern school is every bit as rigorous in teaching survival techniques as is the primitive bush school which we usually associate with painful initiation rites. I suspect the modern school is more traumatic in so far as the modern child's biological passage into adulthood is so ridiculously out of phase with his or her cultural passage. Another thing that makes the modern child's passage more traumatic is the extreme emphasis placed on individual success coupled with the ever present prospect of failure. Be that as it may, the passage from secondary through post-secondary school is a long and arduous period during which students lack the constraints that adulthood normally confers. Young people, therefore, behave accordingly. It is precisely in this setting that Hawaii's various ethnic groups gather to compete for grades and mates, and not necessarily in that order of priority. It is hardly surprising then that ethnic labels find their way into the residues of cloacal and sexual fantasy and abuse in this setting.

From the spatial distribution of the different varieties of graffiti we can posit two rules about the role of ethnic remarks in Hawaiian society. The first rule is that ethnic slurs are extremely antithetical to contemporary norms of Hawaiian society. In fact they are even more antithetical than are scatological abuses. The second rule we can infer from the data is that ethnic slurs aimed at local groups are most antithetical of all.

Ethnographic Confirmation

If we observe other forms of behavior relevant to ethnic group interaction we can confirm these rules which have been derived by and large from archaeological data and method. The first observation involves an episode reported in the local newspaper (Woo 1978:A-1). An unidentified man disrupted a legislative hearing by calling state Representative Tony Kunimura a "Jap." Kunimura followed the man from the House Finance Committee hearing into the attorney general's office where he physically assaulted the man. "I don't care if he calls me a fat little shit,' the stout 5'6" Kunimura said later, "But don't call me a Jap." Kunimura thus articulates the rule, which we have inferred from archaeological data, that racial slurs are more restrictive, forbidden, or liminal than are scatological abuses.

It is relevant that no charges of assault were filed against Kunimura. Given the political nature of law enforcement it would not, however, be prudent to conclude that the sanction against ethnic slurs is also stronger than the sanction against physical assault. We would need more evidence for such a conclusion. Such evidence may be obtained from a study of additional cases. For instance, in another case (Kato 1979:A-3), several local boys beat and choked a white boy unconscious, tied him with ropes and threw him into a pond where he died. The defendant's attorney pleaded extenuating circumstances on the basis that the victim had become belligerent and had begun "insulting Hawaiians." The defendants were found guilty only of manslaughter.

This unfortunate case brings me to the second bit of ethnographic evidence, namely, joking behavior. Ethnic joking is ubiquitous in Hawaii. In contexts where local people are grouping themselves they often joke in the most insulting terms about their ethnic differences. They also joke about whites where whites are entering the group. However, whites cannot as a rule joke about locals in ethnic terms. Whites must utilize nonethnic idioms when joking with or teasing locals. Thus with the exception of whites teasing locals in ethnic terms, ethnic joking is often used to relax ethnic boundaries in order to build interethnic group solidarity. Social scientists have long been aware of how joking relationships enhance group solidarity by allowing mutual expressions of hostility (Coser 1964:64; Radcliffe-Brown 1952: 94-95). Thus ethnic joking, unlike ethnic graffiti, tends to conform to public norms by raising ethnic consciousness in order to defuse it. The rules for joking complement and confirm some of the basic patterns of space and content we observed in the production of graffiti. One of these patterns is the tendency to abuse local groups in the most extreme terms. This pattern suggests that ethnic graffiti tend to constitute a white medium for asserting illegitimate ethnic messages in this land of racial aloha.

Review and Summary

In recent years a number of humanists and social scientists have attempted to determine the sociocultural significance of graffiti. Most of these studies take graffiti at face value as statements of popular opinion. For example, Alan Dundes (1966) reveals basic cultural themes in traditional latrine graffiti which he calls "latrinalia." Paul McGlynn (1972) defends graffiti as private "fragments of truth" which people do not take as seriously as they do the half-truths of commercial advertisements and political slogans. Stocker, Dutcher, Hargrove, and Cook (1972) hypothesize that graffiti express current community norms. Stocker and associates systematically collected and compared nontraditional graffiti from different communities. However, their hypothesis failed to account for the existence of racist graffiti in a liberal university setting (1972:362). This and other such anomolies led Gonos, Mulken, and Poushinsky (1976) to advance an alternative hypothesis: Since lavatory graffiti are a "distorted" and "anonymous" medium, they express the *inverse* of current community norms, a phenomenon which I have examined in some detail and made use of in my analysis. Finally, according to Reich, Buss, Fein, and Kurtz (1977), this hypothesis applies to expressions of opinion on current controversial issues such as race and male homosexuality but not necessarily to the less controversial opinions about lesbianism found in women's lavatories.

While each of these studies test hypotheses by comparing frequencies of graffiti between alleged "liberal" and "conservative" communities, my study posits several rules of social organization by a microscopic examination of the artifactual associations within a single community. I have tried to show how graffiti are essentially behavioral residues; that is they are archeological in nature insofar as they are anonymous artifacts fixed in space and time, and when recovered they lend themselves to quantitative treatments. The question of their normative status hinges on several variables, one of the most crucial of which is their placement in varying spatial contexts. In other words, by combining the archaeological approach to classifying artifacts and noting their distribution in space with ethnological theory of passages in which space is classified as to its usages, I have attempted to infer some elementary rules of social organization in a particular community. I have further verified these rules by observations of on-going behavior.

7

A Herbalist's Shop in Honolulu: Traditional Merchandising in a Modern Setting

Jane Allen-Wheeler

Introduction

In 1975 Reid, Schiffer, and Rathje described four strategies for the study of relationships between human behavior and material objects. Strategy 4 is the analysis of present material objects in order to answer questions regarding present human behavior (1975:866). The present research employs Strategy 4 in order to investigate problems concerned with task specificity and the concept of the activity area.

Questions of interest initially included whether an activity area is reflected primarily by the types of material objects present or by spatial clustering of materials. As research continued, the concept of the discrete, task-specific activity area, represented by a cluster of formally similar material objects, began to seem too simple. An activity area may actually consist of several overlapping activity sets, rather than one unit.

Additional questions connected with task specificity in a marketing situation arose: How are items specific to an activity organized spatially in a shop? Is high visibility correlated with easy accessibility? Are materials specific to certain tasks more visible than others? In a shop dealing in traditional commodities, are traditional items displayed more prominently than more modern materials? Is the primary commodity likely to be imported from traditional sources even if available locally?

In order to answer these questions it is necessary to study not only the

MODERN MATERIAL CULTURE
The Archaeology of Us

materials themselves, but also, from an archaeological perspective, the observable behavior patterns which seem correlated with them. Such a research strategy was facilitated greatly by the high degree of efficiency found at the shop selected for analysis.

The Research

Research was conducted at a site which appeared highly task-specific: the prosperous and busy shop of a Chinese herbalist in downtown Honolulu. The building is located on an old street, surrounded by importers' shops, Chinese markets and bakeries, lei sellers' stalls and other herbalists' shops.

Structurally, the shop appears plain and a bit dilapidated. The French doors are open wide to the sidewalk (Figure 7.1), and the scent of herbs and spices permeates the air outside. Customers entering the shop approach the long counter to their left and request help from either the herbalist or his wife, son or daughter-in-law, who will then dispense the medicinal items requested. Customers do not typically approach the containers of medicinals, which are arranged primarily on open shelving around the room.

The owner of the shop is additionally a prominent, licensed local acupuncturist; he practises his profession in a small room behind the shop. This room and a storage area, both indicated in Figure 7.1, were excluded from the shop study.

The approach used is described by Gould (1968, 1974) as living archaeology: that is, ethnoarcheological research which relies on direct field experience with both current materials and associated behavior. Although interview has been proposed as an integral part of ethnoarchaeology (e.g., Oswalt 1974:3), it has been relegated to a secondary role here, since informant data have been found to be less than completely reliable when tested empirically (Rathje 1974), and also since the goal of the present research is etic, not emic (Gould 1978a:4; Schiffer 1978:234–235). Interview was necessarily relied on for information regarding the geographic sourcing of bulk materia medica and also supplemented opportunistic observation of the contents of drawers not made accessible to research. Labels provided information as to the contents of patent medicinal packages, which could not be opened. Since the goal was not a comprehensive study of Chinese medicinals, herbal materials were not identified to species, but were subsumed under several generalized categories (e.g., dried herbs).

All nonarchitectural objects were described as to form, substance, geographical source, spatial distribution in the shop, and task specificity. Recycling, curation, and discard behaviors were observed whenever possible.

Quantities are described here in terms of "classes" and "units." A class is

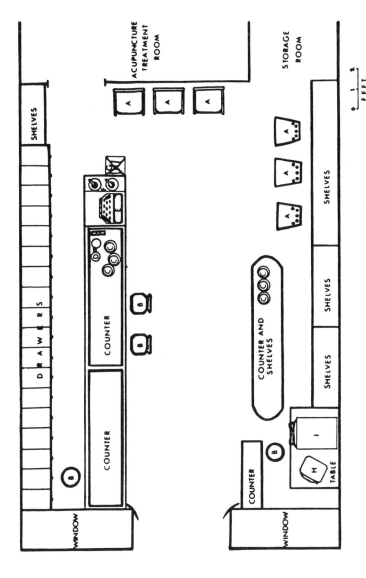

Figure 7.1. Plan of herbalist's shop: A—chair, B—stool, C—jar, D—scale, E—typewriter, F—mortars, G—trash cans, H—television set, I—sterilizer.

an easily distinguished material category; most are general-level categories. Examples include dried herbs, patent ointments, and the steel scale. A total of 142 plain gallon jars containing dried herbs constitute two classes: plain gallon jars and dried herbs.

A unit is an occurrence of a class; the number of units for the class describes its frequency. Each class must have at least one unit and may have many. Among medicinal materials the contents of one container are considered to be one unit. No size reference is implicit in the categories. The contents of 229 jars of dried spices and herbs (Table 7.1) constitute 229 units

Table 7.1
Materials Inventoried

Materials	Classes/Units	Materials	Classes/Units
Bulk medicinals		Patent medicinals	
Dried herbs and spices	2/229	Dried herbs and spices	2/72
Herb and spice		Vegetal powders	3/110
powders	2/162		
Other dried plant		Other dried plant	
products	10/72	products	2/43
Mineral powders	1/3	Mineral powders	1/4
Stones	1/1	Tablets, lozenges	2/60
Sherds	1/1	Gelatin capsules	1/7
Dried fauna	6/6	Ointments	1/113
Seashells	1/1	Topical liquids	2/25
Horn	1/1	Potable liquids	2/8
Deer antlers	1/2	Plasters, bandages	2/13
Bone fragments	1/1	Unknown	2/6
Snakeskin and bones	1/1		
Pelt	1/1		
Unknown	3/3		
Containers for		Equipment for	
bulk medicinals		preparation of herbs	
Plastic canisters	1/20	Porcelain brewing pots	2/8
Plain gallon jars	1/142		
Apothecary jars	3/39	Dispensing equipment	
Other jars	8/36	Abalone shells	1/8
Dishes	3/4	Brass mortars	1/2
String lengths	1/30	Wood pestles	1/2
Boxes	3/56	Rubber covers	1/2
Bags	3/301	Plastic spoons	1/22
Metal cans and bins	3/41	Steel scale and dial	2/2
		Brass and ivory scale	1/1
Patent medicinal		Wood stick	1/1
packages		Metal spool with tape	2/2
Glass bottles	13/149	Metal roller with paper	2/2

Table 7.1 *(cont.)*

Materials	Classes/Units	Materials	Classes/Units
Boxes	36/261	Paper roll	1/1
Wraps	5/17		
Plastic jars and bottles	3/6		
Metal canisters, boxes	3/3		
Tubes, rolls, corks	4/27		
Acupuncture-related		Materials used for	
Objects: For sale		storage of containers	
Plastic models	2/9	Racks	2/15
Boxes	2/7	Shelves	6/40
Stainless steel instru-		Counters	4/5
ments	18/188	Metal strips	1/17
		Foil-covered jars	2/6
Acupuncture-related ob-		Shop-related objects:	
jects: Connected with		Decoration and adver-	
practice on premises		tising	
Chairs	3/7	Vases with flowers	4/17
Steam sterilizer	1/1	Decorations	10/28
Literature	9/91	Signs	3/8
Plastic jug of water	1/1	Clock	1/1
Charts	5/6	Silk curtain	1/1
Shop-related objects:			
Conveniences			
Telephone	1/1		
Swivel chairs	3/5		
Newspapers	1/6		
Bottles and mercuro-			
chrome	2/2		
Shop-related objects:		Objects of unclear	
Sales equipment		functional context	
Spindle	1/1	Novel	1/1
Paper	3/33	Television set—turned	
Cash register	1/1	away from room	1/1
Abacus	1/1	Ball-point pen—in	
Pencils	1/3	corner	1/1
Sign	1/1	Artist's paintbrush	1/1
Credit card imprint			
machine	1/1		
Maintenance items			
Feather duster	1/1		
Garbage can	1/1		
Ashtrays	2/2		
Cloth	1/1		
Cartons	4/4		
Metal hooks	1/6		
Table	1/1		

in two classes (dried spices and dried herbs). The containers themselves are separate classes and occurrences.

Goals

The initial goal was to determine what percentage of objects in a specialized shop is used in a task-specific manner. As research proceeded it became apparent that virtually all items inventoried were task-specific, and that the term needed closer definition. Four major areas of task specificity were recognized: the merchandising of herbals; general, non-herbal medical practice; general merchandising; and structural maintenance. Geographic sources for materials and the distribution of materials in the room were analyzed at each level. An attempt was made to discover whether geographical and spatial considerations reflect social patterning.

Analysis

Functional Classification

Table 7.1 assigns all objects inventoried to categories which describe their actual functions in the shop. The total number of classes recognized was 267; the total for units, 2864. Fairly specific functional categories are presented in order to avoid lumping materials which receive different treatment: for example, containers for bulk medicinals are occasionally curated and remain at the shop, whereas patent packages are typically disposable and leave the shop with the customer.

"Dispensing equipment" is used not for sales transactions but for the physical handling of medicinals. "Objects related to herb use" comprise porcelain pots used in the homes of customers, and not in the shop. Many herbs must be boiled for several hours before consumption.

"Acupuncture-related objects: connected with acupuncture practice on premises" are not used for merchandising purposes. Their location in the shop nonetheless overlaps shop functions and material patterns. Both chairs and literature are occasionally used by shop customers; two of the charts are prominently displayed.

Frequencies and Spatial Considerations

Table 7.2 presents total frequencies for materials in the individual functional categories. Containers account for the largest percentage of both classes and units. Most of the bulk medicinal containers are gallon jars, stored in neat rows on shelves specially designed and crafted to store and display

Table 7.2
Totals for Objects in each Functional Category

Objects	Classes		Units	
	Number	Percentage	Number	Percentage
Bulk medicinals	32	12.0	484	16.9
Patented medicinals	20	7.5	461	16.1
Containers (bulk)	26	9.8	669	23.4
Packages (patent)	64	24.0	463	16.2
Equipment for herb preparation	2	0.7	8	0.3
Dispensing equipment	14	5.3	45	1.6
Acupuncture-related objects				
For sale	22	8.2	204	7.1
Connected with practice	19	7.1	106	3.7
Materials used for storage				
of containers	17	6.3	293	10.2
Shop-related objects:				
Decoration/advertising	19	7.1	55	1.9
Conveniences	7	2.6	14	0.5
Sales equipment	9	3.4	41	1.4
Maintenance items	12	4.5	17	0.6
Objects of unclear				
functional context	4	1.5	4	0.1
Totals	267	100.0	2864	100.0

them. The complete visibility of the contents of the jars through the open doorway would presumably attract passersby. A few of the more interesting materia medica (e.g., seahorses) are displayed prominently in their jars on the counters.

In addition to standardized jars which must have been ordered in quantity, the containers include local *kim chee* jars, as well as U.S. mainland mayonnaise and peanut butter jars probably purchased by the family at a grocery store and recycled to the shop when emptied. These are now used in an entirely task-specific manner related to the merchandising of herbal medicines.

The merchandise itself comprises the second largest category. More materials are used for the physical dispensing of medicinals than for sales transactions. Objects used to dispense medicinals include traditional items such as a brass-and-ivory hand-held scale. Of the sales related items an abacus is stored on the countertop, apparently for display purposes.

The porcelain pots for the boiling of herbs at home are also decorative. They are displayed prominently just inside the door, and help to create a traditional atmosphere in the shop. That they are not actually in great demand is suggested by the fact that all felt dusty.

It would seem that herbalism is highlighted, sales transactions less obviously emphasized, and traditional items used as prominently as possible within each of these task-specific categories.

Shop-related items such as shelving are designed to show off the commodities sold; they are not highly visible in their own right. Counters similarly serve as background elements. Structural features in the shop generally seem to be placed so as to intervene between client and commodity. The visual appearance of easy access to valued commodities may in fact disguise a situation where physical contact is discouraged.

Maintenance objects are in most cases invisible to customers. The items lowest in frequencies and in visibility are those of unclear functional context.

The impression created at the shop is one of conservation of materials used in both display and nondisplay situations. Curation is an ongoing process. The lids of containers for bulk herbals have been painted in many cases; drawers generally present a freshly-painted appearance. The brass-and-ivory scale has been repaired several times, according to the proprietor.

Besides the jars mentioned previously, coffee cans have been recycled to service in the shop. They store medicinals out of view, in drawers. Shipping cartons are reused in some cases; one held items of unclear function. No carton is prominently displayed. Waste is rare, with the exception that patent medicinal packages, designed by the suppliers for high visibility, were also designed for regular disposal.

The shop generally appears efficient, professional, and well organized. Materials in separate functional categories are seldom mixed together. The only obvious cluster of materials from several categories occurs around the cash register, where scales, wrapping paper, receipts, other sales transaction items and a garbage can all appear in close proximity, presumably for easy accessibility, lumping materials for the merchandising of herbals, general marketing, and maintenance. Otherwise, the spatial arrangement of objects of dissimilar functions at the shop tends to separate them distinctly. Objects of like function, most outstandingly objects concerned with the merchandising of herbals, are arranged in a linear pattern around the room, generally behind linear barriers (Figure 7.1), a pattern which reinforces the initial impressions of formality, precision, and a maintained distance between client and merchandise.

Task Specificity

As the study began, the herbalist's shop was considered to be a single highly specialized activity area, a discrete and task-specific unit within a diverse urban setting. Analysis of materials as they function in systemic context within the shop made it clear that the situation was more complex.

Aside from the four items of unclear functional context, all objects inventoried are used in conjunction with at least one of four activity sets: the merchandising of herbals and related medical items, non-herbal medical practice, general merchandising, and structural maintenance. Many objects function in two sets: for example, bulk containers function in both herbal and general merchandising.

Materials used in connection with structural maintenance and in the acupuncture practice on the premises may be seen as representing activity sets separate from but interacting with the two merchandising categories. Within the merchandising sets the arrangement is hierarchical: The merchandising of herbals may be subsumed under general merchandising. Materials involved in the merchandising of herbals are also, by definition, being used in merchandising as a general activity, while materials used in general marketing (e.g., sales equipment) are not specific to herbal shops.

Of the sets of objects listed in Tables 7.1 and 7.2, their observed functions assign the first seven (through acupuncture-related objects: For sale) to the merchandising of herbals and related medical items. The acupuncture practice materials are used in connection with non-herbal medical practice; the items involved here included comfort items (e.g., chairs), educational materials (charts), and objects used in maintenance of acupuncture equipment (e.g., sterilizer), and may be seen as applicable to three separate subsets which fall under the medical practice set.

Items used for storage of containers (e.g., shelves) and shop-related objects are task-specific at the general shop level, and objects listed in the tables as maintenance items are specific to the maintenance activity set.

Examination of these material objects within their systemic context makes possible their assignment to specific activity sets. Such items as dried spices and herbs, individual containers, and the novel are also found in other shop and nonshop situations (e.g., spice shop, kitchen, library), where they function in different sets of activities.

It is often spatial relationships between objects which reveal most about their function and task specificity. While examination of individual material objects in the herbalist's shop did not in most cases clearly associate them with specific activities, analysis of spatial relationships existing among those objects generated several hypotheses which deal with task specificity in market situations. These include the following: *(a)* Client accessibility to primary commodities and objects involved in merchandising the primary commodities is restricted architecturally in shops where there is a need for professional dispensing; *(b)* visibility of the primary commodities substitutes for real accessibility in a shop where dispensing and control over accessibility are important; and *(c)* maintenance items in shops tend to be informally organized (often clustered) and relatively invisible from the vantage point of the client.

Geographic Considerations

Table 7.3 correlates task specificity with geographic sources for materials. Only the frequencies for units are provided, for simplicity's sake. Interview and labels, as indicated previously, provided the data regarding geographic sources. All reported sources are listed; interestingly, no materials were reported from the West outside the United States. "Local" means Hawaii.

According to the proprietor, all bulk medicinals are imported from China, although many substances are available locally. The hills of China are considered the best source area, because pollution and fertilizers have had less effect there than in the lowlands. Excluding unknowns, 75.9% of the patent medicinals ultimately derive from China, Hong Kong, and Taiwan; U.S. intermediaries are occasionally involved in the marketing network. Only 5% come from the U.S. Patent packages agree with their contents. Bulk containers are typically American.

The porcelain steeping pots were manufactured in China. The dispensing equipment most in evidence from the client's vantage point, the brass-and-ivory scale, was brought from China over 50 years ago. All acupuncture commodities displayed for sale were imported from China. Of the items connected with proprietor's acupuncture practice, and visible in the shop, only two objects were definitely imported: charts, which were prominently displayed.

With the exception of American bulk containers, most objects which physically touch herbal substances and acupuncture instruments are imported from Asia. The farther one gets from materia medica and objects which must directly touch them, the fewer objects come from the Asian countries. All storage facilities were crafted locally. General shop-related items and maintenance materials, exclusive of decorative lanterns and two recycled Chinese shipping cartons, were procured locally or from the U.S. mainland. The objects of unclear context were all American.

The most precisely task-specific objects in the shop seem to be those which travelled the greatest distances. Size does not appear to be a major deciding factor; bulk herbal medicinals arrive in large lots, and local materials include both small and large items. Two considerations are likely far more significant: the proprietor's statement that Chinese herbs are chemically more effective, and the perceived benefits of taking medicines grown in the traditional homeland. Items imported from great distances tend to be displayed prominently.

It has been suggested that those items at an archaeological site which had been imported from distant sources may in many cases have had ideational significance to the site's occupants. The present project tends to support this hypothesis. Additional hypotheses concerned with the geographic

Table 7.3

Geographic Sources for Materials, as a Percentage of Units in each Functional Category

| Categories | Units from each source area | | | | | | | |
Number of units	China	Hong Kong	Taiwan	Asia[a]	U.S.	Local	Unknown	Total
Herbal merchandising								
Bulk medicinals/484	100.0							100.0
Patent medicinals/461	27.1	48.1	0.7	8.9	5.0		10.2	100.0
Containers (bulk)/669	27.4	47.9	0.6	8.9	5.0		10.2	100.0
Packages (patent)/463					73.3	23.9	2.8	100.0
Equipment for herbal								
preparation/8	100.0							100.0
Dispensing equipment/45	2.2				15.6	64.4	17.8	100.0
Acupuncture-related:								
For sale/204	100.0							100.0
General medical practice								
Acupuncture-related								
Associated with practice/106	6.6				81.2	7.5	4.7	100.0
General merchandising								
Storage for containers/293					10.9	89.1		100.0
Shop-related objects:								
Decoration/55		3.6			3.6	54.6	38.2	100.0
Conveniences/14					57.1	42.9		100.0
Sales equip./41					14.6	75.6	9.8	100.0
Structural maintenance								
Maintenance items/71	11.8				23.5	5.9	58.8	100.0
Unclear function:								
Objects of unclear								
functional context/4					100.0			100.0

[a] Asia includes Korea, Japan, and Malaysia.

and social implications of the shop's material inventory may be tested in other marketing situations: (a) Where the primary commodity is imported, objects of relatively high visibility which physically contact the valued commodity tend to derive from similarly distant and traditional sources; (b) the greater the distance involved in an object's import, the greater the visibility in the marketing situation.

Conclusion

Analysis of materials found in a highly specialized marketing situation has, by focusing initially on task specificity, produced data that relate to a number of problems, including geographical sourcing for objects in the shop and some possible implications, spatial patterning of materials and material clusters in a merchandising context, and patterns of social interaction suggested by spatial patterning and visibility. The data suggest that even in a highly specialized activity area such as that investigated, task specificity and activity areas need close definition if the researcher is to go on to make meaningful correlations of materials with human behavior.

8

Ideology and
Material Culture

David J. Meltzer

Les idéologies ne sont pas de pures illusions (l'Erreur), mais des corps de répresentations existant dans des institutions et des pratiques [Ideologies are not pure illusions (Error) but bodies of representations existing in institutions and practices]

L. Althusser 1974:114

The National Air and Space Museum in Washington, D.C., was completed and opened to the public on July 1, 1976, with the burning of a red, white, and blue ribbon by an electrical impulse that had originated in the Viking spacecraft then nearing Mars. In addition to its attaining the unique achievement of being one of the few federal buildings in recent memory to be completed on time and under budget, the National Air and Space Museum is also an unmitigated success. Visitors on the Mall are drawn to it, to the tune of some 40,000–50,000 a day *on the average*. The one day record stands at 90,000 plus visitors (July 2, 1978). It generally outdraws the remainder of the Smithsonian Institution complex *combined*.

Why the phenomenal success? Some would argue that it is the elegant architecture which, among other things, magically suspends 10-ton planes from its ceiling. Others would cite the marked interest that the public has in flight and space travel, while still others would advocate the "newness" or pristine nature of the Museum. While I suspect all of these are partially true,

113

MODERN MATERIAL CULTURE
The Archaeology of Us

there is something more subtle operating here which makes this Museum much more attractive than its companions. That feature is an ideological one. There is a message being presented to the visitor that is eminently pleasing. I will examine that message in this chapter.

This might seem a rather peculiar topic at first glance. What, after all, does ideology have to do with material culture, modern or otherwise? It has a great deal more to do with it than one might suspect. Historical disciplines, for example, appreciate that pieces of history, and the "remembering" of history, can reveal a great deal about how a past is *invented* (Lewis 1975). That process of invention is generally attributable to the particular ideological context within which the history is written. The same can be said for the remembering of nonwritten history. One would suppose, therefore, that material-culture studies of such institutions as museums, which record artifacts and events, would yield a significant amount of information about how ideology is projected and enforced through the manipulation of material culture. This kind of perspective forces us to see museums as something more than artifact mausoleums, since the museum not only houses but is, itself, an "ideotechnic" artifact.

It is useful to consider briefly the concept of ideology since, like many of the concepts formulated by Marx (Marx and Engels 1970), it has generated a voluminous critical and discursive literature (e.g., Feuer 1975). The literature varies, it seems, dependent on one's commitment to revolutionary "praxis." From the perspective of the analyst of social phenomena, this is an unfortunate but unavoidable situation; any definition or usage of ideology is sure to offend some scholars, Marxist or otherwise. Nonetheless, the obvious value of this concept, and its commensurate ambiguity, demands its use in some explicit form. I offer the following heuristic framework.

Following a distinction developed by Handsman (1977), the concept of ideology will be used in two ways throughout this essay: in a vulgar sense and in a nonvulgar sense. Vulgar ideology is:

> A system of concepts, beliefs, and values which is characteristic of some social class . . . and in terms of which the members of that class see and understand their own position in and relation to their social environment and the world as a whole, and explain, evaluate and justify their actions, and especially the activities and policies of their class [Mackie 1975: 185];

or:

> a nonunitary complex of social practices and systems of representations which have political significances and consequences [Hirst 1976: 396].

These are admittedly broad definitions, but are so for a reason. In my view, the phenomena of rationalization and justification in all human societies (not just stratified systems) contain universal underlying elements. Restricting the definition of ideology to terms of class society (as is often done), unnecessarily restricts the examination of a potentially valuable parameter of societal function and evolution. A basic assumption of this analysis is that there are no *qualitative* differences in the function of ideology in stratified as opposed to nonstratified societies.

Nonvulgar ideology departs significantly from the "political" or vulgar view of ideology. Vulgar ideology is an element of *subjective* knowledge (c.f. Popper 1972); its reality is an illusion, created and thus dependent on *objective* knowledge, nonvulgar ideology. The nonvulgar ideology is an autonomous and independent theory of knowledge, whose reality is thought to be unquestionable.

> Quel sens avons-nous donné au terme d'ideologie? Une conception idéologique ne porte pas sur le front ni dans le coeur la marque de l'idéologique, quelque sens que l'on donné a cet mot. Elle se présente au contraire comme la Vérité. [What sense did I give the term ideology? An ideological conception carries the imprint ideology neither in its forehead nor on its heart, whatever sense that you give to the word. To the contrary, it presents itself as the Truth] [Althusser 1974:112].

Yet as Handsman argues, nonvulgar ideology is also subject to critical exegesis. What is thus important in an analysis of ideology is not simply to detail elements of vulgar ideology, but to "unmask" the manner in which subjects are created from objects, that is, how the illusion of reality *(Vérité)* is created (Handsman 1977:341). Recognition of the elements of ideology is thus differential: vulgar ideology is notable for its obviousness (Althusser 1971), the nonvulgar ideology is an ontology that must be revealed through its vulgar products.

In this essay, those products which take material form will serve as the focal point of the analysis. This is a materialist analysis of idealist elements. The products I have chosen to examine are one aspect of what Althusser (1971) terms Ideological State Apparatuses (hereafter ISAs). Included in this heading are such institutions as schools, information and communication networks, and cultural ISAs such as museums. These apparatuses are identified as state institutions by their *function;* all serve the maintenance and reproduction of the relations of production. All represent the ruling class ideology, and are unified by political and class identity.

Museums in particular and other ISAs in general serve as concrete forms of otherwise ethereal entities. It is this concreteness that has important implications for the study of both the present (modern-material culture) and the past. Here is the point where materialist and idealist perspectives merge, not just in the material representations of mental phenomena but also in the recognition that the function and evolution of social systems may owe a great deal to "ideas" which do find material form in the archaeological record.

This study, however, does not deal with what we might term an "archaeological ISA." Instead, it focuses on an institution that is a part of our own modern material-culture system, the National Air and Space Museum (hereafter NASM). This study is by no means a conclusive statement on ideology at the NASM, nor does it attempt to provide general observations on American technological museums, nor, for that matter, American museums in general. Rather, the focus is on some of the particular manifestations of a wider phenomena, the predictable (and often unpredictable) means by which we choose to represent ourselves to ourselves. My choice of study area, the NASM, is not based on any higher theoretical principles, and, in fact, is entirely idiosyncratic: I just happen to enjoy the museum immensely.

The Museum As ISA

In their relatively short history, museums have run a gamut of roles from the simple "curio" cabinets for scholars of the sixteenth and seventeenth centuries (Foucault 1970; Rudwick 1972), to public places emblematic of general solidarity and ideology (MacCannell 1976).

One must recognize, however, that there are two avenues through which ideology can appear in the museum sets. On the one hand, there can be a conscious *effort to* promulgate the ideological message; on the other hand, it may be that certain elements or structures are simply a *reflection of* ideological systems. Since societal values are instilled in individuals through the socialization process and everyday life, any social act (building a museum) will surely reflect some ideological constants and constraints. Individuals raised within a particular ideology would not, and probably could not, reflect any other kind of ideology: They reveal their own.

For instance, it is no surprise that at the National Air and Space Museum the underlying structure or theme is a chronological-evolutionary framework; this is simply the manner in which we understand change or progress. Here ideology is a reflection of our basic Western and scientific conception of time. On the other hand, the presence of Julia Child in a museum exhibit (see the following) is clearly an ideological effort. Julia Child, and the message she presents, are not selected randomly.

In fact, one might make the observation that vulgar ideology is, more often than not, an *effort to* present a message, while nonvulgar ideology is largely a *reflection of* our own ontology (ideological ontology). Even though I suspect this generalization is probably valid, it is neither a logical nor analytic distinction, and there are undoubtedly many exceptions.

Regardless, the function of modern museums as ideological sets is not lost on museologists (Fry 1972; Newsom and Silver 1978; Read 1945; Robertson 1972). As Ziontz suggests:

> All societies require the glue of a basic core of values and goals if that society is going to be stable. The museum participates in creating the mythology [vulgar ideology] of nationalism by displaying symbols and objects which glorify the society. The museum helps translate any ideological basis of the nation into simpler patriotic catchwords and mind pictures for the people [1979:28].

This internal recognition of the function of the museums goes a long way toward explaining the concern that museum administrators have for the general absence of lower-income, blue-collar workers from the museums (DiMaggio, Useem, and Brown 1978; Hudson 1977; National Endowment for the Arts 1974). It would seem, at least from this perspective that those who need the ideological pumping the most are getting it the least, and some museum administrators worry about this. Of course, the reverse is also true. A recent study by the Center for Science in the Public Interest decried the blatant ideological messages promulgated at many museums. This included the NASM, which it signaled out as a "temple to the glories of aviation and the inventiveness of the aerospace industry [cited in Broad 1979:1181]."

As social scientists, we can and should view these structures as artifacts of modern material culture; the study can tell us a lot about ourselves.

The National Air and Space Museum

The basic purpose of the National Air and Space Museum, as outlined in Public Law 722 (August 12, 1946), is to "memorialize the national development of aviation; collect, preserve and display aeronautical equipment of historic interest and significance; serve as a repository for scientific equipment and data pertaining to the development of aviation; and provide educational materials for the historical study of aviation." This was later expanded by Public Law 89-509 (July 19, 1966), which added the clause "and space flight" thereby changing the name as well as the function of the Museum.

The focus of the Museum is a highly specialized and technical field. Yet consider that it received its five millionth visitor on December 30, 1976, surpassing in just 6 months time a figure expected to be reached only after a year. On July 9, 1978, the Museum recorded its *twenty-millionth* visitor; in the 2 years after it opened, the NASM drew more people than the Lincoln Memorial, the Washington Monument, the United States Capitol, and the White House *combined* (Bryan 1979). Again, the obvious question to ask is why?

As mentioned, there are a number of factors suggested to account for the Museum's phenomenal success, the one most often invoked being the relative "newness" of the building. Yet in and of itself, age is an insufficient explanation. After all, many NASM visitors are first time tourists to Washington, D.C., and may not have seen any of the other sites. Moreover, the NASM, puzzled by its own success, commissioned a survey of museum visitors, carried out by a national opinion and marketing research organization. In the preliminary findings based on 4000 interviews over a 10-month period, they found that "it is the reputation rather than the newness of the Museum which generates its large audience [Murphy 1978]." While this may be true, especially today, I suspect the reputation had little to do with the millions that entered the Museum in the months shortly after it opened.

In another sense, one might suggest that the concept of newness does play an important role in the Museum's success. This is not newness in terms of the age of the building or the artifacts, but rather in the message being presented within the Museum through the ideological sets. I suspect that the Museum works so well because it presents the new both in time (the future) and in space (the frontier); it shows where we came from (the past), where we are (the present), and most important, where we can expect to go.

Jon Allen noted, in a guide to aviation and space museums around the country, that "the only constant characteristic of the museum scene appears to be change [Allen 1975:11]." Though the comment was strictly about the physical process of opening and closing museums, the observation holds true for the ideological message as well. The message itself is one of change, of progress, and of the future. This Museum has history, but the history goes beyond fossils and Ford Model A's; this is a history still being created. Also, because it is history many of us have taken part in, at least vicariously, it can be calibrated with our own experiences. Virtually everyone can remember and measure events in their own lifetime in terms of Armstrong and Aldrin's walk on the moon. It is, in fact, the very short duration of the chronology, the fact that some of the spacecraft's heat shields still seem "warm to the touch" (Bryan 1979:20), that gives a clear and positive message for our future: "nowhere else in the world has been gathered such overwhelming proof that some of our most elemental dreams can and do come true [Bryan 1979:20]." In the words of the then-Director, Michael Collins (of Apollo 11 fame), before a House subcommittee on appropriations:

> And what better place is there to provide millions of visitors with ". . . [an] understanding of our heritage" or to ". . . quicken the progress toward our horizons. . . ." What better place to accomplish this than a museum dedicated to our air and space heritage. Air and space technology are areas in which our nation has always excelled, and a part of our history which we should emphasize [Collins 1972].

Here, a first level of ideology appears, the Museum contributes to the legitimization of the state by applauding its accomplishments and lauding its efforts and showing its future. It is a state show-and-tell; it operates in a manner that allows the subjects to "work by themselves" (Althusser 1971). In non-Althusserian terms, it allows the natives to be easily absorbed by the ideology and to absorb the ideology. All this is obvious: This is vulgar ideology.

Not so obvious, but present nonetheless, is the hidden or nonvulgar ideology. Here is the basic framework that serves to reify or objectify the presentation of the vulgar ideological scheme. In this case, it is the manipulation of space and time as the backdrop for the "progress" theme.

Vulgar Ideology

As the Museum portfolio says, "the museum is alive with taped voices, films, stagings, labels, lights, and sounds [NASM 1976:45]." It is a media event. Despite the flash, there is a concerted effort made to emphasize authenticity:

> Sophisticated exhibit and presentation units notwithstanding, there is nothing like seeing the actual Wright *Flyer*. . . . In the case of airplanes, all of our exhibited specimens are genuine. . . . However, many spacecraft are not returned to earth when their mission ends. In such cases we exhibit the backup vehicle, an exact duplicate of the original. . . . If the original or backup vehicles are not available, then we try to exhibit a replica *made from actual flightworthy parts.* In those very rare instances when something of lesser authenticity than the original is exhibited, we state explicitly on the label what is being shown [Zisfein 1976:7, emphasis mine].

What is of interest here, from an analytical point of view, is the effort made toward assuring the native (who in many cases wouldn't know better anyway), that he is touching, hearing, seeing, and smelling *actual objects* that were a part of *actual events.* Authenticity per se is undoubtedly not as important to the native as the *perception* that the objects and events are real. It is in this manner that the native becomes a part of the event; the authenticity serves as the mechanism for absorption.

Moreover, as will be discussed, the authenticity serves to complement the "evolutionary progress" message given at the Museum. That message comes across in a number of ways in a number of places. In most general terms, it even structures the layout of the building. At one end of the rectangular Museum are galleries devoted to *air* travel; at the other end are halls devoted to *space* travel. In between the air and space ends is a middle gallery devoted to the Milestones of Flight (air and space). Translating these categories of space into time (as is done repeatedly at the Museum), we can easily track a progressive scheme being formulated between the past (air, historic-local) and the future (space, future-frontier). Mediating these categories is a middle ground, a neutral synthesis of all elements (everywhere, everywhen). It is not at all surprising that the only public entrances to the Museum are through the mediating category, rather than through either of the extremes. One can directly enter an atemporal area, but one cannot enter directly into the past, nor directly into the future.

Many of the individual galleries project the general scheme as well. There are, for example, exhibits on the evolution of air transportation, the evolution of the space program, the development of air mail, and so on. Some galleries, particularly those devoted to specific events, for instance the two galleries devoted to the World Wars, do not fit the scheme.

Regardless, on a large scale, each of the galleries does fit the broader scheme. Galleries 102 through 107 at the air end of the building (first floor) exhibit historic (air) objects and themes. Galleries 109 through 114 at the space end of the building (again first floor) exhibit contemporary objects, but more importantly, are suggestive of the future. Here we find halls devoted to Flight Testing, Satellites, and Rocketry and Space Flight.

This last hall provides one of the better instances of the manipulation of the future. In the gallery is a fantasy-fact slide show. It shows, on one side of a split image screen, an historic drawing or cartoon (perhaps with the likes of Flash Gordon) accompanied by a message, such as "we stepped on the moon." Simultaneously, on the other side of the screen (the fact side) is an actual photograph: in this case a footprint on the surface of the moon. The implication of this is clear. What was once considered science fiction is now a part of our everyday experience. What *we* may consider science fiction is certainly not too far distant. Don't most remember when man had *not* walked on the moon?

It is here that the authenticity is crucial. The *actual objects* serve to reify the progress we have made, and thus will make. The *objects*, together with the scheme of progress, give the native a good conceptual hold on the past, and gives a reign on a whole series of thought to be (or so the native is told are thought to be) inaccessible others, the future and the frontier. The reification of the progress scheme lends credence to the philosophy of manifest destiny:

> "The wide open spaces" have lured Americans from our beginnings. The frontier shaped and molded our society and our people [President Gerald Ford, on the occasion of the opening of the NASM; Ford 1976:1105-1106].

The parallels to Frederick Jackson Turner's thesis are apparent. The frontier is alive and well at the National Air and Space Museum.

> The major attitude that emerged [from a 1964 study group on proposed objectives and plans for the National Air and Space Museum] was that of reorientating the museum from its preoccupation with "famous firsts" to educating the public about aviation and space; instead of merely cataloguing the events of the past it would *influence those of the future* by providing the proper historical perspective [Dooling 1976:255, emphasis mine].

Of course, vulgar ideology is not confined to the "evolutionary progression" which systematizes the Museum. There are other aspects that similarly provide the visitor with the message that the present system is a good and productive one. I will give examples that focus on three different kinds of sets: those with objects, those with people, and those with events.

In terms of objects, perhaps the most significant is *the* moon rock, displayed prominently in the Milestones of Flight Hall. The moon rock is an actual piece of the moon retrieved by the Apollo 17 mission. There is nothing particularly appealing about the rock; it is a rather standard piece of volcanic basalt some 4 million years old. Yet, unlike many other old rocks, this one comes displayed in an altar-like structure, set in glass, and is complete with full-time guard *and* an ultrasensitive monitoring device (or so the guards are wont to say). There is a sign above it which reads, "You may touch it with care."

Everyone touches it. Why? Because this object, perhaps more than any other piece of material culture in the Museum, hails you. The moon rock "marks the most spectacular chapter [of the space adventure] so far [NASM 1976:32]." On one level, it is a metaphor for the space program and, indeed, the extant order. On another level, it is a metonym. As the sign says, touch a piece of the moon. Touching the moon rock is an act of sanctification, an act that the visitor does willingly. In Althusser's terms, it represents the subjection of the subject. Touching it is not significantly different from genuflection.

People as objects of material culture are similarly sacralized. For instance, in the Satellite Hall in a small semi-circular room is a television. On that television is a continuously running "Space Science Report" by Walter Cronkite. We learn from Cronkite that satellites "help children in Appalachia read and write . . . help farmers in India raise better crops . . . and who can deny the untold future benefits" (who *can* deny the untold future benefits?). Cronkite is assuring us that all is good, all has been good, and all always will be good. There is little doubt that if anyone in America can objectify goodness and virtue, and make the message palpable to the masses, Cronkite certainly can. And that's the way it is.

Take another example. As one rounds the corner in the Life in the Universe Hall, one enters a dimly lit, cavern-like room. There is only one object in the room, a large-screen color television. On that television is Julia Child, in her kitchen of course, giving the recipe for the "chemical building blocks of life in primordial soup." At first, her presence in this Hall (in this Musuem!) seems anomalous. Yet it must be recognized that she, like Cronkite, is a real and objective artifact of our culture. Her presence, like Cronkite's, sanctifies but at the same time simplifies. Face it, when Julia Child can explain to us, via television, how life begins, how it began here on earth, and how it can begin anytime anywhere, we are being told we know the past, present, and future . . . and can *create* all three. Bon apetit.

The final kind of ideological set, events, is a large part of the NASM. There is emphasis on both particular events (for example, Lindbergh's solo across the Atlantic in the Spirit of St. Louis, Armstrong's walk on the moon) and more general events (World War I and World War II).

Of more significance than the events that are chosen for the Museum are those events not portrayed. Take the World Wars. Each has an entire gallery devoted to it. They contain not only our planes and our records of flight achievements, but also the planes of our enemies, those who are now our friends (Russian planes are unavailable for exhibition). Moreover, large numbers of books and models in the Museum shop are devoted to these particular wars. Significant planes, such as the *Enola Gay* which dropped the first atomic bomb on Hiroshima, along with a replica of the bomb that was dropped, are pictured and discussed (the actual *Enola Gay* is in the Museum's Silver Hill Facility, which houses the majority of NASM's collection and where restoration takes place).

Yet what of Korea and Vietnam? There is scarcely a mention or artifact of either, with the notable exception of a Douglas A-4C in the Sea-Air Operations gallery. Clearly the technological developments of these wars minimally warrants some small exhibit, if not their own galleries. Korea marked the introduction of jet warfare, while Vietnam saw the creation and extensive use of remote sensing, extremely sophisticated flight weaponry systems, and missile developments. None of this is even hinted at in the Museum. In part, this rather outstanding omission can be "explained" by the fact that the construction of the Museum was significantly delayed by both the fiscal drains of Korea and Vietnam (Dooling 1976:256-257). Or, as some would argue, there were more important advances in the earlier periods, particularly the Second World War (Bryan 1979:289). These explanations are not entirely satisfactory. I suspect more has to do with our conceptions of these wars.

As Walter Mondale implied in his Vice-Presidential debate with Robert Dole (at Houston's Alley Theater, October 16, 1976), World War I and World War II were "good wars" or at least nonpartisan. We now remember them as worthy exercises against honorable opponents. The memories are not painful. The wars that we did not win are not so easily remembered; many choose to forget, as they seem to have at the NASM. The temporal gap between 1976 and 1945 is, in many respects, shorter than the one between 1976 and 1975.

The lack of artifacts from Korea and Vietnam, while not easily justified, is easily explained. The maintenance and reproduction of the relations of production is dependent on the portrayal of imagined relations, those that put the *subject* (the state) in the most favorable light. The justification of the extant order is dependent on its being rationalized and, above all, lauded.

Selective "remembering" (Lewis 1975) through material culture accomplishes this.

Nonvulgar Ideology

In all of the preceding examples, the same pattern of "subjection" comes through, albeit by different means. Ultimately, though, we have to recognize that the various sets, the evolutionary scheme, the moon rock, Walter Cronkite, are all serving a masking function, presenting the *subject* favorably. But at the same time, these sets themselves are being masked. The deeper mask is nonvulgar ideology.

The substance of the nonvulgar ideology is in the time-space framework used as an objective structure for the vulgar ideology. Time and space are treated as objective events, the future and the frontier are tangible qualities. At the same time, these qualities can be demonstrated to be subjective. At the Museum itself they are frequently manipulated and transformed.

Take, for example, the movie *To Fly*, shown continuously at the theater (Gallery 115). It is a great movie. In the more than half a dozen times I have seen it, the audience has responded with applause, a reaction that, according to the theater manager, has been quite common (St. Thomas 1977:8). The 70-mm film is shown to a full house eight times a day, and the high demand has forced the Museum to keep it around for a couple of years past its scheduled closing date.

The movie presents a rather superficial view (combined with some very high-quality filming) of the development of aviation in the United States. It begins, not surprisingly, on July 4, 1831 with a balloon flight; it ends with an animated trip past Saturn and Jupiter. Concurrent with the presentation of the vulgar, progress-evolutionary scheme, though perhaps not as obvious, is the creation and utilization of nonvulgar ideology.

Early on in the film the narrator announces that we no longer think of space in terms of distance, but rather in terms of time:

> Prior to flight, America was the world of the horizontal, and spoke a language of vast distances . . . to conquer that distance we think of space as time . . . we are now in the world of the vertical, the older human scale disappears owing to our new comprehension of things not known to the world of the horizontal [*To Fly*].

What has happened here is that a dialectical opposition, space = time is being simultaneously created and negated. The dialectic is created, in that space and time are thought of as equivalent, hence transferrable and interchangeable. The dialectic is negated, in that time is recognized as a discovered object, while space is seen as a creation or function of time. Here is the denial of equivalence. Of course, there is still the failure to recognize that time also is a creation. In effect, they come close to piercing their own ideology of time and space, by recognizing the essential arbitrariness of those constructs. "The world grows smaller, . . . Hawaii grows nearer."

On a larger scale, that of the Museum in general, time and space are similarly utilized and manipulated:

> Gaze at it (the Wright brothers *Flyer*) with at least a little reverence, then let your eyes drop to the large conical object almost beneath it. This is the Apollo 11 spacecraft, *Columbia* . . . the actual spacecraft flown by the first men to walk on the moon in July 1969. Sixty-six years separate the two events—and the maturity of an entire technological age. About 20 feet separates the two objects here [the translation of time into space; the creation of the dialectic]. And that juxtaposition [the negation of the dialectic] is what the Milestones of Flight—in fact what the whole National Air and Space Museum—is all about [NASM 1976:24].

The NASM has at once broken the boundaries of time, has made the "other" (the future) accessible, but has simultaneously recognized its basic inaccessibility, it is still fantasy, as opposed to fact. The ideology of time and space, which supports the vulgar ideology, has allowed the subject to see the other (both the future and the frontier). In a sense, it makes the subject feel that he has transcended the ideology by viewing the other. We have gone to the moon, we have gone to Mars, we know there is life on other planets, and *Julia Child* tells us how to make it. At the same time, the other is made inaccessible: The basic message of the vulgar ideology is that we must continually evolve and progress, or else we will never get there.

Yet, much as the vulgar ideology is subjective, so too is the nonvulgar ideology, the constructs of time and space. They are created and negated with alarming ease. While the vulgar ideology presents the imagined relations of production, and allows subjection, the nonvulgar ideology presents the structure whereby the vulgar ideology is made objective. Its own subjectivity is cloaked in objectivity *(Vérité)*.

Conclusions

One could easily continue to document examples of "ideological" behavior at the National Air and Space Museum, but I think enough has been said to point out that this kind of phenomena exists and to show some of its varied forms. This chapter does not, and probably could not, document the full range of forms or mediums bearing an ideological message. Regardless, the point would quickly become redundant if one tried. Even though the *form* of ideological expression is varied, the *function* remains the same. The underlying message is essentially constant, though subject to basic economic and political considerations.

Calling the Museum an ideological artifact and analyzing it in this fashion should not cause alarm; this is not a call to revolution. An analysis of this sort can be apolitical. In fact, educators have been analyzing the same phenomena for years, only they term it socialization. Calling the Museum an ideological artifact, as opposed to a socialization artifact, does have the analytic advantage of giving primacy to the economic aspect of the message. It enables us to view our society's manner of reinforcing and reproducing its economic structure. The Museum details our advances and highlights the capabilities of our system. In this way, the Museum serves to make the visitor more appreciative of his role (however small) in our progress, and of the importance of our progress to the individual and to the individual's society (there is a strong underlying current of altruism at the Museum). The Museum is about air and space, but only on a surficial level: It is more properly about us.

The National Air and Space Museum is also, in a real sense, an anachronism. It was conceived at a time when there was great interest in all things aerial, yet it appeared after the flush of enthusiasm for the space venture was complete (the Apollo to the moon missions, in the eyes of many the climax of the space program, ended in 1972). The space program is no longer stylish, even though the Museum is. The next question to ask, is whether Americans will be satisfied to live out the frontier vicariously at the National Air and Space Museum, or whether they will once again make the big push into space. There is always a possibility of a rekindled interest in the space program. For this reason, it would be most interesting to see, if there were a rebound in public interest (and funding), if the NASM played any kind of catalytic role.

The true test of the effectiveness and success of an ideological structure must be measured over the long term. Saying that the NASM works is one thing, showing positive and tangible effects is quite another. I am sure, though it is only a guess, that even the most jaundiced citizen would come out of the Museum with at least some sense of awe and accomplishment; whether this will translate into a substantive change in our conception of the space program only time will tell. For now, all that can be said is that the Museum works, and it works extraordinarily well.

Acknowledgements

For their willing advice and criticism on this, and earlier drafts, I would like to thank R. C. Dunnell, J. P. Dumont, J. W. Fuller, R. A. Gould, D. K. Grayson, R. G. Handsman, G. T. Jones, M. P. Leone, S. L. Siegel, R. J. Wenke, and especially M. B. Schiffer.

Observations of the National Air and Space Museum were made during a series of visits in the spring of 1977. This chapter reflects the structure and exhibits of the Museum at that time.

9

Don't Fence Me In

Patricia Price-Beggerly

Leone (1973) suggests that archaeologists have been in error when they have used as a primary assumption that subsystems such as social organization, subsistence, and ideology determine and are a causative agent for the system of technology. He asserts, that it is a perversion of materialism for investigators to have as their primary concern the use of artifacts to show how they reflect other parts of an extinct or historic system. Instead, he challenges us to consider how the system of artifacts, caused or determined parts of the social or belief system. He proposes that archaeology should study how material culture is used in the present, especially how this use affects present culture. He believes that such investigations will demonstrate the determinative nature of modern technology and will lead to more accurate model building by archaeologists for their use in studying ancient systems. To illustrate these views he presents data from his analysis of Mormon technology as it is reflected in communities located in the Little Colorado River area of eastern and central Arizona.

In his analysis he suggests that Mormon technology articulated the religious culture with the environment with which they had to cope. That the settlement pattern determined some of the relations that Mormons had with each other. That, "Mormonism could not exist without the . . . technological devices that allowed its population to exist [1973:149]." That "every house (indeed every building in a Mormon town and every Mormon house in a Gentile town) had a fence around it. They still do [1973:143]." Based upon

127

these statements, he suggests that an analysis of Mormon technology, particularly the devices they use to parcel out space, could produce general statements regarding the determination of other cultural subsystems by technology.

My argument is not with Leone's goals as I see them. In fact, I find the prospect of studying the determinative nature of technology as it is linked with the archaeological records of extinct systems to be quite exciting. Also, I am in complete agreement with the statements that there is an interplay between the determinative effects of the technological, subsistence, social, and ideological systems of a culture. However, I suggest this interplay in the Arizona data cannot be adequately illustrated or examined by the use of a simple unicausal—A determines B—paradigm. Further, if as I understand it, this is not a particularistic, unique and area-limited study. If Leone is extrapolating from his Arizona data to more general statements about the interplay of technology and Mormon culture universally, then I find several concepts to be in need of further analysis. Perhaps, even modification, because they do not appear to apply to Mormon culture in other localities.

Leone addresses a multitude of anthropological concerns in his paper, that is, the history of archaeological research, the use of archaeology to substantiate national mythology, various theoretical stances of anthropological research, etc. I, therefore, believe it is important to set forth here that this critique examines only the issue of the unicausal determinative nature of technology in a Mormon community, and more specifically addresses a limited number of his statements regarding this issue.

In documenting his data, Leone states that since the nineteenth century every house in a Mormon town had a fence around it. Every building in a Mormon town was surrounded by a fence. Additionally, every Mormon house in a gentile town had a fence around it. And they still do.

Leone suggests, that the act of fence building was, and is a necessary part of the landscaping of a structure. The fence was, and is, an inherent part of the house, and therefore, a building is not complete until it has a fence around it holding it down. From these observations he asserts that Mormon fences are artifacts arranged in predictable patterns surrounding the living and working space of the people.

Additionally, he states, that despite overwhelming changes in Mormon culture and the materials used for fencing that the relationship between a key set of artifacts (fences) and a set of religious symbols has not changed. Fences still keep the same things out; literal things like sand and wind, but also the gentile world and cognitive categories that do not mix. They are also enabling devices that allow Mormons to redeem the earth, manipulate the environment, and reinforce their cognitive categories used to deal with the world.

Leone argues that his data illustrates that Mormon fences (technology) play a determinative role in their culture. Because the Mormons' physical world is divided and compartmentalized by walled interior spaces, yards full of fences and gridded towns and fields, this compartmentalization has a cognitive effect upon them. It is an explicit statement of some part of their religious system. The technology enables them to think in a certain way, to grow crops in a certain way and to articulate themselves with their environment in a certain way.

The last statement which I will address, and perhaps the one which most prompted this research, is one in which Leone states that Mormonism could not exist without the spatial representations set forth here, and the technological devices (fences) that allowed them to exist.

I suggest that although Leone's model might be considered of heuristic value, his conclusions are only acceptable if they can be validated by further research in other Mormon communities. I would argue that these statements are not true for all Mormonism. Although, they may reflect the cultural patterns in the areas he studied, they are not universally valid because they are not borne out by further research. Let me again state that it is my understanding that he did not intend this study to bear conclusions of a particularistic, unique nature; but rather, is using his analysis of this data to support universally true statements about Mormon culture generally.

To argue my case, I would like to present data from two different areas; the first and admittedly most shallow data will involve a two block area of Las Vegas, Nevada. The information is based on settlement patterns present in 1948 and is drawn entirely from my memory of the area as a child. It is presented only to contradict the possibility that the second study from Laie, Hawaii, is aberrant due only to the superposition of the Mormon religion on Polynesian cultural patterns. The second area of data is drawn from the Hawaiian community of Laie. The map, (Figure 9.2) is a partial tracing of a survey made for taxation purposes in 1931 and from this map is drawn the information regarding property lines. The data regarding the presence of fences and hedgerows to divide property boundaries which is superimposed upon the earlier survey map is drawn from a 1977 physical survey of the area in question. It should be stated that, although Zions Securities Corp., the land holding agent for the Church of Latter Day Saints in Hawaii, was contacted in an attempt to secure earlier maps of the community, they could not or would not make these maps available. Further, it should be mentioned that much suspicion was generated by the survey of property lines and residents were not generally cooperative when questioned regarding boundaries of their property. This could be due to recent problems centered around native Hawaiians' rights to property now held by large landholding families, corporations, the church, and the state as well as attempts by some

Hawaiians to gain reparation for lands they believe were unjustly taken from them when Hawaii became a Territory of the United States. It was, therefore, necessary to make this survey from the confines of an automobile and from knowledge gained during a 5-year residence within Area 3. It should also be stated, that the three areas of study in Laie were not chosen randomly, but rather, were areas that were not bounded by the ocean which would have made a natural boundary. Areas 1 and 2 were chosen because they have not been drastically altered by modern (post 1931) subdivision of the land. Area 3 was chosen because it reflects post 1931 settlement patterns.

Although it might seem strange to use Las Vegas, Nevada, to study Mormon settlement patterns, it should be noted that this city was originally established as a Mission of the Church of Jesus Christ of Latter Day Saints (Mormon) whose purpose was to teach farming to the various migratory Indian groups of the area. This missionary experiment failed and the mission was abandoned. Mormons, however, eventually settled in Las Vegas and by 1948 approximately 30% of the population were members of the LDS Church. As can be seen on Figure 9.1, this percentage is reflected in the area of study since 4 of the 11 families are classified as Mormons. Although the percentage of involvement with the church by these families varies, all were presently attending members with three of the household heads being of-

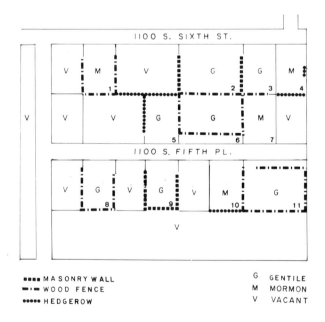

Figure 9.1. *Las Vegas, Nevada, 1948 schematic: Fences and settlement patterns.*

ficers of their Stake and all of the children involved, being educated and enculturated as Mormons. Of the gentile (non-Mormon) families, only three could be classified as active participants of their churches. As indicated by the diagram (Figure 9.1), none of the Mormon families have fenced their yards on all four sides to separate themselves from their Gentile neighbors and only one family has fenced their property on three sides (Number 1). Of the two families that have fenced their property on two sides, Number 4 grew only a partial fence of low, 2-foot (.609 m) shrubbery on a portion of one side of their property and the other family, Number 10 has fenced only the back portion of their property; the second fence is actually the property of a gentile family, Number 11. In all these cases, it might be suggested that rather than fences being a function of separation from gentile neighbors, that fences might function to protect the property from frequent ground winds which blow sand and debris onto their property from adjacent vacant desert lots. It is also noteworthy that two of the seven gentile families have completely fenced their yards on four sides, Numbers 6 and 11, and four of these families have fences on three sides of their property, Numbers 2, 8, and 9.

I therefore suggest, that the Nevada data indicate that (a) every Mormon house does not have a fence around it; (b) the spatial closeness involved in town residence did not cause Mormons to fence their property; (c) buildings were considered complete without fences; (d) Mormons did not draw a clear line between themselves and their gentile neighbors by the use of fences; and, (e) Mormonism does exist and is a viable institution without the spatial representation of fences. Clearly Leone's model is not validated by the Nevada data.

The second area of study is the Mormon owned city of Laie, Hawaii, which is located on the north windward coast of the island of Oahu. The land for this city was acquired by the Church either through direct purchases or by donation from their members. Residents own or rent their houses, they acquire the use of the land through leases from the Church. The area was established in the mid-1800s by Mormons who intended to turn this "desert unfit for agriculture" into a sugar plantation that would help support their efforts to missionize the native Hawaiian population. The sugar cane venture was from the beginning beset by problems. It was only marginally successful when the operation of the mill was transferred to another plantation in 1931. Eventually, the sugar industry was phased out in the area and the lands are now used as a residential sanctuary where Mormon families can raise their children in an atmosphere which more closely meshes with their moral standards than would an area of general population. Today it is also the center of Mormonism in Hawaii and is the site of both the Brigham Young University—Hawaii Campus and the Polynesian Cultural Center. Most important theologically, it is the site of a Mormon Temple complex. Theologically the doctrine of the Church in this city is directed by the Church in Salt Lake City, Utah. Both theologically and socially the Mormons of Laie adhere (from a gentile's viewpoint) to the general basic Utah Mormon theological and cultural pattern. Although an in-depth study of the possible variations of their theology and cultural patterns from that of mainland patterns might be fruitful in analysis of enculturation and change processes, it is beyond the scope of this paper to deal with this issue. For purposes of my analysis, it will be assumed that general Mormon theological and cultural patterns are present in Laie. Considering this assumption, I believe it is illustrated that the settlement patterns stated by Leone for Arizona Mormons and extrapolated for Mormonism generally are not present in Laie; and therefore are not necessary for Mormonism to exist.

As can be seen in Figure 9.2, (a) every building in this community does not have a fence around it; (b) the spatial closeness that enabled cooperation and survival did not also need fences; (c) fence building is not a necessary item for social communication and isolation; (d) Mormon fences are not arranged in regular, predictable patterns; (e) Mormonism is existing and flourishing without the spatial representations and technological devices that are hypothesized by Leone to be necessary for Mormons to exist. They have

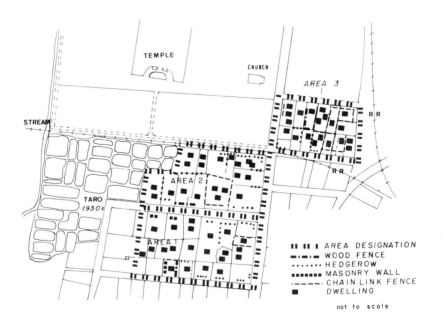

Figure 9.2. *Laie, Hawaii, 1931 map plus 1977 data: Fences and settlement patterns.*

not divided their land into equal parcels. They did not lay out their city into 10-acre squares divided into eight lots. They did not build their houses on the center of the lot 20 feet (6.09 m) back from the property line, and the houses are not back to back facing in opposite directions.

Although many of the cultural patterns suggested by Leone did and do exist in Laie, (a) they did gather in villages; (b) they did cooperate in irrigation systems; and (c) they did provide schooling, worship, and government for their people, other patterns as shown above are absent. It would appear that the same—A causes B—pattern is not present in Laie.

Two further examples of the difference between the Laie patterns and those evident in Arizona might also help illuminate the problem with acceptance of Leone's paradigm.

Between 1972-1977 I resided in Lot 3 of Area 3. During that period the landlord erected a 6-foot (1.82-m) fence which completed the enclosure of that lot on three sides. This fence prevented the inhabitants of the area seaward of the house from "cutting through" the property to the park and church. In 1974, I returned home at the end of the day to find that a large section of the fence had been removed. The fence had not been destroyed, but rather, had been carefully unnailed and lifted from the concrete foundations that held it upright. Most of the lumber was stacked neatly and carefully along the remaining portion of the fence. When questioned, no one had seen or heard anyone dismantle the fence, however, immediately that afternoon the usual procession of people cutting through the yard to the park was resumed. This included children on bicycles and walking, old people and infirm walking, and even young men on motor bikes. The removal of the fence also allowed the continuation of former cultural patterns; such as flower gathering for leis from the plumeria bushes in the yard; harvesting of bananas, coconuts, breadfruit, and sugar cane; and access to outdoor water taps located on the house by young people playing in the park. Based on Leone's analysis of Arizona Mormon behavioral patterns, I would suggest that these are not usual mainland Mormon behavioral habits and would not be a common occurrence in the towns he studied. In the Arizona communities private property concepts are probably much more intensely developed. I believe, these patterns could be attributed to general Polynesian cultural values and should be considered if a new model is developed for Mormon settlement pattern in Hawaii. Or if the role of technology to the totality of Mormon culture in a Polynesian Mormon community is studied.

My last example of the difference between the Laie and Arizona settlement pattern is illustrated by recent development within the city of Laie. Within the last 3 years, a number of homes have been built along the coastline and just inland of the highway. As can be seen on Figure 9.3, this housing represents an area of high-intensity multilevel housing and dense population. Each inland house represents an approximate investment of over $150,000 with those on the shoreline running well over $250,000 plus the charges for leasing the land. As illustrated on Figure 9.3, fences have generally not been used to define property boundaries except to protect the yards from heavy vehicular traffic or to delineate private property from public beach access. It does not appear that they must have fenced yards to be, or to remain Mormon.

In summary, it was the purpose of this research to question the causative role of technology and to test the predictability of Mormon fence patterns and settlement patterns as noted by Leone. Two different areas of Mormon settlement were observed; Las Vegas, Nevada (ca. 1948) which represented Mormon settlement in a Gentile community as well as a main-land versus an Hawaiian community and Laie, Hawaii (ca. 1972-1979) which represents Mormon settlement in a city owned and administered by the Church of Jesus Christ of Latter Day Saints. Both of these areas repre-sent orthodox Mormon communities who take their doctrinal, theological, and cultural policies directly from the Church headquartered at Salt Lake City, Utah. Both of the study areas have religious practices and attitudes

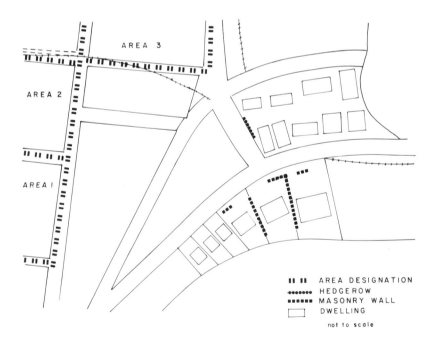

Figure 9.3. *Laie, Hawaii, 1931 map plus 1977 data: Recent residential construction.*

similar to those indicated by Leone for the Arizona Mormons. Important differences existed, however, in their technology. The Nevada and Hawaii LDS communities do not articulate their religious culture with the environment by the use of fences, nor can Nevada and Hawaii fence patterns be predicted from Arizona patterns. The question then is, if Leone is correct and if the Arizona Mormon ideology is determined by their technology (fences, gridded towns, and fields, and settlement patterns) why do Hawaii and Nevada Mormons have the same ideology without the same technology? I would suggest that unicausal explanations are not adequate to illuminate the role of technology as a determinative agent. Rather, the question must be examined holistically within a total system where the actions and reactions of each part of a system and their effects on the whole may be defined and analyzed. In conclusion, although Leone gives lip service to the fact that cause may work both ways and that technology must be considered in a plural context, his entire argument for technological determinism is based on a one-way unicausal relationship. He insists to be Mormon one must be fenced in.

10

The Cemetery and Culture Change: Archaeological Focus and Ethnographic Perspective

Edwin S. Dethlefsen

What Can Gravestones Tell Us about Community?

A cemetery should reflect the local, historical flow of attitudes about community. It is, after all, a community of the dead, created, maintained, and preserved by the community of the living. In many ways it should be a "filtered" and modified reflection of the living community, with an added dimension of controlled chronological depth. At least, the cemetery should have some hints for us about prevailing views of God, acceptable implications of life and death, intensity of status differentiation, and relative values of kin and other social-interactive relationships.

The community cemetery offers some distinctive strategic concerns for the ethnographic observer. Death is rarely taken lightly, but however it is taken, it happens to everyone. Because it is a universal "passage" its associated rituals and materials are likely to be conservatively employed while remaining sensitive to long-range shifts in community value emphases. Because it is subject to changes of fashion, it is a prime target for those interested in studying the dynamics of culture. It is not the dead individual but the living community which determines and maintains the cultural frame within which mortuary practices and perceptions occur. It is ethnographically useful to see the cemetery not only as a historical record but as a current status report, and it is advantageous to conjoin both views to develop syntheses about community-in-process.

137

MODERN MATERIAL CULTURE
The Archaeology of Us

Why the Cemetery?

The graveyard provides a restricted, tangible and controllable body of data. Where the student may be overwhelmed by a multiplicity of potential approaches to the study of the living community, the cemetery is a surface, archaeological site, in that its data are a limited variety of describable artifacts—their attributes and spatial relationships. These are far less subject than is the living community to misinterpretation on account of informant bias, since their "messages" are not so modifiable by the particular accumulation of personal experience the investigator uses to illuminate and through which he interprets what he sees. The cemetery is an eminently manageable body of data, especially for the beginner.

In the 1960s I began to work extensively with Colonial New England gravestones attempting to delineate the kinds of things they might profitably be used to investigate (Dethlefsen and Deetz 1966; Dethlefsen 1969, 1972). At that time I believed I had considered the major features of their anthropological usefulness, and that post-Colonial gravestones were of little study value because their increasingly commercialized production tended to extinguish local, idiosyncratic, vernacular expression. Actually, vernacular developments merely were expressed in new ways, and it is now clear that the delocalization of gravestone production was itself an expression of systemic change in patterns of American material culture as well as of changing directions in our social history (Dethlefsen and Jensen 1977).

While the initial study area probably represents the longest historical sequence in America, dating back to the late seventeenth century, the points I wish to make can be illustrated just as well with data from almost any American community cemetery. In fact, the latter is one of my points. It is not depth of archaeological sequence which need concern us here, but the use of an archaeological perspective in the study of community.

The present discussion involves the idea of "types" at more than one categorical level. This is necessary in order to delineate a model of systemic evolution by which cemeteries may be employed toward understanding the process of community.

The Types of Data: Form and Substance

First there is the shape and material of the grave marker itself. In Colonial New England the material is slate and the form that of a flat tablet. Slate is a densely laminate kind of stone, and it is difficult to imagine any other practical form for it than that of a tablet. The material has had influence on determining the form—and probably vice versa; the tablet form even being evident in grave markers of the Roman Empire. The kind of stone preferred for gravestones has steadily undergone changes since Colonial times, basically from slate or sandstone to marble, to granite, to bronze.

Pictures and Decorations

The design and decoration of the gravestone can be informative in two ways: first, in the kinds of symbolism expressed and what they may indicate as to the values and topical concerns of the community; and second, in the very frequency with which a design element or the overall expression of a particular sentiment appears at any given time. There was a time and a place when a single element—the winged death's head—was practically universal, suggesting that one thing it represented was strong conformity in the community's choice of symbolic expression. In modern illustration of the point we find some cemeteries full of Celtic crosses while others have no such crosses at all, but Stars of David, while yet others have no symbolic statement, sometimes not even decorations. Such observations immediately pose floods of ethnographic hints and questions about the community and suggest deductions we may begin to pursue about the community or about the portion of it served by a particular cemetery.

Size

Other than providing statements about relative status, size is best examined in context with design and/or with other types of data that correlate with size. While famous or wealthy individuals may have larger gravestones for one economic reason, a family may share a large stone for the opposite economic reason. But even here the context requires expansion, for there are other than economic factors involved, which require consideration of more than size alone (e.g., values regarding decoration, landscape design, modesty, status expectations). A powerful U.S. Senator or businessperson might have a fairly modest gravemarker while a famous entertainer would likely have a more flamboyant one, which is itself a historical statement bearing some ethnographic significance.

Using more than size alone, however, one can often trace the histories of ethnic groups through a town's cemeteries more handily than by any other means, provided one understands the cemetery is only a starting point—a place for forming *questions* about community.

Inscriptions

Whether a standard introduction says, "Here lies buried . . . " or whether instead it says, "Sacred to the memory of . . . ," or whether it says merely, "Mother," or whether it says, "Mom" may tell us much, not only about changing views of death and the hereafter, but about variation in the degrees and intensities to which some statuses were overtly defined and the directions in which these recognitions have changed.

Sometimes, too, we can see inscriptions containing more than just vital data like age, date of death, and sex. Even in this regard we might ask why age and vital dates have been universal for so long, and why these statements are disappearing today. At the same time, we should note that sex can be determined with increasing frequency only by inference from a given name. There may be any of a large variety of statements of attitudes toward God, attitudes concerning death, and observations about people's relationships to one another. There is systemic variation through time in a great many aspects of the inscriptions, even to the forms and varieties of calligraphy and to the lengths of epitaphs, as well as to their positions on the stones and to their relationships with the size, shape, and substance of the stone employed.

A large portion of the carpet manufacturing community of East Boylston, Massachusetts, for example, is of recent "Armenian" descent. While the modern gravestones of the surrounding communities place the wives' and husbands' names side by side, those in the East Boylston cemetery place the husband's name *above* that of the wife, with the children and their spouses strung out below, assorted by natal order and sex, the living often listed along with the dead. But before we label the Boylstonians "sexist," let us also note that more than three-fourths of all New England's modern, shared gravestones indicate that the wife lies at the husband's left hand, while in the middle South (where "coeds" yet occasionally may be seen wearing skirts) the decision as to whose name appears first, or at the left side of the gravestone or bronze, appears to be random. There is much food for thought here, not the least of which concerns the role of geography in the interpretation of material culture in systemic evolution.

The Yankee colonials were very economic folk, filling in most of the available gravestone space with words, a virtue they have shared with their British, and especially with their Scottish forebears and colonial contemporaries. The seventeenth- and early eighteenth-century gravestones of Scotland bleed their inscriptions around the edges and onto the backs of the stones, filling all available flat space with inscriptions, while the "man-sized" sandstone tablets of eighteenth- and nineteenth-century Scots Presbyterians may have the vital records of 20 or more deceased inscribed on a single face.

Geography

Another variable among gravestones is their arrangement on the landscape. Sometimes they are set out in neat rows, and sometimes they are scattered about or segregated into discrete clusters. Sometimes two gravestones share a common base. Often certain relatives are buried in some particular spatial relationship to one another as in the case of spouses, just noted. Other times the whole family is buried in an exclusive plot. At yet other times and places there seems no real concern about where in the cemetery any given body is interred. On the other hand, the Moravians of North Carolina employ different sectors of "God's Acre" to segregate adult males from adult females and immature males and females both from adults and from one another. It appears that spatial evidence may vary in its *degree* of significance as well as in its cultural implications from time to time.

Another aspect of the same variable is the place of the cemetery in the physical and cultural landscape. Is it on the hill or beside the church? Is it in the center of town or on the periphery? (Indeed, is it a "cemetery" at all, or is it a mausoleum, or a park?) What, if any, is the correlation of time and place of the cemetery, and what, if anything, does that correlation suggest? Some of these questions have been hinted at by geographers such as Jeane (1969) and Francaviglia (1971).

The Cemetery As a Model

The discovery of variation generally depends upon how closely one looks at one's subject. The closer the scrutiny, the greater the opportunity for differences to be seen, but I have listed the major *kinds* of community data I have been able to distinguish in most cemeteries. Next, the problem is how to use these data.

While I do not care to argue here that culture is organic in the usual biological sense, the generalities of natural selection seem to apply quite frequently and clearly in the case of material culture. If we accept that a community is an adaptive system all of whose parts are more or less delicately adjusted to one another, and then if we look at the cemetery as a limited reflection of the real community, we might begin to see a model of the general workings of the larger system—we might learn how to expose details of synergistic interaction among the "institutions" of a functioning "culture."

The parts of a system are often difficult to perceive. Their "visibility" is in proportion to the viewer's sense of the whole, and they are best seen not in the intricacies of their "structural" details but in terms of their interactive relationships with one another. It was only when I began to see the cemetery as a material expression of the *systemic* history of the *community* that the relationships among the various aspects of observation in the cemetery—spacing, design, form, composition, etc.—began to make themselves visible.

Our model may indeed be useful even if all that it shows is that a given aspect of a system may vary greatly through time and space in the quality and intensity—the *nature*—of the synergy it is required to maintain. For example, during the Federal and Civil War periods in American cemeteries, lengthy and flowery *epitaphs* were very common, while in early Colonial times and in the interval between Federal and Civil War periods, as well as today, they are rare. Thus the frequency of epitaphs, as well as the sentiments expressed, must be taken into account. In Colonial and Federal times, the *design motif* appears rigidly prescribed while in the Industrial Period there was wild variation. (Since it is the variability of artifact attributes that makes those attributes observable at all, the fact that different attributes emerge as significant variables at different times is particularly difficult to observe except in such conveniently "longitudinal" artifact repositories as the cemetery.) Yet today gravestone decoration is often formalized and almost vestigial, while the *sharing* of gravestones between spouses has become almost universal. Thus, for culture-interpretive purposes the *demography* of the gravestone has assumed some of the significance formerly inferred from the *design motif* (compare, for example, traits A1-A3 in the figures and tables—highest frequency of decorative variability precedes predominance of family plots: 1850-1880).

Even the proportion of dead marked by graves at all is suggestive in its variation. Modern reduction in this proportion may imply increased reluctance to confront (or perhaps even to admit) death, or else it may imply a more extensive reintegration of the concept of death and/or cemeteries in the living community, perhaps involving deritualization.

Furthermore, modern cemeteries vary more than ever before in their representativeness of community. Blacks may be separated from whites not only stylistically but geographically, various religious groups (e.g., Moravians, Quakers) have isolated themselves for a long time, and we have every reason to suppose that the users of "lawn" cemeteries and mausoleums form differently constituted community segments which must be taken into account when inferring a systemic synthesis from today's cemeteries.

Thus, in looking at community-*as-process* we may find it worthwhile to keep a flexible focus on our frame of reference. This will help us to avoid serious disorientation when it suddenly appears that a treasured data source has been speaking to us for some time with forked tongue.

Testing the Model Idea

In attempting to define a model to test, I depended heavily on the approach used in earlier studies and particularly on the idea of applying time-frequency techniques to other than decorative types, to see to what extent the significance of a type category might vary independently of types in other categories. That is, I wanted first to know if a given culture trait might be expressed most clearly at one time by one group of typological frequencies and at another time by quite a different set of types. Was what was expressed at one time by *design motif* expressed at another by *stone shape*, by *placement*, or by *inscription?* Did the relationships of typological categories to one another change through time?

Girded with my typologies and attribute lists, and armed with a burning sense of culture-as-system, I quested first through the cemeteries of north central Florida. If my hypothesis was workable it should work *anywhere*, and Florida was where I happened to be, with small enough communities for carrying out some quick test surveys. What I discovered was no single thing I had not seen before, but a set of slowly changing relationships that has seemed to reflect and to generate some interesting ramifications of *allometry* (change rate differential) in cultural dynamics.

North central Florida's white Protestant cemeteries seem to suggest four more or less distinct periods between the Civil War and the present. (I have more than enough data on black and non-Protestant cemeteries to know that these show significant cultural differences that will require separate analytical treatment.)

The Quantitative Data

Four cemeteries of Alachua County, Florida, were tabulated for this study, representing what I thought to be three distinctive forms of community. The Hawthorn group is most cosmopolitan, made up at least in part by retirees from other places. The Micanopy cemetery ($N = 434$) appears to be mostly local "Old Family," representing what I interpret to be the most conservative type of community, "dripping with Spanish moss," while the Ochwilla and Rochelle ($N = 282$) cemeteries are mainly farmers and woods and fishing-camp folks, and a few blacks (the Hawthorn cemetery ($N = 583$) fences the blacks and whites apart, although there is no difficulty distinguishing their graves, and blacks are not in evidence in the Micanopy cemetery).

The means of some of the tabulated attributes for all four cemeteries are summarized in the graphs (Figure 10.10), which provide a general, comparative picture of change in attribute frequencies through time, while separate frequencies for the three community "types" are given in Tables 10.1-10.14. The differences evident in the tables seem to me to be of such interest that I have also calculated the standard deviations and the ratios of the standard deviations to the means, to provide some measure of relative

Table 10.1

Trait A1.   Comparative Frequencies of Burials in a Family Group

Decade	Mic	Roc	Haw	Mean (X)	Standard deviation (S)	S/X
1970-1976	26	28	0	18.00	15.62	0.87
1960-1969	27	23	0	16.67	14.57	0.87
1950-1959	23	33	0	18.67	16.92	0.91
1940-1949	29	35	5	23.00	15.87	0.69
1930-1939	45	17	6	22.67	20.11	0.89
1920-1929	53	48	11	37.33	22.94	0.61
1910-1919	68	50	24	47.33	22.12	0.47
1900-1909	73	31	18	40.67	28.75	0.71
1890-1899	78	26	10	38.00	35.55	0.94
1880-1889	74	64	—	—	—	—
1870-1879	78	50	—	—	—	—
1860-1869	89	—	—	—	—	—

Table 10.2

Trait A2.   Comparative Frequencies of Paired Stones for Spouses

Decade	Mic	Roc	Haw	Mean (X)	Standard deviation (S)	S/X
1970-1976	14	22	12	16.00	5.29	0.33
1960-1969	18	19	21	19.33	1.53	0.08
1950-1959	17	19	52	29.33	19.66	0.67
1940-1949	33	19	27	26.33	7.02	0.27
1930-1939	16	22	40	26.00	12.49	0.48
1920-1929	24	20	22	22.00	2.00	0.09
1910-1919	4	21	14	13.00	8.54	0.66
1900-1909	5	25	16	15.33	10.02	0.65
1890-1899	6	15	6	9.00	5.20	0.58
1880-1889	4	8	—	—	—	—
1870-1879	0	8	—	—	—	—
1860-1869	6	—	—	—	—	—

concurrence among the community types with regard to the relative time stability of specific attributes. Thus, low differences between means indicate that frequencies of attributes are similar in all three cemetery types, while high differences suggest at least different rates of change within the community types. While I have only considered a few very obvious attributes here, there are many more that are possible, including such considerations as

Table 10.3

Trait A3.   Comparative Frequencies of Shared Stones for Spouses

Decade	Mic	Roc	Haw	Mean (X)	Standard deviation (S)	S/X
1970-1976	40	11	51	34.00	20.66	0.61
1960-1969	40	26	34	33.33	7.02	0.21
1950-1959	39	38	35	37.33	2.08	0.06
1940-1949	19	19	16	18.00	1.73	0.10
1930-1939	14	33	14	20.33	10.97	0.54
1920-1929	8	12	4	8.00	4.00	0.50
1910-1919	12	4	2	6.00	5.29	9.88
1900-1909	7	0	4	3.67	3.51	0.96
1890-1899	12	4	3	6.33	4.93	0.78
1880-1889	0	4	—	—	—	—
1870-1879	0	0	—	—	—	—
1860-1869	0	—	—	—	—	—

Table 10.4

Trait BI.   Comparative Frequencies of Use of Term of "Mother," "Father"

Decade	Mic	Roc	Haw	Mean (X)	Standard deviation (S)	S/X
1970-1976	14	22	12	16.00	5.29	0.33
1960-1969	3	12	8	7.67	4.51	0.59
1950-1959	12	14	2	9.33	6.43	0.69
1940-1949	15	16	0	10.33	8.96	0.87
1930-1939	13	28	9	16.67	10.02	0.60
1920-1929	8	16	28	17.33	10.07	0.58
1910-1919	16	14	9	13.00	3.61	0.28
1900-1909	10	31	9	16.67	12.42	0.75
1890-1899	16	0	15	10.33	8.96	0.87
1880-1889	9	4	—	—	—	—
1870-1879	0	17	—	—	—	—
1860-1869	0	—	—	—	—	—

epitaph sentiment, decoration (both in stone and supplementary), and a host of demographically related variables.

Summarizing the data from four cemetery samples from north central Florida, the graphs illustrate frequency variations through time of several type categories, including: A, Spatial Relationships of the Burials; B, Kin and Other Affiliative References; C, Presence of an Epitaph (a lumped category

Table 10.5

Trait B2.   Comparative Frequencies of Use of Term "Wife"

Decade	Mic	Roc	Haw	Mean (X)	Standard deviation (S)	S/X
1970-1976	3	0	3	2.00	1.73	0.87
1960-1969	0	5	0	1.67	2.89	1.73
1950-1959	0	0	3	1.00	1.73	1.73
1940-1949	4	3	0	2.33	2.08	0.89
1930-1939	4	6	3	4.33	1.53	0.35
1920-1929	8	8	7	7.67	0.58	0.08
1910-1919	18	14	20	17.33	3.06	0.18
1900-1909	21	19	22	20.67	1.53	0.07
1890-1899	19	19	9	15.67	5.77	0.37
1880-1889	27	20	25	24.00	3.61	0.15
1870-1879	18	13	—	—	—	—
1860-1869	18	—	—	—	—	—

Table 10.6

Trait B3.   Comparative Frequencies of Filial and Other Kin Terms

Decade	Mic	Roc	Haw	Mean (X)	Standard deviation (S)	S/X
1970-1976	3	0	0	1.00	1.73	1.73
1960-1969	0	0	1	0.33	0.58	1.73
1950-1959	0	0	2	0.67	1.15	1.73
1940-1949	2	3	8	4.33	3.21	0.74
1930-1939	6	0	1	2.33	3.21	1.38
1920-1929	12	0	2	4.67	6.43	1.38
1910-1919	21	14	9	14.67	6.03	0.41
1900-1909	19	6	20	15.00	7.81	0.52
1890-1899	39	4	35	26.00	19.16	0.74
1880-1889	23	12	13	16.00	6.08	0.38
1870-1879	0	17	—	—	—	—
1860-1869	0	—	—	—	—	—

that could be broken into a number of epitaph types); D, Composition of the Gravestones; E, Shape of the Gravestone. Because the graphic indicators are themselves so expressive of cultural macroevolutionary change, and because I have attempted a broad interpretation of their systemic significance elsewhere (Dethlefsen and Jensen 1977), I leave their detailed interpretation to the reader.

The tables show some clear distinctions among the community types,

Table 10.7
Trait B4.   Comparative Frequencies of Fraternal or Military Affiliation

Decade	Mic	Roc	Haw	Mean (X)	Standard deviation (S)	S/X
1970-1976	16	17	26	19.67	5.51	0.28
1960-1969	11	16	26	17.67	7.64	0.43
1950-1959	18	24	24	22.00	3.46	0.16
1940-1949	6	14	10	10.00	4.00	0.40
1930-1939	17	6	11	11.33	5.51	0.49
1920-1929	2	12	9	7.67	5.13	0.67
1910-1919	8	4	15	9.00	5.57	0.62
1900-1909	4	6	7	5.67	1.53	0.27
1890-1899	0	7	0	2.33	4.04	1.73
1880-1889	0	4	—	—	—	—
1870-1879	0	0	—	—	—	—
1860-1869	0	—	—	—	—	—

Table 10.8
Trait C.   Comparative Frequencies of Epitaphs (any Length)

Decade	Mic	Roc	Haw	Mean (X)	Standard deviation (S)	S/X
1970-1976	21	17	23	20.33	3.06	0.15
1960-1969	36	7	13	18.67	15.31	0.82
1950-1959	16	14	7	12.33	4.73	0.38
1940-1949	10	16	17	14.33	3.79	0.26
1930-1939	25	11	17	17.67	7.02	0.40
1920-1929	16	20	50	28.67	18.58	0.65
1910-1919	70	54	39	54.33	15.50	0.29
1900-1909	66	63	44	57.67	11.93	0.21
1890-1899	90	44	71	68.33	23.12	0.34
1880-1889	92	60	50	67.33	21.94	0.33
1870-1879	89	63	—	—	—	—
1860-1869	100	—	—	—	—	—

especially with regard to their comparative rates of change in the various descriptive type categories, but also with respect to the time periods in which the rates themselves change most. As a very simple measure of the latter I have used the ratio of the standard deviation (S) to the mean (X) of all the cemeteries for each decade and type where data are available and meaningful, in each type category. A high figure in this column (Column 7) indicates a low concordance of means among the three community types,

Table 10.9

Trait D1.   Comparative Frequencies of Marble Markers: Selected Sites

Decade	Mic	Haw	Mean *(X)*	Standard deviation *(S)*	*S/X*
1970-1976	5	0	2.50	3.54	1.41
1960-1969	16	2	9.00	9.90	1.10
1950-1959	22	13	17.50	6.36	0.36
1940-1949	17	15	16.00	1.41	0.09
1930-1939	44	34	39.00	7.07	0.18
1920-1929	37	48	42.50	7.78	0.18
1910-1919	84	87	85.50	2.12	0.02
1900-1909	90	78	84.00	8.49	0.10
1890-1899	97	82	89.50	10.61	0.21
1880-1889	96	—	—	—	—
1870-1879	100	—	—	—	—

Table 10.10

Trait D2.   Comparative Frequencies of Granite Markers: Selected Sites

Decade	Mic	Haw	Mean *(X)*	Standard deviation *(S)*	*S/X*
1970-1976	95	82	88.50	9.19	0.10
1960-1969	84	66	75.00	12.73	0.17
1950-1959	75	73	74.00	1.41	0.02
1940-1949	83	64	73.50	13.44	0.18
1930-1939	54	46	50.00	5.66	0.11
1920-1929	57	35	46.00	15.56	0.34
1910-1919	13	17	15.00	2.83	0.19
1900-1909	10	17	13.50	4.95	0.37
1890-1899	0	4	2.00	2.83	1.41
1880-1889	0	—	—	—	—
1870-1879	0	—	—	—	—
1860-1869	0	—	—	—	—

which in turn suggests that the corresponding time period may be one of higher-than-usual overall, systemic stress-instability.

Because in any dynamic system the nature of the complex of componential interactions is always changing at a correspondingly complexly integrated variety of rates, I think comparative figures on rates can bring us closer to an internally comprehensive model of community cultural dynamics through time. For example, a rapid glance down the columns of means (Col-

Table 10.11

Trait E1.   Comparative Frequencies of Tablet Form

Decade	Mic	Roc	Haw	Mean (X)	Standard deviation (S)	S/X
1970-1976	0	11	2	4.33	5.86	1.35
1960-1969	0	0	2	0.67	1.15	1.73
1950-1959	10	19	5	11.33	7.09	0.63
1940-1949	2	11	2	5.00	5.20	1.04
1930-1939	13	22	9	14.67	6.66	0.45
1920-1929	6	16	13	11.67	5.13	0.44
1910-1919	29	43	26	32.67	9.07	0.28
1900-1909	38	38	41	39.00	1.73	0.04
1890-1899	48	67	44	53.00	12.29	0.23
1880-1889	77	60	—	—	—	—
1870-1879	88	71	—	—	—	—
1860-1869	91	—	—	—	—	—

Table 10.12

Trait E2.   Comparative Frequencies of Pulpit Form

Decade	Mic	Roc	Haw	Mean (X)	Standard deviation (S)	S/X
1970-1976	0	0	0	0.00	0.00	0.00
1960-1969	3	0	0	1.00	1.73	1.73
1950-1959	2	5	3	3.33	1.53	0.46
1940-1949	2	0	0	0.67	1.15	1.73
1930-1939	0	11	0	3.67	6.35	1.73
1920-1929	2	12	17	10.33	7.64	0.74
1910-1919	26	25	20	23.67	3.21	0.14
1900-1909	21	13	11	15.00	5.29	0.35
1890-1899	29	7	15	17.00	11.14	0.66
1880-1889	5	0	—	—	—	—
1870-1879	13	0	—	—	—	—
1860-1869	0	—	—	—	—	—

umn 5) indicates that Hawthorn has responded most rapidly and most completely to change in all type categories, while the older cemeteries are more conservative—they are slower to respond and are less thoroughly invested in their response. Since Hawthorn is a twentieth-century community, one might expect it to be more "adaptively experimental" than the others. Where Hawthorn diverges most from the others is during the 3- or 4-decade period

Table 10.13

Trait E3.   Comparative Frequencies of Obelisk Form

Decade	Mic	Roc	Haw	Mean (X)	Standard deviation (S)	S/X
1970-1976	0	0	0	0.00	0.00	0.00
1960-1969	0	0	0	0.00	0.00	0.00
1950-1959	0	0	0	0.00	0.00	0.00
1940-1949	0	0	0	0.00	0.00	0.00
1930-1939	0	0	0	0.00	0.00	0.00
1920-1929	11	0	2	4.33	5.86	1.35
1910-1919	23	4	33	20.00	14.73	0.74
1900-1909	23	19	20	20.67	2.08	0.10
1890-1899	18	11	21	16.67	5.13	0.31
1880-1889	0	24	2	8.67	13.32	1.54
1870-1879	0	21	—	—	—	—
1860-1869	0	—	—	—	—	—

Table 10.14

Trait E4.   Comparative Frequencies of Block Form (All Types)

Decade	Mic	Roc	Haw	Mean (X)	Standard deviation (S)	S/X
1970-1976	89	79	83	83.67	5.03	0.06
1960-1969	98	92	71	87.00	14.18	0.16
1950-1959	87	63	76	75.33	12.01	0.16
1940-1949	89	59	80	76.00	15.39	0.20
1930-1939	73	61	70	68.00	6.24	0.09
1920-1929	85	48	46	59.67	21.96	0.37
1910-1919	24	25	18	22.33	3.79	0.17
1900-1909	18	6	24	16.00	9.17	0.57
1890-1899	6	7	9	7.33	1.53	0.21
1880-1889	5	8	—	—	—	—
1870-1879	0	0	—	—	—	—
1860-1869	0	—	—	—	—	—

centering on 1920. This represents a major "cross-over" period, where the shorter, squatter, battleship-shaped frequency curves of Hawthorn expand or attenuate out of phase with those of Micanopy and Rochelle-Ochwilla.

The Federal Period

Turning now to a sequential examination of the changes, I have found little evidence of pre-Civil War occupation of central Florida, but other

Figure 10.1. *Tablet representative of early to mid nineteenth-century gravestone forms.*

southern cemeteries provide some continuity with data from earlier periods in the Northeast. To accentuate this continuity, I begin with the Northeast Federal Period, lasting in the cemetery to about 1840. During this time the urn-and-willow motif fades from its beginning as a universal design around 1780. (For a good summary of archaeological examination of this and earlier design types, see Holton 1979.) The gravestone *material* began as slate and ended as marble during this same period, while the *form* remained that of a simple tablet, with gradual alterations in silhouette (Figure 10.1). The burials were generally in rows, with little or no spatial differentiation of family members from other members of the community. Husbands and wives were buried side by side more often than not, but the cemetery gives a general impression of community uniformity and "solidarity" (at least in selection of gravestone attributes) during this time, hinting that while family was certainly important, community orientation was also an important aspect of world view. (Incidentally noteworthy in this regard is that the number of white males in America has increased more than fiftyfold between 1790 and 1970 (U.S. Bureau of the Census 1975:16) and the number of females has increased more than sixtyfold. In the 19th century it was probably still possible in most communities for one to know one's neighbors and to be involved with them.)

The Civil War Period

Another period which can hardly be seen except as a backdrop for observations of later changes begins with the coincident explosion of northern industry in the 1840s. Now there is some sculptural experiment with design elements, but the basic tablet form continues up to about 1875 (Figure 10.2), and emphasis returns to highly verbose epitaphs and pictorial motifs, after their near extinction toward the end of the Federal Period. Otherwise the gravestones remain relatively austere in form and they are unsegregated from communal rows. There is a high emphasis on religious symbols, but instead of a single, universal *motif*, as in the case of the earlier urn-and-willow,

Figure 10.2. *A tablet form typical of the middle to late nineteenth century.*

there are many, beginning around mid-century. Most of these suggest peace, love, and comfort in the afterlife. Doves, lambs and flowers, clasped hands, crowns, crosses, heavenly gates, etc., are all popular, and Masonic emblems, military, and other signs of nonfamilial associations make their first regular appearance.

Relatives are grouped helter skelter. The small number of surnames in most of these "frontier" communities probably makes family-segregated groupings seem more real than they actually were.

The Industrial Expansion Period

By the 1890s the industrial culture of the North had made its way to expression in the northern Florida cemeteries, and from that time on we see emphases again changing. This period began earlier in New England (Dethlefsen and Jensen 1977:35). Epitaphs are reduced, but not decorative motifs, and families are segregated into clearly marked plots, often complete with iron fences or stone borders. Gravestones change both in form and in function, as tablets are replaced by obelisks (Figure 10.3), pulpits (Figure 10.4), and a wide variety of other sculptured representations, well illustrated in a variety of current cemetery "art" books. The sculpturability of marble is extensively exploited up to about 1925 (again, a decade or so later than in New England), the large, three-dimensional monuments sometimes serving whole families, while individuals are also marked with smaller, supplementary stones, labeled "Mother," "Father," "Little Fannie," etc., with surname and vital data often only on the larger, family monument. At the same time footstones disappear from the cemetery or are incorporated into plot borders.

While females and youngsters had been generally associated with paternalistic heads of household (e.g., "Wife of . . . ," "Son of . . . ,") ever since

Figure 10.3. *Obelisk form of grave marker, generally representing an entire family and accompanied, in a family plot, by small, individual grave markers. Typical of late nineteenth and early twentieth century.*

Colonial times, we now find for the first time frequent references to fathers, husbands, and friends, as well as to membership in fraternal organizations—Masons, Woodmen, American Legion, etc.—and such references are almost entirely associated with adult males (compare traits B1–B4 in the figures and tables). Flowery epitaphs have given way before a reduction in available flat space on these three-dimensionally conceived monuments. Where they do appear they are religious, eulogistic, or biographical.

Figure 10.4. *Pulpit-type grave marker of the late nineteenth and early twentieth century, generally marking an important individual ("Mother," "Father") in a family plot where the family obelisk was not employed.*

"Father" receives the biggest monument and is in general the object of major attention, although motherhood is more frequently made explicit. Lambs and doves are reserved for small children, although the latter are also associated with young adult females. Age-sex patterns of design selection emerge clearly during this period. In earlier times there was little or no sexual or rank distinction in the sizes of markers. Although age and economic status probably always had some influence on selection of size, design, or both, acceptable ranges of variability seem by contrast to have been very small, increasing markedly during this period. Spatially there is no particular diad favored in the family groupings, although "Father" and "Mother" generally have larger individual markers.

The period today seems particularly one of sculptural superfluity and soppy sentimentality, but it also expresses, at least in the cemetery, aggressive experimentation, economic competitiveness and strong familial orientation. Old concepts of death have been abandoned in favor of "Gone Home," "Called to Jesus," "Resting," and "Waiting on the Other Side."

The "Reform" Period

Sometime in Florida's 1920s the ostentation of marble sculpture became distasteful, and in the 1930s it is clearly no longer fashionable for individuals to display wealth quite so lavishly in the cemetery. It is an intriguing coincidence that the wealthy were expressing themselves less flamboyantly in other areas of material culture as well. During the 1920s through the 1930s there is rapid change in almost every aspect of the community cemetery. If one cannot quite see socialism creeping across the cemetery, the effect and speed with which changes do occur is nonetheless startling. I am tempted also to think of the latter part of this period, the 1930s to 1950s, as suggesting "incorporation," as there is a clear retreat from expressions of individuality; class distinctions, if not fading, are more subtly expressed. Perhaps too we are seeing the growth of America's "Middle Class" expressed

Figure 10.5. *Granite block with polished, inscribed face—early twentieth century to the present.*

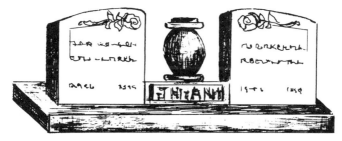

Figure 10.6. *Dual gravestone, usually representing pairs of spouses in middle to late twentieth century.*

here, while lawn cemeteries and mausoleums are emerging in response to the demands of other segments of American society.

Throughout America there is in the same period a growing, flamboyant elite of "entertainers." Hank Williams' 10-gallon hat and all his "hit" records are carved in stone over his grave, and the individuality of the "Industrial Expansion" period is increasingly restricted to this emergent group of "heroes."

The substance of the gravestone is changed very rapidly from marble to granite, and the form becomes a massive block of fairly uniform size (Figure 10.5), with much the same uniformity illustrated by slate and marble before 1870.

Surnames, first separated from given names during the Industrial period, remain so (Figures 10.6 and 10.7) and for the same reason that the stone frequently represents more than one family member. The new, granite stones most frequently represent only spouses. Other relatives are rarely to be seen among these new ranks of couples. The family plot is gone. The children are likewise gone, or banished to some corner of the cemetery often referred to as the "Nursery" or "The Singles." Epitaphs are either gone altogether or are reduced to such terse and standardized phrases as "At

Figure 10.7. *Joint gravestone, usually representing pairs of spouses in middle to late twentieth century.*

Rest." Interestingly, God is now almost as rare in the cemetery as are sons and daughters, and design motifs are most often merely floral borders. Epitaphs, when present at all, are generally such one-liners as, "Not Dead but Sleeping."

The "Lonely Crowd" Period

Finally, in our contemporary period, we find the changes of the 1940s and 1950s are fixed, but complemented by changes in new directions, representing new culture-systemic adjustments. Rank upon rank of couples march in granite rows across the landscape, and the living are represented along with the dead, often in greater numbers. Among the granite stones there is here and there a glimpse of religious concern, but more often we see a couple's stone inscribed with their wedding date and such words as "Memory Lane," the design motif is of a couple strolling hand in hand into a sunset (Figure 10.8), and one or both of those whose names are inscribed is still alive. Today, as a rule, only the years of birth and death are given, and specific dates are ignored. On the other hand, never before has the wedding date been part of the gravestone inscription.

In the expanding "Memorial Lawns" we see a complementary increase in a variety of designs: membership emblems (women now are displaying affiliations other than with such as Eastern Star), occupational symbols, and, especially among the younger set, such symbols of their concerns as guitars, firearms, and even a motorcycle. The number of single adults has risen in these cemeteries, especially in proportion with the number of explicitly non-religious symbols employed. (Religious symbols are now distinctly associated with females far more than with males.) Variety of decorative motif is again on the rise, as the granite gravestone cemetery is gradually replaced by that of small, flat, bronze or granite lawn-markers. One can begin even to seek ethnic distinctions among the types and arrangements of plastic flowers that

Figure 10.8. *Granite, shared-gravestone type of the late twentieth century.*

Figure 10.9. *Paired stones of spouses as employed during the late nineteenth to mid twentieth century (a variety of silhouettes).*

sprout from the markers in memorial lawns. The apparent conservatism of modern granite gravestones is more than balanced by emerging expressions of individuality in the lawn cemetery.

Concepts and Applications

I have only touched upon the remarkable array of cultural data available through a careful examination of a community cemetery, and I have emphasized those general, cultural historical interpretations that are least

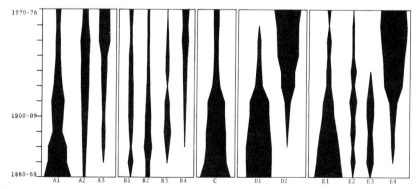

Figure 10.10. *Graphic representation of the means from Tables 10.1-10.14. The dates range from 1860 at the bottom of each "ship-shaped" curve to 1976 at the top. The space within each curve represents the mean proportion of gravestones exhibiting the trait at any given time within that period. The broader the space within the curve, the greater the proportion represented. The base of curve C represents 100% in 1860-1869. All the gravestones of that decade bore epitaphs. The proportions may be compared visually. See the tables for precise figures.*

Traits represented: A1. Burials in clearly identifiable family group. A2. Paired stones for spouses. A3. Shared stones for spouses. B1. Use of term "mother" or "father." B2. Use of term "wife." B3. Filial and other kin terms. B4. Fraternal or military affiliation. C. Epitaph of any length. D1. Marble stone. D2. Granite stone. E1. Tablet form. E2. Pulpit form. E3. Obelisk form. E4. Rectangular block (all variants).

argumentative because they are so easy to illustrate. Although at this stage in the development of material-culture studies we are still learning how to perceive data, we may begin to give very practical attention to the historical and philosophical applications of data such as these from the graveyard. Historical trends in community psychic orientation and group dynamics are evident in the cemetery, as are changes in the apparent role of religious belief in the evolving community. How we choose to examine and record the data depends upon whether we are interested in micro- or in macrosystemic evolution. Whatever one's goal a visit to the cemetery may bring readjustments in one's view of the magnitude and significance of observed ethnic and geographical differences.

On a "macro" scale I have wondered why photographic reproductions of the deceased are so common on the gravestones of one part of the country and of the world, and not of another, and what their connection with particular religious preference has to do with some aspects of world view shared across many, but not all, communities. Why does the southeastern Irish gravestone almost inevitably include the town of the deceased's nativity, while American gravestones hardly ever do, *except for foreigners?* What does this observation have to do with understanding differences in our ways of seeing community? Why is it that the Englishwoman of Worcestershire was already putting "Husband" on her deceased spouse's gravestone fifty years before a few daring American women did it in the last decade? What kinds of ethnographic questions does that pose for us on the nature and identification of sex roles in our two cultures?

The graveyard is a microcosmic material history of the systemic evolution of the living community. On a microevolutionary scale, I might look first in the cemetery for clues to the history and strength of ethnic and religious distinctions, of relationships of economic status with popular surnames, of attitudes towards innovation versus conservatism, of family roles and relationships, and to be reminded of a host of questions I may not yet have thought to ask. Following are a few examples.

"Miscellaneous" Observations

Grave markers have been made often of wood, sometimes in the form of tablets, other times in shapes of crosses. These show geographical, social, socioeconomic, and technological variation, as does the occasional use of hollow-cast metal, cast concrete, and, most interestingly, of pottery "tombstones" and cemetery urns specifically in Eastern Tennessee (Smith and Rogers 1979; also Ann Toplovich and Victor P. Hood, personal communication).

Then there is the category of grave "goods" or "extras." Modern cemeteries often have their most recent graves marked with metal stake-markers whose characteristics vary from place to place and from mortuary to mortuary. There is a time when the American Legion swept the nation's cemeteries with its flag-decked iron standards. There are times and places where plastic flowers replace fresh ones, and others where mason jars breed mosquitos among the brown stalks of last year's geraniums. There are places where children's toys are left upon their graves, and times when an entire section of the graveyard is set aside for children. This year (1980) I saw an Easter basket, complete with "sacrificial" candy, on the grave of a two-year-old who died in 1978.

Seashells seem particularly popular grave decorations in some parts of the world, including our own Southeast and Middle South. They are employed in a remarkable variety of ways reflective, without doubt, of a variety of long-standing traditions. On the Gulf Coast of Florida a fresh burial may be mounded high with sand and paved with even rows of clam-shells and headed by a cedar board of distinctive local pattern. In Georiga bleached conchs may outline a nineteenth-century grave headed by a marble tablet, while a black cemetery anywhere in the "Bible belt" may have periwinkles pressed, alongside marbles and bits of colored pottery, into the colorful face of a homemade concrete cross. All along eastern coastal America one may find seashells placed on or near gravestones dating back even to the first half of the nineteenth century, and the practice is much the same in southern England and southwestern Ireland.

While the variety of observations to be made about material culture in the cemetery is practically limitless, one of my own most important discoveries is that practically all of it is meaningful in terms which reflect the cognitive, systemic evolutionary history of the community itself. Whether a statement is expressed at a single grave (as at the Bronson, Florida, grave that employs a toilet bowl as a "footstone," or the stock car, number "34," complete with crossed, checkered flags on a granite marker in Denbigh, Virginia) or at many (as with the countless Eastern Stars and Masonic emblems on the spouse-shared bronzes of a modern "Memorial Lawn"), there are historical anthropological inferences to be made about the nature of community systemic evolution since Europeans first established themselves here.

Acknowledgments

I am indebted to Kay Dethlefsen for critical comments on an earlier draft of this paper and to Kenneth Jensen for assistance in gathering the data. Janet Valerius King drew Figures 10.1–10.8.

11

Pennies from Denver

Nan A. Rothschild

Archaeological explanation and interpretation usually begin with an analysis of a collection of artifacts in terms of a series of formal attributes. The analysis is used to place the assemblage (and the site from which it derives) in a temporal framework and establish parameters for comparison with other assemblages. This paper will treat a collection of modern artifacts in a similar manner. It has several aims. One is to demonstrate the capabilities and limitations inherent in this traditional mode of analysis. Another is to show how interpretations of a data set change as new categories of information become available. The third, and most relevant for this volume, is to suggest that the anthropological archaeological perspective, normally constrained by the absence of many types of data, may offer unique insights into modern behavior in a complex society.

The specific data set consists of about 1000 U.S. pennies, in four separate samples. The data are interpreted first as physical objects having certain characteristics. This analysis yields certain insights, but leaves many questions unanswered. Additional knowledge of the function of these objects, and their place in an economic system, suggests that they may most productively be analyzed in terms of assumptions about economic behavior. Since there are documentary records available to supplement the physical data, these are examined. Two interpretive models are evaluated for their ability to increase our understanding of cultural behavior and decision-making processes.

MODERN MATERIAL CULTURE
The Archaeology of Us

The Data and Their Collection

The data were collected in New York City, in two households in which an archaeologist resides. For the purposes of this analysis they can be seen as trial samples. The pennies were accumulated by placing excess pennies in places other than pockets and change purses as their numbers increased. There was no conscious selection principle (e.g., certain years being saved, or "shiny" pennies being saved). They were collected in dresser drawers, old socks, and the like over a more than 20-year period. There are four samples, three of them collected in one household. Sample sizes range from 174 to 350 pennies apiece, and the total number in all sets is 1070. The terminal dates of the collections are 1957, 1973, 1974, and 1979. The 1979 collection was accumulated over about a 1-year period, the 1973 and 1974 collections over about 2 years each, and the 1957 collection over 2–3 years. None of the members of either household traveled extensively during the collection period, but during each such period, one or more household members made about two trips to the western part of the United States (California, the Southwest, etc.).

Description and Analysis: Physical Attributes

Examination of the physical attributes of the pennies reveals that they are uniform in size and weight. Their composition is almost uniform; copper accounts for 95% of the coin by weight, and zinc, with occasional small irregular quantities of tin, makes up the remainder. The coins vary in degree and type of wear, but for the most part, the degree of wear is related directly to the age of the coin. Some surface indications suggest that pennies are occasionally used as tools, with asymmetrical scratches seen in the rim implying a twisting motion.

Surface decoration varies in several ways. Date and place of manufacture are indicated on the head side of the coin. Sixteen percent of the pennies have either a small "D" or "S" below the date, denoting manufacture in the Denver or San Francisco Mints. All others are minted in Philadelphia. Other elements of design can be assumed to reflect cultural values (Wobst 1977). It is interesting to note a design change in 1959 (Figure 11.1) in which a domesticated plant (wheat) surrounding the large, centrally placed letters "ONE CENT" is replaced by a centrally placed structure with many pillars, with the letters above and below it.

While we cannot as yet pinpoint the shift in cultural values which this design change represents, it appears that agriculture lost its dominant status in the society and is replaced by a symbol of social unity or the dominance of

a

b

Figure 11.1. *The reverse side of a Lincoln-head penny, (a) before and (b) after 1959.*

a political-religious institution. Not only do the letters "ONE CENT" lose their central position, but they become smaller in size, suggesting a decrease in importance for the concept represented. It seems clear, at least, that the society in 1959 (although the change may have occurred prior to 1959) is one that represents a new value system and a new mode of organization with more centralized institutions, and it may be more hierarchical than the earlier society in form.

Variation in Dates

When we plot the dates of manufacture of the coins by sample (Figure 11.2), the samples are seen to share certain common characteristics. The dates on all four samples span a period of between 32 and 60 years in length, but the distribution curve is very skewed with most of the sample dating from the latter part of the time range. From 58 to 84% of the sample is found in the final 20 years of the samples. The histograms also vary in width; in general the distribution is more tightly clustered in later samples. Without overinterpreting the data at this point, this change in curve width simply implies an increasing proportion of later-dated objects.

In each sample, the largest group within the sample (15-22%) has the penultimate date for the collection. The next most frequently occurring dates are either the final year or the third year from last. Aside from these, there are also certain dates which represent some sort of elevated levels in two or more samples: 1944-1946, 1961, 1964, 1969. Pennies minted in 1975 also represent a very large proportion of the 1979 sample (11.1%). Although we have not yet discussed the manner in which these objects are

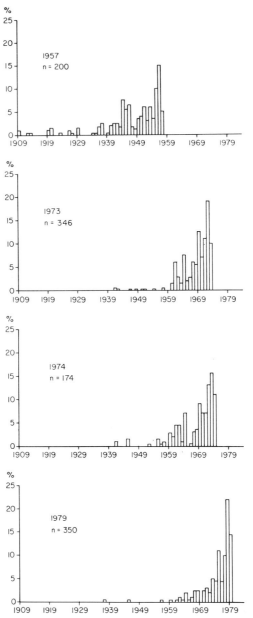

Figure 11.2. *Frequency distribution of four samples, by date of minting.*

circulated, it seems that their maximum circulation is achieved a year after they are dated. An alternative explanation is that the collection process stopped before the end of the ultimate year.

Variation in Mint Location

As for the pennies made in Denver and San Francisco, they are more frequent in some samples than others, with the range from 7 to 27.5%, combining both western mints. The letter "D" appears 18 times as frequently as the letter "S" (all samples combined), and the latter is missing entirely from two of the four samples (Table 11.1; Figure 11.3). The distribution of Denver pennies does not follow the same pattern as the distribution of plain (Philadelphia) pennies, with the former type at its maximum in 1964 and 1969. Equally important to note, there are no Denver or San Francisco pennies from the years 1965 to 1967.

One obvious conclusion is that in penny collections accumulated in New York City, very few pennies come from the San Francisco Mint. As for the Denver pennies, if the assumption is made that the variations in frequency of these pennies are indicative of varying interactions, or trade, one can assert unequivocally that something has interrupted this interaction for a 3-year period. (There are other years which may represent the same interruption of circulation, but there can be no doubt about the interference during this period since it falls between two peak years for Denver penny production.) We can speculate as to the cause of the interruption in the flow of pennies. Does this imply a war between Denver and New York from 1965 to 1967, followed by increased trade between the two communities? It may also be that the periodic peaks in frequency of Denver coins followed by lows or interruptions (1947, 1955, 1958) suggest a self-regulating cycle in which negative feedback is operative. Or perhaps a catastrophic social upheaval took place in Denver between 1965 and 1967. Since we know that there was neither a war between Denver and New York nor an upheaval in Denver, a better explanation is needed.

The problem is part of a larger question concerning the movement of things within a cultural and spatial unit, or trade. Since pennies are small objects, of little, and ever-decreasing value, one may assume that there would be little to interfere with their movement, and that their distribution would be a direct reflector of the movements of people and the exchange of commodities in a typical market system of exchange (Polanyi, Arensberg, and Pearson 1957). It is not surprising in this light to find so few pennies made in San Francisco; as Renfrew notes, the frequency of occurrence of an exchanged item will decrease with the effective distance from the source (1977:7).

Table 11.1
Distribution of Pennies in All Samples by Mint and Year

1957	1973	1974	1979
1909— 2	1941— 2	1941— 2	1919— 1(S)
1912— 1	1942— 1	1945— 3	1937— 1
1913— 1	1946— 1	1952— 1(D)	1945— 1
1919— 2	1948— 1	1955— 3	1956— 1
1920— 3	1950— 1	1956— 1(D)	1959— 2(1D)
1923— 1	1951— 1	1957— 2(1D)	1961— 3(1D)
1926— 2	1954— 1	1959— 5(3D)	1962— 4(1D)
1927— 1	1956— 3	1960— 4(1D)	1963— 3(1D)
1929— 3	1957— 2(D)	1961— 8(3D)	1964—14(6D)
1934— 1	1960— 6(2D)	1962— 8(4D)	1965— 2
1935— 1	1961—21(11D)	1963— 2(D)	1966— 4
1936— 3(1S)	1962— 9(1D)	1964—12(3D)	1967— 9
1937— 5	1963— 6(4D)	1966— 1	1968—10(1D)
1939— 1	1964—26(5D)	1967— 5	1969— 6(4D)
1940— 4	1965— 7	1968— 6	1970—11(1D,1S)
1941— 5	1966—10	1969—16(10D)	1971—10
1942— 5(1D)	1967—21	1970—12(2D)	1972— 9(2D)
1943— 3(1D)	1968—20(3D)	1971—12(2D)	1973—19(1D)
1944—15(1D,2S)	1969—43(18D)	1972—23(2D)	1974—18(1S)
1945—11(1D,1S)	1970—25(3D)	1973—27	1975—41(2D)
1946—13(1D)	1971—38(5D)	1974—20	1976—16
1947— 3	1972—67(2D)		1977—36(1D)
1948— 2(1S)	1973—34		1978—77
1949— 7(2S)			1979—52(1D)
1950— 8(1D,2S)			
1951—12(8D)			
1952— 6(4D)			
1953—12(8D)			
1954— 7(5D)			
1955—20(1D)			
1956—30(12D)			
1957—10(2D)			

From this perspective a classical economic analysis which considers factors of production, distribution, and consumption should prove insightful. In fact, it can be anticipated that analysis of these factors should answer any remaining questions about variations in the composition of the samples.

Production, Distribution, Consumption

There are a number of factors which will influence the quantity of pennies minted in one city and turning up in another. *Production* is a critical element and is affected by the availability of raw materials and labor, and the ex-

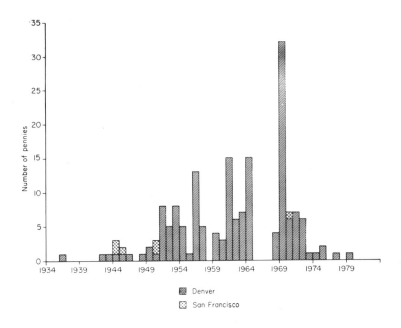

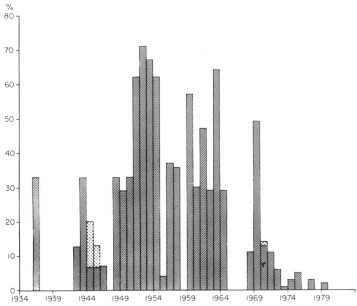

Figure 11.3. *Frequency distribution of Denver and San Francisco pennies, all samples combined.*

isting technology. *Distribution* needs to be examined in detail, so that methods of distribution and the availability of transportation are considered. Both production and distribution are controlled by decisions based on assumed needs (or *demand*) and economic priorities. Finally, *consumption*, or the use of pennies should be investigated. All of these factors will be examined in terms of changes which took place during the period of interest. Obviously in a paper of this scope, these things can only be considered briefly.

Supplementary documentary material was consulted in two steps. It was believed at first that distribution and use patterns for pennies would be unlikely to have changed radically over the period of 20 years, and that, therefore, the answer to remaining questions of interpretation of the sample distribution curves would be found in production figures. A readily available source, namely a coin collector's handbook, was consulted for the yearly production, by mint, of pennies. Examination of these production figures is enlightening. For one thing, it indicates as anticipated that several of the sample characteristics are direct reflectors of population characteristics (Figure 11.4).

Of the distribution noted previously in which several dates showed up in one or more samples as unusually highly represented (and not related to the characteristic quantitative dominance of the last 3 years of a sample), all reflect production peaks. Production data also explain some of the variation in the appearance of pennies from Denver and San Francisco. For example, the hiatus in the presence of Denver pennies in the samples matches a 3-year hiatus (1965-1967) in their production, and in addition, although the San Francisco sample in our collections is too small to analyze, there is a 12-year interruption of production by the San Francisco Mint (1965-1967).

Thus while confirming the reliability of the samples, and suggesting that production practices have changed during the period studied, as anthropologists we are not much closer to understanding certain aspects of the behavior reflected by the distribution of pennies. Specifically, in this case, why did production at two western mints stop for periods of several years in length?

Decision-Making at the Mint

It was decided, therefore, to examine the published records of the Bureau of the Mint for insight into the reasons for changes in production, specifically for major increases or decreases of production. The Director of the Mint issues a report each year which tabulates many types of information for the year, including the number of coins and medals struck during the year. The reports

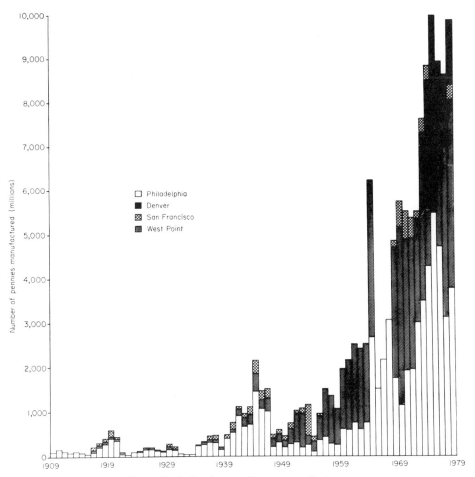

Figure 11.4. *Production of pennies at all mints.*

vary widely as to some of the material presented, but they all contain certain basic data relevant to the production and distribution of coins.

Production is influenced by factors such as the availability of raw materials, the labor supply and technology. These elements were considered first to see if the interruptions in production were correlated with changes in any of these factors. The main ingredient of a penny is copper, mined in a number of western states, chiefly Arizona, Colorado, Utah, and Montana (U.S. Mint 1955, 1956). This might suggest that penny production would be less expensive, and therefore larger, in western mints, as the latter are closer to the major raw material source (Christaller 1966). However, while the minting of money is affected by considerations of cost-effectiveness (see following), there is evidence that other considerations are operative also. The location of raw material sources does not seem to be a dominant factor in production decisions. The labor supply also seems to have no impact on production; it varies as needed (mostly in relation to automation) and is never mentioned as a constraining element in any of the Mint reports.

While no single factor accounts for production changes, a combination of factors resulted in the decision to close the San Francisco Mint in 1956. Being larger, the Denver Mint was able to purchase copper in larger ingots, which are less expensive per unit of measurement. And having a newer plant, modern machinery was more readily installed at Denver, which meant that penny production in the latter Mint was more economical. Of further significance was the fact that the demand for pennies in San Francisco was lower than the supply, so that excesses were shipped elsewhere, making it more cost-effective to manufacture pennies in Denver and ship them, as needed, to San Francisco, than to make them in San Francisco (U.S. Mint 1964:177).

Since production of pennies resumed in San Francisco in 1968, it is clear either that cost effectiveness was no longer the dominant factor, or that something had changed regarding production or distribution costs. The stated position of the Mint is that changes in production are based on "need" (Alan Goldman, Assistant Director, U.S. Mint, personal communication). Need is measured both at local commercial banks and in Federal Reserve banks and branches by the amount of coinage on hand, and by demand. The supply of coins is normally kept, more or less automatically at a level equaling 20% of the total money supply, with 80% of all money being paper money (U.S. House of Representatives 1964:44), and penny production normally accounts for about two-thirds of all coin production (U.S. Mint 1964:130; 1968:3). The supply of money is also regulated in accord with the Quantity Theory of Money, postulated by David Ricardo, which, briefly stated, says that the value of money varies inversely with its quantity (Ritter and Silber 1970).

Measuring the "Need" for Pennies

In order to discuss the perceived "need" for coins, a brief discussion of how coins are distributed, or get into circulation, is necessary. Each of the two major mints (and the minor mints) ships coins to the Federal Reserve banks, of which there are 12, and their branches, of which there are 24 (Figure 11.5); these units of the Federal Reserve System then distribute coins among local commercial banks in their area. Separate figures on shipments of pennies to each Federal Reserve unit are not available for most years, but

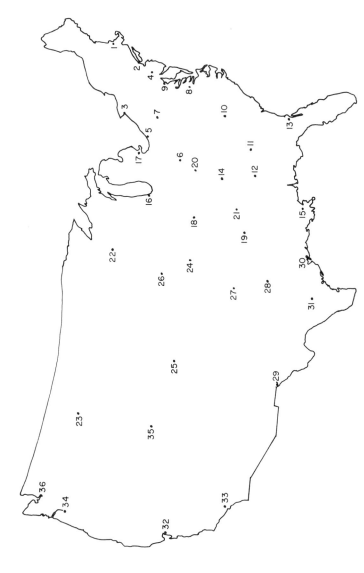

Figure 11.5. Map of Federal Reserve banks and branches. *Key: 1. Boston. 2. New York. 3. Buffalo. 4. Philadelphia. 5. Cleveland. 6. Cincinnati. 7. Pittsburgh. 8. Richmond. 9. Baltimore. 10. Charlotte. 11. Atlanta. 12. Birmingham. 13. Jacksonville. 14. Nashville. 15. New Orleans. 16. Chicago. 17. Detroit. 18. St. Louis. 19. Little Rock. 20. Louisville. 21. Memphis. 22. Minneapolis. 23. Helena. 24. Kansas City. 25. Denver. 26. Oklahoma City. 27. Omaha. 28. Dallas. 29. El Paso. 30. Houston. 31. San Antonio. 32. San Francisco. 33. Los Angeles. 34. Portland. 35. Salt Lake. 36. Seattle.*

during the one 3-year period there is an increase of 48% in the number of pennies shipped to all components of the Federal Reserve system (Table 11.2).

This increase in production, reflecting an increase in need, can be attributed to several factors (although it should be noted that without figures

Table 11.2
Pennies Shipped to Federal Reserve Units (in Millions)

	1963	1964	1965
Boston	163.3	164.1	144.6
New York	275.9	273.1	412.9
Buffalo	52.8	53.1	58.5
Philadelphia	141.4	137.1	199.4
Cleveland	67.4	54.5	109.8
Cincinnati	66.3	71.5	94.1
Pittsburgh	27.1	34.2	78.8
Richmond	69.4	86.6	131.4
Baltimore	51.4	65.7	59.2
Charlotte	35.6	44.2	68.6
Atlanta	46.8	56.3	79.6
Birmingham	27.6	35.6	43.9
Jacksonville	94.3	101.2	155.0
Nashville	28.1	35.3	35.9
New Orleans	60.3	73.4	83.1
Chicago	269.7	274.1	474.2
Detroit	85.8	90.6	149.0
St. Louis	63.6	74.5	99.5
Little Rock	13.1	14.5	24.6
Louisville	26.1	35.2	47.9
Memphis	29.6	34.0	50.6
Minneapolis	68.3	71.6	87.9
Helena	6.3	6.0	16.1
Kansas City	36.1	40.9	60.3
Denver	62.8	49.2	47.3
Oklahoma City	23.9	27.5	30.2
Omaha	19.3	21.3	22.8
Dallas	41.3	44.4	79.8
El Paso	14.5	11.1	22.2
Houston	30.6	33.6	53.3
San Antonio	16.1	21.0	25.7
San Francisco	131.8	138.2	199.7
Los Angeles	223.8	228.3	243.6
Portland	29.2	36.2	38.5
Salt Lake	15.9	15.5	31.9
Seattle	40.2	45.6	50.6

before and after this period, it is difficult to assess the significance of the increase). Population has, of course, increased (from 180.7 million in 1960 to 216.8 million in 1977; U.S. Department of Commerce 1978:xiii), while coins are more frequently used in American society for vending machines selling many things: telephones, coin changers, laundry, parking meters, and the like (U.S. Mint 1964:130). Some of these have, at least in the past, required pennies, although the use of pennies in such machines has decreased as inflation has spiraled upward.

Withdrawal from Circulation

Other factors to be considered are those which cause the withdrawal of coins from circulation, either because they are worn out, or because they are kept out of circulation, intentionally or unintentionally. Banks remove heavily worn coins (called "uncurrent") from circulation; the criteria for "heavy" wear are not made explicit. The available statistics indicate that such withdrawals are very small and there is no reason to assume that the withdrawal rate has ever been of major significance (Table 11.3). The other means by which coins are withdrawn from circulation, either nonpurposefully in dresser drawers, etc., or purposefully by coin collectors and hoarders, clearly have an important effect on the flow of coins. The 1974 Mint Report notes that 62 billion pennies had been produced between 1959 and 1974. Since the life of a coin, on the average, is 25–30 years (U.S. Mint 1965:69), these should still have been in circulation in 1974, and yet at that time, less than half that number was estimated to be available (U.S. Mint 1974:9). There are no comparable figures on the proportion of pennies minted but not in circulation in earlier periods, but the possibility that this lack of circulation may be related to the decreasing value of a cent should be considered (Figure 11.6).

Hoarders are here defined as people who keep coins for the value of their component metals. Between 1962 and 1974 (especially between 1972–1974), the price of copper rose 250% and the price of zinc doubled (U.S. Mint 1974:120). The cost of producing pennies rose to more than a cent apiece. The rising cost of copper exacerbated an existing shortage of pennies and led to extraordinary measures on the part of the Mint to improve the situation, exhorting the public to search their usual hiding places for pennies, which in fact produced most of the data for this paper.

In addition to hoarders, influenced by the price of copper, and normal withdrawal from circulation in dresser drawers, pickle jars, and the like, there has also been an apparent increase in the practice of coin collecting and investment. (The latter involves saving uncirculated or specially struck "proof"

Table 11.3
Pennies withdrawn by Federal Reserve Unit (in Thousands)

	1964	1965	1967
Boston	350	65	135
New York	145	80	65
Buffalo	250	50	85
Philadelphia	170	130	155
Cleveland	140	65	80
Cincinnati	65	—	20
Pittsburgh	190	—	—
Richmond	—	83	201
Baltimore	53	49	68
Charlotte	77	47	165
Atlanta	290	87.5	—
Birmingham	140	68.5	—
Jacksonville	—	480	—
Nashville	679	—	—
New Orleans	19	112	187
Chicago	470	390	625
Detroit	95	60	118
St. Louis	105	75	809
Little Rock	25	—	—
Louisville	55	—	—
Memphis	25	—	—
Minneapolis	170	145	102.5
Helena	30	—	22.5
Kansas City	145	50	165
Denver	110	40	75
Oklahoma City	30	40	55
Omaha	15	21	56.5
Dallas	80	65	249
El Paso	5	15	8
Houston	30	15	105
San Antonio	—	55	10
San Francisco	185	115	400
Los Angeles	415	300	530
Portland	90	—	90
Salt Lake	—	50	50
Seattle	65	55	160

coins for profit, while the former focuses more on rare and unusual coins.) The increase in this behavior was noted in the mid 1960s, and relates to coins in general, rather than pennies specifically (Robinson and Young 1965:17). Coin dealers were described as using false names to circumvent the restrictions on distribution, and were sending for multiple sets of mint

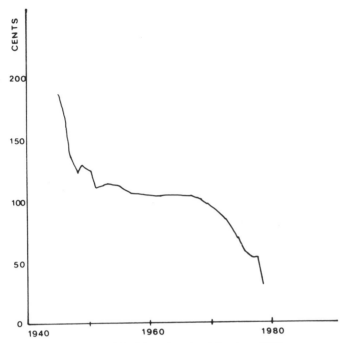

Figure 11.6. *The value of a dollar, base 1960.*

issues, while people coming to banks were asking for rolls of new coins, rather than single coins (U.S. Mint 1964:138). The number of proof sets made (and sold) per year offers a rough quantitative measure of interest in coin collecting, increasing from 180,300 sets in 1954 to 4.1 million sets in 1976 (U.S. Mint 1954, 1976). Some of this interest in coin collecting would not be likely to affect the flow of coins, as it focuses on currency which was never meant to circulate. However, the interest in this type of coin may reflect interest in other types of collections.

In terms of the problem being considered here, namely the impact of this behavior on the Mint's perception of "need" for increased penny production, the relevant fact is that collecting and investing have increased at almost 100 times the rate of population increase (U.S. Department of Commerce 1978), and a 20% population increase between 1960 and 1977 was outmatched by a 500% increase in penny production. This suggests that collecting has taken on the characteristics of a "fad," based at least in part on irrational or emotional elements. The relevance of this insight for archaeologists is that these elements are not usually accessible to us. One could model all the other factors noted above having an impact on production, distribution, and consumption, but there is no way to predict the popularity of (and there-fore the impact of) collecting.

However, it is this unpredictable element which is responsible in some measure for the two decisions of the Mint remaining to be explained. One is the resumption of penny minting in San Francisco in 1968 and the other is the apparent closing of the Denver Mint between 1965-1967. The former was necessary because the capacity of the two other mints, even with shifts working around the clock, was insufficient for the demand (U.S. Mint 1974:9) and coin reserves by 1968 had become very low. This situation con-tinued, aggravated by the rising price of copper, so that in some years the mints had to suspend production of other coins to keep up with the demand for pennies (U.S. Mint 1974:59).

Some form of collecting (including hoarding) can be seen to have in-fluenced the reopening of the San Francisco Mint, but the apparent closing of the Denver Mint can be explicitly linked to "collector behavior." In fact the mint was not closed, but was observing a 5-year legal prohibition on the use of mint marks on any coins, put into effect when the new "clad" coins (dimes, quarters, and half dollars) were first manufactured in 1965 for fear that the public would collect the new coins rather than circulate them. The prohibition was suspended in 1967 when it was clear that the coins had been accepted. The $2.00 bill, the Eisenhower dollar coin, and most recently the Susan B. Anthony dollar coin have all failed as currency because they were collected rather than circulated, and something similar is said to have hap-pened in certain areas with the 50-cent piece. (U.S. Mint 1976:6). Public opinion reported recently indicates that the Anthony dollar's failure is due to its variance with stereotypic concept of the size, weight and value of the dollar (New York Times, 10 October 1979). C. Kramer suggests that this is a reflection of the Mint designers' failure as typologists (personal communica-tion).

The expected behavior of collectors caused another perplexing decision by the Mint to date coins made in 1965 as "1964," and those made in the first half of 1966 as "1965." This decision is indirectly visible because the 1964 output is 2.5 times as great as 1963 production, and 4 times as great as the 1965 output, and appears quite out of place in the context of the whole, rather evenly increasing, yearly total penny output. The decision to falsify dates of manufacture was presumably related to the issue of new coins. The planned increased output of 1965 would have made the relatively rare 1964 pennies desirable to collectors, aggravating the shortage rather than alleviating it. Creating an excess of 1964 pennies would not notably increase the desirability of any other coins.

It is clear that in considering the flow of coins through this economic system, the most difficult factor to model accurately is consumption, because one aspect of consumption relates to a use of the product which is unexpected. The behavior of coin collectors (defined broadly as previously) is responsible in part for the increasing shortage of pennies, for the apparent hiatus in penny output from Denver, for the reopening of the San Francisco Mint, and for falsely dating output at all mints for 1.5 years. The penny samples reflect the parent population quite well as far as other elements of production and distribution are concerned. This long digression and exploration of decision-making processes at the Mint finally yields explanations for all residual variation in the samples' composition.

Since money is minted for use, and is supposed to generate use, reflecting faith in the system, coin collectors are in one sense working in opposition to these goals and assumptions. They are reflecting faith in the monetary system but are operating in a different time framework than is expected. They (some proportion of them) are counting on the inflationary spiral to continue, and make the collected objects more valuable in the future than they are in the present. On the other hand, some collectors (the inadvertent ones) are operating as if the pennies had no value by storing them. Neither of these modes of operation fits behavior expected by those responsible for the circulation of currency. In rejecting, finally, the notion of a war between New York and Denver by explaining the apparent break in production by the latter Mint, it seems that some of the key elements of the explanation are found in unpredictable behavior patterns.

Interpretive Models

A number of models could be used to better understand some of the behavior described previously. Two are investigated here. Both are employed by anthropologists; one assumes basically rational bases for actions, the other does not. The first is the body of theory developed by geographers with reference to the location of various elements in market systems of complex societies. The method of coin manufacture and distribution fits some aspects of both Central Place Theory (Christaller 1966; Loesch 1954) and Wholesale Theory (Kelley 1976; Smith 1976; Vance 1970). The latter type of theory assesses the location of raw materials, energy sources, labor and markets, and transport costs in modeling market locations. While much of Wholesale Theory describes dendritic systems found predominantly in rural areas or underdeveloped countries, Vance feels that the development of much of the western United States was affected by wholesale considerations in which the supplier of goods dominates trade (Smith 1976:34-35). Central Place Theory may be more relevant for the locations of Federal Reserve System units in the eastern portion of the United States, presumably selected on the basis of existing population centers which would have developed in accord with central place assumptions. While the coin distribution system fits neither Wholesale nor Retail systems perfectly, it does have two of five characteristics postulated by Kelley for dendritic systems (1976:221), namely, more low-level centers than predicted by the central place model, and the orientation of each lower-level center to only one center in the next level.

Whichever is the relevant system, it was hoped that locational analytic theory might provide insight into some aspects of the system of coin distribution. It is clear that the system consists of a three-level hierarchy of central places, including the mints, the Federal Reserve system (its banks and branches are equivalent in level) and the local commercial banks. Pennies and coins in general are sent from the mints down through the system and into general circulation (Figure 11.7); they are also withdrawn from circulation in the same way, reversing the procedure. The volume of movement in the system can be seen in the fact that the normal return flow of coins was 9 times the number of new coins minted (U.S. Mint 1964:3).

An example of the explanatory power of this body of theory is seen in a discussion of changes in coin circulation. The 1965 Mint Report notes that the usual practice was for any local coin excesses (above need) to be returned to the nearest Federal Reserve unit for redistribution. In 1965 it was reported that some commercial banks were redistributing coin excesses among themselves (using the medium of a common armored car company

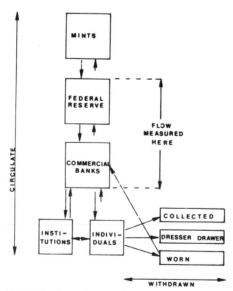

Figure 11.7. *The flow of coins, from production to consumption.*

as the vehicle of exchange), thus creating an apparent disappearance, or reduced return flow, of coins (U.S. Mint 1965:69-70).

This practice can best be understood as a change in the hierarchical system, by means of which the commercial banks were moving up to a more "central" place (in functional terms) than previously. It can be assumed that the manifest goal of this move was to increase speed, and therefore efficiency, of redistribution. This is behavior which is expected of a rational system and also suggests closer analogy to retail marketing than wholesale. However, at another level, the coin distribution system does not, and cannot be expected to, behave in a rational manner, simply because the production and distribution of coins is, first of all, a government monopoly, and second and more important, *the system is not directed by a profit motive*. Wholesaling networks have some of the same characteristics as redistributive systems found in complex societies such as chiefdoms. Steponaitis has described the imperfect fit of central place principles in one such society (1978). Another equally important source of lack-of-fit is when conditions other than those assumed to be dominant (competitive, market-based, rational economic behavior) may apply.

Money as Ritual

A second model to lend insight into the interpretation of these data is one based on Douglas' notion that money is analogous to ritual (1966):

> Money provides a fixed, external, recognisable sign for what would be confused, contradictable operations; ritual makes visible external signs of internal states. Money mediates transactions; ritual mediates experience, including social experience. Money provides a standard for measuring worth; ritual standardises situations, and so helps evaluate them. Money makes a link between the present and the future, so does ritual. . . . Money is only an extreme and specialised type of ritual [p. 69].

It would appear that the behavior identified above as irrational and inexplicable from an "economic" point of view can be readily seen as conforming to the "money as ritual" concept. In order for currency to work, that is, for it to circulate and intensify economic exchange (Douglas 1966:69), its users must believe in it. A lack of trust in a currency is often a sign of failure of belief in a social system, as in the efficacy of ritual. Collectors are acknowledging the aspect of money that is like ritual rather than the purely rational, more "economic" aspect. By collecting it, they may be doing several things: expressing doubt in the system of which it is a part, expressing reverence for it (and the system), or acting in a very rational manner and predicting that its component elements will be more valuable in the future than in the present.

A final possibility is simply that the value of the penny is so small that in many cases it is simply being ignored, and is not circulated because the labor needed to exchange it for larger currency is not thought to be worth its potential value.

Summary and Conclusion

It is this set of multiple explanations for a single set of facts that makes the interpretation of this data set so challenging. This research began with a corpus of objects and the aim of explaining variations in a number of attributes and in the composition of the samples. Initially, some changes in design, perhaps reflective of symbolic meaning were noticed. Some patterning in relation to the age of the objects was also noted, as were some locational differences in the source of the objects.

At this point, the mode of analysis shifted to an examination of the implied trade patterns and flow of pennies throughout the United States. The expectations of this analysis were that (a) the sample characteristics should, for the most part, reflect the production characteristics of pennies as a whole, and (b) any residual variation in the distribution of pennies in the samples should be explicable by reference to other economic factors. The first of these expectations was fulfilled, but the second was more problematical. A detailed analysis of all components of production, distribution, and consumption, seen in the internal records of the Mint, showed that neither production costs nor distribution problems account for changes in production by the Mint. Rather, a nonrational and often noneconomic element, the popularity of coin collecting, has had a major impact on such changes.

Analysis of the formal attributes of the penny samples yields a fairly reliable reflection of the output of pennies on a national scale. However, any unusual aspects of these sample distributions (such as the absence of pennies from Denver) are not explicable simply from the physical data. They also are not explicable when viewed as elements in a rationally determined set of relationships making up a regional economic system. The application of Marketing Theory sheds light on the part of the system related to distribution, but some portion of the behavior of which these penny samples are the ultimate result can only be understood with reference to the concept of money as ritual. This situation may very likely obtain whenever currency is being evaluated. It may also help to interpret the distribution of any material objects used in ritual context, or as media facilitating exchange, or in any other situation in which objects may have a symbolic value not necessarily connected to a pragmatic value.

Pennies themselves are probably well along the road to extinction. It was recommended in the 1976 Mint Report that their production be stopped, as their utility had declined greatly. However, some of the insights of the present analysis may be useful in understanding the "inexplicable" portions of some other data analyses. Further, this examination of modern artifacts demonstrates both the strengths and the weaknesses of a basic archaeological approach to a set of data, as well as offering some interpretations of the behavior and decision-making process of those responsible for the manufacture of currency in the United States.

Acknowledgments

I would like to thank Carol Kramer and Ed Rothschild for many pennies, and Robert Bettinger, Anne-Marie Cantwell, Gregory Johnson, Carol Kramer, Ed Rothschild, Bert Salwen, and Howard Winters for comments on various forms of this chapter. Thanks also to Jon Morter for Figures 11.2, 11.3, and 11.4.

12

The Raw and the Cooked:
The Material Culture
of a Modern Supermarket

Joyce E. Bath

Introduction

Where ". . . chaos—a tumult of events which lack not just interpretations but interpretability—threatens to break in upon man at the limits of his analytic capacities [Geertz 1972:172]." Intense or sustained bafflement, according to Geertz (1972), radically challenges the proposition that life is comprehensible.

Geertz was discussing religion; I am going to talk about a supermarket. While this may seem an abrupt descent from the sublime to the ridiculous, the principle involved in both instances is the need to perceive order in one's environment. This need must be fulfilled to enable man to function effectively and to keep chaos at bay.

Indeed, it requires an act of faith to walk for the first time into a strange supermarket with the confident expectation of locating the desired items on one's list out of an inventory which must number in the thousands. But we all do this many times in our lives, and expect success. Our expectations are, clearly, rooted in the unconscious assumption that there are underlying organizational principles guiding the distributions of items. All one needs to do is crack the code.

The initial impetus for this ethnoarchaeological project was personal aggravation, as a stranger in a strange land, over the length of time necessary

MODERN MATERIAL CULTURE
The Archaeology of Us

to crack the code. The supermarket responsible for the aggravation and therefore the subject of this study, is a branch store of a supermarket chain.

The overview of the store led to the title of this paper and suggested the analytical methodology. There is a clear, obvious spatial separation between the raw foods and the cooked foods (Figure 12.1). In the course of analysis and in the body of the paper, the "cooked" category (with apologies to Levi-Strauss) became "processed."

In the introduction of *The Raw and the Cooked,* Levi-Strauss' opening comment is:

> The aim of this book is to show how empirical categories—such as the raw and the cooked, the fresh and the decayed, the moistened and the burned, etc., which can only be accurately defined by ethnographic observation and, in each instance, by adopting the standpoint of a particular culture—can nonetheless be used as conceptual tools with which to elaborate abstract ideas and combine them in the form of propositions [Levi-Strauss 1964:1].

Methodology

Levi-Strauss' oppositional approach is employed here to arrive at general propositions—or principles of order—both overt and covert, operating in the supermarket world. This method is linguistic, analyzing the grammar of the market's empirical shelf arrangements to achieve an understanding of the deep structure—the underlying organizational principles. Tree diagrams provide the analytical tool and illustrate the oppositional relationships.

The exclusive strategy of tree diagram analysis yields a hierarchical structure of categories, from the general to the particular. The overview of the market (Figure 12.1) provides the two most general oppositions:

1. food versus nonfood items, and
2. raw food versus processed food.

The analysis of individual shelves (Figures 12.2 through 12.8) provides the lower level oppositions:

3. solids (edibles) versus liquids (drinkables);
4. immediate consumption versus delayed consumption (or foods requiring no preparation versus those requiring some sort of manipulation such as heating, thawing, or combining);
5. element versus compound (actually a four-component opposition based on origins of foods, that is, vegetable, animal, and fruit elements versus compounds of two combined elements or chemi-

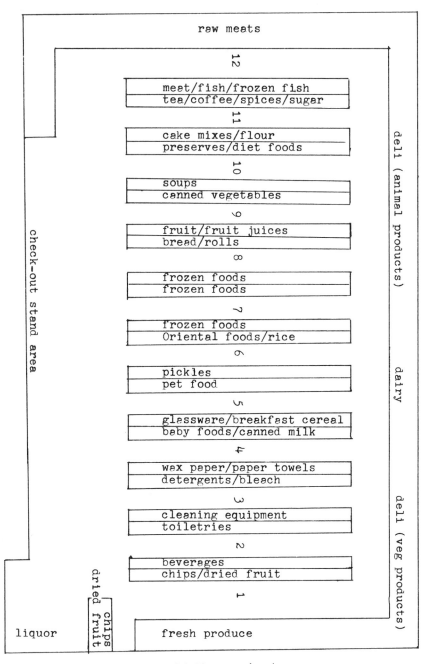

Figure 12.1 *Plan view of market.*

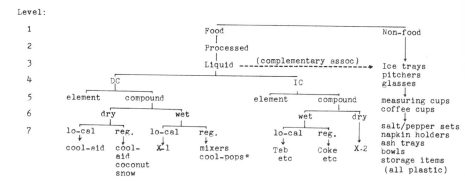

Figure 12.2 *Aisle 2: Beverages.*

cally derived products, such as soft drinks. Elements may also be opposed to each other);

6. wet versus dry (processing method as indicated by type of
   container);
7. low-calorie variants versus regular products.

Finally, the anomalies that are apparent after the regularities are accounted for within the diagrams provide three associative principles: *(a)*
ethnic (where a complete hierarchy is appended onto a staple food); *(b)*
coat-tail (where a category too small to rate a major display is appended onto

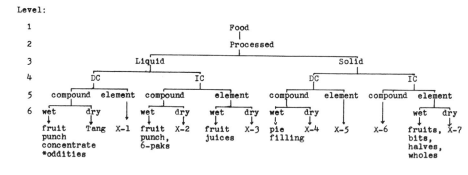

Figure 12.3 *Aisle 9: Canned fruit.*

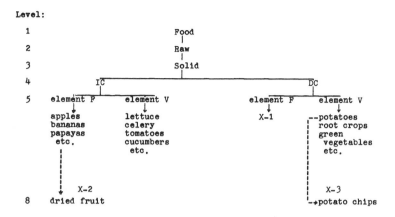

Figure 12.4 *Aisle 1: Dried fruits, potato chips.*

a large grouping of the same general nature); *(c)* complementary (where a small grouping is attached to a major grouping, different in kind but suggestive of an association).

Data Analysis

In order to keep the project to a manageable size, the nonfood category is arbitrarily excluded from analysis, with the exception of nonfood items occurring in complementary association with food categories. Also arbitrarily, a sample of shelves within the food category is selected for analysis.

Each tree diagram (Figures 12.2 through 12.8) represents a single display shelf unit and is identified with the supermarket's own category label and numerical classification. The hierarchical level at which analysis of an individual shelf starts depends on the shelf content. Consequently, the levels at which the diagrams differentiate are variable. For example, in Figure 12.2, the breakdown within the food category starts at Level 4, as the beverages can be separated into two exclusive categories: those which are ready to drink and those which require mixing or dilution. In contrast, the items on the Aisle 9 shelf (Figure 12.3) differentiate at Level 3, as both liquids and solids are found on the same shelf.

Below the level of differentiation, categories that drop out on the diagrams are marked by an x and numbered, that is, x-1, x-2, x-3, etc. These designations are keyed to the texts accompanying the figures, and discussed in order of occurrence. Associative categories are also labeled with an

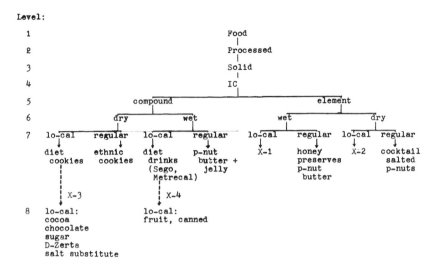

Figure 12.5 *Aisle 10: Preserves, diet food.*

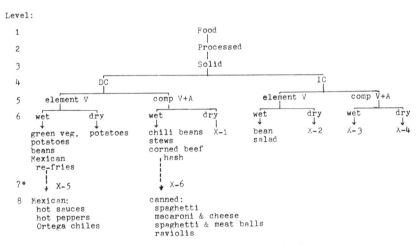

* No low-calorie variants of these foods are on the shelf

Figure 12.6 *Aisle 9: Canned vegetables.*

188

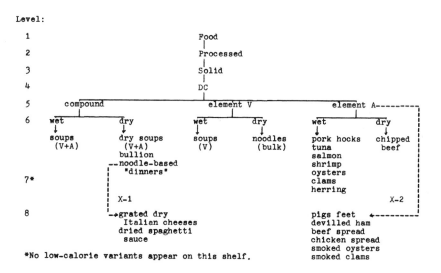

Figure 12.7 *Aisle 10: Soups.*

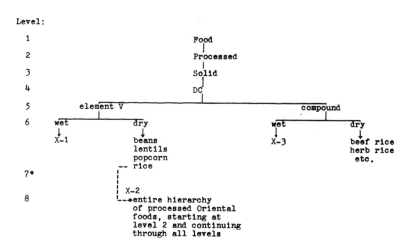

Figure 12.8 *Aisle 6: Oriental food, rice.*

x digit to key into the text. Specific food items discussed appear on the diagrams below level 7, where applicable. Abbreviations used are:

IC	=	immediate consumption,
DC	=	delayed consumption,
ELEM V	=	vegetable origin,
ELEM A	=	animal origin,
ELEM F	=	fruit origin,
ELEM	=	element, origin not specified,
COMP	=	compound,
LO-CAL	=	low calorie variant,
REG	=	not low calorie.

The items on the aisle shown in Figure 12.2 are all "drinkables." The immediate consumption category consists of both bottled and canned soft drinks. The delayed consumption category consists of both wet items (such as quinine water or Tom Collins mix) and dry powdered items. These include punch bases (Kool-Aid) and powdered mixers to be used with alcohol (coconut snow, or mai-tai mix).

The nonappearance (x-1, x-2) of drinks of fruit, vegetable, or animal origin predicts that either such products do not exist, or are a large enough category in themselves to require separate shelving. The absence of low-calorie alcohol mixers (x-3), given the presence of low-calorie soft drinks, allows for the prediction that such products do not exist.

The category indicated by x-4 is a logical inconsistency produced by the system used here. By definition, a dried form of soft drink would belong on the other side of the opposition, under delayed consumption. Alternatively, if left under the immediate consumption side, a dried form of soft drink would qualify as an edible rather than a drinkable. In defense of this category, I offer the case of teenage competitors at swim meets eating Kool-Aid and Jello straight from the package between event calls. And, in fact, there is a product called Pixie Stix, a flavored loose powder packaged in straws, usually found at the candy counter in a dime store or at snack stands at Little League baseball games.

The presence of Kool-pops is logically consistent in that the item can be characterized as a wet concentrated punch base. It is anomalous in that Kool-pops are not destined to be diluted and drunk, but to be frozen and eaten as a sucker.

The chemically derived wet fruit punch bases, which logically should be located here in opposition with dry fruit punch bases, are in fact shelved on Aisle 9 with the fruit juices. This may reflect a perceived purity, or closeness to the category of real fruit origin, notion with regard to wet fruit punch bases. Alternatively, it is possible that real fruit is used in the manufacture of liquid fruit punch concentrate.

The most prominently displayed nonfood items (ice cube trays, plastic pitchers, and plastic glasses) on this shelf complement (x-1) the category of liquid "drinkables." The further appended items, which do not bear any functional relationship to the beverages displayed here, are also all plastic, which suggests a nonfood organizational principle of material type (plastic) accounts for their placement. These items relate, then, to the ice cube trays, pitchers, and glasses, rather than to the beverages.

Although the store label on the aisle shown in Figure 12.3 specifies "canned fruit," both canned fruits and canned and bottled fruit juices are found on this shelf.

The delayed consumption category within the liquids is very small, consisting primarily of the oddities. These logically should be liquid compounds with a fruit component, requiring either dilution or mixing. Grenadine and Rose's lime juice fit these requirements, in that both are not consumed straight from the bottle, but are mixed with or diluted by alcohol. The reconstituted lemon juice can also be accomodated in this category, in that it is a compound of dried extract of lemon, water, and preservatives, and is not drunk straight either.

The absence (x-1 and x-2) of fruit juices in the "dry" categories reflects the same problem encountered and discussed in Figure 12.2. A dried immediate-consumption liquid would classify as an edible.

The lack of dried fruits for either immediate consumption or delayed consumption (x-4, x-5, and x-7) suggests that fruits are neither dried nor combined with other elements. Subsequent exploration, however, would show that these products are shelved elsewhere, that is, dried fruits in the fresh produce section, frozen fruit pies in the ice cream section, etc.

The store label indicating that the aisle shown in Figure 12.4 is devoted to dried fruit and potato chips is misleading indeed. The shelf is actually allocated to fresh produce, which occupies at least 90% of the available space. Potato chips and dried fruits are located on the shelf unit labeled "0" in Figure 12.1, and on the remaining 10% of the fresh produce shelf.

The proximity of the liquor department as an explanation for the placement of potato chips (x-3) was considered but discarded because of the solid nature of the physical barrier between the two departments. Further, this explanation would not have accounted for the association of dried fruit and potato chips which is so blatantly expressed by the store's label and the physical proximity to fresh produce on the shelf. Analysis suggests that what is really operating here is the "coat-tail" principle (x-2, x-3), based on the vegetable and fruit origins of the products.

The immediate-consumption versus delayed-consumption principle would predict that green cooking apples would be separated from red or yellow eating apples (x-1). Although apples are sorted into separate bins by type and color, they are all adjacent to one another and spatially located with fruits, not tubers. This suggests that all kinds of apples are perceived primarily as snack foods and only secondarily as cooking ingredients. It would be interesting to compare this particular spatial distribution with an example for the midwestern United States, where apple pie approaches the status of religion.

The initial difficulty in analyzing the organization of this shelf (Figure 12.5) revolved around the co-occurrence of notoriously fattening foods (peanut butter, jelly, jam, and honey) and diet foods (Metrecal, Sego, Figurines, etc.) After seriously considering the possibility of sadistic tendencies on the part of store personnel, working through the hierarchy of oppositions indicates that this co-occurrence can be explained by the fact that quantitatively, the major items on the shelf are immediate-consumption foods.

The loss of low-calorie components on the right-hand side of the diagram (x-1 and x-2) predicts that these items do not occur in low-calorie form. This prediction is made even more explicit by the fact that a complete hierarchy of diet foods occupies another part of the shelf.

By extension of the idea of "diet," other low-calorie foods (x-3), including salt-free and low-sodium medically prescribed products, are included by the complementary principle. It is postulated that the snack-type diet foods are principally responsible for the association.

In terms of total shelf space, peanut butter is quantitatively predominant. This suggests that a combination of the origin principle and the immediate-consumption principle accounts for the placement of salted cocktail nuts on this shelf. Unsalted nuts for use in baking are elsewhere.

Canned vegetables, dried vegetables, and canned prepared dinners are the products actually found on the shelf shown in Figure 12.6. Quantitatively, beans predominate.

The absence of dried prepared vegetable plus meat dinners suggests that items in this category (x-1) are not produced. This type of product can be found, however, in back-packing supply shops. When and if these products find their way onto supermarket shelves, a space is ready and waiting.

The absence of items in these three categories (x-2, x-3, and x-4) can be explained only as noncategories. The prediction would be that vegetables are not dried and eaten in the same manner as fruit, while the notion of immediate consumption of chili beans or stew out-of-the-can, unheated, does not titillate the salivary glands.

The ethnic association principle can be seen operating in the case of the Mexican refried beans (x-5), where those things associated with the ethnic category of Mexican food are dependent on the presence of the refried beans.

The pasta items (x-6) are not logically out of place, in that they are vegetable plus animal-based products. However, they would be more logically placed on Aisle 10 where noodle-based products predominate, than here where bean-based products predominate. The similarity of processing type and resultant container type probably accounts for this appearance here, under the coat-tail association principle.

The quantitative predominance of canned beans on this shelf points up the absence of dried beans, leading to a prediction that dried beans are not produced, or constitute a large enough category to be shelved separately elsewhere.

The direct association of grated dry Italian cheeses with noodle-based prepared dinners on the aisle shown in Figure 12.7 (only some of which are Italian derived) suggests the ethnic principle is in operation. A recheck proved that a token number of dried spaghetti sauce packets are also displayed here. Bottled wet-process spaghetti sauces, however, are found on the "pickle" shelf with other tomato-based products. This supports the precedence of the wet-dry opposition and the element-compound opposition over the associative principles.

The delayed consumption violation (x-2) represented by the appearance of canned and bottled snack meats can be explained by the coat-tail association principle, which suggests that snack meats represent a small category.

Low-calorie variants of items on this shelf do not appear at all, predicting that they are not produced. Two other predictions that could be made are soups are eaten, not drunk, and dried meats (represented by a single item) are not a large part of this society's regular diet.

Powdered bouillon is found with the dry soup mixes, while bouillon cubes are not. This suggests that the powdered variety is perceived as a soup, and the cubes as ingredients to be used in cooking. In effect, bouillon exhibits a dual character, which implies that the immediate-consumption–delayed-consumption opposition might more accurately be characterized as a triad: *(a)* snack foods (IC), *(b)* heat and eat convenience foods (DC$_1$), and *(c)* cooking ingredients (DC$_2$).

The organizational level at which the break-down starts in the aisle shown in Figure 12.8 confirms the prediction made for Aisle 9 (Figure 12.6): that dried beans would be found elsewhere in the store. In turn, the co-occurrence of dried beans and dried rice here taken in conjunction with the non-co-occurrence of canned rice and canned beans on Aisle 9, allows for the prediction that rice is not cooked and canned in this society.

The attachment of the entire stock of canned, bottled, and dried oriental foods (x-1) is a confirming example of the operation of the ethnic association principle. Rice could be identified as the staple dictating the association both by total quantity (percent of dried rice relative to beans), and by comparison of container size. The largest package of beans is two pounds, while packages of rice range up to 25-pound sacks.

The dropped categories (x-2 and x-3) predict either noncategories or fairly large assemblages elsewhere. And, in fact, canned beans are found in Aisle 9, and wet-processed rice is a noncategory, as noted above.

The interrelationships of these three shelves suggest that within the vegetable element, a "staple" dichotomy exists (Aisle 10 noodles, Aisle 6 rice, and Aisle 9 beans), which accounts for the majority of the distributions on the three shelves.

Discussion

One of the more interesting results of this analysis that has emerged in the discussion of individual shelves, is that the sins of omission—or missing items—are what yield predictive power. This is demonstrated by the fact that in three instances, when analysis predicted an item should be present, a recheck of the shelves proved that the item had been missed in the initial mapping phase. An absence of a logical oppositional category predicts that either the society does not make use of the category (as in a language where not all possible phoneme combinations are utilized), or that the category contains a large enough number of items to require separate shelving. With a large enough sample, the either/or situation can be resolved.

Conversely, the sins of commission—a violation of a higher principle in shelf placement—yield explanatory power. The presence of an item which is not predicted or accounted for by analysis represents an anomaly. The nature of the association between the anomaly and the distributional pattern then suggests explanations. This can be seen in the formulation of the three associative principles (ethnic, coat-tail, and complementary) postulated here.

Anomalies also allow for contingency propositions, when quantitative data are added. For example, the total percentage of shelf space given over to nonfood items is so small that a comparison of relative percentages would immediately suggest to the researcher that the consumer population of this market would be a mobile population—that is, one which would have access to some means of transportation to other locations for the acquisition of nonfood products. A comparison of this market with a country store (see Cleghorn, Chapter 13, this volume) would tend to confirm this hypothesis.

It is possible that a researcher would also be able to predict that the consumer population of this market is composed of two dominant ethnic groups,

Caucasian and Oriental. The proportions predicted would tend to be skewed in favor of the Caucasian population due to the marketing policies of the supermarket chain. The Mexican ethnic food category is too small quantitatively to predict a resident ethnic population, but its embedded position on the shelf is too obvious to be missed.

Prior to writing the discussion and conclusions, the tree diagrams and list of derived principles were submitted to a marketing analyst for comment. Discussion of the resulting comments follows.

The raw-processed principle postulated here reflects the marketing strategy known as the "important purchase." Marketing research has shown that raw meats are the consumer's first and most expensive selection, followed by dairy items and fresh produce. Supermarkets are spatially arranged so that by the time the shopper has been to these three areas, the farthest reaches of the store have been visited (Faison, personal communication).

The distinction made between immediate consumption and delayed consumption in this analysis is also a marketing principle, and is, as suspected, a triad. There are three marketing categories called "table ready" (snack foods), "oven ready" (heat and eat convenience foods), and "kitchen ready" (staples such as flour, sugar, and rice) (Faison, personal communication).

Processing method (wet-dry) also serves as an organizational marketing principle, and it was pointed out by Faison that the divisions are finer than postulated. For instance, within the dry category there are freeze-dried, sundried, and dehydrated items, and the method affects shelf organization.

Although the postulated principle based on food origins drew no comment, the analysis made here suggests that this principle most profoundly affects distributions. The absence of response, while perhaps not significant, is strongly suggestive that a covert principle is in operation.

In the introduction, reference was made to cracking the code. This is the process by which individuals, consciously or unconsciously, sift clues in the environment. The object is to arrive at an understanding of the principles of order involved and gain thereby some predictive power. Without this, chaos prevails.

Further, it has been shown that we impose order on the cultural environment by the formulation and utilization of principles of categorization. The spatial distributions of material culture items, or artifacts, constitute the clues to understanding. Thus it is possible not only to play the game, whatever it might be, but to reconstruct the principles governing the formulation of it.

13

The Community Store: A Dispersal Center for Material Goods in Rural America

Paul L. Cleghorn

Introduction

Ethnoarchaeological research on the nature of material goods found in the community store of the relatively isolated, rural community of Maunaloa on the island of Molokai, Hawaii was conducted during the Spring of 1977. Following arguments put forward by Adams (1973), the study began with the assumption that the community store, as the dispersal center of material goods, would carry only items that its customers would buy. The primary goals were to determine the wants of the community, the purchasing power of the people in the community, and the economic networks that connect this small community with the rest of the economic world, through an analysis of the material goods present in the community store. Besides these rather specific goals, the study generally aimed at discovering general propositions relating material items found in the store with the behavior of community members.

The present research is not the first anthropological research to be carried out in Maunaloa. In 1959, Edward Norbeck published his ethnography, *Pineapple Town: Hawaii,* which is primarily a description of the plantation community of Maunaloa. The main concerns of his work were to characterize the community, describe the social relationships within the community, and to explore the influence of pineapple husbandry techniques and the demands of industrial employment on the lives of the people residing in the

MODERN MATERIAL CULTURE
The Archaeology of Us

community (1959:vii). These aims are clearly different from those of the present study.

Maunaloa is currently experiencing a period of change. The days of the pineapple plantation, to which the community owes its existence, have been over since September 1976. The pineapple plantation was almost the sole employer for the people of the community (Norbeck 1959:41). When it phased out its operations, the people had to adjust and look elsewhere for work. Given these conditions, Maunaloa may be described as being in an economically depressed state, and as such provides an excellent opportunity for studying a store in operation during a period of stress.

Maunaloa is an isolated community located at the west end of Highway 46, 27.4 km (17 miles) from Kaunakakai; the only urban center of any kind on the island. Maunaloa may be viewed as a system (Figure 13.1), in which the majority of material goods enter the community and are housed at the store. These items are then sold and dispersed throughout the community, where they are utilized in people's homes. When the goods have fulfilled their functions, they are discarded either into refuse containers within the community or transported directly to the community dump. The refuse in the containers is collected periodically and also transported to the dump.

Approximately 800 people presently live in Maunaloa; the population is composed primarily of Filipinos, though there are also people of Japanese, Chinese, and Caucasian racial extractions. There are eight enterprises in

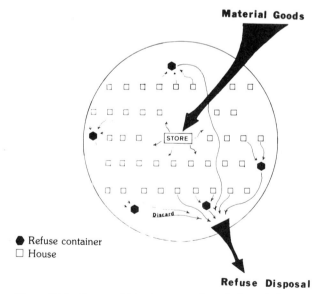

Figure 13.1. *Flow model tracing material goods through the community system.*

Maunaloa that provide employment for some of its residents: Molokai Ranch, which owns the town; a Chevron service station; a post office; a Molokai Community Federal Credit Union; a pool hall; a laundromat; the Taro Patch store, which sells craft jewelry and some clothes; and the Friendly Market, the locale for this study. Besides the limited number employed within Maunaloa, approximately another 200 people commute to other areas to work, and some 70 men are retired and living on social security benefits and company pensions. There are an undetermined number of people on unemployment compensation.

Methodology

In order to achieve the objectives of this study, the merchandise of the Friendly Market was inventoried; information on number, price, and origin of items was recorded. Yardage and clothing merchandise was not inventoried because of time restrictions and the great amount of material in this category. The store's structural features and spatial distribution of goods were also mapped, and an inventory of nonsalable, store support items was made. Ethnographic interview was rarely used, and then was limited to questions pertaining to the functions of different areas and structures of the store, and to the census estimates given earlier.

When the data collected from the inventory were examined, it became obvious that some method of categorizing the materials was needed. All of the inventoried merchandise was classified into the following 18 categories: *consumables*—consist of foods, for example, meats, fruits, vegetables, and food stuffs, for example, sauces and spreads, whose ingestion results in the liberation of energy (after Schiffer 1972:157), *maintenance items*—include all implements used in the preparation, serving, consumption, and storage of consumable items (after Binford and Binford 1969:71), both items with a long use-life such as pots and pans, as well as items with a short use-life such as "food wraps" are included; *extractive items*—consist of tools used for opening containers for consumables (after Binford and Binford 1969:71), included in this category are "multi-purpose" tools (Gould 1978b) that open more than one type of container, for example, cans and bottles; *electrical conveniences*—are items requiring electrical input, which function to reduce the effort expended by the user in accomplishing various specific tasks; *decorative items*—consist of items that function primarily to decorate people's homes, such as vases and figurines; *refuse disposal items*—include all items associated with the removal of refuse from the home, and are generally containers of some kind, for example, rubbish cans and trash bags; *socio-relationables*—consist of elements that serve the purpose of making one's self presentable or tolerable to other persons, such as, cosmetics and deodorants; *medicines*—include items that are either taken internally or applied externally and function to aid the health of the user; *child care items*—are nonconsumable items associated with the care of children; *structure conservation items*—include tools and materials used in the construction or repair of buildings and their associated features; *pet care items*—are items associated with the care and keeping of pets, items range from pet foods to "kitty litter"; *eliminators*—consist of tools and materials used for the elimination of pests and odors in the home; *cleaners*—are implements and materials used for washing, scrubbing, and polishing; *indulgences*—consist of tobacco and alcoholic goods; *garden items*—include implements and materials associated with growing plants; *recreation items*—consist of material items that function for amusement or diversion; *time items*—are items that measure the passage of time, excluding those that require electricity to function and materials associated with these items, for example, watch bands; *miscellaneous items*—are items that do not fit into the preceding categories. Some items could have been placed into more than one category, for example, electrical conveniences and time; these items were placed into the one category that best represented their most salient properties.

The Friendly Market

Structural Features (Figure 13.2)

The core of the store consists of the store proper (17.0 by 16.5 m) and the adjoining main storeroom (14.0 by 10.5 m). Off the storeroom is a toilet room. Attached to the west side of the structure is a room housing motors for a large walk-in refrigerator-freezer, and a storeroom filled with empty boxes. An attached fenced-in area contains empty cardboard boxes and other discards. A covered area under which trucks can park adjoins the fenced-in area to the south, with a freight-loading platform located at the entrance to the main storeroom.

Located 3 m south of the main structure, and connected to it by a fence, is a vacant corrugated iron structure (11.5 by 3.5 m). It was explained to me that this structure was used long ago, before electricity was installed in Maunaloa, by Chinese men who cooked on wood-burning stoves. It is not currently in use and remains vacant and locked.

Spatial Distribution of Goods

The first impression one gets of the organization of the public portion of the store is chaotic confusion. The contents leave one feeling staggered; the variety of goods extends from pigs' heads to frozen pizza, and from nuts and bolts to electronic calculators. The store contains food, alcohol, bolts of cloth,

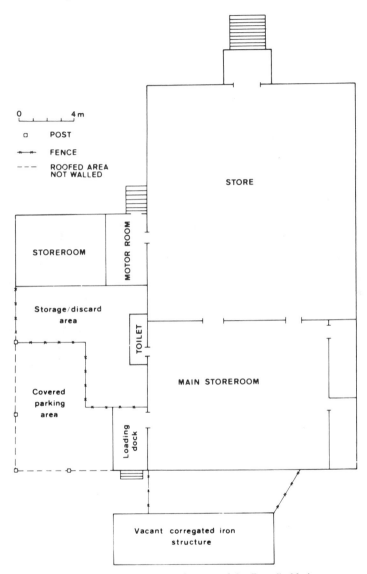

Figure 13.2. *Structural features of the Friendly Market.*

hardware, radios, stereos, and televisions in great quantity. The interior is a maze of shelves, cases, and appliances, with goods stacked almost to the ceiling (Figure 13.3). It is enough to strike fear into the poor wayward archaeologist who has undertaken the task of inventorying this mess!

A closer look, however, reveals that there is organization to this confusion (Figure 13.4). The store can be separated into seven major sections,

Figure 13.3. *Scene from public portion of the Friendly Market.*

listed with their corresponding relative percentages of floor space: yardage and clothing (18.24%); structure conservation (5.11%); alcoholic indulgences (4.47%); consumables, including some maintenance and extractive tools (45.99%); a small storage room (6.26%); the office and check-out area (4.60%); and a general work area (15.33%).

There is a positive correlation between the amount of space allocated for a category of goods and the amount of use that section gets. I observed that the consumable section was frequented more than the yardage and clothing section, which in turn was more popular than the structure conservation section. An apparent anomaly of this correlation is the alcoholic indulgence section, the smallest section in the store, which seemed to be frequented more than either the structure conservation or yardage and clothing sections.

Store Support

In addition to the salable items in the store, a small percentage of items function solely toward operating the store. Specifically, these items function to preserve and display salable items, move goods, clean the store, and facilitate monetary transactions.

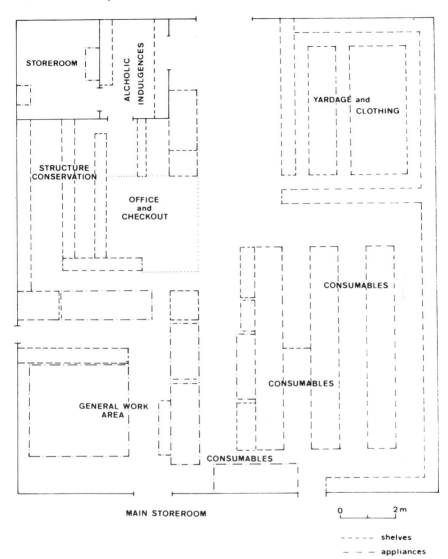

Figure 13.4. *Floor plan of public portion of the Friendly Market.*

Approximately 13% of the support items are related to the butchering of meat; all of these are located in the restricted space labeled "General Work Area" in Figure 13.4. Butchering items include a meat scale, a meat slicer, display refrigerators, a walk-in refrigerator-freezer, a chopping table, a hanging fan, and a butcher paper dispenser. This area has the appearance of task specificity, that is, the butchering of meat. The appearance is misleading; meat is not butchered here. Prebutchered meat is shipped directly to the store and the only type of butchering conducted here is the grinding of hamburger. One of the display refrigerators now contains milk, juice, cheese, etc.; the chopping table is usually stacked high with cardboard boxes; and the walk-in refrigerator-freezer is used for some consumable items as well as for keeping beer cold. The area is now used as a general work area and for wrapping precut meats.

Primary Merchandise: Consumable Items

Table 13.1 summarizes the analysis of food items found in the Friendly Market. The types of food—meat, fruit, etc.—are listed along the vertical axis, and the manner in which the food has been processed—canned, frozen, etc.—is listed along the horizontal axis. The Number column is the number of items per type; the V column is the percentage per vertical category, for example, canned; the H column is the percentage per horizontal type, for example, meat.

The majority of food items are present in canned and dried forms (88.99%), with few goods in fresh and frozen forms. The total percentage of Seasonings combined with the total percentage of Sauces-Spreads equals 19.34%, which is higher than any other type of consumable.

Table 13.1
Consumable (Food) Items

	Canned[a]			Frozen		
	Number	Percentage of vertical category	Percentage of horizontal category	Number	Percentage of vertical category	Percentage of horizontal category
Meat[b]	790	21.11	66.50	235	48.06	19.78
Fruit	240	6.41	85.11			
Vegetable	596	15.92	68.82	42	8.59	4.85
Soup	214	5.71	50.95	47	9.61	11.19
Juice	451	12.05	82.30	50	10.22	9.12
Prepared Meal	277	7.40	75.89	88	18.00	24.11
Cereal-Cracker						
Sauce-Spread	656	17.53	100.00			
Baking	106	2.83	49.30			
Seasoning						
Milk	113	3.02	67.26			
Nuts	84	2.24	100.00			
Starch[c]				27	5.52	21.43
Drink[e]	216	5.77	73.72			
Other						
Total	3743	99.99		489	100.00	

[a] Includes both metal and glass "cans".
[b] Includes meat, fish and poultry.
[c] That is, noodles, taco shells, rice, and potatoes.
[d] Goods present, but number not available.
[e] That is, coffee, tea, and coco.

Fresh vegetables were present in limited quantity and variety; a large number and great variety of vegetable seeds (ca. 100 packages, 21 types) were available in the store. Given these observations, one might predict that the people in the community supplement their diets with garden produce. This prediction was verified through a tour of the community; most homes had vegetable gardens.

Purchasing Power

An estimation of how much money people are willing to spend at the community level may be determined by examining the prices people pay for goods at the store. One might think that consumable items would make a good category for such a study, since food is needed by all members of the community. However, this category is unsatisfactory because of the prevalent use of "food stamps" at the store, which possibly affects the amount of money people are willing to pay for food.

Electrical Conveniences have been chosen to illustrate the maximum amount of money that people are willing to spend on material items at the community level. These items tend to be the most expensive in the store and are apt to be of a luxury nature. There are 46 items in this category (Table 13.2), ranging in price from $7.95 for a heating pad to approximately

	Dried			Fresh			Total		
Number	Percentage of vertical category	Percentage of horizontal category	Number	Percentage of vertical category	Percentage of horizontal category	Number	Percentage of vertical category	Percentage of horizontal category	Total percentage of each type
44	2.32	3.70	119	56.94	10.02	1188		100.00	18.74
42	2.21	14.89	—d			282		100.00	4.45
228	12.02	26.33	—d			866		100.00	13.66
156	8.22	37.14	3	1.44	0.71	420		99.99	6.63
33	1.74	6.02	14	6.70	2.55	548		99.99	8.65
						365		100.00	5.76
244	12.86	100.00				244		100.00	3.85
						656		100.00	10.35
109	5.75	50.70				215		100.00	3.39
570	30.05	100.00				570		100.00	8.99
42	2.21	25.00	13	6.22	7.74	168		100.00	2.65
						84		100.00	1.33
99	5.22	78.57	—d			126		100.00	1.99
77	4.06	26.28				293		100.00	4.62
253	13.34	80.83	60	28.71	19.17	313		100.00	4.94
1897	100.00		209	100.01		6338			100.00

Table 13.2
Cost of Electrical Conveniences

Number	Item	Price (dollars)
3	Blender	32.50
7	Calculator	9.99–12.95
1	Can opener	12.98
1	Clock radio	59.95
2	Color television	ca. 400.00
2	Dry iron	17.95
2	Fry pan	32.99
1	Hair dryer	13.95
1	Heating pad	7.95
1	Hot lather machine	19.95
2	Infant nite lite	11.49
8	Portable radio	14.95–54.95
2	Radio	54.95–84.95
9	Rice cooker	24.95–34.95
1	Standing fan	98.50
1	Toaster	23.50
1	Toast master oven	61.50
1	Waffle iron	38.50

$400.00 for a color television set. Many of these items are tucked away, hidden from clear view, which may indicate that they have been in the store for a long time and that they are not in great demand. But the mere presence of these items is an indication of purchasing power, if not at this time, then at some more prosperous time in the past.

Origin of Goods

To explore the economic networks that connect the community of Maunaloa with the rest of the world, the world was first divided into a series of 1000-km wide geographical zones, with the exception of western Europe which was lumped into one 4000-km wide zone (Zone XII, Figure 13.5). The merchandise, classified by material category, was then tabulated by geographical zone of origin (Tables 13.3 and 13.4). For a similar treatment of economic networks, see Adams (1976:78–97).

Material goods in the Friendly Market originate from 4 Hawaiian Islands, 34 continental states, and 19 foreign countries. Goods range from those locally produced on the island of Molokai (bakery goods and charcoal) to items imported from areas as far away as Yugoslavia, some 20,000 km distant (dog tie-out chains). Of the 12,649 salable items that were inventoried,

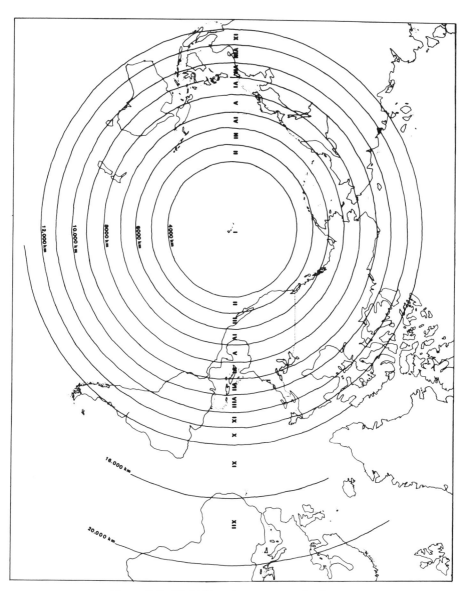

Figure 13.5. *World Map, showing geographical zones.*

Table 13.3
Origin of Domestically Produced Material Goods

Material Categories (18)	U.S. geographical zones								Total	
	I (No.)	II (No.)	III (No.)	IV (No.)	V (No.)	VI (No.)	VII (No.)	VIII (No.)	Number	Percentage
Consumables	794ᵃ	882	197	6	58	1121	1769	124	4951	46.65
Maintenance Items	30	76		12	1	641	552		1312	12.36
Extractive Items		3				1	17		21	0.20
Electrical Conveniences					3		2		5	0.05
Decorative Items		2			3				5	0.05
Refuse Disposal Items						37	7		44	0.41
Socio-relationables	40	10	11	20		234	423	54	792	7.46
Medicines		6			5	11ᵃ	33ᵃ	21	76ᵃ	0.72
Child Care Items	1	1		1		510	198		711	6.70
Structure Conservation Items		33		4		153	568		758	7.14
Pet Care Items		196		4	4		40		244	2.30
Eliminators		4				92	162		258	2.43
Cleaners	34	128		13	11	203	261		650	6.13
Indulgences	—ᵃ	—ᵃ				—ᵃ	—ᵃ		—ᵃ	—
Garden Items	1					190	27		217	2.04
Recreational Items				11			9		21	0.20
Time Items					19	91	49		140	1.32
Miscellaneous Items	75	2		3		206	102		407	3.84
Total	975ᵃ	1343ᵃ	208	74	104	3490ᵃ	4219ᵃ	199	10,612ᵃ	100.00
Total percentage per geographical zone	9.19	12.66	1.96	0.70	0.98	32.89	39.76	1.88		

ᵃ Additional items present, but numerical information not recorded.

Table 13.4
Origin of Foreign Produced Material Goods

Material categories (18)	Foreign geographical zones								Total	
	V (No.)	VI (No.)	VII (No.)	VIII (No.)	IX (No.)	X (No.)	XI (No.)	XII (No.)	Number	Percentage
Consumables	581		106	50		26		4	767	37.65
Maintenance Items	537	77		31				18	663	32.55
Extractive Items	1	5							6	0.29
Electrical Conveniences	17	1							18	0.88
Decorative Items	73	8		15					96	4.71
Refuse Disposal Items	4								4	0.20
Socio-relationables	22		2						24	1.18
Medicines	1								1	0.05
Child Care Items	59			9					68	3.34
Structure Conservation Items	78	8	1	8				5	100	4.91
Pet Care Items								3	3	0.15
Eliminators	31								31	1.52
Cleaners	3		9	21	9			20	62	3.04
Indulgences	—[a]			—[a]				—[a]	—[a]	—
Garden Items	10	4	2						16	0.79
Recreational Items	155	4							159	7.81
Time Items									0	—
Miscellaneous Items	18	1							19	0.93
Total	1590[a]	108	120	134[a]	9	26	—	50[a]	2037[a]	100.00
Total percentage per geographical zone	78.06	5.30	5.89	6.58	0.44	1.28	—	2.45		

[a] Additional items present, but numerical information not recorded.

the majority (83.90%) were produced domestically (USA). The majority (72.65%) of these domestic goods originate from geographical Zones VI and VII, which encompass the Eastern seaboard and the industrial centers of the midwest; Zone II, the West coast, is the next most productive zone; Hawaii (Zone I) produces only 9.19% of the domestically produced items in the store. Most items of foreign origin come from Zone V, Japan (78.06%).

Discussion and Conclusions

The small isolated community of Maunaloa is not really isolated when viewed in terms of the material goods present in the community. Maunaloa is connected to most of the economic world through a complex set of trade and distribution networks. Raw materials are produced in one area, transformed and manufactured in another, shipped to large dispersal centers, which then ship the goods to the store at Maunaloa. Here they are sold and dispersed throughout the community, used, and finally discarded at the local refuse site. This connection with the economic world is a one-way proposition— goods are being imported into Maunaloa, but no goods are being systematically exported out of the community.

It was seen that the majority of goods in the Friendly Market originate from places 7000–10,000 km distant, which include the Eastern seaboard and the industrial centers of the midwest United States, and the country of Japan. These figures are indicative of the importance these areas have in the worldwide economic market, and are not at all surprising. What is surprising is the finding of 50 plus items originating from 16,000–20,000 km distant (western Europe); all of these items can and are manufactured in places closer to Maunaloa. The question to be asked then is: Why are these items present? The presence of these items cannot be explained by Schiffer's utilitarian explanation, which states that when a trade network is in existence, one would expect a decrease in the consumption rate as the distance from the source increases and that the rate will reach zero when other comparable resource loci are encountered (1976a:164–165). The presence of these items in Maunaloa is an anomaly that cannot be explained at this time.

The analysis of consumable items (Table 13.1) showed that the majority of food items were present in canned and dried forms, with low percentages of foods occurring in fresh and frozen forms. Factors that may influence these proportions are that canned and dried foods do not need the special appliances fresh and frozen foods require for preservation, and that foods that are either canned or dried run a much lower risk of spoilage than either fresh or frozen foods. The relative proportions of consumable items are best explained as risk-minimizing behavior on the part of the merchant, who, for economic reasons, does not want to risk having a quantity of merchandise spoil.

The study showed that the combined total percentage of seasonings and sauces-spreads was greater than any other type of consumable. This figure may be indicative of people's tastes, that is, people like their food highly seasoned and/or covered with some sort of sauce that either masks or adds to the original flavor of the food.

The research revealed that there is a strong correlation between the amount of space allocated for particular types of goods and the amount of use that section receives. This correlation suggests the nature of the wants of the people who utilize the site, that is, the people want consumable and yardage items more than structure conservation items. Thus, a general proposition may be made: The greater the spatial allocation for a particular category of goods, the more important these goods are to the people using the site. It may be possible to extend this proposition to include different activity areas in a nonspecific site: The greater the relative space used for a particular activity, the more important that activity is to the inhabitants of that site.

The alcoholic indulgence section of the store is an exception to the space allocation proposition. Though I do not have an explanation for this, several factors may be involved. This section of the store does not allow free access; a counter separates the customer from the merchandise, which necessitates that a store worker wait on the customer; and additional stock is kept in the adjacent small storeroom and in the walk-in refrigerator-freezer (Figure 13.4).

Not all parts of the store structure are now functioning in the capacities originally intended. The Chinese cookhouse, still erect and attached, is vacant and nonfunctioning; the butcher shop no longer functions as a butcher shop, but is used for other purposes. A persistence effect is in operation. The persistence of the Chinese cookhouse may be explained in terms of energy expenditure; it requires energy to remove or destroy the structure, and this will not be done unless there is a compelling reason to do so. Recycling behavior, on the part of the store owner, best explains the persistence of the appliances that were associated with the now nonexistent butcher shop.

The persistence effect carries over to some of the goods found in the store. Many of the decorative (e.g., vases and figurines) and electrical convenience items are tucked away from clear view and covered with dust, indicating that they are not in much demand. It is likely that these items are a carry-over from a more prosperous time, but are not selling now. The original assumption of this study, that the community store would carry only items that its customers would buy, has been shown to be incorrect. An inventory of a store will include merchandise that its customers will not buy as well as items people will buy. The dust-covered items may indicate past preferences and/or reduced purchasing power. Alternatively, their presence may simply be the result of the store owner's poor judgment in ordering items. In any case they can be conceived of as persisting items that the store owner has difficulty in selling.

Finally, two additional general propositions, based on this study of a community store, may be offered:

1. The longer and more intensively an area is used, the greater the likelihood that this area will contain some items and features that have ceased to be utilized or that are now being used for purposes other than originally intended.
2. The greater the quantity and variety of material goods found in an activity area, the greater the number of people using or frequenting this area.

The general propositions raised in this study may be tested through similar ethnoarchaeological studies in other societies and may ultimately prove useful in interpreting archaeological sites of the past.

Acknowledgments

I would like to thank Richard Gould for introducing me to the field of ethnoarchaeology and for his guidance, suggestions, and criticisms of this study. Edward Norbeck wrote letters of introduction to people in Maunaloa, which greatly facilitated my research. In Maunaloa, Mrs. Sunn and Mr. Acoba are thanked for their information on contemporary community affairs, and Mrs. Sunn is further thanked for her hospitality during my stay. Mr. and Mrs. Jinnai, the owners of the Friendly Market, are especially thanked for giving me complete freedom in their store; without their generosity, this study could not have been accomplished. Earlier versions of this paper were critically read by Richard Gould, Michael Schiffer, Patrick McCoy, Joyce Bath, and Jane Allen-Wheeler. Myra Tomonari-Tuggle assisted in the drafting.

14

A Microarchaeological
View of Human Settlement
Space and Function

Alice W. Portnoy

Studies of the contemporary use of space by living people can contribute not only to an understanding of their way of life and to the possible improvement of their living conditions through appropriate planning and design, but also to our interpretation of the archaeological record. Such studies can help us identify, make explicit, and examine our assumptions and perhaps recast them as testable hypotheses. They can shed light on just how the archaeological record is formed, that is, what kinds of remains certain activities leave, how these remains are patterned and what accounts for this patterning. They can also suggest some categories of interpretation that may be more fruitful than others. For example, Yellen (1977), in his study of the !Kung, states:

> Although unique activities are rarely relegated to mutually exclusive areas within a camp and may occur in more than one place, I have demonstrated that underlying social rules are clearly reflected in the spatial patterning of activities. Because of this, it is possible that the seemingly "abstract" aspects of social organization may be more easily reconstructed from camp debris than such supposedly more simple aspects as delineating the nature and range of activities that took place [p. 135].

Yellen (1977:125) developed a model of a !Kung camp which shows its socially organized use of space. He described the material remains associated with the camp and its activities and showed how clusters of camp debris could be interpreted.

213

MODERN MATERIAL CULTURE
The Archaeology of Us

In 1975, I conducted a field study of the use of space in contemporary American homes (Portnoy 1975). As the theoretical framework for this study, I used a model of social interaction-space developed by Goffman (1959). At that time, I also applied the model to several studies done in various societies; in this paper I have also applied it to Yellen's (1977) study of the !Kung. In this paper, I shall redefine Goffman's model and then develop a general model of settlement space, activity location, debris clustering and social interaction.

The Goffman Model

A rationale for classifying activities and the spaces that contain them is given by Goffman (1959) in his concepts of "front regions" and "back regions." These concepts are useful for studying spatial behavior and may help to explain certain "clustering" of activities.

Goffman analyzes social interaction by describing it in the language of the theater. Each individual is seen as an actor, or performer, presenting himself in a performance to other individuals who serve as his audience. This person uses various techniques for fostering particular impressions of himself that he wants his audience to receive. Individuals may act together as a team in fostering an impression and putting on a performance, as does the cast of a play. All performances occur in a specific place, or setting. One part of the setting is where the performance is presented to the audience; it is called the "front region" and may be likened to a stage. The appearance of this front region affects the success of the performance, just as stage scenery and props do. The other part of the setting is where the actors prepare for the performance and is called the "back region"; it is like the backstage area of a theater. Behavior differs in each region: a careful "front" is maintained in the front region while relaxation of performance standards is expected in the back region. Activities which meet "performance standards" are called "front region activities"; those which do not are called "back region activities." Some places function sometimes as front regions, sometimes as back regions, just as the theater stage becomes a back region during rehearsals, but in most cases they keep their character most of the time.

Goffman assigned various parts of the contemporary American home to front or back regions. Back regions include bedrooms, bathrooms, kitchen, and back exterior areas (back yard and porch) (1959:121, 123). He did not specifically name front regions, but stated that they are those places where performances are presented to persons outside the family (p. 123). These are probably the front yard and porch, front entry hall, living room and dining room.

Different societies and sometimes groups within societies define front and back region activities differently and the investigator must be careful not to classify activities according to the rules of his or her own culture. For example, our own society has a full range of front-back behavior for cooking in the home (in restaurants, kitchens are definitely back regions, dining rooms are front regions). Home cooking can be done in (back region) kitchens by servants or particular family members, then served in separate (front region) dining rooms. Sometimes guests joins the host and/or hostess in the kitchen and even help cook; then all may eat the meal in an adjoining, open "dining area." Sometimes the cooking itself is a major part of the performance, as at some outdoor barbecues. I would expect that in many societies, cooking is usually considered either a front or a back region activity.

I believe that a few activities seem to occur in the same regions in most societies. The reception and entertainment of guests is usually a front region activity. Back region activities often include most adult (nonritualized) sexual activity, adult defecation and to a lesser extent urination, messy activities such as butchering of large animals, disposal of messy or smelly waste products, and most long-term storage of relatively low-value items. Evidence of such activities may be "markers" of back regions and we shall see that other back region activities may be expected to take place there. Also, antisocial behavior engendered by strong emotions is considered inappropriate in front regions in many societies (cf. Douglas 1973; Gregor 1974; Lewis 1961). This often includes fighting between spouses, (nonritualized) displays of rage, crying, sulking, and scolding.

The division of space into front and back regions with their associated activities is becoming an important concept in architecture and in urban planning and design (cf. Portnoy 1979; Rapoport 1977). The concept has also been applied to problems encountered while doing ethnographic field work, where the ethnographer is particularly interested in gaining access to back regions for a more complete understanding of the society, while the informants are trying to keep up a "front" for various understandable reasons and therefore try to confine the ethnographer to front regions (Berreman 1962:11).

The Field Study

In 1975, I conducted a field study of lower- and middle-class White, Black, and Mexican-American families in a small Texas city in order to discover, describe, and analyze relationships between family behavior patterns and physical settings (homes). The study was based on participant-observation and home interviews with 12 families (Portnoy 1975).

One of the subjects investigated was the actual location of specific activities. Although contemporary American (and other) homes are fairly standardized in types of rooms and in layout, people use the space available to them in "nonstandard" ways. For example, in this study, a dining room was used for sewing, a kitchen for arts and crafts, a garage for children's play and toy storage. While the permanent and semi-permanent equipment or furnishings in a room may indicate some uses, for example, a cookstove in a kitchen suggests that cooking is done there, many other activities either require no specific equipment, use portable and/or temporary equipment which is stored in various places between uses or is discarded elsewhere after use, or use equipment for other activities in unexpected ways.

For each home in the study, a table (too large to present here) has been composed to show how each of the rooms was used. The table lists the "name" of the room (as designated by family members), how it was furnished, what activities took place there, what equipment was used for these activities, and where this equipment was stored between uses.

For each home, another table (too large to present here) has been composed to show how I attempted to categorize rooms as front or back regions, based on my observations and interviews. It also shows whether these areas were physically located in the front (street side) or back of the house.

These tables show that rooms and other areas were usually multi-purpose, but that activities often clustered into front or back regions (both physically and conceptually). When they did not, as in one home I visited, chaos resulted.

One family, a mother with six children, lived in a two-bedroom house where there was very little differentiation of space use, as evidenced by both the furnishing and the activities. Only the bathroom and the kitchen were recognizable as such, and even so, a large freezer stood in the living room. Beds, clothing, food, toys, cooking utensils, and everything else were distributed and used fairly evenly throughout the house. Collier (1967:81) noted that this condition may reflect "confusion and disorder in the minds of the people." Indeed, I later found out that the mother in this family is severely disturbed and is regularly visited by a psychiatric case worker.

It is interesting to note that another family (father, mother, and six children) was living in an even smaller house (living room, one bedroom, tiny kitchen, bathroom) that they kept perfectly neat and clean. The crowding of necessary back region activities into all areas (for example, four children slept in the living room) severely curtailed adult social life (there was no front region for evening entertaining when the children were in bed) and created other problems. The family made great efforts to define areas, prevent conflicts, and keep everything as "nice" as possible under extremely difficult conditions.

One room seemed to be "ambiguous"; this was the "formal living room" in those houses which also had a "den" or "family room" (6 of the 12). In all cases, less living went on in this room than in any other, even though it was usually the best furnished room. It was located in the front (street side) of the house in all six cases.

This room has retained the character of the old fashioned parlor, a space formally furnished and too sacred for any but the most solemn occasions, such as a visit from the minister or one's rich aunt, a wake, or a meeting of the ladies' church circle. But these occasions have either disappeared, been moved to places outside the home, or become informal enough for them to take place in the den or family room, and the living room is left for the most part unused. This was true in all three ethnic groups in the families of middle-class status who had these living rooms.

With rising construction costs, this room is tending to disappear. The family room or den, originally designed as a family back region (entertaining of guests was supposed to be done in the front region living room), is taking over the front region social functions. I believe there is a trend for some back region activities originally planned for the family room or den (e.g., arts and crafts, other hobbies) to move out into special areas such as small studios and workshops. This is probably because front and back region activities are often incompatible, and guest entertaining, as it becomes more informal, is taking over the family room and turning it into a front region, even in houses where a separate front region (the living room) is available.

Another use of space that is rather ambiguous concerns where children do their homework. In the six families whose school-aged children either have a room of their own or share it with only one sibling, five sets of parents have provided each child with a separate study desk in his or her bedroom. In the three families who have school-aged children but do not have the space (where there are more than two children in each bedroom), all parents expressed a desire for separate study desks in the children's own bedrooms. No child in any of the nine families with school-aged children regularly uses a study desk in his room for homework. Those who have them generally use them as just another storage-play area. Most children do not do homework in their bedrooms at all, despite their parents' desires and requests. The most common places to do homework are the dinner table and the den-family room (or living room if there is no den) floor. This ambiguity may be explained by the classification of homework as a front region activity by children and a back region activity by parents.

Other Studies

Parts of several studies which I believe illustrate front region-back region concepts will be briefly described here. Gregor's (1974) study is the only one of these which utilized Goffman's (1959) concepts.

Cooper (1967) studied and described activities in small yards and porches in a public housing project. In a sample of households, she listed all activities and their frequencies reported for each area. She found that the back yards were used most often for household maintenance activities, such as clothes drying, storage of infrequently used furniture, tools, and play equipment, and the confinement of dogs and small children. The back yards were also used to barbecue food which was brought inside to be eaten. The front porches were used for single-age group social gatherings (e.g., small children during the day, teenagers in the evening), and the front yards for display of status (e.g., lawns and flower beds), observation of neighborhood activities, and casual interactions among neighbors.

Cooper noted that most complaints were about the back yard and centered on "lack of privacy" for sun bathing and for entertaining guests at barbecues. She recommended improvements in the fencing. Greater privacy achieved by different fencing might make the back yard more suitable for sun bathing, but if, as indicated in her study, the other back region activities which take place there are necessary for household functioning and there is no other place for them, then I would predict that the back region activities would probably interfere with entertaining and other front region activities (equipment might have to be moved, the area might have to be cleaned for each occasion, etc.).

The locations of activities listed in Cooper's study suggest that activities tend to cluster into those suitable for either front or back regions.

An interesting example of this clustering can be found in Embree's (1939:130-131, 215-218) description of a funeral and its preparation in a Japanese village. At the time of a death in the family, the neighbors helped to prepare the coffin, the grave, and the funeral feast, with all the relaxed behavior associated with back region activities, while the family received relatives and friends in a dignified, ceremonial manner. In this case the front region was the front entrance and front rooms of the house; the back region was the kitchen and other back rooms of the house and the exterior yard and barn. The working (and socializing) neighbors in the back region were visible and audible to the mourners in the front region, but their presence was ignored, even when they continued to drink and talk during the funeral service (p. 131). The "barrier" was purely social but the front and back region activities were clustered together and spatially separate from each other.

A study of the functions and design of the contemporary American bathroom (Kira 1966) shows how a back region (the bathroom) designed for a specific function (personal hygiene) is also used for other back region activities. It is used for sulking and crying, withdrawal into daydreams, uninterrupted reading, and for relief from social roles. It is also a common place for suicides to occur (p. 182). It has assumed this privileged character (nearly absolute privacy) because our society has such strong norms concerning privacy for personal hygiene activities.

Various strategies for obtaining privacy in a society where houses offer few back regions have been described in a study of a Brazilian Indian village (Gregor 1974). The domestic life of these people is highly visible; they live in unpartitioned thatched houses which shelter several extended families. Both house-mates and neighbors have access to much information about each other. These people try to keep up appearances or "front" while in the village. They use trips out of the village for back region activities such as personal hygiene, extramarital affairs, and arguments and fights between spouses. If they cannot avoid such back region behavior while they are in the village, observers will act toward them as if they have not seen them, although they will gossip to others about what they saw. Discretion and tact are highly valued, but much gossip is indulged in. The researcher concluded:

> In highly exposed settings, managing information that would undermine social relationships is not a simple task. Active strategies must be developed to control others' knowledge of one's activities, whereabouts, and attitudes. The visibility of social action must therefore be regarded as an important factor in the definition and maintenance of social relationships [p. 347].

Yellen's Study and Model

The !Kung live in constantly moving camps organized by very fluid bands of nuclear families and related individuals (Yellen 1977:41-49). They build small grass shelters mostly for light temporary protection from wind, rain, and sun. They spend very little time in them, not even sleeping in them at night during good weather. They also use them to store their small amount of property (p. 87). They leave little debris in these huts (p. 92).

The hut can be seen as a family or individual "back region." It is obvious that this back region does not provide much in the way of privacy—even less than does the Brazilian thatched house. However, it is extremely mobile. When a !Kung family or individual is in conflict with other camp members, it can move its hut away from the offenders or even join another band.

The area directly in front of the hut contains the hearth, the focal point of family activities. Here, families prepare, cook and eat food (Yellen 1977:87, 90). Groups of men gather at various hearths to visit and to make or mend tools (p. 90). Groups of women gather at various hearths to visit and to make ostrich shell beads (p. 90). Yellen notes (p. 95) that debris from both subsistence and manufacturing activities are found in the hearth areas. The social contexts in which these tasks are performed define them as front region activities and we see that they have clustered in a front region.

Yellen (1977:95) has called these family areas, which we have divided into front (hearth) and back (hut) regions, the "nuclear activity area." He has also designated two areas of a !Kung camp as "communal activity" and "special activity areas."

The communal activity area is in the center of the camp (usually within a rough circle of huts) and is used for dancing and first distribution of meat (p. 90). We can designate these as front region activities. These activities leave no debris (pp. 90, 91).

The special activity area is outside the circle of huts and is used for messy and/or space consuming activities such as skin pegging and drying, head roasting, and quiver making (which involves warming roots) (p. 92). These may be seen as back region activities. This area is also used on a short-term basis for any other kind of casual activity if it provides more shade during the hottest part of the day than do other camp areas (p. 92). It has light and varied debris.

Yellen (1977:125-130, Figure 12) proposed a spatial model of a !Kung camp called "The Ring Model," with an "inner ring"—the "communal area" and "nuclear area"—and an "outer ring"—the "special activity area."

Yellen (1977:93) described !Kung children's play activities as disruptive factors in the formation of the archaeological record: They play all over the camp and scatter their own play materials and other debris. This is also true in our own society, although attempts are made on both communal (e.g., playgrounds) and family (e.g., bedrooms-playrooms) levels to segregate these activities. Children's play is usually treated as a back region activity by adults (it is often messy and noisy). However, it is certainly viewed by children as a front region activity, even if performance standards are different.

Redefinition of the Goffman Model

My field study and the other studies described suggest that Goffman's model can be redefined. The front region as Goffman (1959:123) defined it for the contemporary American home can be called the "family front region" (the hearth for the !Kung). I would add a "communal front region," for example, the sidewalk and street in our residential areas, the central open space in a !Kung camp. The back region as Goffman (1959:121, 123) defined it can be called the "family back region" (the hut for the !Kung). I would add a "communal back region," for example, alleys and vacant lots in our residential areas, the "special activity area" in the !Kung camp.

The general activities associated with each region could then be described as follows. Family (sometimes another social unit) front region activities are social, often involving the reception and entertainment of non-family members as guests. Family back region activities are private, "backstage," "nonperformance" activities of family members. Communal front region activities are public and often ceremonial in nature. Communal back region activities are those which are necessary for community functioning, but not suitable for other places. They are activities which might interfere with communal front region activities (e.g., too messy, noisy, smelly) and/or cannot be accommodated within family back regions (e.g., needing too much space).

A General Model

Yellen's (1977:Figure 12) center-and-ring-shaped activity areas can be expressed in a model with center-and-ring-shaped family and communal front and back regions. This can serve as a general model for circular settlements (Figure 14.1).

We can also adapt this model to settlements organized in ways other than circular. If we "cut and straighten out" the circular model, we get a model for linearly patterned settlements (Figure 14.2), such as those formed by many Northwest coast American Indian villages which faced bodies of water and by some Aztec villages along lake shores.

Many settlements have a double linear (facing) arrangement (Figure 14.3). The "ends" of this type of settlement are sometimes well defined, resulting in a rectangular pattern; this is seen in many villages (cf. Fraser 1968). The double linear model lends itself to extension on the ends and by repetitions of face-to-face-back-to-back regions (seen in many contemporary

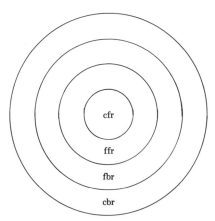

Figure 14.1. *General model for a circular settlement. Key to all figures: cfr—communal front region: ceremonial; ffr—family front region: social; fbr—family back region: private; cbr—communal back region: necessary.*

cbr
fbr
ffr
cfr

Figure 14.2. *General model for a linear settlement.*

Western, especially U.S., urban and suburban settlements) as in Figure 14.4. The simplest model for the common "plaza" plan and its variants is shown in Figure 14.5.

Conclusions

Activities tend to cluster into what we have referred to as "front regions" and "back regions." These designations are based on the participants' criteria of whether or not a particular activity meets "performance standards." Goffman's front and back regions have each been divided into "family" and "communal" areas in order to extend the model from the individual home to the community. Several versions have been illustrated to fit different community arrangements.

These models reflect not only debris clustering and activity locations but also types of social interaction and behavioral norms. This illustrates Yellen's statement (1977) "underlying social rules are clearly reflected in the spatial patterning of activities . . . [p. 135]."

We can suggest how certain societies categorized specific activities as appropriate to front or back regions when we identify some debris clusters. For example, if human coprolites are found in one area, we can postulate that

cbr
fbr
ffr
cfr
ffr
fbr
cbr

Figure 14.3. *General model for a double linear (facing) settlement.*

cbr	alley or open space
fbr	back yard
ffr '	house
	front yard
cfr	sidewalk/street
ffr	front yard
	house
fbr	back yard
cbr	alley or open space
fbr	back yard
	house
ffr	front yard
etc.	

Figure 14.4. *Example of a repeated double linear (facing) settlement (U.S. urban).*

this was a back region which precluded certain front region activities and that associated debris probably indicates other back region activities.

If evidence of structures or patterning of debris clusters (such as the rings of similar debris which show up in the !Kung camp) suggests a particular layout for a settlement, we can use the appropriate model to formulate hypotheses about activity clustering and location.

The models could be tested by applying them to various home and community maps and plans on which activities are located (or can be inferred) to see if family and communal front and back regions can be delineated. Any information about how the inhabitants might classify (or might have classified) their activities or areas in "front-back" terms would be extremely valuable. Sometimes such information is available in or can be inferred from ethnographic, ethnohistoric or historic accounts of activities. A few possible sources are noted in the following.

Fraser (1968) provides a large variety of village plans from ethnographic

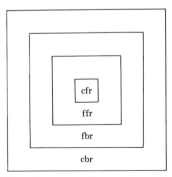

Figure 14.5. *General model for a plaza settlement.*

and ethnohistoric sources which could be utilized. Recent ethnoarchaeological studies (e.g., Gould 1978; Kramer 1979) could be even more valuable because they collect and report more specific data about locations of activities and associated debris. Archaeological studies especially concerned with the use of space (e.g., Clarke 1977) could also be appropriate. Other studies that come to mind are those of Shafer and Bryant (1977) at Hinds Cave in Texas and de Lumley (1969) at Terra Amata on the French Riviera. Some of Sanders' (1965) Aztec "line village" and Flannery's (1976b) Oaxacan settlement studies also might be appropriate as extant sources of data.

Using front-back region concepts allows us to ask new questions of our data, the answers to which may help us to interpret other data. A general subject area that might lend itself to such treatment is that of mortuary practices, where we could ask questions such as: Are primary mortuary activities, such as initial preparation of the corpse, usually done in back regions? Do societies who practice secondary burial tend to do the first stage in back regions (such as using communal open spaces for exposing the body for reduction to bare bones) and the second stage in front regions (such as public or family display or deposit of ancestral remains)?

The answers to such questions may suggest that we use evidence of certain activities as "markers" of front or back regions. Identifying what other activities took place in these regions (reflected in the debris clusters) may lead us to inferences about social rules and interaction. Although we have learned that residues which are found together cannot be assumed to have been deposited at the same time, by the same individual, or from the same activity, we can at least make a cautious and tentative assumption that they were likely to have been deposited in either a front or a back region, which we might be able to identify on the basis of "markers."

In this chapter, I have been concerned with "front-back" concepts at the scale of small settlements, for example, camps and villages, and of small areas within larger urban settlements, for example, individual homes and residential neighborhoods. I have rather loosely termed such small settlement areas, "communities." Rapoport (1977) uses front-back concepts at the scale of the large urban settlement (town or city). I believe that this usage is valid.

Archaeologists and others have devised and applied other models of the use of space in complex societies (cf. Fletcher 1977; Flannery and Winter 1976; Flannery 1976a). Utilization of the family and communal front and back region model can add a social dimension to our interpretation of material culture in both living systems and in the remains and traces of such systems in the archaeological record.

15

The Archaeological
Significance of Counting Houses:
Ethnoarchaeological Evidence

Jeffrey L. Eighmy

As archaeological interpretation becomes more sophisticated, the limitations of current ethnographic data relating material culture and social behavior emerge. In many respects archaeological field technique and observations are far more precise than is warranted by current information concerning the behavior–material-culture interaction. Why, for instance, record point provenience of artifacts when we know so little about the meaning of artifact distributions within sites and habitations? Or why take numerous pollen samples when we know nearly nothing about the impact of social behavior on pollen distributions? This ignorance has led to many important experimental studies; so that archaeologists have discovered on their own some of the behavioral significance of artifactual variation. An important aspect of ethnoarchaeological study continues this interest in discovering the behavioral regularities underlying material-culture patterning. While the results of such studies are often discouraging to the prehistoric archaeologist due to the unexpected complexity in sources of material culture variation, ethnoarchaeological discoveries have given new and unexpected meaning to lifeless patterns in artifactual distributions. Nowhere is this process of discovery and new understanding better illustrated than in the ethnoarchaeological study of domestic structures.

225

MODERN MATERIAL CULTURE
The Archaeology of Us

Estimating Population From Domestic Structures

The domestic structure or house has been important to archaeological interpretation for many reasons, one of which has been in estimating population size (e.g., Gregg 1975) and population change (Plog 1974). Unfortunately, for the archaeologist looking for neat solutions to the population size problem, accumulating ethnoarchaeological evidence indicates that estimating population from number of domestic structures is more complicated than it seems at first glance. Rather than being able to simply multiply the number of domestic structures by mean household size, it now appears that household size varies along a number of parameters important to archaeological interpretation.

First, mean household size is culturally and regionally specific. Cook and Heizer (1965) were the first to point out this fact when they found considerable regional variation in mean household size even within the California cultural area. Based on this evidence Roberts (1977:167) argues the best use of a conversion factor would be based on data specific to regions, cultural groups, and domestic types. From an informal survey of the Human Relations Area Files, we find considerable variation within and between different subsistence types. Hunting and gathering average household size for 21 societies has a standard deviation of 1.38, 6 pastoral societies has a standard deviation of 1.39, 13 horticultural societies exhibited a standard deviation of 5.04, and agriculturalists revealed a standard deviation of 3.86. Average household size of the subsistence types varied from 4.91 for hunters and gatherers to 6.69 for agriculturalists.

Second, the domestic structure–household size relationship for a specific region, culture, and structure type depends on community size and cannot be expressed by a simple mean for the group. As communities increase in size, the average number of people per dwelling changes. Both Cook and Heizer and Roberts develop different conversion formulas for large and small communities.

Third, data gathered by the author and presented below indicate that the average household size changes through time as a function of typical family composition.

Mean Household Size through Time

The concept of mean household size has had an interesting impact on archaeological interpretation of population change. When constructing demographic records, it has been assumed that mean household size is constant through time. With a good record of the trend in number of domestic structures, converting to actual population change figures becomes an unnecessary complication (Plog 1974:94; Longacre 1975:72). Since mean household size is assumed to be constant, it can be argued that the value of domestic structure trends lies in their shape and not in their ability to predict the actual size of population change. For most questions of change, information concerning periods of relative population increase, decline, and stability and relative rates of change are often as important as actual population figures. Still, it is assumed that these curves reflect in some regular way population change. It is argued that the record of site and room use reflects population change because the number of people per habitation room remains constant over time. Considering the importance of demographic reconstruction and the variability already noted in mean household size, this assumption deserves testing.

To test the assumption, synchronic and diachronic data on the domestic structures of a large number of Mennonites living in Mexico were collected (Eighmy 1977). The Mexican Mennonites (the Old Colony Mennonites of Manitoba Colony, Cuauhtemoc, Chihuahua, Mexico) live in 45 separate villages averaging 36 houses per village and 6.12 people per house. Interestingly enough the average people per house seems to predict fairly well village populations in 1977 for the Mexican Mennonites. There is very nearly a 6.12 to 1 correlation across the entire range of village sizes for this specific group. Despite a regular, nearly linear relationship of houses and number of people for 1977, diachronic data on Mennonite housing and population (Eighmy 1977) show that from the time of first settlement (1922) mean household size among Manitoba Colony Mennonites has changed dramatically (Figure 15.1). Over the past 50 years mean household size has increased by about 50%. It appears that even though houses and people may show a nearly linear correlation at one point in time, it cannot be assumed that mean household size is a constant through time, and the model for predicting population size from the number of houses is more complicated.

This change in average household size can be related to change in typical family composition. The Manitoba Colony Mennonites immigrated to Mexico between 1922 and 1926. Immigrant populations are usually composed of a relatively higher proportion of young adults and males than mature populations. For example, between 70 and 80% of all immigrants into the United States between 1860 and 1924, were between the ages of 15 and 40 at a time when only about 40% of the host population was in this age category. Further, this same immigrating population contained a 60% male bias (Willcox 1969:221-223). If similar selection for young adults and males occurred among the Mennonites immigrating to Mexico, then the migrating population probably contained an unusually high proportion of unmarried adults and small families. Through the 1940s and 1950s the average family

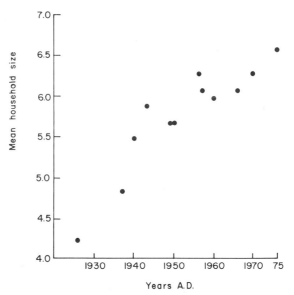

Figure 15.1. *Change in mean household size through time among Manitoba Colony Mennonites, Chihuahua, Mexico, 1926 to 1975. The low periods around 1950 and 1960 are probably related to periods of outmigration to new colonies established by the Altkolonier Church in 1946 and 1958. The emigration of hundreds of families would have decreased mean household size. Based on a 10% random sample.*

size could have increased until the population became demographically stable in the 1960s and 1970s. Since the Mennonites usually live in neolocal, independent households, a high proportion of small families would appear as a high proportion of small households.

The case is interesting to archaeologists not as an instance of simple ethnographic analogy but as an illustration of what might be going on during periods of major social change, and these are precisely the periods of extreme interest to prehistorians (Plog 1974:8–11). Due to the very instability of these situations archaeological inference is much more difficult. Factors which may be considered a *constant* in interpreting synchronic variation for a specific group from site to site during stable periods may be *variable* through time due to changing social conditions.

The case of Mennonite migration may have more direct application to archaeological problems. In the Southwest, for example, it has been suggested that a succession of communities were settled, expanded, and abandoned (Matson and Lipe 1976; Mendeleff 1900; Reid 1973). Estimating the population size of these prehistoric colonizers should include some consideration of the change in household size as the settled population matures.

The Mennonite data reveal further diachronic regularities of interest to

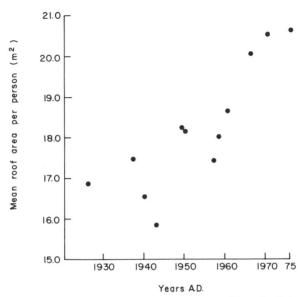

Figure 15.2. *Change in mean roofed area per person among Manitoba Colony Mennonites, Chihuahua, Mexico, 1926 to 1975. Based on a 10% random sample.*

archaeologists. It might be tempting to assume that as mean household size increases, mean roofed area per person declines. As a matter of fact, among the Manitoba Mennonites mean roofed area increased despite the increase in mean number of people per house (Figure 15.2). This increase is probably a result of two separate factors. First, remodeling had the effect of increasing the size of existing houses. The roofed area of 31 of the oldest houses increased from around 90 m² in 1928 to 2520 m² in 1975, an average increase of 60.6 m² per year (Figure 15.3). Second, the per person increase in roofed area is probably also a function of the partial abandonment of some roofed space. As families grew and left home to establish their own neolocal households, the old house was gradually vacated until the senior generation died.

The Significance of Counting Houses

What then of counting houses? Are comparisons of number of houses only useful synchronically to deal with variation in population size within a social system from community to community? Obviously not. Synchronic variation in housing styles has always been an important means of sociological inference for archaeologists (e.g., Trigger 1968:58–59), and the

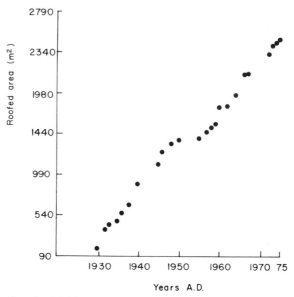

Figure 15.3. *Growth of 31 houses built between 1922 and 1927, Manibota Colony Mennonites, Chihuahua, Mexico.*

full potential in this regard is only now being recognized (Bastian 1975; Rickert 1967). But beyond synchronic sociological inference and despite the difficulty in dealing with changing population size, the ethnoarchaeological study of Mennonite houses and population indicates that counting houses can be useful in diachronic analysis also. The diachronic significance of counting houses stems from the fact that the house site, even though a poor predictor of household composition and size, gives a clear and unambiguous indication of a household itself, and the household, as a unit, is an important feature in ecological analysis (Hole and Heizer 1977:314).

If we agree with Hole and Heizer that the household, particularly in simple societies, is the major unit of production, then the founding of a household, no matter what its size, composition, or stage of development, is a significant ecological event. It indicates the current subsistence strategy is still viable and encouraging new participants—whether by immigration or natural increase. In recent discussions of the niche and population concepts by human ecologists (Love 1977; Montgomery 1977), the household, as opposed to individuals and populations, is the more important analytic unit. For Love, small farmer households compete with retirement farmer households for land while Montgomery describes the structure of the Yelnadu Reddi population through an analysis of variation in "commensal family units." Thus, the prehistoric trends described by Plog (1974), Longacre (1975),

Gumerman (1975), Eighmy (1979), and others from changing habitation variables may still reflect important ecological developments even if the trends are inaccurate representations of population change. The trends may reflect periods of expansion and contraction in the number of households participating in a subsistence strategy even if population grows and declines at slightly different rates. Ecologically, the changes in number of household units are as important as actual population figures.

Further, the ethnoarchaeological evidence suggests that quantifying number of domestic structures (and by implication number of households) may allow the archaeologists to differentiate subsections of a social group which would be overlooked by a preoccupation with estimating actual population figures. Most social groups are divided into economically or ecologically important subunits. These groups can often be seen in different domestic structure types (Bastian 1975), and changes in the relative proportion of structural types may indicate important demoecological change. For example, among the Manitoba Colony Mennonites, houses can be separated between those with agricultural lands (farmsteads) and those with none (lot houses). Lot houses are small, located at the end of villages, have no associated pasture-field and a few (small) barns. One new village, Lowenfarm, has nothing but lot houses and as a result it is a much more compact settlement. For the Manitoba Colony Mennonites the difference between lot

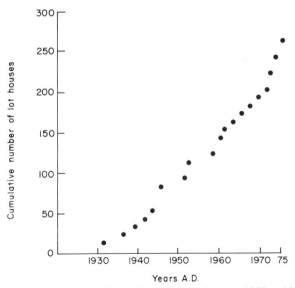

Figure 15.4. *Cumulative number of Manitoba Colony lot houses, 1922 to 1975. Based on a 10% random sample.*

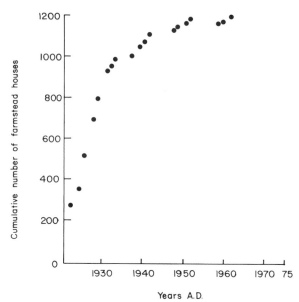

Years A.D.

Figure 15.5. *Cumulative number of Manitoba Colony farmstead houses, 1922 to 1975. Based on a 10% random sample.*

houses and farmsteads reflects a classic social difference—that between landed farmers and wage workers. Households living in lot houses are landless; a few rent farmland, but most are wage workers in the growing Mennonite service and industrial sectors. Services such as retailing and repairing have been available since the earliest years, but the number and variety of these services has been growing recently. Factory work is a more recent addition to the Mennonite economy (Eighmy 1977:32 and Figure 9). When the founding dates for lot houses are accumulated through time, the pattern clearly reflects the wage labor growth trend (Figure 15.4). The circa 1940 acceleration of the wage labor shift is also clearly predicted from the cumulative trend in number of farmsteads (Figure 15.5). As Manitoba Colony land was saturated by farms, it would be predicted that some of the new households would shift to new economic pursuits not requiring additional land. Domestic structures were clearly sensitive to this shift in households even if inaccurately reflecting the change demographically.

Conclusion

Two things can be gained from data presented in this chapter. First, the data and analysis increase our understanding of the relationship between domestic structures and population by showing that the population inhabiting a given number of domestic structures may be quite variable and that estimating population change (even relative change) is more complicated than currently assumed. Second, and possibly more important, the contribution illustrates the place of ethnoarchaeological research in archaeological interpretation. Ethnoarchaeology does not aim to show why material culture is uninterpretably complex. Quite the contrary, for ethnoarcheology to have any place in the science of human behavior it must (a) increase our understanding of human behavior and (b) expose the behavioral order expressed in material culture. The ethnography of material culture has not left the archaeologists with a morass of complicated and unexplainable variation. In this case, the modern studies of domestic structures specified some of the conditions effecting the variability in mean household size. Further, the ethnoarchaeological evidence has pointed to a more profitable approach to the order inherent in change in number of prehistoric houses. Given the close relationship between habitation structures and the domestic unit of production, houses may reflect in a fairly direct fashion subsistence strategy growth, decline, and differentiation. Thus, the house site does not lose its archaeological significance in the study of prehistoric change just because it may be insensitive to household composition and size. It may still be a valuable index to shifting subsistence activity among households.

Acknowledgments

Several people read early drafts of this paper. Their comments were extremely helpful in writing the final version. The remarks of Ken Kvamme and Pierre Morenon were particularly useful. To Kevin Thompson goes the credit for looking through data on over 150 societies in order to derive some impression of the variability extant in household size among the world's cultures.

EXPERIMENTAL APPROACHES

We do not ordinarily think of archaeology or anthropology as experimental sciences. In the case of archaeology, we must destroy the site we excavate, with no possibility of digging it over again. We must do an adequate job of archaeological reporting the first time, since an excavated site is not an experiment that we can go back and repeat. This fact violates the requirement that all scientific experiments must be repeatable. In social and cultural anthropology, we are dealing with people, whose rights and dignity must be protected. The first rule of ethical conduct for an anthropologist, as stated in Part 1 of the *Principles of Professional Responsibility*, is:

> In research, an anthropologist's paramount responsibility is to those he studies. When there is a conflict of interest, these individuals must come first. The anthropologist must do everything within his power to protect their physical, social and psychological welfare and to honor their dignity and privacy [American Anthropological Association 1971:1].

Experiments in contemporary human behavior are constrained by this principle, and scrutiny by government agencies and universities whenever medical or psychological experiments on human subjects are planned is commonplace today.

Given such compelling and rigorous constraints, what possibility remains for the effective application of the experimental method in studying contemporary and past human behavior? The papers contained in this section

MODERN MATERIAL CULTURE
The Archaeology of Us

demonstrate that ample scope exists within the framework of a modern material-culture approach to carry out useful experiments in human behavior without violating either of the restrictions described above. Claassen offers a general rationale for such experimental studies along with some well-chosen examples including an experiment of her own design involving vessel breakage under controlled conditions. These experiments are mainly of the "byproduct" variety (Tringham 1978:175), involving controlled testing of different materials by subjecting them to varying mechanical and other forces. Such experiments provide a basis for assessing the regular occurrence of wear patterns, breakage, and other forms of mechanical and chemical alteration of materials in relation to different kinds of naturally or humanly induced actions. These kinds of experiments more closely approach experimental science as carried on in fields like physics and chemistry than any others that anthropologists are likely to encounter and are less directly involved with human subjects than any other kind in the field of social science. At the same time, these kinds of experiments offer some of the most reliable results available to us, and they represent a productive and rapidly growing component of archaeology.

Claassen rightly notes that the usefulness of such experiments with contemporary materials does not reside in their direct application as analogues to the past. Instead, their value depends upon the uniformitarian assumption that these relationships between different forces and materials will produce the same results whenever and wherever they occur. Indirectly, therefore, one can infer which forces produced particular results and make reliable judgments as to whether those results were produced by nature or by man. It is this indirect use of the uniformitarianist assumption rather than the direct application of experimental results by analogy that makes by-product experiments of the sort described by Claassen scientifically valid and useful.

Claassen's account of Hill's experiment to discover individual variation in designs by potters in Tijuana and Baker's cement block reduction study are examples of well executed "behavioral" experiments (Tringham 1978) applied to modern materials. These experiments involve human subjects *as experimenters* themselves. In each case, we can see how various motor patterns and other behavioral considerations affect the material product under controlled conditions. It should be noted that the controls in such cases are less tight than is possible under the laboratory-like conditions of a by-product experiment, since human motor patterns and selective criteria (e.g., for different sized hammerstones) are bound to vary somewhat from one episode to the next. While perhaps less uniformitarian in their results, these kinds of experiments offer useful ideas about human behavior in relation to materials, many of which can be tested by further, by-product experiments.

Ingersoll's study departs from the others by providing an experiment to test analytical methods used in archaeological sequence-dating. This rather technical study is important to any archaeologist-anthropologist who wishes to establish reliable criteria for observing and measuring change in prehistoric and historic materials. The Puddle Dock project, described by Ingersoll, addressed this problem in relation to eighteenth- and nineteenth-century ceramics from a well-documented site in Portsmouth, New Hampshire. Among other things, this research provides an assessment of different, alternative techniques that are widely used for measuring changes in archaeological and historic materials. Ingersoll's study not only reveals the ambiguities of the cumulative graph method, but it shows how controlled archaeological findings from historic sites can be used to construct an experiment to test different methods of analysis in studying changes in man-made materials.

These three chapters demonstrate that the experimental method does have a viable place in modern material-culture studies and ought to be regarded as part of the conceptual and methodological "toolkit" of anyone who wishes to study the "archaeology of us."

R.A.G.

16

Experimentation
with Modern Materials

Cheryl P. Claassen

The purpose of this chapter is to argue the validity and necessity of using modern materials for experimental studies in archaeology. If experimentation is to develop into an important analytical tool for archaeologists, several assumptions about its utility must change and the scope of the situations in which experimentation is thought appropriate must widen. In brief, there are no archaeological problems, whether the concern is with natural processes or cultural processes, that cannot be better understood by a well-executed experiment.

Several years ago, Schiffer (1973b) presented a research strategy that would allow archaeologists to investigate, if not explain, the relationship between human behavior and material culture. Furthermore, this relationship could be investigated in any society without regard to temporal and geographical boundaries. The strategy he proposed, behavioral archaeology, validates the study of modern materials for the purpose of deriving hypotheses and proposing laws.

Perhaps the two earliest research projects which focused exclusively on modern materials for data applicable to more traditional archaeological problems were Rathje's (1974) garbage project and Baker's (1974) experiment in lithic reduction. The latter project was executed the same year John Coles (1973) published his handbook for experimentation in archaeology. As the reader will soon see, these events represent two radically different theoretical views on the utility of experimentation.

239

MODERN MATERIAL CULTURE
The Archaeology of Us

Coles (1973) outlined several procedural rules to be followed by any experimenter in archaeology to ensure the reliability of the test results. The first of these rules was that the materials used in the experiment should be those considered to have been locally available to the ancient society that produced the problem. To fail to do this was to interfere with the applicability of the results. His second rule was that the methods used in the experiment to reproduce the ancient materials should not exceed those presumed to have been within the competence of the society in focus. Clearly Coles, as well as Ascher (1961), does not envision experiments that would use modern industrial objects. More importantly, they do not design their experiments to test the relationship between variables. Their imagination limits archaeological experimentation to being merely replication. Its greatest potential is for understanding the degree of dependence of the variables on one another.

Coles' objection to the use of modern materials in experimentation and possibly the reader's as well are overcome when the experimental process is viewed as an examination of relationships between variables. Schiffer (1973:175) says one or more of the variables under examination should be potentially measurable in the archaeological context. But it seems that at least for "the basic testing of hypotheses on the mechanical properties of materials [Tringham 1978:175]" or "low-level" testing, a carefully devised experiment will result in *all* variables being observable. Properties such as hardness, compactness, tensile strength, degree of sphericity are held in common by past and present objects and these objects can be examined in light of variables such as angle of inclination, point of impact, water absorption, ad infinitum. The degree of dependency of the relevant variables on each other can then be investigated. An example of the results derived from such an approach would be that obsidian flakes held at angle X are damaged in the observed way (quantifiable) when used against materials of hardness values A, B, and C. These three hardness values are only three points along a continuum of all the possible hardness values and are, as a result of the experiment, reference points for other archaeologists examining edge-wear data. The materials used for the hardness variable could be anything, including concrete, linoleum, and plastic for instance. It is not necessary to test all substances, but it is necessary to test all numerical values on the hardness scale. Edge damage produced by use against some unknown material of hardness D can now be seen to be harder than material A or B but softer than C. The low-level testing thus provides the necessary background theory for higher-level behavioral testing.

Before the argument for the use of modern materials can be considered complete, one more important assumption currently held must be eliminated. Tringham, Cooper, Odell, Voytek, and Whitman (1974), in discussing the source of their materials for their extensive and very well conceived lithic experiments say "the source of the hypothesized behaviour and the selection of testable variables lies in the ethnographic and historic data [1974:21]." Furthermore, "we have tried to test the tools on as many materials as possible that would have been available and modified by flint edges [1974:14]."

An archaeological problem is not most efficiently addressed by using only and as many ethnographically valid objects or substances as possible but by using representatives of several points in the range of the variable being tested. If one restricts the source of the experimental materials to a specific ethnographic area, then the test results will only be applicable to that specific area. This creates a need for someone interested in a second area to repeat the experiment simply for the sake of different materials. What is called for is an understanding of the experimental materials and questions. It is feared that those who strive to replicate only the ethnographic record are failing to understand just what are the variables in question and are hoping that quantity will provide for significant or positive results which are often merely replication. (Tringham *et al.* [1974] are notable exceptions to this generalization.)

Mary Gay Sprague (1979) conducted a test to distinguish plant residues at the genus level on grindstones. She terminated the experiments when she exhausted her supply of grindstones. Her failure to recognize that grain size was the key variable in the experiments prevented her from finding a substitute material such as sandpaper which comes in a wide range of grain sizes. On the other hand, she did use nonethnographic foodstuffs to complete her sample of representatives from each of the different classes of vegetables. This aspect of the experiment, that is, testing representatives from each class of vegetable, is that which gives Sprague's work its value.

Tringham (1978) has since argued that it is not necessary to restrict one's self to a similar environment or geographic area for ethnographic analogy. I would go further and say that it is not necessary to restrict one's self to the ethnographic record at all in either analogy or experimentation. This is a point made in the initial presentation of behavioral archaeology, but its implication in experimental research is rarely realized. Beyond this, it can be said that it is not even necessary to restrict one's self to *analogy* apart from the sharing of variables between past and present objects and behaviors.

Tringham's (1978) recent theoretical paper on experimentation calls for an increase in "low-level" testing or by-product testing. In addition to by-product testing, she distinguishes "behavioral experimentation," tests of the relationship of human operators to materials. Both kinds of experimentation can and have been undertaken using modern materials. I believe that in all cases of negative or inconclusive results in the experiments about to be discussed, the reader should hesitate to hold the modern materials at fault.

Rather than the materials, the structure of the experiment (time allotted, sample size, unskilled participants, etc.) can be held accountable and future experimental sessions with the same materials would yield more satisfactory results. The experiments to be discussed are three in number: Bonnichsen's bone fracturing experiments, the author's pottery fracturing experiments, and Hill's artistic style experiments. A fourth exemplary experiment is Baker's lithic extraction-reduction experiments using a concrete block and modern hammers. Since this research is discussed by him in this volume, only summary remarks will be made here.

Bonnichsen, who has also done pioneering work in lithic experimentation (see particularly 1977), conducted a series of glass fracture tests and eventually applied the techniques and results to a study of bone fracture (1973). He points out that glass is particularly well suited for the study of fracture propagation since it has a uniform structure: The molecules of the material have a random orientation in space and have the same properties in all directions (1973:13). He began by creating fracture in glass plates using a hammerstone. In reconstructing the plates he found that he had delivered the maximum load at what was the convergent point of numerous small triangular pieces.

The next step was to approximate a long bone by subjecting glass tubes of several sizes to the hammerstone. Some tubes were held by one end, others were supported between two wooden anvils. The fracture pattern was the same in both cases. Again, the triangular-shaped fracture occurred at the point of impact in the wall directly underneath the blow and was explainable in terms of transverse radial fracturing.

The final stage was to experimentally treat long bones in the same manner, supporting them in various ways and cracking them with a hammerstone. The fracturing pattern was the same on bone as it was on the glass tubes. Conical step fracturing and splintering were further noted on the bone.

Bonnichsen hypothesized that it would be possible to determine whether bone found in an archaeological context was fragmented as a result of human or carnivore behavior. The experimental approach was used in an attempt to develop a fracture model for explaining a particular kind of bone-fracture pattern. Bones chewed by animals were collected from a game farm for a comparative sample. It appeared to him that the two agents of breakage were distinctive.

Without treating other methods of human bone fracture or animal fracture he cannot say conclusively that humans always fracture bone in a way distinct from that of carnivores. However, the understanding he now has of bone fracture is due to the use of a modern material whose properties are well understood.

Several years ago the author conducted an experiment in ceramic fracture. The question to be answered was whether different causes of breakage left identifiable clues for the archaeologist. The constants in the experiment were the ceramic form and the speed of fall after release. The variables were distance from target point or *height of fall, point of impact* on the vessel, and *surface of impact*. During each stage of the experiment only one of these actually varied. It was thought that the breakage pattern, defined as the number of pieces and the extent of their spread, might vary for each combination of the three variables.

The vessels used were 6-in. flower pots with a 1-in. rim. Each vessel was painted a different color over four quadrants, on the base, and on the rim to facilitate recognition of the origin of each sherd in the scatter. Vessels were dropped from heights of 1, 3, or 5 feet either base first or side first onto a surface of either packed earth, planking or asphalt. On each surface was drawn a large circle divided into 23° segments. After a pot was dropped the maximum spread was measured and each sherd was mapped as to degree of the circle and distance from the center of the circle. The number of pieces was counted, the quadrant was noted, and in several instances the vessel was reconstructed.

The Mann Whitney U test was then used to assess the significance of the results. The null hypothesis was that the variables would among themselves show no significant differences in either the number of sherds produced or in the extent of their spread. For the variable, *height of fall*, the null hypothesis was rejected. Vessels dropped from 1 foot ($N = 12$) could be distinguished from vessels dropped from 3 feet ($N = 20$) by the number of pieces (.01 significance level). The spread of the sherds was only slightly less informative (.05 sl). There was insufficient data on the 5 foot drop. For the variable, *point of impact,* a pot dropped on its base could be distinguished from a pot dropped on its side by the number of sherds (.01 sl) and less securely so by spread of the sherds (.05 sl). It was not possible to test the significance of the results generated for the variable, *surface of impact*. However, *surface of impact* is apparently the most significant variable since no vessel broke when dropped on its base on wood from any height or on its side from 1 foot. Furthermore, no vessel broke at all on packed earth.

Other results were rather interesting as well. A point of impact was evident on all vessels dropped from higher than 1 foot. It is very similar to what has been noted for bone (Sadek-Kooros 1972), that is, crumbling of the material at that point rather than a clean break. Many of the pieces generated at that point will have a crumbled edge. Furthermore, exactly as Bonnichsen found in his glass experiment, the ceramic pieces closest to the point of impact were triangular in shape. Polygons were the next closest shape. Curved breaks, rather than strictly linear ones, occurred at a height of 3 feet or more. For vessels dropped on their sides, the quadrant of the vessel which met the surface first shattered into the most pieces. Finally, the majority of pieces (78%) came to rest inside-up.

Even though the experiment was not exhaustive, the data generated are still of use. The reader may think that since no prehistoric vessel would have the combined qualities of the vessel type employed here the results are not applicable to a prehistoric context. Quite the opposite conclusion is proposed. The main elements of this experiment, such as vessel attributes (i.e., strength), point of impact, and surface of impact attributes (i.e., compactness) can be transformed into a formula requiring only that the next investigator "load" the formula with her or his own data.

Although these data cannot be applied immediately to that from an excavated house floor, neither can the data from the flint experiments of Tringham et al. (1974) be used directly on obsidian or andesite. Altering the vessel type is the next step in this experiment. However, had an attempt been made to approximate or utilize some specific non-Western culture's pottery, the other variables would still have to be examined and material would still need to be altered in subsequent tests. There is now, however, an idea of the importance of the several different variables. The breakage pattern of this pottery type falling from this range of heights, on these two parts of this vessel type on this range of surface hardnesses has now been observed.

Bonnichsen's and the author's experiments represent by-product testing. Baker and Hill both undertook experimentation with modern materials which tested behavior. Baker (1974) devised his experiment to provide information about the prehistoric activities of lithic raw material procurement and chipped stone tool manufacture. The experiment, Baker thought, was important for demonstrating a way in which behavioral data can be obtained. Past activities were simulated under controlled conditions for the purpose of testing and refining hypotheses related to these activities.

The final experiment will be examined only briefly since it is the most visible of all those included here (Hill 1977, 1978) and since its rationale is more easily argued and accepted. Hill (1978:247), wishing to determine if it would be possible to distinguish individual prehistoric artisans, utilized modern behavior and materials to investigate the possibility. He purchased 75 ceramic vessels from a shop in Tijuana, Mexico, and had one painter paint four designs on a single vessel. Five painters then painted 15 pots each, attempting to make exact copies of the first vessel. The pots were subsequently broken. Cluster and stepwise discriminant analysis grouped together the sherds from vessels painted by an individual artist.

Suspecting that a painter's motor performance characteristics might change over time to the degree that analysis would indicate two different people, Hill used long-term change data from handwriting. His sample for this phase of his experiment came from letters written at 8- to 10-year intervals by four British novelists. Taking several measurements on the "th" combination, Hill subjected eight groups of measurements, early and late for each author, to cluster and step-wise discriminant analysis. These tests grouped the "th" cases by individual rather than time period.

The application of these experimental results and results of future experiments to prehistoric data is a simple transition:

> A great deal more research must be done to further test the results presented here (all of them). We especially need more experimentation in controlled situations in order to learn more about the nature of the variables that can be ascribed to subconscious (and conscious) individual variation. If it is possible to establish a reliable relationship between specific kinds of variations and individual motor-performance, we can then simply apply the results to prehistoric data without the need for testing the relationship itself with independent archaeological data [Hill 1978:255].

The objective of this set of experiments was, in Hill's own words, "to discover which *kinds* [original emphasis] of variables are best for distinguishing the works of individuals [1978:247]." Once again, modern materials are being utilized to examine variables, to understand relationships. As a result of this testing attitude, the experimental results are free of temporal or spatial constraints.

Conclusion

If experimentation is to develop into its potential as an analytical tool, then archaeologists must free themselves of the notions of adherence to the ethnographic record. Testing of relationships, as demonstrated here, can lead to the formulation of mathematical models. As Saraydar and Shimada (1973:350) have pointed out, when enough basic data have been generated, models can be built which simulate the functioning of specific aspects of the past.

Saraydar and Shimada outline the procedure for an input–output analysis of subsistence systems by computer. The process involves seven steps. The first two are the technology (defined as a given tool complex and the efficiency of that complex) and the efficiency of methods of manipulating the tool complex. In both of these steps completely modern materials (and, necessarily, modern behavior) can be used to generate data for several points along the continuum of tool complex efficiencies and tool use efficiencies. The data that result can be manipulated mathematically.

Another advantage in using modern materials in experimentation is that the properties of most industry-produced materials are known or knowable and thus offer a better chance at understanding the interaction that is observed. Many materials that were used by prehistoric peoples have been studied by modern sciences only insofar as there are currently economically viable reasons to do so. Our lack of relevant knowledge about many aspects of stone, both silicious and nonsilicious, reflects this situation. The known properties of clay are much more relevant to archaeologists because it is still manipulated in ways similar to the past. But it will be archaeologists who add to the information pool data on clay decay.

When testing is done to refute an hypothesis, the practice of limiting the experiment only to ethnographically valid materials becomes unwarranted. The use of modern materials, by themselves or in addition to ethnographic materials allows the investigator to simulate a wider range of properties and/ or more points in the range of one variable.

Furthermore, any proposed regularity between a by-product and human behavior must be tested with data from points all along the time line. We are looking for regularities which are free of time-space constraints but those must be constantly tested. Experiments utilizing prehistoric materials and offering the results as explanation must still be performed altering the materials. Given the limitations of time, and, more importantly, money for research, it is much more efficient to begin the search for those regularities in our own culture.

Last, and most importantly, these experimental results are important, in and of themselves, exclusive of any application to prehistoric data or problems. Archaeologists are slowly becoming aware that ours is a field which is distinctive from all others because we examine the relationship between objects (and materials) and their human manipulators. In the history of our discipline, this has meant the study of the prehistoric or even historic (provided it were distant enough) relationships. Undisturbed data from the past, however, are rapidly disappearing. While experimentation with and studies of modern objects and behaviors *should* be pursued for the benefit of studies based on data from the past, there is no need to abandon the discipline with the demise of the data base. Within the next several decades it is highly probable that there will be archaeologists who earn their living studying the *modern* relationship between humans and their objects who serve in the capacity of government policy advising, marketing, advertising, inventing, product development, and architectural consulting. Archaeologists validate their endeavors when necessary by claiming to be examining and unraveling the details of past human adaptations, problems and mistakes, knowledge which will benefit contemporary and future societies. May we not overlook the other ways we can continue to serve in that capacity.

Acknowledgments

I wish to thank Carol Spears and Tom Burke who read and commented on an earlier version of this paper.

17

A Simulative Experiment in Simple Product Manufacture

Charles M. Baker

Experimental archaeology is defined by Ascher (1961:793) as a "category of experiments [that] entails operations in which matter is shaped, or matter is shaped and used, in a manner simulative of the past." Such experiments are designed to test "beliefs about past cultural behavior." Recent experimental studies in archaeology have demonstrated their potential for deriving principles by which past human behavior may be illuminated. Although automobile junk yards (Ascher 1968b), residential garbage dumps (Rathje 1974), supermarkets (Salwen 1973), and libraries (Schiffer 1973a) perhaps provide atypical research laboratories, the behavioral activities responsible for their characteristics, when identified and explained, increase the degree to which archaeologists can make valid inferences regarding the nature of analogous material culture deposits in the archaeological record. In an effort to produce information that might be useful for understanding the behavioral correlates of past material assemblages, an experiment designed to simulate certain activities associated with simple product manufacture was performed.

Simple product manufacture is defined as a process by which a solid raw material is purposefully selected and altered through a reduction process to yield a finished product of desired form. In simple product manufacture, the basic properties of the raw material are not changed although the finished product is always smaller than the original raw material.

This process characterizes a type of prehistoric industrial activity well

247

MODERN MATERIAL CULTURE
The Archaeology of Us

known to most archaeologists, that of flaked stone implement manufacture. In addition, however, it characterizes activities such as shell bead manufacture, the production of ceremonial stylae, or the manufacture of wooden canoes. For this reason, a close examination of the general process of simple product manufacture potentially offers insight into the nature of many prehistoric manufacturing pursuits.

The Simulative Experiment

The experiment chosen to investigate simple product manufacture was structured to allow the observation of particular behavioral responses to a controlled work situation. Observations recorded pertained to raw material selection and reduction, fabrication implement use, product blank production and selection, blank shaping, and blank refinement to a finished product.

Participants chosen for the experiment included 10 male undergraduate students. The raw material provided for each was a standard 30-pound cement block. The set of fabrication implements made available included four steel hammers of differing weight in the proportion of 4:2:2:1. All hammers had blunt striking surfaces with the exception of one middle sized hammer which, in addition, had a pointed end. Using reduced portions of the cement block, each participant was instructed simply to produce to exact scale each of two geometric design models, a square and a triangle, using any of the hammers he desired. During the raw material reduction and design replica production processes, waste materials of various size and form were expected to result. The purpose of the experiment was to determine the ways in which the manufacturing activities were patterned and the degree to which the resulting products and waste materials reflected the behavioral responses observed.

In preparation for the experiment, each participant was presented an information sheet that generally described the events to follow. A cement block, the four hammers, and the geometric designs were placed nearby for reference. Each person was then allowed a 3-minute period to practice breaking up a piece of a cement block. This enabled the participants to acquaint themselves with the fracture characteristics of the material and also to evaluate the capabilities of each hammer. Following this procedure a second information sheet was provided that indicated the initial task would be to produce blanks of such size and form that would be suitable for further refinement. Instructions specified that blank shaping should not be a concern at this stage. During this initial process, hammer selection and use were noted and the hammer blow frequency for each implement used was recorded.

Also, the amount of time required was assessed. Following this activity, the produced blanks and the resulting waste materials were collected.

The next stage of the experiment began by assembling all blanks together for inspection. The participant was told to select only one blank for manufacturing the square and one other for the triangle. Following selection, the outline of each chosen blank was traced on paper for later comparison with the shapes of blanks that were not selected. Also, the weight of each was recorded for calculating manufacture waste weight proportions. A final instruction sheet was then provided indicating design replication requirements and also that a 5-minute limit would be imposed for the production of each item. The design models were provided for reference but only visual inspection of these was allowed.

As in the initial manufacturing stage, hammer selection and hammer blow frequencies were recorded during each period of design replication. These observations were noted separately for the first 2 minutes of the activity periods and for the remaining time used. Following the production of each design replica, the waste materials were collected. The experimental procedure was now completed.

Summary of Observations

It is reasonable to expect that the size of a fabrication implement employed in product manufacture will vary according to the methods and techniques followed for reducing the raw material being altered. It might also be anticipated that larger implements will be used for initial raw material reduction while smaller ones will be reserved for the final reduction stages. Observations made during the experiment indicated that while hammer selection and use were patterned in certain ways, these activities did not necessarily conform totally to the above expectations.

Selection of the largest and smallest hammers most clearly conformed to the anticipated behavior. The largest hammer was selected by nine of the participants for use during the initial reduction of the cement block. Only two persons selected the largest hammer for the initial reduction of the blanks, and no one selected this implement for the refinement of the design replicas. Alternatively, the smallest hammer was selected by only one person for use during the initial reduction of the block, while all participants used this hammer during the subsequent stages of manufacture. It was more difficult to see a pattern in the frequency with which the middle-sized hammers were selected. Although these hammers were chosen more often during the initial stages of design manufacture and less during the later stages, there was considerable variation in choice among the individuals. Certainly, a strong correlation between use of the middle-sized hammers and the intermediate stages of manufacture was not clearly evidenced.

Hammer blow frequencies for the different implements also varied in interesting ways. Overall, the largest hammer was the most infrequently used, followed by the blunt middle-sized hammer, the smallest hammer, and the pointed middle-sized hammer. During the initial reduction exercise, the largest hammer was usually used first for a limited number of blows, followed by extensive use of the pointed hammer and less frequent use of the blunt hammer. A similar pattern was observed for the initial blank reduction stage of the square manufacture except that the largest hammer was used less frequently and the blunt middle-sized hammer was used more frequently. For the latter stage of the square manufacture, the blunt hammer use frequency decreased while use of the smallest hammer tripled in frequency. For the initial stage of the triangle manufacture, the pointed hammer was used most frequently followed by the smallest hammer. The blunt middle-sized hammer was used least frequently. For the latter stage, the blunt middle-sized hammer was used most frequently, however, the smallest hammer was used almost as much. The pointed hammer was used the least.

These observations indicate that the selection and use frequency of different implements for different stages of raw material reduction vary in manners that do not neatly conform to an expected order. While it is acknowledged that the experimental situation was artificial and foreign to the participants, the implication is that implement size and raw material reduction stage do not necessarily correspond.

Based upon these findings, it is suggested that the size classification of manufacturing implements found in an archaeological context (e.g., hammerstones at a stone quarry or workshop site) will only generally reflect the production stage usage of these tools. At localities where the size distribution of manufacturing implements is extremely skewed, with either uniformly large or small tools predominantly represented, an inference regarding raw material reduction activities will probably be more sound than where a greater range in implement size is represented.

Observations pertaining to blank selection revealed that all participants chose blanks that, expectedly, were larger than the design models. For manufacturing both the square and the triangle, 6 persons selected blanks that were larger than the other blanks available for use. An opposite trend was actually expected. It was anticipated that blanks requiring minimal reduction would be chosen over those necessitating greater alteration. However, since all 10 participants had produced at least one other blank that was similar in shape to the square design but smaller, and the same situation held for 6 persons choosing triangle blanks, the factor of size would appear to have been a predominant consideration. This inference is further supported by the observation that only 3 persons chose blanks for manufacturing the triangle that were similar in shape to the triangle model.

The implication of these observations is that a least-effort principle related to anticipated work required for blank reduction does not necessarily affect blank selection. It may be that the larger blanks were chosen in anticipation of possible mishaps during the manufacturing exercise so that a suitable matrix might still be available should breaks occur. On the other hand, because four participants did make blank choices that conformed to the expectation, evaluation of the observations remains uncertain.

Another finding was that seven persons chose blanks for the square that were larger than the blanks they chose for the triangle. It is pointed out here that the square design model was 100 cm^2 in surface area while the triangle design model measured only 50 cm^2. These data suggest that the raw material matrix selected for manufacturing a product will be directly proportional to the anticipated size of the product when finished. The archaeological implication of this relationship should be relatively obvious. Simply, the proportion of manufacturing waste to the size of the blank selected is a function of the size of the products manufactured. Should values for either of these variables be known, it might be possible to predict values for the others.

In the present experiment, it was found that the waste weight proportion for the triangle was greater (72%) than for the square (66%), although the absolute weights were very similar (square waste weight: 1392 g; triangle waste weight: 1276 g). These data suggest that when information is available regarding the sizes of the products that were manufactured and/or the sizes of the raw material matrices chosen for reduction, waste occurrences at production localities measured by weight or volume might yield data bearing on site use intensity or duration. Clearly, a comparison of absolute waste weights or volumes within or among different production localities would probably not allow distinction of particular manufacturing activities.

A final set of findings to be discussed resulted from the analysis of waste materials produced during the manufacturing processes. The discussion will center on the overall counts of waste elements of varying size for the different reduction exercises. As noted, waste materials were collected following the block reduction as well as after completion of the design replicas. During the manufacture of the triangle replica, waste was collected twice, once after 2 minutes and again at the end. For the analysis, waste size categories were established, waste items were measured by template reference (measuring the greatest dimension of a waste element), and waste element frequencies for each category were obtained. Mean counts were then computed on the basis of all 10 participants (Table 17.1).

Frequency variation in the waste size classes indicates several interesting

Table 17.1

Frequencies and Percentages of Waste Elements in Different-Size Categories for the Various Stages of Product Manufacture

	Waste element size categories[a]				
Manufacture stage	1	2	3	4	5
Block reduction	84 (79%)	14 (13%)	3 (2%)	1 (2%)	2 (4%)
Square manufacture	33 (78%)	5 (9%)	1 (5%)	1 (3%)	1 (3%)
Triangle manufacture	42 (81%)	5 (9%)	2 (3%)	2 (3%)	1 (2%)
Triangle (Stage 1)	37 (78%)	5 (10%)	2 (4%)	2 (3%)	1 (2%)
Triangle (Stage 2)	17 (89%)	1 (6%)	1 (2%)	1 (3%)	0 —

[a] Size categories measured in centimeters: (1) 0.5–2.9 (2) 3.0–5.9. (3) 6.0–8.9. (4) 9.0–11.9. (5) 12.0+ .

patterns. First, it is readily seen that smaller waste materials were much more abundant as a result of initial block reduction. By percentage comparison, however, these elements occur in similar proportions for all stages of manufacture. This pattern does not hold true for the other waste element size categories. A comparison of waste materials resulting from the square and triangle manufacture indicates both a greater count and percentage of smaller waste elements for the triangle. While the differences are slight, this may suggest that increased numbers of small waste materials can be expected where item production requires greater reduction and refinement of a raw material. In the present experiment, the smaller size of the triangle and its more acute angles certainly required such treatment. A final observation pertains to the different stages of the triangle manufacture. Here it can be seen that waste element frequencies in all size categories are greater for the initial stage. Interestingly, however, the percentage of the smallest waste materials is greater for the latter stage where the manufacture of the product was near completion.

It is perhaps significant to find that the frequencies and percentages of waste materials in different size categories do not readily provide a basis for distinguishing among different stages of product manufacture. This would minimally indicate that simple correlation between waste element size frequency and stage of manufacture does not exist. Many production analyses (e.g., those concerned with flaked stone tool manufacture) focus on the sizes of the waste elements that occur at production localities. Similarly, in the present analysis, the three largest waste elements that resulted from initial block reduction and each stage of the triangle manufacture were selected and measured. The mean maximum dimension of these for each production stage were found to be 15.4, 9.7, and 8.5 cm, respectively. Thus, the trend of reduced waste element size for the progressive stages of manufacture is obvious. On the other hand, it takes little imagination to see that if overall mean sizes of waste elements for each manufacturing stage were computed, the initial stages would be characterized by lower mean size values. Accordingly, common characterization of manufacturing stages as primary or secondary based upon selected item measurement must be regarded somewhat tenuous.

One possible reliable measure of production stage as might be represented at a given locality, where overall waste material occurrences are considered, is the standard deviation of waste element frequencies for the different size categories. As an example, for the smallest waste size category in the present experiment, the standard deviations of waste element frequencies for the block reduction and the two stages of triangle manufacture were found to be 46, 16, and 9, respectively. Thus, while counts and percentages only minimally distinguish the various production stages, the standard deviations of waste frequencies indicate relatively significant variation.

It is readily conceded that in any similar analysis, the size of waste elements represents only one criterion that should be considered. Morphological variation in waste elements, for example, is often a key indication of activity stage differences within and among production localities. Indeed, in the present analysis the resemblance of waste materials to the original morphology of the cement blocks was taken into account and the frequencies of elements with angular shapes were greater for the initial reduction stage. Even here, however, the findings were not absolute indicating that any single measure of production stage variation is inadequate to support conclusive inference.

Discussion and Summary

The experiment discussed here was intended to provide insight into the relationships between production behavior and the materials that result from simple product manufacture. It is admitted that many limitations inhere in the design of the experimental procedures. Nevertheless, it is believed that useful information did result from the investigation.

Perhaps the most important general finding was that the relationships between behavior and its material consequences are exceedingly complex. Simple approaches to the study of material items, particularly the by-products of manufacture, do not appear to be adequate to yield supportable inferences regarding product manufacturing stages within and among archaeological localities. Also, simple classifications of items that vary in size and shape for the purpose of interassemblage comparison would appear to require considerable reevaluation. Further, simple quantitative comparisons of material types will not necessarily reflect specific differences in manufacturing stage. While firm conclusions concerning relationships among selected production variables are not possible at this time due to low sample size and other deficiencies in the experiment, several informal hypotheses having potential explanatory value were indicated.

This experiment, following Ascher (1961), is believed to demonstrate a useful method by which behavioral information can be obtained for the purpose of testing ideas concerning past human behavior. Minimally, as shown here, simulative experiments are excellent tests of preconceived notions that are often unfounded. Of course, the focus on experimental analogues is not a new innovation. In the late nineteenth century, for example, observations of the behavior of gun-flint manufacturers in Europe formed the basis for inferences concerning the activities of aboriginal stoneworkers (Evans 1872). On the other hand, the potential of similar investigations would seem to be largely disregarded. If inferences regarding past behavior made use of experiments in which presumed past activities were simulated under controlled conditions in order to test and refine notions pertaining to those activities, it would appear possible to gain additional support for the logic and validity of our conjecture. Accordingly, experimental archaeology is believed to provide an excellent opportunity to acquire data for explaining past behavior associated with archaeological phenomena.

Acknowledgments

A research assistantship granted by the Arkansas Archeological Survey provided partial support for this research while the author was enrolled in graduate school at the University of Arkansas. Also, at one time or another, various persons have provided comment on the study as well as editorial assistance on manuscript drafts. Foremost among these are Michael P. Hoffman, Stephen C. Saraydar, Michael B. Schiffer, and more recently, Richard A. Gould. Each contribution has been greatly appreciated.

18

Cumulative Graphs and Seriation

Daniel W. Ingersoll, Jr.

Perhaps the first use of the cumulative graph in archaeology was by Bordes and Bourgon (1951), who employed it to make typological and descriptive comparisons between two paleolithic industries. Previously, Bordes had constructed histograms for such comparisons. When Bordes first began using cumulative graphs, the trend lines were not superposed, but each line was shown on a separate graph. Artifacts were ordered along the horizontal axis in typological rather than chronological order. Later, Jelinek modified the layout of the cumulative graph to show temporal progression. If the "artifact types are placed in general order of chronological appearance, the temporal factor becomes significant in comparing samples, and an orderly progression of curves may be interpreted as a temporal progression [1962:243]." To construct the graphs, the chronological order must be known beforehand; then sites or strata may be "dealt with quickly by entering them on a cumulative graph based on this information [1962:243]." It is clear from Jelinek's article that for components to be orderd, the types must first be ordered chronologically by using stratigraphic or other data. Others since Bordes and Jelinek have also utilized the cumulative graph (Fitting 1968; Irwin and Wormington 1970; Tixier 1963).

Brose (1967) adapted the Jelinek graphic technique for ordering rifle cartridges, historical ceramics, pressed glass, and faunal remains from the nineteenth-century Custer Road Dump site in Michigan. The first graph Brose presented showed rifle cartridges according to their frequencies in

255

MODERN MATERIAL CULTURE
The Archaeology of Us

eight natural layers. Apparently, the cartridge types were arranged in order of appearance along the horizontal axis (left to right), because Brose discussed their independently known dates of onset of manufacture (1967:70). Two types, judging by Brose's discussion of dating, are reversed when the horizontal axis is read from left to right. These are the "Phoenix" and the "Tinned Case" cartridges as read on the graph. The former was made only in 1876, and the latter was made 1874–1885 (Brose 1967:70). An explanation for this inversion has not been found. Brose concluded that "all the changes of cartridge type frequency are seen to be highly correlated with the postulated level dates established independently from these dated cartridges [1967:72]."

In the cartridge graph, Brose possessed independent chronological data for the artifact types which he could use to construct his graphs. In the next two artifact categories presented, Brose attempted to derive chronological orders of ceramic and pressed glass types from the graphs themselves, employing the assumption that "where the order of appearance of artifact types is not independently certain, their arrangement on a cumulative graph into non-overlapping curves representing stratigraphic levels should produce horizontally the desired chronological sequence of popularity or use [1967:72]." With this assumption the technique clearly seems to deviate from the one Jelinek outlined. It may therefore be considered an experiment with a graphical technique.

The final type of graph employed by Brose illustrated five faunal types (1967:Figure 10), each given a trend line across a base line of stratigraphic levels (from levels 0–8). This graph was not employed for dating purposes; the component ordering on the horizontal axis, in this case by actual stratigraphic order, should already be correct.

In Brose's first and last cases, the chronological orders were not the object of investigation. In the cases concerning glass and ceramics, the graphic technique was intended to elicit an ordering of types. Brose felt that:

The chief value in this type of chronological study does not lie in a classification of the material culture of a late nineteenth century military post in the Great Lakes. Of course, that should be one result of this paper. The major value of this report, however, should be the establishment of a tightly defined chronological ordering of artifact types (such as historic ceramics and glass) which are generally present at all historic sites. It should be possible by frequency distribution studies of these artifact types to construct a cumulative graph for minimal vessels of each diagnostic type at any historic site in the Great Lakes area. By comparison of curves representing distinct components on a cumulative graph with those curves representing well-dated components (such as those described here) it should be possible to date the unknown component to within 3 years of its date of deposition. . . . Frequency distribution studies expressed as easily compared cumulative graphs can greatly increase the precision of such dating [1967:76].

With the "extremely good communications in the entire northeastern United States," the results "obtained from this location may apply over a rather extensive area [Brose 1967:72]."

According to Schuyler, one of the desirable objectives or goals in historic sites archaeology is to use a site as a test case for archaeological techniques, and he commends Brose for achieving this objective "by applying a cumulative graph technique originally developed by Jelinek for prehistoric sites. Not only are the results positive, but unlike Jelinek, the author is able to check his findings against historic data to explain the relative popularity of given types [1970:179]." In the cartridge example, independent data were employed to order the artifacts. In addition, stratigraphic order was known. The curves did not cross, and therefore Brose might argue that his variation on the Jelinek method works. On the assumption that the method did work, apparently, Brose used the graphs to order the ceramics and glass. If Brose's orders are correct, not only will we know more about ceramic history, but we also will have a method which could be used by all archaeologists who have well stratified multicomponent sites at hand. Was one test sufficient?

I decided to test Brose's ceramic data further. To do this, I devised two tests, one of which involved using the ceramic historical literature to independently date the ceramic types. The other involved quantifying a sample from a tightly dated site in Portsmouth, New Hampshire, called Puddle Dock, and preparing a cumulative trend line from the site to compare to Brose's Custer Road Dump site ceramics trend lines.

In the first test, I used documentary data to independently date the ceramics. Ceramic historians have produced a voluminous literature on eighteenth- and nineteenth-century ceramics. Most of this literature relates to fine arts objects of the sort rarely found by historic sites archaeologists, but there is still much valuable information that can be abstracted from this literature that concerns utilitarian wares. As part of the Puddle Dock research project, information relating to late eighteenth- and nineteenth-century ceramics was collected and synthesized. The kind of information available includes type names (emic), dates and location of manufacture, materials, technological process, etc. Examples of the kinds of sources which were employed are contained in Bemrose (1952), Godden (1963), and Spargo (1926). The synthesis of ceramic data will not be reproduced here but is located in Ingersoll (1971:176–213).

The next step was to relate Brose's type names to the forms described in the ceramic literature (Ingersoll 1971:225–227), and to correlate these with dates from the synthesis mentioned above. Then the ceramic types A–M from Brose's cumulative graph's horizontal axis (1967:Figure 7) (see Figure 18.1 this chapter) were organized according to earliest date of manufacture, as was the case with the cartridges. (The cutoff date for continuing types was set at 1895, the approximate end of deposition at the Custer Road Dump site.) This order can be read from earliest to latest, bottom to top, in Table 18.1, Column 1. If Brose's methods were performing as predicted, the order as derived from the ceramic historical literature should run as Brose's cumulative graph's horizontal axis: A,B.C, . . . , M (see Figure 18.1). As can be seen, the order based on the literature bears no meaningful relationship to Brose's: E,A.G.M, . . . , D (see Table 18.1, Column 2). The rankings were compared by means of a rank order correlation coefficient *(p)*. In this comparison, $p = .270$, which value falls far short of the 5% level of $\sim .620$ for $N = 11$.

It might be argued that the dates for the types are only approximate, but close inspection shows that adding or subtracting even a decade to the types furthest from "home" would not greatly reorganize the seriation based on the literature. It might also be argued that the use of a median date, rather than a beginning date, could correct the ordering difficulty, but such is not the case (see Table 18.1, Column 3). The rank order according to median or central date is changed little, with $p = .071$, which falls even further short of the 5% level of $\sim .620$ for $N = 11$. The orders by date (Table 18.1, Column 2) of first manufacture and by median date (Table 18.1, Column 3) differ little from each other. In this rank comparison, $p = .899$, which exceeds the 1% level of $\sim .785$ for $N = 11$. Without shifting to an etic typology (it is possible to come up with much finer subdivisions of each of the types A–M), the

Table 18.1

Order by cumulative graph (Brose: 1967; Figure 7) (1)	Order by date of first manufacture (Ingersoll: 1971:247) (2)	Order by median date (3)
A. Brown transfer print	E. (1863–1895)	E. (1879)
B. Red or green transfer print	A. (1835–1895)	G. (1863)
C. White, clear glaze, repoussé	G. (1830–1895)	M. (1863)
D. Oriental	M. (1830–1895)	F. (1863)
E. Decalcomania	F. (1830–1895)	A. (1865)
F. Underglaze painted	B. (1825–1895)	B. (1860)
G. Rockingham or Bennington	L. (1800–1850)	J. (1842)
H. Blue transfer print	J. (1788–1895)	K. (1835)
L. Spatterware and banded ware	K. (1774–1895)	L. (1825)
K. Feather-edge	H. (1755–1895)	H. (1825)
J. Raised glaze	D. (1700–1895)	D. (1798)
M. Common yellow	C. (range unknown)	C. (range unknown)
Other	Other (?)	Other (?)

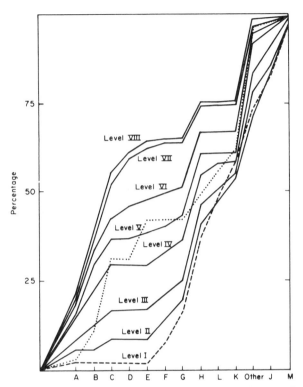

Figure 18.1 *Horizontal axis = Ceramic types A-M, Custer Road Dump Site and Puddle Dock. Vertical axis = Cumulated frequencies of ceramic types. Trend lines = Levels I-VII, Custer Road Dump Site, natural strata, 1876-1895. Superimposed trend line (dotted line) = Puddle Dock, Layer II, 1899-1900. (Redrawn from Brose 1967: Figure 7.)*

Brose order does not seem to accomplish its aim: to produce a correct chronological order of types.

It could be supposed that even if the graphical form did not produce a correct order of types, perhaps it could give a chronological position to an unknown component. In the second test, a "known" component was treated as a "postulated unknown." The component (layer 11, square 1, cut 1) from Puddle Dock was dated by several means independent of the ceramics (oral tradition, newspaper archives, and actual bits of newspaper and playbills and pollen from layer 11) and a deposition period from summer 1899 to early spring 1900 was determined (Ingersoll 1971:36-51, 237). The ceramics were quantified as closely as possible to Brose's scheme. This meant leaving out all undecorated vessels as well as some decorated vessels which Custer Road Dump produced but which were not employed for analysis (see Brose

1967:Table IV), or which Puddle Dock produced but which were not present at Custer Road (not very many). The comparable Puddle Dock sample was set at 100% and then entered on Brose's Figure 7 as an additional or super-imposed trend line. This line can be found in Figure 18.1 in this chapter. It can be seen that this additional line falls generally in the center of the lines for Levels I-VIII, and crosses over several of them.

If the graph were employed as a dating device for an unknown, the unknown here would have been dated to about 1885, approximately mid-way between the date span for Levels I-VIII (1876-1895) at the Custer Road Dump site. This is simply an estimate, since the picture is complicated by cross-over. The "postulated unknown," however, dates to 1899-1900. The graph should have placed the new trend line above the Level VIII line, and clear of it and the others. It is apparent that the graph did not correctly place the postulated unknown. How might this be explained?

Could Puddle Dock be so far removed in space from the Custer Road Dump site, that the graph technique would not work? Brose pointed to the "extremely good communications in the entire northeastern United States," as quoted earlier. It would be hard to believe that ceramics from English or American manufacturing centers would arrive at Custer Road more than a few months later than Portsmouth, N.H. If anything, with Portsmouth as an Atlantic seaport, English ceramics would arrive sooner, which would cause the Puddle Dock site to appear even more "recent" in a comparison to Custer Road. This was not the case: Puddle Dock actually appeared to be older on the graph. Slow communication does not seem to explain the shape of the trend line. Could the Puddle Dock or Custer Road excavation units have been misdated? This seems to be highly unlikely, since in both cases there is much internally consistent evidence apart from the ceramics to sup-port the layer or level dates.

There is the possibility of problems caused by different observers apply-ing typological labels; all that can be said here is that every effort was made by the author to use the same criteria as employed in the Brose classification. I feel that typological assessments cannot account for the ordering anomaly.

Consideration will now be given to the graphical technique itself. A number of workers have pointed to difficulties with the graphical technique. Both Schuyler (1970:180) and Fontana (1968:126) have expressed the reaction that the cumulative graphs are difficult to interpret, and Schuyler feels that Ford's battleship-shaped curves are superior "disregarding whatever faults the assumptions underlying the system contain [1970:190]." For example, when cumulative graphs are used to compare artifact frequen-cies, it is a chore to isolate the frequency of a single type. This can only be done by finding the bracketing cumulated frequencies for the type and then taking their difference. This is a time-consuming operation. There are other drawbacks involved in reading the cumulative graphs (Ingersoll 1971:219-220), but of course these of themselves are not related to the questions here. However, while pondering the difficulties of estimating frequency changes from angle changes between 0 and 90° on cumulative graphs at each data entry point, it occurred to me to conduct some simulation experiments with imaginary samples. One of the results discovered during experimental manipulation was that for a cumulative graph to continue to maintain separate and continuing trend lines, and thereby define a chronological position for the artifact types entered, the first type entered on the left of the horizontal axis would eventually have to approach 100% and 90°, with the subsequent types approaching 0%. You can do this for yourself by progressively adding trend lines to any prior trend line. You can also reverse the process. From this simple simulation it is possible to see that the cumulative graph cannot portray the kind of data seen in a typical lenticular or battleship-shaped curve as used by Ford and others, without causing lines to crosscut each other. That is, a type may increase or decrease but not increase from zero (reach a peak) and then decrease in popularity to zero, without having the lines cross on the cumulative graph. If cumulative graphs are to be used for this kind of data, new assumptions will have to be made concerning notions of popularity of artifacts. Thus, without using any archaeological data it is possible to show that this particular graphical technique is not able to do what Brose wants it to do and illustrate artifact frequency changes according to the view that artifacts or attributes appear, reach a popularity peak, and then fade from use. Ford's battleship-shaped curves would probably be somewhat better, but as McNutt (1973:47-48) has shown with simulations, there are also serious problems involved with this graph technique.

This discussion has related mainly to the use of cumulative graphs to generate or represent chronological orders. Can cumulative graphs be used for other purposes with artifacts such as comparing assemblages as Bordes (1969), Irwin and Wormington (1970), and Fitting (1968) have done? Could the ceramics graph employed by Brose be used as another kind of representation? Several authors expressed strong reservations. Kerrich and Clarke (1967) have discussed five areas where there may be dangers: sample errors, percentage errors, ordering errors, typological errors, and perceptive errors. To a certain extent these errors can appear in any situation involving quantification, qualitifaction, and manipulation. One of these categories, ordering errors, which is particularly relevant to cumulative graphs, will be discussed here.

Kerrich and Clarke (1967:60-66) demonstrated with simulated data how ordering errors may occur. Since the arrangement of artifacts on the horizontal axis is arbitrary, there are many possible arrangements *(n!)*. Different orders can produce many different shaped trend lines; the shape of the trend lines can influence what interpretation may be drawn. The question is, which of the n! orders should be selected? There is no logical relationship between the artifacts—they do not grade one into another—so how will the selection be made? In Brose's case, how is one out of 13! orders located? Some orders may produce crossing lines while others do not. If all graphs with crossing lines are eliminated, how is a selection to be made from those left? What do the different shapes mean? Because these shapes seem difficult to interpret, there may be the temptation to apply statistical methods to help resolve the chaos. Such application would lead to further complications, since the use of the graph in this way is questionable.

The reason cumulative graphs are not trustworthy in the kinds of situations described, as Thomas (1971:207) has pointed out, is that these cumulative curves have treated nominal data as if it were ordinal. Cumulative graphs must employ ordinal data if they are to work properly. In a cumulative graph, one data point entry influences the position that all subsequent data points will occupy. This makes sense if test scores, wages, or other scaled data are used, but not if the data points represent arbitrarily related frequencies. The problem caused by employing nominal data here as if it were ordinal is like the old problem of trying to add apples and oranges. You can do it, but the results are not very useful.

All this does not mean that cumulative graphs do not have a place in archaeology. They are helpful when it is necessary to show how many cases are above or below a certain value. A recent study by Brose (1975) has employed cumulative graphs to illustrate the relationships between flake-wear striation, flake rejection, and the passage of time. Although Brose did not follow the convention of placing the frequencies or percentages along the vertical axis (Blalock 1960:42-43), the graph does not employ ordinal data (time) along the other axis, and the comparisons are assisted by locating how many cases occur below a certain value, something which frequency polygons do not readily show. Certainly, there are many other instances in which archaeologists could use this cumulative graph technique as a data presentation device. The important thing is to make sure that requirements for their appropriate use be met, and this can be done by checking with standard statistical references.

Before going on, I would like to make several comments concerning David Brose's work which I employed in the first section of this paper. Brose felt that the greatest contribution his Custer Road Dump Site report might make would be the chronological ordering of historic ceramics found in many parts of the world. The results of the present study indicate that that order was not generated. Did Brose's report fail according to his own standard of judgment which ranked chronology at the top? I feel that the site report is one of the best available to historical archaeologists. For example, the interpretations of the fauna and of the vessel forms and the interrelationships of the two categories are very imaginative, although these interrelationships might be described as synchronic ones. And as far as ceramics are concerned, Brose gives sufficient data that others may rework them for comparative purposes, as was the case here. All in all, I regard the report as excellent.

Conclusions

Cumulative graphs have been examined and have been found wanting in regards to several functions expected of them by archaeologists. It is concluded that cumulative graphs are not appropriate for assemblage or artifact comparisons, since to date there is no way to determine how to order the horizontal axis on which types, etc. are represented. With frequency seriation, the additional problem of graphical inability to represent rising and falling frequencies in one type without line crossing arises. It is recommended that cumulative graphs only be used where data requirements as described in statistical references can be met. As far as artifact or assemblage comparisons or frequency seriations are concerned, it is suggested that all previous interpretations and explanations which involved cumulative graphs as devices to represent or manipulate data be reconsidered (for an example of a reconsideration, see Thomas 1971).

In this paper two major kinds of approaches to experimentation have been employed to examine cumulative graphs: One approach involved simulation, and the other involved "real" data. Kerrich and Clarke showed with simulated data that horizontal axis ordering presented problems (1967:60-66), and Ingersoll showed that the graphs could not represent increasing and decreasing frequencies without noise (1971:224). In two experiments employing "real" data (Ingersoll 1971 and this chapter), cumulative graphs did not succeed in accurately chronologically ordering ceramic types. In this case, both simulations and real data experiments confirmed each other. With simulations, variables are easily manipulated, data are easily restructured, no excavations are required, and costs are low. There is, however, the problem of credibility, for many archaeologists may feel that simulations do not relate to real world problems. In this sense, real data experiments may be more effective, but much more time and energy is required. In another sense, some research problems may be very difficult to assess without real data experimentation, since there may be many "invisible" or unknown variables operating which are not located or incorporated in a simulation study. Nevertheless, it is hoped that this study which has employed both simulation and real data studies will help to illustrate the effectiveness of simulation as an approach to experiment and evaluation. Simulation studies ought to be devised to evaluate all qualitative and quantitative techniques in use by archaeologists now. Even more importantly, such studies should be devised to evaluate the assumptions which are made prior to application of manipulative techniques, so their power may be explored.

Further Implications

Turning more generally now to the topic of assemblage or artifact comparison and chronology, there are problems since two popular graphical techniques which have been used for assemblage or artifact comparison and frequency seriation, battleship-shaped curves and cumulative graphs, have received serious criticism concerning their representational appropriateness. If these two graphical techniques are not appropriate for their desired uses, what others should be substituted? In reassessing Irwin and Wormington (1970), Thomas suggested that they "may have been misled by their cumulative measures of the Agate Basin complex [1971:208]." Thomas substituted Q-mode phenograms generated by a computer in his re-representation of the Agate Basin complex data.

McNutt (1973:60), in his study of frequency seriation argued that the computer applications employed the same or similar assumptions as the simpler battleship-shaped curve graphical technique, and thus could share the same faults. On the whole, McNutt is pessimistic about the underlying assumptions made concerning frequency seriation and the battleship-shaped curves. The only suggestions McNutt offered were that if collections could be assigned to classes and subclasses carefully, and if these could be dated independently, "it may well be possible to (a) deduce the dynamics of ceramic change mathematically, although not by inspection, and (b) isolate gross difficulties in typology [1973:60]." He added that this may have been what Phillips, Ford, and Griffin (1951) did, "by inserting stratigraphic data into seriation diagrams and by 'creating' types so they would reflect 'historical reality' [1973:60]."

Both Thomas and McNutt have looked toward mathematics or computers for possible answers, but there are still several kinds of problems. The first problem is that the manipulations performed by statistical tests and computers may not be understood by the archaeologist employing them. It is very easy and tempting these days to solve problems with canned programs. The results impress many as being scientific, and the mystique of math or statistics can distract many from their primary responsibility of examining underlying assumptions made before any manipulative devices are applied.

If the underlying assumptions have been carefully evaluated, then, the next step is to make sure the statistical and computer operations are understood. This is not impossible although it may be difficult. If the statistical-computer tools which have been substituted for earlier simpler but unsatisfactory techniques are not understood, the chances that misapplications would be discovered would seem to be reduced, especially in this age of rapidly accelerating computer use. Given undetected computer misapplications, there is the danger of a following flood of faulty secondary, tertiary, etc., manipulations, with subsequent inference, interpretation, and synthesis built upon them. In this respect, the tremendous increase in computer applications in archaeology is somewhat alarming, not because the tools are difficult or complicated, but because the very assumptions archaeologists have made prior to application have not been properly identified or evaluated.

A second problem is that, unfortunately, archaeologists often do not consciously recognize many of their assumptions, and if they do recognize them, they may be unwilling to evaluate them. Where assumptions have been drawn into the field of consciousness, there are several possibilities. Logic and simulation may be employed to evaluate assumptions. McNutt's study (1973) is a good example of logic and simulation applied to several levels of assumptions: McNutt deals not only with assumptions concerning a graphical technique, but also with assumptions concerning the possibility of frequency seriation itself. Real data experiments also can contribute.

All levels of assumptions are worth investigating, if we believe as social scientists we should always be attempting to discover and describe our assumptions and then prove or falsify them, but the earlier in a hierarchy of assumptions proof or falsehood can be suggested or established, the more sure we can be of what we are doing. In any case, we do not want to found cultural and processual explanation on unsurveyed ground, even if it means living with a good deal of pessimism while evaluation is going on.

A third problem involves becoming aware of our unconscious biases and assumptions as social scientists. As anthropologists, we can press to advantage our cross-cultural knowledge and approaches, to help isolate some of these biases and assumptions. Anthropologists have barely touched the topic of "own" culture, that is, they have looked outward, but have not carefully looked inward. Looking inward with the cross-cultural method as a tool can help in two ways. First, we can improve our general understanding of our own culture, its symbols, motive forces, and central concepts. Second, we can attempt to understand our own peculiar roles as social scientists. With a better understanding of what moves us, we should be able to ask better questions of the data. Such work is difficult to do, and there has not been much done in archaeology, but one contribution from social anthropology, Needham's *Belief, Language, and Experience* (1972) will serve as an illustration.

In that volume, Needham evaluates the meaning of "belief" in our culture and in anthropology. One of Needham's major points is that, "the first task of social anthropology is precisely this: the undermining of categories throughout the entire range of cultural varieties in the conception of human experience (1972:302)." As archaeologists who are first anthropologists, this is also our responsibility. This sounds like a destructive process, but it is not in the long run. In the case of the word "belief," we learn from Needham that the word cannot be glossed simply, that the word cannot be used uncritically by the analyst who is interpreting another culture. But, the reader of Needham's book comes away with a clearer idea of what our culture is like in respect to a category ("belief") which is highly loaded indeed, and with a new awareness for what meaning may or may not be located in another culture's symbols. The analyst—the social scientist—has profited by the "undermining." Social anthropologists hopefully will continue following Needham's model with "belief" to examine other central Western concepts such as love, conscience, knowledge, reason, and truth. Archaeologists can profit by keeping up with this literature, but in addition, they might actively contribute in areas in which social anthropologists have exhibited little interest. The topic of this paper, cumulative graphs, suggests one such area: time. Why are Westerners so enthralled by time, the future, change, and process? What does time mean to us that we devote so much effort to marking its passage? Why is it so important to know how old something is? What other questions should we ask besides how old something is? We can ask ourselves such questions as ethnoarchaeologists, as archaeologists conducting living archaeology, as ethnographers, and as informants in our own culture. The answers can help us to discover assumptions that form the ground of our social science.

Acknowledgments

I would like to thank the National Science Foundation, Strawbery Banke, Inc., and the Peabody Museum of Cambridge, Massachusetts, for generous support of the Puddle Dock research project. University of Massachusetts students Catherine Flataker, Petra Drewski, and Brona Simon assisted in experimenting with graphical simulation models. James Mielke prepared Figure 18.1 redrawn from Brose (1967). Permission to redraw Figure 18.1 was kindly granted by Professor Brose and the Michigan Archaeological Society. Thanks are due to the Division of Social Science, St. Mary's College of Maryland, which helped to prepare this chapter, and to Betty Knight who typed it.

TRADITIONAL TECHNOLOGIES
IN THE PRESENT

The most long-standing research orientation of ethnoarchaeology is the investigation of ancient technologies, such as chipped-stone tool manufacture and use, that survived into the present in a few isolated places. Such studies have always had a close link with the archaeology of prehistoric sites where often the remains of similar technologies are found. Opportunities for direct observation of certain manufacturing traditions have diminished in recent years, with the rapid changes in material culture that societies undergo as they become incorporated into the world economic system. Nevertheless, the possibility of investigating surviving technologies is far greater than many would suppose. Traditional crafts sometimes still flourish, both to fulfill domestic needs as well as to supply items for use as status symbols in the more fully industrialized nations. Although two of our three chapters treat traditional technologies in traditional societies, the same kind of research could just as easily have been carried out on Ozark basketmakers, builders of log cabins in Alaska, or urban potters who use nonindustrial methods. What these studies have in common is a focus on the production and sometimes use of handmade craft items; although important, the societal context in which these technologies are found plays a secondary role.

Richard A. Gould shows that the Brandon gunflint industry, long studied by archaeologists, can still yield interesting information and can contribute to the formulation of general principles. This stimulating piece of research alerts us to a poorly studied aspect of technology, the character of a

267

MODERN MATERIAL CULTURE
The Archaeology of Us

dying industry. Gould presents a lively discussion of the last Brandon knapper and his manufacturing techniques. On the basis of historical accounts and his own quantitative observations, Gould shows that as the industry underwent the transition from producing utilitarian items in times of war to supplying the smaller hobbyist market today, it also became more standardized and conservative. Gould generalizes these findings into a law-like hypothesis concerning "archaisms." When comparative studies are carried out, as Gould suggests, they may lead to the recognition of widespread regularities in technologies as their end draws near.

In the next chapter Thomas R. Hester and the late Robert F. Heizer describe an alabaster workshop at the upper Egyptian village of Sheik Abd el Gurna. There craftsmen toil to shape chunks of imported alabaster into delicate vases for sale to tourists. The authors explore the connections between this modern industry and those reaching back into Egyptian antiquity, but the results are equivocal. In a sense, the end seems near for this traditional craft, as mechanization reduces the role of skilled craftspeople in the production process.

It is perhaps fitting that the concluding chapter in this book, by J. Desmond Clark and Hiro Kurashina, should concern the manufacture and use of chipped stone tools. Their study is based on fieldwork carried out at the homestead of a Chawa tanner, located in a village on the Southeast Plateau of Ethiopia. The tanner is a specialist, engaged in tanning hides for farmers and herders. Of particular interest to the archaeologist is that the hides are dressed with retouched obsidian flakes. Clark and Kurashina detail the processes of tool manufacture, use, and discard. They are able to show, for example, that drastic changes in scraper morphology accompany the retouch process, and from this they draw clear lessons for archaeological typology. The authors' microwear study takes on special significance because the scrapers were used in a single task by a skilled worker under realistic conditions. Such good controls are difficult to achieve in experimental situations. Another noteworthy finding pertains to refuse disposal. Clark and Kurashina show that all of the exhausted scrapers as well as the bulk of the debitage and retouch debris come to rest archaeologically as secondary refuse. The deposits thus formed might be easily mistaken for work areas; the latter, however, would in fact be devoid of obvious archaeological signatures.

The studies in this part call attention to the vast potential that traditional crafts, practiced in distant societies or in our own backyards, offer ethnoarchaeology. In the future we can expect that ethnoarchaeologists in greater numbers will exploit the details of craft production and use for testing general principles of human behavior.

M.B.S.

19

Brandon Revisited:
A New Look at an Old Technology

Richard A. Gould

The gunflint manufacturing center of Brandon, in Suffolk, England, has attracted the attention of archaeologists since the 1870s (Skertchly 1879), and more recent studies (Clarke 1935; Knowles and Barnes 1937; Oakley 1967:25–27) have described the technology of Brandon gunflint making in detail. Homogeneous, black East Anglia flint has been used in tool-making since Paleolithic times. Early studies by Skertchly proposed a continuous evolutionary sequence of technological development from discoidal neolithic scrapers to historic gunflints and strike-a-lights, followed by anthropometric studies in 1879–1880 on the physical and racial characteristics of the modern residents of this area of Suffolk. As might be expected, the results of this latter survey were inconclusive, although certain Welsh characteristics were noted (Clarke 1935:42)! Attempts to support or disprove continuities between prehistoric and historic toolmakers in Suffolk provided the impetus for studies from the 1870s to 1935. Subsequent observations from a more purely technological point of view followed these, and today we can look back over a hundred years of detailed, albeit intermittent, observations of the Brandon gunflint making industry.

Historic documentation in such detail over such a long period is uncommon for any technology, especially one involving stone tools. Once aware of the literature on this subject, I thought it would be appropriate to visit Brandon and attempt to locate any remaining flintknappers who might still be producing gunflints. Oakley's more recent account suggested that such work

269

MODERN MATERIAL CULTURE
The Archaeology of Us

might still be going on. In particular, this was an opportunity to see what, if any, changes had taken place in the industry since the last detailed descriptions of it in the 1930s. With this question in mind, I traveled to Brandon in February 1978 and eventually met Mr. Fred Avery, the last gunflint maker at Brandon.

There are estimates that 200 flintworkers were employed at Brandon during the Napoleonic Wars (Clarke, 1935: 51), which was probably the all-time peak of production there, but by 1837 the number of flintworkers had declined to around 70-80, to revive briefly in 1846 to around 100 flintworkers. Following this minor resurgence, decline has continued to the present day (56 employed in 1868, 22 employed in 1907, and 7 in 1924). These figures include both the actual flintworkers and miners who quarried flint at neighboring localities like Thetford and Lingheath. As Clarke commented:

> A study of the numbers employed in the flint industry at Brandon is of some interest as a register of the vicissitudes of war and peace and the march of invention during the last century [1935:51].

With this point in mind, one can ask: What is Mr. Avery's role as the last Brandon flintworker in relation to the demand structure for gunflints today? This study represents a preliminary attempt to answer this question by examining Mr. Avery's technological behavior in relation to the market he produces for and the distribution of the items he produces. The technological aspects of gunflint making are relevant here only as they relate to wider questions having to do with general relationships between materials and human behavior.

Some scholars have questioned my interest in the Brandon flint-knappers, arguing that, because of the extensive literature on this topic, we already know all we need to about the subject. I was at pains to explain that it was precisely the detail and duration of this literature and the presence of an active flintknapper in Brandon today that provided an opportunity to discover and posit general relationships between materials and human behavior. Certainly one could view this as an arcane subject for research, since gunflint manufacture has always been a minor industry in the world and since it has little, if anything, to do directly with the production of ancient types of stone tools that might be of interest to the archaeologist. What, indeed, could we hope to learn from Mr. Avery that we did not already know?

Brandon: The Setting

The town of Brandon, while not a cosmopolitan center, is hardly the sort of isolated setting in which one might expect to find traditional crafts being maintained. It is readily accessible from London, Peterborough, Norwich, and other major centers by road and rail, and it has several large military air bases located nearby. Nor is Brandon a tourist center of any kind, since it has relatively few historic or architectural monuments. In short, Brandon is a medium-sized residential and light-industrial center like many others in East Anglia, with the same general degree of involvement in modern British society.

Yet residues of the old flintknapping industry are visibly present in many parts of the town. Although walls constructed of flint nodules are a common feature in many parts of East Anglia, in Brandon there is an unusually large number of polyhedral flint cores which have been cemented into walls with their striking platforms facing outward. Sometimes one sees entire walls constructed this way, resulting in a smooth exterior wall facing of much greater regularity than usual with flint walls. According to the publican at "The Flint Knappers," a licensed hotel in the center of Brandon, many of the buildings in town were constructed of discarded cores derived from refuse heaps where flintknapping was done. One also sees walls made of dressed blocks of flint laid in regular courses like bricks in many places in Brandon. Clarke (1935:56) mentions that a large industry in building flints had grown up in Brandon by 1904, and Mr. Avery's primary occupation today is as a bricklayer and sometime producer and layer of flint wall blocks.

So, aside from a pub called "The Flint Knappers" and the extensive use of trimmed flint cores and blocks in wall construction, there is little to distinguish Brandon from other East Anglia towns of comparable size, at least to the casual observer. Many of the local people I spoke with in Brandon and nearby areas were unaware that there had ever been a flourishing flintknapping industry there, or else they knew very little about it.

Fieldwork in Brandon

Although the reader may have noticed that a certain amount of interviewing was done in pubs, most of this study was done in the small workshop behind Mr. Avery's home. Mr. Avery demonstrated his manufacturing techniques to me, allowing me to ask questions and photograph as he worked. On later visits I learned how to produce acceptable gunflints using the same techniques, although I never attained the speed of production shown by Mr. Avery. My earlier training and practice in stone toolmaking was invaluable, both for establishing rapport with Mr. Avery and also in acquiring a firsthand understanding of the technical problems of gunflint manufacture. Mr. Avery spoke readily about his experiences as a gunflint maker in Brandon as he worked, and these "rock-busting" sessions were the focal point for finding out about present-day activities connected with this craft.

The approach used here was informal and nondirective, and the reader is cautioned to regard this study as nothing more than a preliminary view of the subject. It does not presume to be a rigorous or systematic attempt to study Brandon flintknapping. Rather, it is intended to alert scholars to the possibilities of applying a modern material-culture approach to traditional kinds of technological behavior.

Flint Procurement

Mr. Avery complained that the flint available today is inferior in flaking properties to what was obtained and used formerly by Brandon flint-knappers. The best material was opaque black flint with virtually no flaws and with a fine, smooth texture that was superior to the somewhat more coarse textured flint he was using for most of his work. The finer material used by the old Brandon knappers he referred to as "floorstone" (see also Clarke, 1935:43), which he said was obtained from greater depths in the local chalk deposits than is generally possible today. He had a large piece of the fine material which had been given to him several years before, and he proceeded to demonstrate his argument by producing a core and gunflints from it, providing a ready contrast with the more commonly available flint in the area today. At the present time, Mr. Avery obtains his supplies of flint from a chalk quarry near Thetford, not far from Brandon, where the quarrymen, who are friends of his, set aside any nodules of flint they find for Mr. Avery to collect periodically in his station wagon. Since the Thetford chalk quarries are not as deep as the old flint mines of Lingheath and other localities, they do not reach the "floorstone" material. Although less smooth-textured than "floorstone" flint, Mr. Avery says the Thetford chalk quarry flint produces functional gunflints which can be shaped about as rapidly and accurately as the best "floorstone." His complaints about Thetford flint versus "floorstone" were based mainly upon esthetic considerations of finish and neatness of appearance, as well as a suspicion that the Thetford flint is softer than the "floorstone" and wears down more quickly in the flintlock.

Of course, it can also be argued that without other flintworkers and miners to help him, Mr. Avery is compelled by circumstances to use inferior flint and that his qualified acceptance of this material for gunflint making is only an effort by him to rationalize by making virtue of necessity. It would be useful to carry out some behavioral[1] experiments in core-reduction to see to what extent the production of usable gunflints vis-á-vis the weight of the core varies with each of these raw materials as well as by-product experiments to determine what, if any differences there may be in the use-lives of gunflints of

---

[1] For a discussion of behavioral versus by-product experiments in archaeology, the reader is urged to consult Tringham (1978).

these two grades of raw material. It was beyond the scope of this preliminary study to carry out experiments of these kinds, although as the study progressed various possible experiments aimed at quantifying important aspects of the core reduction and flakemaking process began to emerge. Experiments of this kind could be essential in assessing the utilitarian aspects of this technology. In other words, there is still important work to be done in studying the technology of gunflint making at Brandon.

Manufacture

The first step in the core reduction process involved drying, essential in the damp East Anglia climate. In this case, Mr. Avery kept the flint nodules he planned to work inside his shed, where a small electric heater aided this process (instead of the large fire mentioned by Clarke [1935:49]). Mr. Avery said it was impossible to work the flint when it was wet, but he could not be more specific about why. (Personal experience suggests that slippage and loss of control occur when one attempts to flake wet flint, but there may be more to it than this.) The dried nodules were then "quartered"—a term used by Mr. Avery and appearing in the literature on Brandon flintknapping to describe the use of a short-handled, flat-faced steel hammer weighing about approximately 2 kg (4.4 pounds) to break open large nodules into smaller and more manageable pieces. This was done by bringing the hammer down rather gently on the center of the flattened side of the nodule, causing cone-splitting or a break along an existing fracture line and producing several thick chunks with more or less 90° edges, each of which then served as a core.

During the course of my observations I saw Mr. Avery "quarter" several nodules of Thetford flint as well as the large nodule of "floorstone" which he had been saving (Figure 19.1). This latter piece weighed about 20 kg (44 pounds) before "quartering." I observed six "quartering" operations, five with Thetford flint and one with "floorstone," and all were successful in that they produced usable core pieces and did not shatter, as Clarke (1935:49) indicates sometimes happened. In all "quartering" operations, Mr. Avery worked in a seated position, resting the nodule on one leg on top of a thick cloth pad strapped to his thigh to cushion and steady the work.

Each chunk was then further reduced by means of direct percussion with a pointed-face soft steel hammer weighing about .68 kg (1.5 pounds). Working around the perimeter of a single striking platform, each chunk soon became a regular polyhedral core (Figure 19.2) as elongated, parallel-sided flakes up to 13.9 cm (5.5 in.) long were removed in sequence. Some wastage occurred in the initial row of flakes, since many of these contained cortex material. Approximately equal numbers of single- and double-ridged

Figure 19.1. *Mr. Avery preparing to "quarter" a piece of floorstone.*

flakes were produced as flake removal proceeded around and around the core until the flakes averaged less than 1.8 cm wide, whereupon the core was abandoned. It would have been possible to produce additional flakes from these cores, but, as Mr. Avery pointed out, a gunflint below this minimum width would not fit into the slotted fitting of any flintlock rifle, pistol, or strike-a-light. At this stage in the work, Mr. Avery tossed all usable flakes into one bucket and all rejected flakes and exhausted cores into another.

The next step involved use of a short-handled steel hammer with a broad, flat blade about .5 cm thick in conjunction with an upright anvil constructed of a flat bar of steel about .5 cm thick and 3 cm wide set into the

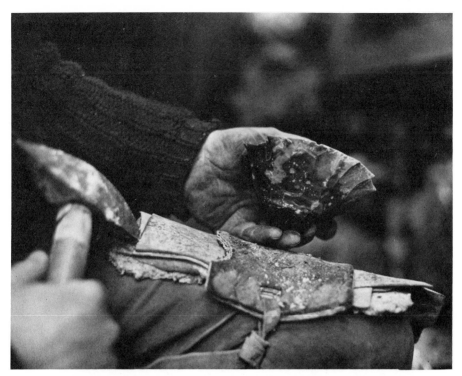

Figure 19.2 *Core prepared by Mr. Avery for flake removal. Note the steel hammer used for this operation.*

top of a flat wooden table and with a cloth pad laid across its base (Figure 19.3). The anvil bar stood 13.5 cm high. Each flint flake was placed horizontally on the flat-topped anvil with the bulbar face upward and held on one side of the anvil while on the opposite side the hammer descended vertically to make a clean break across the entire flake. After each blow was struck, the flake was fed in across the top of the anvil, and the next blow was struck (Figure 19.4). In each case, the blow was directed at a point equal in distance from the last blow and to the width of the flake, resulting in a square or nearly square section of the flake. Each of these square pieces was a finished gunflint, and to minimize damage to these finished pieces a cloth pad was positioned under the tabletop anvil to catch each piece as it fell.

During this phase of the operation, Mr. Avery had three buckets arranged on the table, and he tossed different gunflints into these buckets according to size. The largest gunflints I observed during this operation averaged 2.5 cm in width, the intermediate-sized ones averaged 2.1 cm in width, and the smallest averaged 1.8 cm wide. Mr. Avery worked rapidly and with great accuracy, although it would be useful to measure the variability of the

Figure 19.3. *Mr. Avery sectioning flakes on a vertical anvil-bar. Note the flat hammer used for this operation.*

gunflints within each size category over an extended series of manufacturing operations. By inspection, it was apparent that variation was minimal, and work was done to very close tolerances. As Mr. Avery pointed out, however, if he made a mistake and made a piece too small, he would always trim it a bit and place it in the next smaller category—although, in fact, I never saw this happen. Table 19.1 summarizes the numbers of usable gunflints obtained from the core-reductions of Thetford flint by Mr. Avery.

Limited as they are, these two sets of observations suggest that there may be considerable variation from one core to the next in the numbers of usable gunflints produced, and further quantitative studies of this would be useful, as would controlled observations of the numbers of flakes produced

Figure 19.4. *Detail of flake-sectioning on vertical anvil-bar.*

from each core and the average number of gunflints in each size range produced from each flake. It appears, too, that one of the penalties of working to such exacting templates is a high degree of wastage, since in each case the total weight of the waste material (i.e., cortex flakes, residual core, and residual flake material from gunflint shaping) exceeded 50% of the total core

Table 19.1
Usable Gunflints

Core weights	Number of gunflints			
	Size range 1 (avg. 2.5 cm)	Size range 2 (avg. 2.1 cm)	Size range 3 (avg. 1.8 cm)	Total gunflints
No. 1 2.79 kg	64	30	78	172
No. 2 2.29 kg	43	50	22	115

weight. Specifically, Core 1 produced 1.26 kg of usable gunflints, while Core 2 produced 851 g of usable gunflints. Another general observation from this pair of core reductions was the uniformity of overall average gunflint weights, which varied from 7.3 per gunflint for Core 1 to 7.4 for Core 2. Of course, a sample of two cases is inadequate for any general conclusions, but these trial observations should indicate specific ways in which variability in this stone-working technology can be measured.

Discard

Mr. Avery said that he would periodically gather up the debris and dump it in a pit which he dug into the ground "in order to confuse some future archaeologist." Most of his work was done at a workshop about three-quarters of a mile from his home, and the discard pits are in that general area, but I did not actually observe any discard behavior of this kind. Mr. Avery has been visited before by archaeologists.

Production

Mr. Avery works at gunflint-making for about 1.5 hours each weekday evening, and he estimates that he produces between 150,000 and 200,000 gunflints each year, mainly for gun clubs in North America. He says that when he is showing off at fairs he can produce over 300 usable gunflints in an hour, although his normal rate of production is closer to 200. This estimate parallels that offered by Clarke (1935:53). He does not retail his products directly but has a middleman who arranges for sales and passes the orders on to be filled. The sizes of the different gunflints reflect the sizes of the fixtures on the flintlocks these gunflints are intended for.

As the foregoing description suggests, there is little capital investment required by Mr. Avery in this craft. This a true cottage industry in which all of the work is done with simple hand tools and locally available raw materials which are inexpensive to procure. Likewise, Mr. Avery's investments of labor in this craft are not overwhelming, although one ought to regard investments of skill, difficult as they are to measure, as significant in this case. Finished gunflints from Mr. Avery's workshop travel between 2500 and 5000 miles to their intended destinations, despite the fact that flints suitable for gunflint manufacture are available in many natural locations in North America—that is, much closer to their intended users. In relation to labor and capital investments, this long-distance transport of materials seems to defy ordinary expectations based upon laws of supply-and-demand or principles of least effort. The long distances traveled by these items to their sites of intended use seem disproportionate to the effort expended to produce them, especially in light of the fact that usable flint is readily available closer at hand. Another apparent anomaly arises when one considers the relatively short use-lives of gunflints, at least when used by gun collectors who actually fire their weapons. According to several antique gun collectors I have spoken to about this, gunflints are generally not kept or recycled once they are worn down. The only exception has to do with some collectors who keep a fresh gunflint in a weapon that is for display only and is never fired. But such cases, while numerous, do not lead to an ongoing demand for gunflints. So we cannot really argue that longevity of use-life is what might be "pulling" gunflints across the Atlantic.

Perhaps it is the element of Mr. Avery's skill, based in this case upon a long tradition of such skill, that is decisive here. It would be hard to calculate the investment of effort represented by Mr. Avery's flintknapping skills or the tradition that produced them, but it would be foolish to overlook them. Moreover, these skills have been applied to a highly specialized craft. So specialization in relation to a specific demand is also an important factor in any attempt to explain this pattern of low investment of effort in production compared with the distances these items travel.

The Principle of Archaisms

A comparison of Mr. Avery's gunflint-making techniques with those described in the literature about Brandon over the last 100 years indicates that his methods are identical to those of his predecessors. If anything, Mr. Avery's work is even more stereotyped than that of many of the earlier Brandon flintknappers, whose skills extended into such virtuoso items as flint fishhooks and complete alphabets (A–Z) made of letters fashioned of chipped flint. According to Clarke (1935:56) these fishhooks were used to catch perch on the Ouse River! Mr. Avery produces only gunflints and flint building blocks, and the gunflints he makes conform to the rigid specifications described earlier. In relation to the methods used and the regularity of the items produced, Mr. Avery's work represents an extreme case of both precision and conservatism in flaked-stone technology.

This extreme conservatism of technique is related to the demand structure of the market for which Mr. Avery produces, namely, collectors of antique weapons. These weapons, mainly pistols, muskets, and rifles (like the famous Kentucky Long Rifle) are often over 200 years old and have been carefully preserved or restored by their owners. An essential characteristic of such collecting is that these weapons are restored as nearly as possible to their original working condition, down to the last detail. Thus we may regard the practice of antique gun collecting, whether by individuals or groups, as an archaism—that is, a conscious attempt to retain and even, to an extent, reenact some aspect of the past (see also Leone's discussion in this volume of the reenactment of firing a flintlock at Colonial Williamsburg). Mr. Avery's flintknapping represents a specialized technology that serves to support this archaism.

Archaeologists have studied archaisms in various ways, ranging from their recognition, on stylistic grounds, of archaisms in pottery associated with prehistoric gravelots in Peru (Rowe 1962:135), to ethnoarchaeological studies of "curation" among the Nunamiut Eskimo (Binford 1973:242-243) and the "heirloom hypothesis" as applied to a Diegueño Indian shaman's wand (Thomas 1976:128-132). These studies point out how items which have been retained beyond their normal use-life within a cultural system can produce stratigraphic and/or associational anomalies in archaeological sites. Although the case of Mr. Avery's gunflints has obvious archaeological implications, it is of interest here mainly as a way of discovering general processes of contemporary human behavior in relation to materials. In this case we can see more clearly the linkages between archaisms such as the maintenance and restoration of flintlock weapons and the technologies needed to support these archaisms.

So, on the basis of this single case, we can posit a general principle: *As a cultural institution becomes archaic, the technologies supporting that institution assume an increasingly standardized and stereotyped character.* We might refer to this as the "principle of archaisms," and it is a relationship that can be tested cross-culturally in any contemporary society where archaic practices occur. Assuming, for the sake of argument, that cross-cultural testing proves that such a principle exists, we can then apply this principle as an explanatory prediction to archaisms in the archaeological past. The principal aim of this study has been to posit the existence of this general relationship between certain aspects of human behavior and the handling of materials, in this case, gunflints.

The End Is Near!

This is not a dire prediction of the end of the world but a simple statement that when Mr. Avery ceases to manufacture gunflints the Brandon tradition of flintknapping will be over. Mr. Avery has no competitors or apprentices, nor are any likely to appear in the near future. In the past, several youngsters showed interest in learning the craft from Mr. Avery, but they were discouraged by their parents with the argument that many of the early Brandon flintknappers died at an early age from silicosis arising from inhalation of flint dust while working. Clarke (1935:52) notes that seven out of eight men in one workshop died of this ailment within 4 years. Accurate figures are not available, but the fear seems well founded. Mr. Avery takes the precautions of limiting his flintknapping to short periods and working in a well ventilated area, in contrast to the oldtimers, many of whom worked long hours in enclosed areas. As the work proceeds, it is possible to see the flint dust rising from the work area, and prolonged exposure entails obvious risks. Mr. Avery is philosophical about this risk, and, as he hastened to point out, he smokes a lot, too.

So perhaps the initial hypothesis can be extended to suggest that technologies which support archaisms become most conservative and stereotyped when the end is near.

Whether or not one accepts such propositions, this paper should serve to alert anthropologists and archaeologists to the fact that there is still much that we can learn from the case of the Brandon gunflint industry. Above all, this new look at the old and much-described Brandon flintknappers should awaken interest in studies of material culture that go beyond particularistic descriptions of technique and begin to deal with general principles of human behavior in relation to materials. The approach used here resembles what Schiffer (1976a:8-9) has referred to as the "Strategy 4" approach to behavioral archaeology. This involves studies of present-day cases to posit a general relationship between behavior and materials in the *present-day*, that is, as a case of contemporary ethnology from a modern material culture perspective. As this example shows, a single case may be used to posit such general relationships, although one must be willing to extend and test these relationships cross-culturally and archaeologically before they can be regarded with the sort of confidence we attribute to scientific laws.

Acknowledgments

This paper benefited from discussions with Professor Charles McBurney, Dr. Ian Hodder, and Dr. Geoffrey Bailey, although I remain responsible for any errors of fact or interpretation that may exist in this paper. I also wish to thank Cambridge University Press for allowing me to recycle some of the information that first appeared on pages 232-235 of my book, *Living Archaeology* (1980).

20

Making Stone Vases:
Contemporary Manufacture of
Material-Culture Items in Upper Egypt[1]

Thomas R. Hester and Robert F. Heizer

In 1971, during the course of a research project involving the Colossi of Memnon (Heizer, Stross, Hester, Albee, Perlman, Asaro, and Bowman 1973), we visited a small workshop area in the village of Sheik Abd el Gurna on the western plain of Thebes in upper Egypt.[2] At this workshop, vessels and other objects of alabaster were being made by hand. We took a number of photographs and recorded some initial observations regarding the workshop activities. We were struck by the fact that the craftsmen were producing these stone artifacts by hand, utilizing techniques which seemed to us little different than those we had seen depicted in reliefs on the walls of Old Kingdom tombs.

In February, 1972, when we returned to Egypt to continue our study of the Colossi of Memnon, we decided to make a detailed record of the alabaster workshops at Sheik Abd el Gurna (Figure 20.1). The research at the workshops had two major goals: *(a)* a thorough photographic documentation accomplished by taking black and white photographs and color

---

[1] This paper is derived from our more detailed monograph, *Making Stone Vases: Ethnoarchaeological Studies at an Alabaster Workshop in Upper Egypt*, Undena Publications, Malibu, Calif. 1980.

[2] The Colossi of Memnon research was supported in 1971-1972 by grants from the National Geographic Society, Washington, D.C.

MODERN MATERIAL CULTURE
The Archaeology of Us

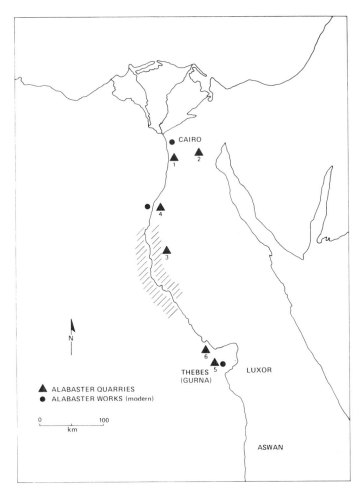

Figure 20.1. *Locations of ancient alabaster quarries and modern alabaster works in Egypt. 1. Helwan. 2. Cairo-Suez desert. 3. Hatnub vicinity (many quarries, apparently on both sides of the river). 4. East of Maghagha (at Wadi Moathil). 5. Three miles from Wadiyien, opposite Luxor. 6. Mountains of Nag' Hammadi.*

slides, and by making a record of the alabaster-working on 16-mm film;[3] *(b)* a careful written account, through direct observation and informant interviews, of the techniques and sequence of alabaster vessel manufacture and an overall study of the alabaster industry.

It was our hope that this research with contemporary vase-making

---

[3] Our film-making efforts met only moderate success. The rented camera turned out to be faulty and only about one-half of the exposed footage turned out to be of any value. This still awaits editing.

technology would benefit the study of alabaster industries in ancient Egypt Such studies of material culture, in contemporary and nonindustrial societies, designed to aid in archaeological interpretation have been done in various parts of the world for many years. More recently, this field of investigation has intensified and broadened and has become known as ethnoarchaeology (see Hester, Heizer, and Graham 1975:10); a sample of some important studies includes the publications of Donnan and Clewlow (1974), Yellen (1977), and Gould (1978a).

Ancient Egyptian Use of Alabaster

Alabaster was extensively utilized by the ancient Egyptians. As a construction material it was used for lining passages and rooms, this beginning in the early dynastic period and lasting well into New Kingdom times (Lucas and Harris 1962:59). Large sculptures were sometimes made of alabaster. An example is the 60-ton alabaster statue of Djehutihetep, depicted in a twelfth-century tomb painting at El Bersheh (Heizer 1966:Figure 10). Another major use was in the manufacture of vessels destined to be placed as funerary offerings in elite tombs (Harris 1961:77). According to Montet (1925:147) the manufacture of stone vases had been perfected to a high degree in the first dynasty and still flourished in the Ramesside period. Even later manufacture of alabaster vases and containers continued into the fourth century B.C.

An example of just how extensively the alabaster resource was used comes from the Old Kingdom, the site of Saqqara. In one of the galleries of the third dynasty Step Pyramid of Zoster at the site, about 30,000 alabaster vessels (roughly 90 tons) were found (Firth, Quibell, and Lauer 1935:130; Quibell 1935:76-77).

Geologic Sources of Alabaster

Egyptian alabaster is, in geologic terms, a calcite. According to Lucas and Harris (1962:59), it is a "compact crystalline form of calcium carbonate, white or yellowish white in colour, translucent in thin sections and frequently banded." The same authors (pp. 59-60) have described in some detail the various geologic sources of alabaster exploited by both ancient and modern-day Egyptians. They note its occurrence in the Sinai and at a series of localities on the east and west sides of the Nile. The approximate locations of these sources (and ancient quarries) are shown in Figure 20.1. They include a locality in the Cairo-Suez desert (also apparently used in modern times); a source near Wadi Moathil (a branch of the Wadi Sennur), due east of

Maghagha; an area of about 90 miles from Minia to south of Asiut in which there are signs of many quarries, with the most important being at Hatnub (15 miles east of El Amarna; the Hatnub source was the principal one up to the time of the New Kingdom, according to Harris 1961:78) and at Guata near Wadi Asiut; a source in the mountains near Nag' Hammadi; and a quarry used in modern times 3 miles béhind Wadiyein (a branch of Wadi el Muluk, on the west side of the Nile opposite Luxor). There is also an important ancient alabaster quarry at Wadi Gerrawi near Helwan (Erman 1894:470).

Undoubtedly, some of the alabaster used in contemporary alabaster workshops is derived from quarries opened in ancient times. Others, like the one at Wadiyein near Luxor, have been utilized only in modern times. However, it does not appear to have been the source for the alabaster used in the workshops we studied.

Alabaster-Working in Ancient Egypt

The widespread use of alabaster and the sometimes massive numbers of objects from it, required the development of a craft specialization centering on alabaster-working. Unfortunately, we do not have any very good accounts, from excavations, of ancient alabaster workshops at Egyptian sites. There are some brief mentions of excavated areas which probably functioned as such, for example, at Meydum (Petrie, MacKay, and Wainwright 1910: 44) and Hierakonpolis (Quibell and Green 1902; Adams 1974a,b).

While we have inadequate archaeological data on alabaster (and other stone) workshops, a rich record of the manufacture of stone vessels is preserved in bas relief sculptures on the walls of Old Kingdom tombs (cf. Blackman 1914:Plate 5; Blackman and Apted 1953:Plate XVII; Davies 1902: Plate 14; Klebs 1915:Abbildungen 66). Analysis of such scenes, along with the study of excavated vase borer bits and alabaster artifacts, have permitted several archaeologists to comment on the stone vase-working process. Our knowledge of ancient Egyptian vase-manufacturing technology is still quite limited (cf. Harding 1971:242).

First of all, there are a number of tomb reliefs that depict the vase-drilling process (Blackmann 1914:Plate V; Blackman and Apted 1953:Plate 17; Davies 1902:Plate 14; Guimet 1909; Klebs 1915:83; Montet 1925:295; Morgan 1896:165; Rowe 1931:41). In these the craftsmen are shown working singly, that is, without an assistant (we suspect, on the basis of our research reported later, that at least two individuals would have been needed for drilling tasks earlier in the process). The borer is not clearly depicted in these reliefs, although it is shown to be composed of a vertical rod-like element, curved near the top, to which is attached (at the top) two counter-weights, and at the bottom, a drill bit of some form. The pictorial evidence suggests there may have been some intermediate component, or shank, into which the drill bit was inserted. The hieroglyphic symbol depicting the vase borer is obviously stylized, but reveals the components which we have just noted. However, in this symbol, the drill bit is shown as a rod-like horizontal piece inserted in a cleft at the distal end of the borer (Figure 20.2b).

It should be noted at this point that a preserved, intact vase-boring tool has never been found in Egypt. However, grooved stones which are apparently the counterweights noted earlier have been recovered (Borchardt 1907:143; Rowe 1931:41, Plates XV,I). Experiments by Hartenberg and Schmidt (1969) have shown that the curious curved boring tool, with such

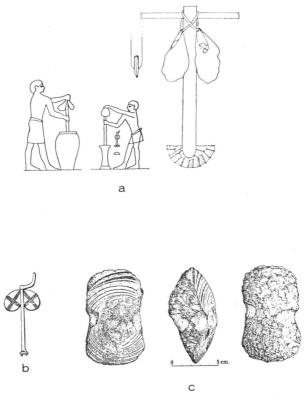

Figure 20.2. *Stone vase manufacture in ancient Egypt. (a) Adapted from Hodges (1970: Figures 100-101); the detail of the vase-boring tool on the right suggests the use of a chipped stone crescent as the drill bit; (b) the hieroglyphic sign for ancient stone vase workers; (c) three examples of sandstone vase "borers" or bits, from Borchardt (1907:Abb. 123-124).*

weights attached, would indeed function as a vase-drilling implement. Their research indicates that the tool functioned much like a modern brace-and-bit; the intermediate component mentioned by us above, was probably a sleeve connecting the forked shank holding the drill bit with the long, curved upper section of the borer (Hartenberg and Schmidt:163).

A problem that we see in reviewing these various accounts of the vase-boring technique is the assumption of many authors that the drill bit was a "crescent" (see Figure 20.2a)—a chipped flint lunate (cf. Caneva 1970; Firth 1930:105; Firth, Quibell, and Lauer 1935:126; Hodges 1970:110-111; Lauer and Debono 1950; Petrie 1902:12; Piperno 1973:71). Use-wear observations that we have made of museum specimens and examples we were able to view in Egypt indicate no evidence of such arduous wear (cf. Hester 1976). We believe, as do Petrie (1910:79; 1917:Plate 52), Quibell and Green (1902:17, Plate 62), Quibell (1905:Plate 63), Petrie, MacKay, and Wainwright (1910:44, Plates 39,2) and Borchardt (1907:Abb. 129), that lenticular conical pieces of quartzite, sandstone, diorite, and limestone were used as the primary boring bit; further, it is our opinion that varying sizes of these bits, perhaps in a graded series were employed to obtain different diameters in the vessel interiors (cf. Davies 1902; Caldwell 1967:188). A number of examples (Figure 20.2c) have been found at Egyptian sites (cf. Borchardt 1907; Quibell and Green 1902; Adams 1974a). They are notched or constricted at midpoint, and this feature would have facilitated their attachment to a shank, and then to the boring tool. Petrie (1917:95) suggests the drill bit was fashioned so that it could "be slipped through a (vase) neck and then turned flat to drill a wider hole. It was rotated by a forked stick holding the contracted point." Petrie also stated that these borers were of "sandstone, used along with sand for boring out the interior of vases [p. 95]." Similar vase-grinders or bits from late Minoan times on Crete were fastened with wedges to the boring tool (Warren 1969:156, Figure 5A,B).

The wear striations clearly observable on these quartzite or stone bits in published illustrations closely match the types of interior striations noted on ancient alabaster vessels in Egypt (cf. Adams 1974a:45).

However, despite our belief that the "crescents" were not the primary tool in ancient Egyptian vase drilling, we must call attention to the data reported by Caton-Thompson and Gardner (1934) from gypsum works in the Fayum depression. Theirs is a detailed study, parts of which we have reprinted in our monograph (Hester and Heizer 1980). In the excavations of the Old Kingdom workshops and related areas at Umm-es-Sawan two major types of flint tools were found and were linked to gypsum-working, including the production of vases. "Pebble hand-picks" were apparently used in extracting the gypsum. Crescentic flints, numbering close to 2000 and often caked with gypsum (Caton-Thompson and Gardner 1934:105), were classified as "drills" or "grinders." The crescents were discovered in contexts that indicate their use in gypsum-working, perhaps the drilling (or "grinding," as the authors describe it) of platters, vases, and other objects.

This fascinating study by Caton-Thompson and Gardner represents, as far as we know, the only case in which there appears to be detailed evidence for the use of the chipped stone crescents in stone vase manufacture. However, we would like to see detailed wear pattern studies done of such crescentic specimens extant in museum collections in order to more fully ascertain their role in this technology.

Other tools available to the vase-makers would have been copper and metal chisels (Petrie 1901:24). Petrie (1917:46) notes limestone bowls of Ptolemaic age which had been hollowed out with chisels. As seen later in this paper, contemporary alabaster workers use an iron chisel to carry out the preliminary shaping of vessel interiors. Warren (1969:158-165) in his description of Minoan stone vase manufacture, notes the use of chisels and the shaping of vessel preforms with a hammer or chisel. Such tools were probably also used in a similar fashion by ancient Egyptian vase-makers (cf. Quibell 1935:77-78).

The fine finish which is observed on ancient alabaster vessels was probably accomplished with the use of files made of sandstone blocks or of similar abrasive stone. The reliefs in some tombs depict the use of such smoothing implements on vessel exteriors and interiors. Petrie (1901:19), in his study of stone vessels from the cemeteries of Diosopolis Parva, noted that the vessel interiors "were ground out by blocks of sandstone or emery." The modern vase-makers of Gurna still use such sandstone blocks for the final smoothing of the vessels.

Contemporary Alabaster Technology

The manufacture of alabaster vessels has had a long history in Egypt. Periods of great emphasis on their production occurred, as in the Old Kingdom, and it seems that perhaps the craft waned in the late centuries B.C. Just when the making of alabaster objects was revived we do not know. However, we strongly suspect that it was in the early part of the nineteenth century when forgery of artifacts was begun in earnest in Egypt, particularly in the Thebes area where tomb-robbing and the sale of antiquities were rampant (cf. Rhind 1862; St. John 1852:292; Wilson 1964:35-35,51,53-54). Such practices continues unabated in the Gurna area of Thebes today; and since there are few tombs left to rob and a scarcity of genuine artifacts to peddle, there has been a great increase in the manufacture of fakes of various kinds (cf. Muhly 1975). Some of the forgeries are quite good, requiring much time and skill; among these are some of the fine alabaster vases produced in workshops such as the one we studied. However, much of the effort in alabaster workshops goes toward the production of small vases and bowls, ashtrays, shoddy replicas of pharaonic busts and the like (cf. Noel-Hume 1974:298-299). A small shop adjacent to the alabaster workshop specializes in the production of limestone scarabs; these are far superior to the glazed green scarabs (imports, we were told, from Czechoslovakia!) which are sold to most tourists. We observed no serious attempt to pass off these modern alabaster objects as ancient, and we suspect that most of them are purchased simply as souvenirs. In the case of the fine vases and bowls produced in the Gurna workshop which we studied, most of the items are sold to curio shops in Luxor, or are bought by passing tourists who are attracted to them as works of art.

We believe that the alabaster workshops of Gurna represent a dying industry. For example, in the tourist shops in Cairo, the alabaster artifacts offered for sale have been manufactured with the use of lathes and possibly other mechanical equipment. Warren (1969:164-165) has noted a similar situation on Crete. Unlike the vessels made in Gurna, these have a "plastic" appearance. We were told that they were made in the Cairo area and in the vicinity of Beni Suef (Figure 20.1). It seems to us that it will only be a matter of time until mechanization replaces handicraft at Gurna.

The Setting

A string of small settlements, known collectively as Gurna, are situated on the edge of the desert (and thus on the fringe of the fertile floodplain) on the western bank of the Nile opposite Luxor (Figure 20.1). Many of the mud-brick houses sit atop or near tombs of the New Kingdom. Nearby are a wide variety of archaeological monuments, such as the Ramesseum, Deir el Bahari, the Tombs of the Nobles, and the Colossi of Memnon (cf. Heizer *et al.*, 1973).

The workshops we selected for study are situated in Sheik Abd el Gurna, on a hillside overlooking the western plain of Thebes. We had briefly visited these workshops in 1971. Arrangements for the study described here were negotiated with the head of the main workshop, Sheik Mahmoud, with the aid of Ahmed Younes, a vice-president of the Bank Misr in Cairo (Younes also served as our interpreter). The sheik agreed to let us carry out our study, and later, sold us a set of vase-making tools, vases, and other artifacts relating to the workshop.[4] These are now in the Lowie Museum of Anthropology at the University of California, Berkeley.

[4] The purchase of this museum collection was somewhat difficult to arrange, as the sheik thought that we were aiming to set up a rival vase-making operation. "Why else," he asked, "would anyone want to buy a set of tools?"

Quarrying of the Alabaster

The alabaster used in the workshops is reported to come from the mountains of Nag' Hammadi, on the way to Akaba. Because of military restrictions in force on Americans in Egypt in 1971 and 1972, it was impossible for us to visit this source. Our interviews at the workshop yielded the following details about the quarry and the quarrying process.

The quarrying and transport of alabaster to the Gurna workshops involves six men. Three men accompany a donkey train to and from the quarry (actually, a series of quarrying localities), while three remain at the quarry to work the stone. Once the caravan has made a round trip, the men switch tasks. According to the sheik who administered our workshop, this process goes on year-round without interruption. We did not determine whether these quarry workers supplied both Sheik Mahmoud's workshops as well as others in the area, although we suspect this to be the case. The distance to the quarry area is approximately 50 km, and the trip takes about 24 hours, with frequent rest stops. Each donkey in the train is loaded with either two pieces of alabaster (the examples we saw were about 14 in. long and weighed 30–35 kg) or with several (up to six) smaller chunks. The sheik claimed that the maximum load was 80 kg per animal. According to the men who arrived with a donkey train at the workshop during our study, the alabaster is quarried out in large pieces and is then trimmed for transport to Gurna. These quarry workers spoke of many different sources of alabaster in the mountains near Nag' Hammadi, stating that once a particular source was exhausted, they simply moved on to another. According to them, there is still "much alabaster" in the region.

At the quarries, a large pry bar (over 1 m in length) is used, and is hammered at one end with a large sledge; with these two basic tools, large chunks of alabaster are detached. Sometimes they use a small chisel (about 50 cm long) to chip an opening or notch in a large exposure of alabaster; then, the large pry bar is pounded in, opening a larger crack in the exposure, and eventually splitting off a suitably-sized chunk.

Once secured through quarrying, the alabaster chunks are roughly hammer dressed, loaded on the donkeys in wide-gauge netting and transported to the workshops. We were unable to record the payment received for these blocks when delivered at the workshops.

The Workshops

Although the workshops we studied initially appeared to us to represent one single workshop setting, further investigation (reported in the following) revealed that there were actually two, one controlled by the sheik, the other by his nephew. A plan of the workshop and adjacent buildings is shown in Figure 20.3.

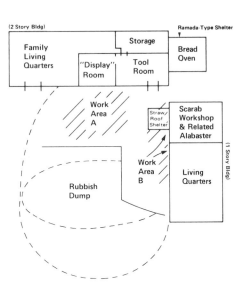

Figure 20.3. *Plan of the alabaster workshop, 1972, and associated buildings related to the workshops studied in 1972. Not to scale.*

The workshops are located in the open, with only a small portion shaded by a straw roof extending from an adjacent building (see Figure 20.3). Tools, however, were stored inside a large room where they were scattered in the dust in a state of great disarray. In a small room adjacent to the tool room was a small display area, containing a table with curios and small vessels made of alabaster and limestone. Inquisitive tourists are led to this room to observe some of the products of the workshops. A small back room served as a storage facility for unworked alabaster, and was filled with chunks and roughly shaped pieces of varying sizes.

The largest of the two workshop areas, that controlled by Sheik Mahmoud, is shown as workshop A in Figure 20.3; the smaller, but immediately adjacent, workshop controlled by the sheik's nephew, is shown as workshop B. In this second workshop, there is also a small-scale scarab-making industry (mentioned previously) going on inside the building shown in Figure 20.3.

At the corner where these two workshops meet, there is a ramada-like structure in which is located a bread oven. This is used by the alabaster workers during the final stages of vessel production.

A widely dispersed rubbish heap is observed at the front (east side) of the two workshops (Figure 20.3). Although we carried out no excavations in this mound, we checked the surface carefully and noted little in the way of broken workshop debris. In fact, we recall observing only a single small piece of a ruined vase. Some additional comments on this phenomenon are provided later.

The Manufacturing Sequence

We have previously noted that the alabaster arrives from the quarry in roughly shaped blocks. The worker selects a block from the storeroom and proceeds to trim it, using a short-handled double-pointed hammer. With this tool, the block is given further shape and is reduced until the general, though still irregular, vessel outline can be seen. The vase "preform" is then prepared for the hollowing-out of the interior cavity. The most common practice we observed is as follows: Melted glue is applied to the exterior of the preform and on this alabaster dust is liberally sprinkled. Strips of glue-soaked cloth are then wrapped tightly around the preform. This coating of glue, alabaster dust, and cloth is then allowed to dry and harden. The workers believe that this coating helps to prevent breakage of the vessel preform during the hollowing-out process.

Once a bowl or vase has been coated in this manner, and the coating allowed to dry and harden, the forming of the interior can then begin. Initial hollowing is done with a hand-held three-pronged iron chisel. Once a rough and fairly shallow concavity has been formed in this manner, the interior is coated with a concoction of glue and alabaster dust, which, according to the workers, "goes inside the stone and hardens it." Given the porous nature of this rather poor quality alabaster, there may be some value to this practice.

For drilling out the interior (or in some cases, for boring and smoothing the interior of a hand-chiseled concavity), a brace-and-bit tool is used. The various components of this composite tool are shown in Figure 20.4. Depending on the type of vessel to be bored, the worker will select (from the tool room) the needed drill bits and insert them into the shank, where they are held in place with short iron keys or wedges. The assembled tool is then turned in a rotary motion to enlarge the interiors of the vessel (Figure 20.5). While turning the crank drill, the worker would occasionally reverse the motion, though it was mainly clockwise due to the fact that all of the workers were right-handed.

Before the drilling process begins, the workmen (usually two are involved; see Figure 20.5) locate a shallow, previously dug pit in the earth in the workshop area, scoop out the accumulated dust and dirt and set the vessel in this. For boring the interior of a deep vessel, a single broad drill bit, with serrated edges, is used. To bore out the basin of a shallow bowl, three crescentic-shaped serrated bits are assembled. During the boring or drilling

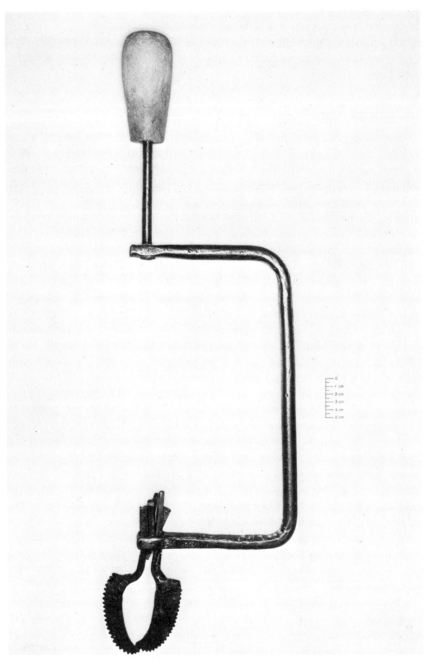

Figure 20.4. *Assembled vase-drilling tool. Components of the vase-drilling tool, including the curved metal drill bits and the short iron keys or wedges that hold them in place.*

Figure 20.5. *Two workers at the alabaster workshop are using the vase-drill tool (see Figure 20.6) to drill the interior of a vase.*

process, the bits may be changed, or their arrangement altered, several times. For example, in boring the basin of a bowl, a worker first assembled four crescent-shaped blades and turned the brace-and-bit for a few minutes until a minor degree of smoothing had been accomplished. The accumulated alabaster dust was then poured out and the drill blades reassembled, this time removing one of the original three. After 20 additional minutes of basin-grinding, the drill component was reset with two crescent blades. But, some 20 min later, the three-blade arrangement was again used until the boring–grinding process was completed. On vases and other specimens the size of the drill bits will occasionally vary in order to make the inner contours of the vessel. See Figure 20.6 for an illustration of some of the various types of bits.

After the interior of a vessel has been bored out, the glue and cloth coating is stripped off, using the short-handled pick-hammer; this usually takes about 20–30 min for a large vase. At this point, attention turns to finishing the exterior of the vessel. The vessel, during manufacture, has a roughly shaped exterior which is suggestive of the final form it will have. The drilling out of the interior initially produces a thick-walled vessel with a rough exterior, though often the walls are not more than 1.5 cm thick at this point.

Figure 20.6. *Tools from the alabaster workshop. A series of the different kinds of drill bits, used in drilling the interior of vases, bowls, and jars (all specimens are in the Lowie Museum of Anthropology, University of California, Berkeley).*

Steel, rat-tailed files are used to provide a roughly smoothed exterior surface, with the workman bracing the vessel with his feet and with short pegs driven into the ground. But, to provide a smooth finish, a sandstone polisher is used. A large basket of sandstone chunks (which the workers told us came from the nearby ruins of Medinet Habu) is brought out, and a suitable piece (unshaped) is selected for use as a vessel polisher. The ultimate polish is given the exterior with a piece of coarse commercial sandpaper. The vessel is next placed in a bread oven in the nearby ramada and is heated for about 5 min. It is then brought back to the workshop and candle wax is applied to the surfaces, melting into the heated stone. The wax used in these two workshops is "Alexandria Wax," described by the workers as "having a good smell." The wax serves to enhance the color of the stone (turning it a light brown), and the workers believe that it "removes" any alabaster dust remaining on the specimen. The finished, waxed vessel is then polished with a piece of cloth.

Socioeconomics and Organization of the Workshop

The alabaster industry studied by us actually consisted of two workshops, side by side, claiming to be of one family, yet manifesting a rivalry of sorts between the two. Sheik Mahmoud claimed that all the alabaster workshops in the Gurna vicinity were controlled by a single family. He asserted that his father had invented the tools of the trade, a fact we could not substantiate. At least in the two workshops that we studied, all of the workers claimed to be related. The sheik had been in the alabaster workshop industry for most of his 80 years. He told us that he had eight sons, four of whom were dead, with the surviving four presently employed in alabaster-working. We inquired as to the health of the workers, as we found it hard to believe that there is no effect on the lungs of breathing the fine crystalline dust. Sheik Mahmoud denied this when we asked him, and said that in fact the alabaster powder was good for you. And as evidence, he leaned over, scooped up a handful, put it in his mouth, chewed and swallowed it.

The adjacent workshop belongs to the sheik's nephew, but retained a considerable degree of autonomy. Separate negotiations had to be conducted with the nephew in order for us to film and to talk with his workmen. The sheik told us that his brother had a workshop on the south side of Gurna, and the two other workshops in the village were also administered by family members. We did not have a chance to visit these. In the sheik's workshop were five workers and in the adjacent nephew's, there were three. According to the sheik, his brother's workshop had four workers, and there were three and two workers respectively at the other workshops mentioned above.

The work-day at the sheik's workshop was from 7 A.M. to 12 noon. Each worker received 50 piastres to 1 LE compensation per day, plus, the sheik claimed, 30 piastres an hour for "overtime." This seems to be their primary (if not sole) means of support. He informed us that the average income (profit?) for his workshop was about 70 LE per month. In addition to paying the workers' salaries, the sheik also provided their lunch. According to the sheik, he absorbs the financial loss if a vessel is broken during manufacture, that is, it is not deducted from the worker's salary. We could not independently verify this assertion. However, it seemed to us that there was very little broken. We noted in the rubbish dump a single fragment of a small vase broken during the drilling process (the exterior was covered with the glue and cloth coating). We suspect that any fragments resulting from a broken vessel are usually reworked into smaller alabaster artifacts.

Based on our observations, estimates and prolonged conversations with the workshop personnel, it apparently takes about 7 days to make a vase roughly 11.5 in. high and 6.5 in. in diameter. A shallow bowl 12.5 in. in diameter and 5 in. high takes about 4 days to manufacture. The vase would sell for about 5 LE, and the bowl for about the same amount. The glue which is used for coating and hardening the stone comes in sheets adhering to chicken-wire and costs about 70 piastres per kilogram.

Because of the erratic nature of production at the workshop, it is hard to ascertain just how many vessels are made and sold each month. We did not

Figure 20.7. *Vessel from the alabaster workshop. A well-made large vase, of the finest form produced in the workshop. Height of specimen 232 mm. (Lowie Museum No. 5-11380.)*

observe a workman taking a vessel preform and following through with manufacture in a continuing sequence. Rather, each workman, or apparently several workmen, will work on several vases simultaneously, each vessel often at a different stage of manufacture. We would estimate perhaps as many as 100 or as few as 60 vessels are made in a month in these two workshops. In addition to making the various large and small vases and bowls (see Figure 20.7), the workers also produce alabaster ashtrays replete with a pharaonic head on one side and an obelisk on the other, small sphinxes, and other curios. These are generally sold to the passing tourist; on occasion, a large vessel will be sold to a tourist. However, most of the vessels apparently go to curio shops in Luxor. The dealer pays 5-6 LE for the vessel, and then marks up the price in his shop to around 18 LE. Sheik Mahmoud believed that the products of his workshop were often represented by the curio peddlers as ancient pieces.

We noted no particular specialization among the workers, each being able to handle any of the tasks required during the manufacturing process. Workers often start as young as 12 years of age (at present, the sheik's youngest worker is 17 and has been employed for 5 years). Sometimes younger children of the workers are pressed into service to aid in the polishing of the vessels. As we noted above, in the actual sequence of production, a vessel is rarely (if ever) taken from beginning to completion by one worker. We observed vessels started by one man being worked on by another and other vessels casually passed around and worked on by various craftsmen.

Sheik Mahmoud was very interested in mechanizing his workshop, as he claimed he could not meet the demand for its products. He had heard of the alabaster workshops nearer to Cairo in which lathes and other mechanized techniques are being used to turn out alabaster vessels. There seems little doubt that within a few years the mechanization of the alabaster folk-industry at Sheik Abd el Gurna will have been accomplished.

Concluding Comments

We have provided here a description of a contemporary alabaster-working technology in a small village in Upper Egypt. We have also summarized a variety of information pertaining to ancient alabaster vessel manufacture in Egypt. Where the data permit, we have attempted to relate certain aspects of the contemporary technology to the ancient industry (cf. Stiles 1977:90). In the text, we have put forth certain observations or inferences derived from our ethnoarchaeological research, but we have not offered—and indeed cannot offer within the scope of the present study—any generalized "laws" of the sort called for in a recent review paper prepared by

Schiffer (1978). There are several reasons for our reluctance to offer further generalizations or speculations. First of all, our study is an incomplete one. We focused in our 1972 research on the manufacturing process. We need more first-hand information on quarrying activities. We also need more data on the social organization and economic structure within which the quarrying and manufacturing system operates. We were able to study two adjacent workshops, and did not then have the time (or since, the funding) to examine the other workshops in the vicinity. We think that such comparative studies would be essential to an understanding of the overall context within the alabaster craft functions.

We are also aware that the contemporary industry operates under different social and economic pressures than those of dynastic times. Ancient workshops may have been more highly specialized, both in terms of organization and in production goals (e.g., mass production for funerary use, although some must have made utilitarian vessels). The contemporary workshops produce, often at a rather leisurely pace, a limited number of vessels for sale to tourists. Finally, the contemporary workshops are comparatively "recent" in origin, with the revival of alabaster-working beginning around 100 years ago as best we can tell. Arab villagers at Gurna apparently began making the vessels as the supply of ancient examples decreased, while the demand from tourists and collectors persisted. There may be, then, a gap in organized alabaster working of about 2000 years. However, we are fascinated by the persistence in Egypt and adjacent areas of certain other folk art and customs. Emery (1948:17) points out that modern Nubian graves contain pots of water and food, just like the C-group Nubian graves of 1600–2270 B.C. In the Sudan, a leather shield found at the site of Qustul is identical to those still used by the Beja tribes of the area (Emery 1948:44), and there is persistence—over a period of 1500 years—of special forms of ivory dice markings and wooden camel saddles. Winlock (1942:193) records the persistence of basket forms from dynastic times to contemporary Nubia, and comments (p. 207) on what he considers to be special hairdress modes found both in Egyptian tombs and in modern Nubia (this spanning a period of some 4000 years). It may well be that while the Arab conquest of Egypt introduced new political systems, religious beliefs, etc., many basic items of material culture continued to be important in the villages and farming communities. We cannot be sure that alabaster-working has not continued since dynastic times in one form or the other; we simply do not have the evidence to support such a possibility.

As we have repeatedly noted in our discussion, there are some remarkable similarities between the ancient and contemporary alabaster technologies, and the basic techniques of manufacture have actually changed very little. Until sophisticated excavations of ancient alabaster workshops are done in Egypt, little can be done to compare the structure and organization of our workshops with those of the past.

Our study, then, is a preliminary one. We regret the lag between field-work and publication but, like many other archaeologists, we have had other deadlines and other research with which to deal. In fact, we had hoped to return to the Gurna workshops for studies of other workshops, and par-ticularly the socioeconomic aspect of alabaster production, in 1973, but funding could not be obtained. Colleagues who have visited the area in more recent years indicate that the workshops are still functioning (cf. the photo-graph in a *National Geographic* article by Hall 1977:311). In a symposium held at the Society for American Archaeology meeting in New Orleans in May, 1977, Patty Jo Watson described her studies of folk industries in the Near East, reporting a situation in which the "traditional crafts are rapidly vanishing." In that same symposium, Frederick Matson reviewed his ethnoarchaeological research among contemporary potters in Afghanistan, noting the new economic pressures they were facing, the intrusion of new and innovative techniques in pottery-making, etc., and he observed that this is "the last decade for learning about village potters" in that region. We share these pessimistic views as regards the future of ethnoarchaeological research at Gurna, where the same kinds of external pressures are coming to bear. We hope that more intensive field studies can be done before mechanization replaced hand technology in the production of alabaster vessels.

Schiffer (1978) has recently pointed out that ethnoarchaeological studies "are nowhere near . . . approaching their full potential." While we have no apologies to offer, especially since the research reported here was an offshoot of a major project in which we were both involved at the same time, we certainly feel that a more broadly conceived and detailed field study should be done while the Gurna alabaster workshops remain in their present behavioral and technological contexts. We have noted above some of the areas that still need to be explored. And, since political tensions and restric-tions on travel have eased in the area, it is also to be hoped that any future research could involve visits to the alabaster quarries, excavation in the con-temporary middens associated with the workshops and other aspects of this fascinating technology which was not possible in the political climate of 1972.

Acknowledgments

We are grateful to Professor J. Desmond Clark for his careful reading of earlier versions of this manuscript, and for alerting us to the Caton-Thompson and Gardner (1934) reference. We also wish to thank Dr. Sandro Salvatori (Venice) for his comments on this study and for sharing with us his views of alabaster technology observed at Bronze Age sites in Iran. Professor John A. Graham aided in the recording of field data.

This manuscript was completed in the early summer of 1979, shortly before the death, on July 18 of that year, of Professor Robert F. Heizer. Even though Bob had been ill with cancer for many months, he had a keen interest in seeing this study, and its counterpart monograph, through to completion. He had been, since our first visit to Egypt in 1971, very enthusiastic about the alabaster workshop research and felt that the study constituted a useful record of a dying technology. The investigation of ancient and contemporary nonindustrial technologies held great fascination for Bob, as is evidenced by a number of his publications. Such analyses, he believed, added new dimensions to the study of ancient human societies (T.R.H.).

21

A Study of the Work
of a Modern Tanner in
Ethiopia and Its Relevance for
Archaeological Interpretation

J. Desmond Clark and Hiro Kurashina

Introduction

It is often mistakenly thought that, in order to be able to use ethnographic evidence, it is necessary to be dealing with a group that is in "pristine" condition within its environment. But must we restrict our studies to contemporary societies which have not been subjected to external pressures that will have drastically affected the traditional patterns of behavior and material culture, so considerably altering their original form? Such pressures may, of course, bring about the disappearance of important lines of evidence, such as those relating to stone tool manufacture, but this does not affect the evidence on site formation processes and the spatial distribution of artifacts, refuse, and other features. Models can still be set up to explain the dynamics of specific and general archaeological situations and, in addition, may be mentioned the frequency with which artifacts are made, and their average life-expectancy and final disposal.

Of course, it should never be assumed, or indeed expected, that the processes which can be observed at work on occupation sites today are necessarily the same as were those that contributed to the formation of any archaeological site. However, the later the archaeological site the greater is the possibility that the processes which contributed to its formation resembied those which can be observed today. When we are dealing with early man sites of the Plio–Pleistocene, however, there is much greater reason for cau-

303

MODERN MATERIAL CULTURE
The Archaeology of Us

tion. Probably the most reliable reconstructions are those where a direct relationship can be established between the ethnographic present and the archaeological contexts through historical record. Such is the case with Gould's interpretation of aboriginal Australian settlements in the Western Desert where the same kinds of artifacts were being made over a long period of time and where the functions and associations can be established from the way in which this aboriginal group behaves today (Gould 1971).

Obsidian Scrapers and Ethiopian Tanners

There are few surviving examples of stone tool manufacture today and fewer still where the artifacts are carefully retouched. It is all the more interesting, therefore, to find an important and most valuable piece of evidence concerning stone flaking and tool use in association with data on the complete process involved, coming from central Ethiopia where obsidian is still used to manufacture scrapers for cleaning hides. In February-March 1977 in the course of paleo-anthropological investigations on the Southeast Plateau, we were fortunate to have been able to make a brief study of the methods and of the resulting accumulation of obsidian on the site where these activities were carried out. Among the Cushitic-speaking Oromo-Sidamo peoples of central and southern Ethiopia there are several minority groups of specialists—iron-workers-smiths, grindstone-makers, tanners, and magicians. One of these groups is that of the Fuga (Guraghe) or Chawa (Oromo) tanners or hide-cleaners. In some ways they are underprivileged—for example, no Oromo will break bread (eat food) with a Chawa although both are Muslims, they do not intermarry, and the Chawa are generally considered to be rather bad luck. In other ways, however, their rights are defined and observed by the superior group as, for example, among the Guraghe on the Ethiopian Plateau where remnant forest still exists and the Fuga have a monopoly of hunting (Shack 1966:8-12). In fact, it has been suggested that the derivation of these minority groups may be sought in the late prehistoric hunting-gathering populations of the Plateau and Rift (Shack 1966:8).

The homestead of the Chawa tanner discussed here is situated on the Southeast Plateau, east of the Galla Lakes section of the Ethiopian Rift, on the Gadeb Plain (7° 02′-7° 13′N: 39°15′-39°28′E) in Arussi-Bale, where the Oromo farmers keep cattle, sheep, and goats (as well as horses) and cultivate barley and some wheat and teff in the montane grass plains at altitudes of between 2300 and 2500 m. Small groups and individual tanners are widely dispersed over both the Ethiopian and Southeast Plateaus wherever the need exists for skin clothing and hides for bedding. Now, skin clothing is mostly confined to Sidamo and this is where the greater number of tanners are concentrated, but hides for bedding and other purposes—saddles, bridles, etc.—are still a necessity in Arussi-Bale—so that tanners are to be found here also, though more widely dispersed. In an area of some 900 km² in northern Bale there were three individual tanners in the countryside and a group of several more in a village west of Adaba on the main highway.

Interest in their craft centers upon their use of obsidian for scrapers with which to dress the hides. Obsidian is excellent for this purpose providing sharp, but not too sharp scraping edges that can easily be resharpened. The archaeological evidence suggests that the characteristic scraper form is of some antiquity, as is shown, but, today, the craft is beginning to die—children are often not following in the profession of their father—so that a systematic study should not be delayed.

Our own is not the first study of this kind. Gerrard Dekker, a United Nations water conservation expert, first brought to our notice this continuing use of obsidian and made a film of the process in a village near Addis Ababa. Next, Gallagher (1977) from Southern Methodist University made a study of tanners among the Guraghe, Sidamo and Arussi in connection with his work on Later Stone Age assemblages in the region of Lake Zwai. More recently still, Randi Haaland of the National Museum, Bergen, has worked with a tanner at Soddo among the Sidamo. The account that follows is based upon our own observations at Gadeb.

The hides to be cleaned are brought by individuals to the homestead and after argument, a price is agreed. If the hide is wet it has first to be pegged out to dry. If it is very dry—that is, 8 months old or more—it is flattened on the ground, wetted, and pounded with a stone to smooth it and flatten out the creases. The work of cleaning is carried out inside a work hut, the hide being stretched with ropes on a vertical frame. It is held taut—but not too taut—by the tanner's standing on two ropes attached to the lower edge of the hide (Figure 21.1).

The scrapers to be used are mounted on either side of the head of a curiously shaped wooden handle, well polished by use (Figure 21.2). The name of the handle is *gundalla* and those used by our tanner, Kadir Alaki, were made from a tree (*kadida*[1]) growing on Mount Badda some 40-50 km to the north in Arussi. The two scrapers (*chabbe*, i.e., obsidian) are mounted in rectangular sockets with the aid of mastic. Kadir Alaki got his mastic from a tree *(hadama)* growing in the Bale mountains to the south; this tree produces a white juice and may be a species of *Euphorbia*. To mount a new scraper Kadir Alaki removed the old one by hand, took the end of a sickle made hot in the fire and plunged this into the socket. This quickly made the mastic soft and malleable so that the new scraper could be pushed home and the mastic pressed down and round it with the thumb. On cooling, the mastic sets hard

---

[1]The botanical names of these trees are not available.

Figure 21.1. *Chawa tanner scraping stretched hide with gundalla, Gadeb, northern Bale, Ethiopia. The white lines indicate the width of the scraper edge coming into contact with the hide.*

and holds the scraper at an angle of about 110-120° to the line of the handle.

The skin to be scraped is kept continually moistened by blowing water onto it with the mouth from a tin which he keeps by his side. The tanner, standing and holding the wooden handle of the tool with both hands, scrapes off long shavings from the inner, fatty part of the skin. These shavings are devoured by dogs and chickens but occasionally some are kept and eaten, boiled, by the tanner and his family. To clean a cowhide takes one complete day—that is, some 8-10 hours—and the two mounted scrapers are exhausted at the end of this time and have to be replaced. A skin is considered cleaned when the whole of the inner fatty layer is removed.

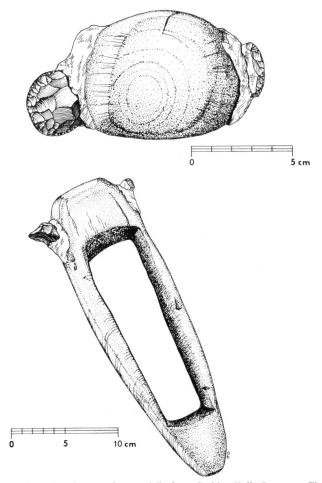

Figure 21.2. *Side and end view of a gundalla from Soddo, Kaffa Province. The left-hand scraper is of obsidian and unused; that on the right is of bottle glass and is worn out after resharpening and ready to be discarded.*

Scrapers are made from flakes struck from a large block of obsidian by free percussion with a stone or iron hammer, the block resting on a skin on the ground. The flakes are removed randomly and are generally broad and thickish. Kadir Alaki obtained the obsidian blocks from Shashamane, an important market center in the Rift, about 85 km to the west. They were brought up for him by bus to the nearest town on the main road by a middleman; a block about 45 cm in diameter and 20 cm thick cost the tanner E$10 (U.S. $5.00).

After the flaking, suitable examples are selected and retouched into scrapers using a flat piece of soft iron as a fabricator; this is shaped like a

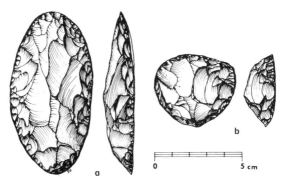

Figure 21.3. *(a) Unused and (b) worn out and discarded obsidian scrapers from Gadeb, northern Bale, Ethiopia.*

blunt knife blade and is about 22 cm long, 3 cm wide, and 5 mm thick. An evenly shaped, usually oval to subrectangular scraper is quickly formed by flaking with this tool all round the circumference of the piece to give the scraper a planoconvex section and a relatively low angle to the scraper edge situated on one end, sometimes on both ends, of the piece (Figure 21.3a).

After 15-20 scrapes the scraper has to be resharpened and this is done by "brushing"[2] the edge with the iron fabricator. Sometimes—when the angle between the ventral and dorsal faces becomes too steep—a rejuvenating flake is struck that removes the whole of the scraping edge. Although the retouching of the working edge—the "brushing"—removes only extremely small flakes the length of the scraper is gradually reduced to that of a short convex scraper, by which time it is discarded (Figure 21.3b).

All the flaking was done into an old, flat winnowing basket so that the debitage could then be taken away from the working area and dumped on a midden.

Sometimes larger, broad flakes were retouched as hide scrapers and, when this happens, they are not mounted in the handle but used directly in the hand but in the same way. Kadir Alaki made us some 20-30 scrapers and it is clear that there is a considerable amount of variation in morphology within what the maker obviously regards as a single type of tool.

Morphological Characteristics of Hide Scrapers

From the plotted midden (Figure 21.6) in Kadir Alaki's homestead, approximately 8 kg of obsidian artifacts were collected in February 1977. Among these artifacts were 55 complete, used, and discarded hide scrapers. A sam-

[2] That is, lightly flaking by minimal contact.

ple of roughly one-quarter of the total assemblage, 393 pieces, reflects the overall frequency distribution of the main artifact types: (a) hide scrapers (4.1%), (b) broken hide scraper fragments (1.5%), (c) flakes (27.9%), (d) flake fragments (62.9%), (e) cores (.8%), and (f) chunks (3.8%). Of the total 55 complete hide scrapers, 30 were submitted to a more detailed attribute analysis involving preliminary edge-wear studies; they were also compared with 14 ·unused obsidian hide scrapers manufactured by Kadir Alaki. The purpose of this analysis is first to provide a descriptive record of these rare stone hide scrapers from the ethnographic present and, second, to search for traces of the behavioral patterns of the maker-user as represented in these stone implements. Ethnographic examples can provide a unique opportunity to study the range of morphological variability and the effects of edge-wear within the natural environmental settings in which the function, the manner of manufacture, use, and discard are well documented.

As can be seen in Figures 21.3 and 21.4 and the statistical summary table (Table 21.1) there are apparent morphological differences between unused and used obsidian hide scrapers. The used and discarded tools are reduced in volume considerably and altered in outline shape from oval to an inverted triangular shape, often having sharp projecting corners at both ends of the working edge. The reduction in size is due to the constant resharpening required for the maintenance of the working or scraping edge. This results in an average decrease of 25 mm in maximum length whereas there are only minor quantitative changes in breadth and thickness, -6 mm and -2 mm, respectively. While the mean length $\times$ breadth $\times$ thickness measurement for unused scrapers is $65.3 \times 42.3 \times 16.8$ mm, the equivalent dimension for used and discarded scrapers is $39.9 \times 36.5 \times 14.8$ mm. The minimum size is regulated by the need to secure the scraper firmly in the handle by means of mastic. A decrease in the number of flake scars and circumference length is evident due to this size reduction. What are also affected by the size reduction are statistically significant (t test: $p < .005$) changes in the breadth/length and thickness/length ratios which are important shape defining indices.

Because of the constant edge-wear and resharpening, the working edge formed by the dorsal and ventral faces becomes increasingly steep. There is a difference of 13° in the average working edge angle between used and unused hide scrapers, 44° with the former and 57° with the latter scrapers. It is interesting to note that this range of edge angles closely approximates the 46-55° range observed by Wilmsen (1968:159) among Paleo-Indian "skin preparation" scrapers. Edge angles taken at other lateral and proximal edges do not show any noticeable difference between the unused and used scrapers.

In locating the actual working or scraping edge on used and discarded

Table 21.1
Fuga-Chawa Tanner's Obsidian Hide Scrapers

Attribute	Unused scrapers (N = 14)	Used and discarded scrapers (N = 30)	Total sample (N = 44)
Length (mm)			
Mean	65.3	39.9	48.0
Standard deviation	16.3	5.5	15.6
Range	40.0-91.0	31.0-56.0	31.0-91.0
95% C.I.	55.0-74.7	37.9-42.0	32.5-43.3
Breadth (mm)			
Mean	42.3	36.5	38.3
Standard deviation	13.8	7.0	9.9
Range	24.0-82.0	22.0-51.0	22.0-82.0
95% C.I.	34.3-50.2	33.8-39.1	35.3-41.3
Thickness (mm)			
Mean	16.8	14.8	15.4
Standard deviation	4.4	2.4	3.3
Range	10.0-27.0	10.0-21.0	10.0-27.0
95% C.I.	14.2-19.3	13.9-15.7	14.4-16.4
Breadth-Length			
Mean	0.66	0.93	0.84
Standard deviation	0.16	0.19	0.22
Thickness-length			
Mean	0.26	0.38	0.34
Standard deviation	0.03	0.07	0.08
Thickness-breadth			
Mean	0.41	0.42	0.42
Standard deviation	0.11	0.08	0.09
Working edge angle			
Mean	44.2	56.6	52.7
Standard deviation	6.7	8.3	9.7
Range	34.0-56.0	43.0-79.0	34.0-79.0
95% C.I.	40.4-48.1	53.5-59.7	49.7-55.6
Arc length (mm)			
Mean	—	43.9	—
Standard deviation	—	8.1	—
Retouch scar no.			
Mean	83.93	59.8	67.5
Standard deviation	16.3	8.1	15.9

scrapers, one must consider not just one but several morphological characteristics: *(a)* edge angle, *(b)* edge-wear, *(c)* striations, *(d)* retouch flake scars,
(e) projecting corners formed by edges, and *(f)* transparency or translucency
of edges. Along the working edge of used and discarded specimens, the
edge angle is steeper than adjacent edges; the retouch tends to be more
semi-invasive than stepped; striations often originate along the scraping

edge; the working edge is defined by two sharply projecting corners; the light emittence is low along the working edge; and the polish caused by working on "soft" material may be recognized.

Analysis of Edge-Wear

All the hide scrapers under discussion were examined using the binocular microscope at magnifications ranging from 12 to 45×. For much of microscopic analysis this range of magnification proved adequate and useful for the present analysis. However, to meet the strict demand of micro-edge-wear analysis proposed by Keeley (1977) a higher magnification range of 100 - 400× should be accommodated in any future analysis.

The character of edge-wear may be dependent on the various conditions in which the tool is used. If the raw material used is variable, then for each raw material petrographic properties such as hardness, resilience, and the amount of impurities must be noted. If, on the other hand, the raw material is not variable, as in this assemblage of hide scrapers which are made on black obsidian, then the raw material can be considered as a constant. The obsidian used for the hide scrapers is smooth and highly vitric with overall black color, having a somewhat greenish tinge that may be seen along the thin parameters when placed against the light.

Although the majority of specimens are fresh, there are a few used and discarded examples which show signs of patina both on ventral and dorsal faces. The patina must have developed after these specimens were discarded in the midden, exposed to sunlight and atmosphere and, also, having direct contact with soil, ash, and other elements. Although the exact duration of direct exposure to and contact with these natural and chemical processes cannot be determined, the formation of a shallow whitish patina is apparent on a few discarded specimens. Since the patina is only weakly formed, the microrelief of the surfaces of these specimens remains virtually unaltered. Effects of the patina to traces of use must be considered minuscule. The objects on which the scrapers were used are restricted purely to animal skins ranging from cow to sheep and goat. It is, therefore, possible to preclude the differential wear caused by working on wood, antler, or bone in this analysis. The material scraped may also be controlled broadly as a constant variable, assuming there is regularity in the hardness and texture of animal skins. A note of caution must be sounded here in that the hardness of skin could vary to some extent since the amount of moisture in the hide controls the expansion and reduction of fibers. Even on a single piece of hide, irregularity of hardness may exist as the skin is wetted by water blown from the tanner's mouth.

The working edge of the hide scraper is always semicircular or convex, which would yield a greater working edge length or arc length than a straight edge by a factor of 1.2, by our calculation, and the convex edge provides a firmer and easier penetration into the fat and muscle fiber than the straight edge does. Although the hide cleaning activity takes place inside a work hut, the stretched hide can still be subject to dust and soil particles from the earth floor and thus minute sandy grit may be trapped on the skin. Inclusion of these sand grains must also contribute to the cause of edge-wear and surface attrition. The character of the wearability of hide scrapers must, above all, be determined by human factors such as the amount of force exerted on the scraper during use, the angle of the scraper edge in relation to the hide, and the speed and frequency of strokes. Due to the combination of these factors, the scraper edge must be resharpened every 15–20 scrapes in our ethnographic example involving Kadir Alaki. Resharpening is accomplished by "brushing" the edge with the iron fabricator or striking off a rejuvenation flake, particularly when the edge angle formed by the ventral and dorsal faces becomes too steep. An individual rhythm of scraping, resharpening, scraping . . . seems to be a well-established part of this craft tradition.

Wear, as observed in the used and discarded hide scrapers, constitutes "micro-deformation" of the working edge (Semenov 1964:13). The intensity of wear is variable from tool to tool and yet there is a fair uniformity in the character of deformation. "Polishing" is evident on all the used and discarded hide scrapers and the very fine alterations of working edges become clearly visible under the binocular microscope using magnification greater than $22\times$. Polishing is evident on the ridges between flake scars near the extremity of the working edge. Gloss from use could well be present along the working edges; however, the natural luster of obsidian makes it virtually impossible to determine whether "gloss" exists or not. What is also noteworthy is that fat from the skin seems to have been trapped in the hinges created by step flaking. Dust particles and minute shavings have subsequently also been trapped and adhere to these hinged areas. Needless to say, an unused scraper edge appears pristine even under high magnification. Also present among used and discarded scrapers is more noticeable edge damage resulting in an irregular edge outline. Edge damage is extended to the removal of minute chips creating small scars or "microscarring" (Tringham, Cooper, Odell, Voytek, and Whitman 1974:185–187) mostly on the dorsal face and occasionally on the ventral face. While the microscars are continuous and scalar along the working edge, they are discontinuous and roughly triangular along nonworking edges, particularly along the edge opposite the working edge where the scraper is hafted into the handle. This slight deformation is most likely to be caused by the abrupt contact and friction the obsidian scraper makes with the wooden socket. There are some randomly distributed flake scars which are visible microscopically in some used and discarded specimens, indicating the possible effects of trampling by people and domestic stock.

Another form of deformation found in the used and discarded scrapers is striation. The striations are minute grooves or scratches found on the ventral face of the scrapers. As a rule, the ventral face of scrapers is always the release surface of flakes or flake fragments, the primary forms or blanks being either side-struck or end-struck flakes. Most commonly the original striking platform, or its remnant, is found at the proximal end of the scraper which is inserted into the hafting socket and covered with mastic. Striking platforms of original flake blanks are sometimes, however, positioned on the working edge itself. In such cases these platforms are point platforms having extremely thin platform thickness. When working on a relatively soft and plastic material it would seem that no scratch marks are produced under normal circumstances. In open-air working conditions accidental intrusion of sand grains is quite conceivable and they could become intermediary abrasive agents contributing to the surface attrition of hide scrapers. Minute chips are constantly generated by friction during the course of the work and these not only dull the working edges but also contribute to edge damage and cause striations as they become abrasive agents. There are some definite orientations found in the traces of striations which give an indication of the direction in which the hide scraper was pulled. Among the 30 used and discarded scrapers 17 (56.7%) showed double orientation in the pattern of criss-cross parallel lines as illustrated in Figure 21.4. These striations or scratch marks reflect the tanner's kinematic behavior associated with scraping activities. There are two kinds of strokes or movements governed by the stance adopted when cleaning hides. Although the scraping appears vertically unidirectional from the top down, this is achieved by periodically alternating the stance of the tanner from left to right in relation to the hide and, consequently, rotating the working edge of the obsidian scraper. Alternating the manner of stroke relates to the minimization of the strain on one particular hand and arm and facilitates the even distribution of edge-wear. Effective cleaning may thus be done by changing the direction of strokes and this aspect of behavior is clearly imprinted in our ethnographic example. The average angle formed by the two orientations seen in the scratch marks on the ventral face is 56°. Of the remaining 13 used and discarded scrapers, 6 show striations running from upper left to lower right, 4 from upper right to lower left, and the remaining 3 show no signs of striation. It was found that the absence of striations is correlated to the concavity of the ventral face and, conversely, that the presence of numerous and deeply incised striations relates to the convexity of the ventral face, often created by the bulb of percussion.

Figure 21.4. *Worn out and discarded obsidian scraper: the frontal view (top) and the ventral face (bottom).*

The Chawa Homestead and Disposal of Obsidian Waste

We plotted the disposition of all structures, features and obsidian at Kadir Alaki's homestead and this is shown at Figure 21.5: a dwelling house, a working hut used also for storage, grain silos and bins of split bamboo for winnowed grain, a stock pen (he owned a few cattle), haystacks, a winnowing area, a tethering area for horses and/or donkeys, and three midden areas. Kadir Alaki had lived here 16 years—the old, turf-walled stock pen dates to an earlier occupation.

It is apparent that there is practically no obsidian in the living and workshop areas which are kept free because of the danger of cutting the feet. There was no opportunity for careful examination and plotting of the floor of the work hut which might have yielded a few small obsidian fragments though none were readily visible. The three midden areas had been arbitrarily selected except that they had to be downwind as ash from hearths was regularly dumped there also, as well as bone and other waste materials. The oldest midden had very little ash and was where Kadir Alaki dumped his obsidian waste, close behind the area where he was working. The next oldest midden was that to the west while the area to the northwest was in current use. Before we left he had started to use the westernmost midden again. Figure 21.6 shows the distribution of obsidian and ash on this midden. The small dots are debitage and the larger triangles are the discarded, worn out scrapers. It can be observed that the midden is expanding from west to east, and most of the debitage was being dumped at the end nearest to where the obsidian was being worked. Individual basketfuls can still sometimes be recognized. Discarded scrapers exhibit a random distribution. All debitage and worn out scrapers were collected from this midden and the results of the analysis are reported above. The complete process of manufacture can be reconstructed and will be of considerable use for comparison with later prehistoric debitage where hide scrapers are present.

Most interesting, perhaps, for archaeologists is what happens to the obsidian when the midden is deflated by the removal of the ash by wind action and when more perishable organic materials have disappeared. The bone and stone become concentrated and compacted on the ground surface and, in due course, become covered by soil processes. In another area we examined just such a midden that was 25 years old and this concentration had come about. What would the excavation of Kadir Alaki's area have suggested to us if it had been in archaeological context and we had had no ethnographic observations as a basis for reconstruction? There would probably have been few who would not have interpreted the middens as the places where stone flaking had been carried out and, because of the scraper distribution, as places where these tools had also been used, most likely on the bones. In other words, this would probably have been interpreted as the activity area of the site. Of the dwelling and work huts, little would be preserved except hearth stones, the foundations of grain bins; the pounding stones used for straightening out the hides, some postholes and, perhaps, compacted dung ash in the stock pen, if it had been burned, would be all that would remain besides the debitage and bones. From Pleistocene times most of even this slender evidence would not be available.

A closely similar situation was observed in the excavation of a Middle Stone Age quarry workshop site at K'one (Garibaldi) caldera complex west of Metahara at the southwest corner of the Afar Rift. Here, excavations ex-

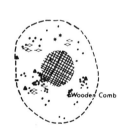

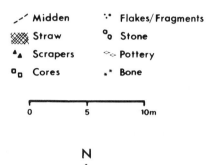

⟋⟋	Midden	∵·	Flakes/Fragments
▨	Straw	°₀	Stone
▲▲	Scrapers	⬦⬦	Pottery
▫▫	Cores	₊*	Bone

```
|—————————|—————————|
0         5         10m
```

N
↑
●

Wooden Comb

Midden 1
(plotted)

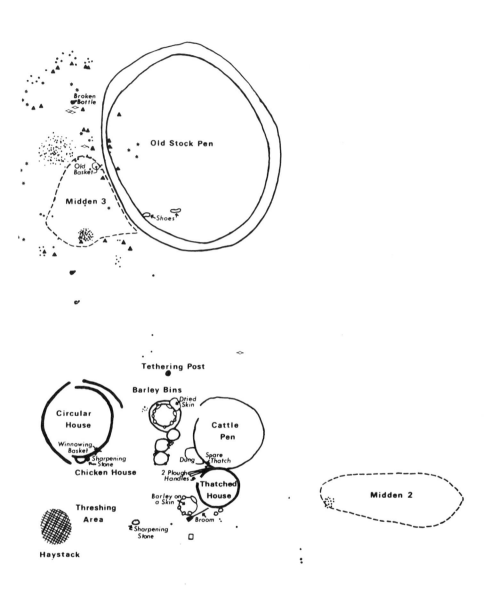

Figure 21.5. *Plan of Chawa tanner's homestead at Gadeb, northern Bale.*

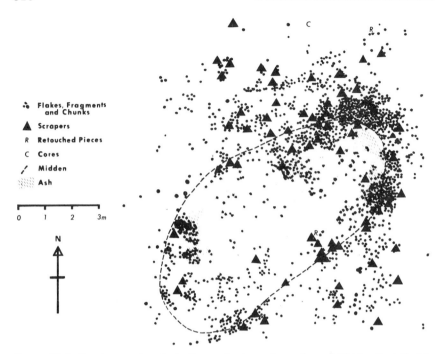

Figure 21.6. *Distribution plot of obsidian and ash on the surface of Midden 1 at Gadeb, northern Bale.*

posed a general scatter of debitage and artifacts (often broken in process of manufacture) and small, compact concentrations of obsidian flaking waste about 20–30 cm in diameter. The question arises as to whether these concentrations should be interpreted as the places where individual knappers sat and worked or as the flaking from an individual's activity that had been carefully dumped away from the working area?

Another interesting study that was possible has to do with the quarrying and distribution of the obsidian—in other words, the trade in obsidian. The main source today is in the Galla Lakes area (Chabbe Volcano). This was visited with the Gadeb tanner and we have a record of Kadir Alaki's opencast working, the rough dressing of the obsidian, and its sale in Awasa market. The roughed out blocks prepared for transport to the market closely resembled the proto-Levallois cores found with some Upper Acheulian assemblages.

One last observation concerns the peeling of the inner hide resulting from the scraping activities and the use of the shavings sometimes as food by the tanners. Since this practice is looked down upon and derided by Amharic speakers, it is probable that the use of these scrapings as food was much more common in the past than it is today. It does, however, provide an analogue to one possible use for the many small scraper forms found on the Oldowan and later sites at the Olduvai Gorge and on other Plio-Pleistocene sites in Africa—namely, for removing portions of the fatty, inner layer of dryish hides for use as food. It is hardly necessary to add that hides are regularly eaten by San Bushmen and other African peoples.

Archaeological Evidence for Hide Scrapers in Ethiopia

Additional significance attaches to the activities of the Fuga-Chawa tanners because of the time depth through which their characteristic scrapers can be traced. The worn out, short convex scraper forms have been found on what is probably a pre-fifteenth-century fortified Iron Age site in the vicinity and also at the fortified town of Mole in the Chercher Mountains (Joussaume and Joussaume 1972) dating around 1450 A.D. These are mostly made from chert and some 3000 were collected in a small area which has been interpreted as the "flint-knappers' quarter."

Considerable numbers of similar short convex scrapers are found at Axumite sites in northeastern Tigre, some as late as the mid seventh century A.D. (Puglisi 1946). Other concentrations are reported from an urban complex close to Axum and from the capital itself (de Contenson 1959:28). It seems probable that these scraper assemblages associated with Axumite and medieval urban centers and found concentrated in one part of the complex can be interpreted as waste products from the tanners' quarter. Besides attesting to the long persistence of this kind of scraper in association with hide cleaning, the concentration of these tools may also indicate that the Fuga-Chawa minorities were segregated at least as long ago as the early centuries of the present era.

Archaeological evidence suggests that the use of this kind of scraper for hide cleaning is of even greater antiquity. Typical worked-out scrapers have been found in the Gobedra Rockshelter near Axum dating to 1000 B.C. (Phillipson 1977:81) and examples have been reported by Blanc (1938) from the Later Stone Age site of Modjo. In Kenya also the so-called double-ended Wilton A scrapers reported by Leakey (1931) from the Naivasha-Nakuru Rift are similar and we ourselves in our 1974 excavation at Lake Besaka, Metahara, found similar short convex scrapers dating from 1500 B.C. Because of the great preponderance of these scrapers over microliths at the Lake Besaka site, as well as the probable presence of domestic cattle there, it would seem that by 1500 B.C. the earlier purely hunting-gathering economy was being replaced by pastoralism with a consequently greater use being made of hides.

Conclusion

What emerges from our field observation and laboratory examination of ethnographic hide scrapers in obsidian is that it is possible to define the range of morphological variability created by a single tool maker-user. Given the first-hand knowledge that these stone implements have a culturally specific function, namely, cleaning hides, it was possible to describe the particular kind of edge-wear on obsidian due to a single function. Microscopic analysis enabled us to identify the technological signs of the kinematic movement of the user, which was already known from field observations.

In interpreting the prehistoric function of end-scrapers, several possible uses have been suggested, ranging from chopping to cutting, scraping, chiseling, and grooving (Bordes 1969:18; Semenov 1964:85). It has been argued that they were probably fixed or hafted in handles; with end-scrapers made on elongated blades, however, it is thought that direct use would also have been possible. Concerning the direction of use, frontal movement (pushing forward) is more favorably implied as in the ethnographic Eskimo examples reported by Nissen and Dittemore (1974). In our ethnographic example the end-scrapers found in Gadeb are single-function tools which are hafted in wooden handles. Relatively long scrapers represent the unused or very initial stage of use but they are also hafted. Small specimens represent either the near terminal or discarded stage in the life-span of these scrapers. If found in archaeological context it is likely that the used and unused scrapers might easily be treated as separate and distinct artifact types by typology-oriented archaeologists because of apparent shape and size differences. Invariably the scraping movement is not frontal at Gadeb but involves pulling toward the user rather than pushing forward or outward for cleaning the hides.

The relatively greater wear on the right side of these tools is evident as the used and discarded scrapers are lopsided when compared to the more symmetric unused examples. This indicates that Kadir Alaki, who is right-handed, exerted more force with the right hand which caused tilting of the scraper slightly to the right during use. It is interesting to note that the greater wear on the right side of end scrapers has been remarked by Semenov in the material from Kostienki I, Timonovka, and other Soviet sites as well as from Upper Paleolithic sites in Europe and North Africa (Semnov 1964:86-87).

A great deal still remains to be undertaken in respect to studies of Fuga-Chawa obsidian working and use and it can be expected that much of significance for archaeological interpretation will result from such studies, since these scrapers are one of the very few kinds of regularly retouched tool still being made from stone in the world today. Lines of approach that trace the continuity from the present through the historic past to prehistoric times will certainly help to interpret the distribution patterns and variability observed in Later Stone Age and Iron Age contexts in Ethiopia and will also have some general cautionary message to convey to archaeologists from further afield.

References

Adams, B.
  1974a *Ancient Hierakonpolis.* Warminster, England: Aris and Phillips.
  1974b *Ancient Hierakonpolis. Supplement.* Warminster, England: Aris and Phillips.
Adams, E. Charles, and Frank W. Eddy
  1977 A design for a sophomore teaching laboratory in archaeology. In *Teaching and training in American archaeology: A survey of programs and philosophies,* edited by William P. McHugh, *Southern Illinois University at Carbondale, University Museum Studies 10.* Pp. 210-224.
Adams, William H.
  1973 An ethnoarchaeological study of a rural community: Silcott, Washington, 1900-1930. *Ethnohistory 20*(4):335-346.
  1975 Archaeology and the recent past: Silcott, Washington, 1900-1930. *Northwest Anthropological Research Notes 9*(1):156-165.
  1976 Silcott, Washington: Ethnoarchaeology of a rural American community. Ph.D. dissertation, Washington State University.
Allen, J. L.
  1975 *Aviation and space museums of America.* New York: Arco.
Althusser, L.
  1971 Ideology and ideological state apparatuses. In *Lenin and philosophy,* by L. Althusser. New York: Monthly Review Press. Pp. 127-186.
  1974 *Elements d'autocritique.* Paris: Hachette Litterature.
American Anthropological Association
  1971 Professional Ethics: Statements and Procedures of the American Anthropological Association. Washington, D.C.

Ascher, Robert
   1961   Experimental archaeology. *American Anthropologist 63:*793-816.
   1968a   Teaching archaeology in the university. *Archaeology 21:*282-287.
   1968b   Time's arrow and the archaeology of a contemporary community. In *Settlement archaeology*, edited by K. C. Chang. Palo Alto: National Press. Pp. 43-52.
   1970   CUES I: Design and construction of an experimental archaeological structure. *American Antiquity 35:*215-216.
   1974   Tin can archaeology. *Historical Archaeology 8:*7-16.
Baerreis, David A.
   1963   Teaching techniques. In *The teaching of anthropology*, edited by David G. Mandelbaum, Gabriel W. Lasker, and Ethel M. Albert. *American Anthropological Association, Memoir 94.* Pp. 253-259.
Baker, Charles M.
   1974   A study of aboriginal novaculite exploitation in the Ouachita Mountains of south-central Arkansas. M.A. thesis, University of Arkansas, Fayetteville.
Barker, R. G.
   1968   *Ecological psychology: Concepts and methods for studying the environment of human behavior.* Stanford: Stanford University Press.
Bastian, R. W.
   1975   Architecture and class segregation in late nineteenth-century Terra Haute, Indiana. *Geographical Review 65*(2):166-179.
Baumgartel, E. J.
   1955   *The cultures of prehistoric Egypt.* London: Oxford University Press.
Bellah, Robert N.
   1970   Civil religion in America. In *Beyond belief.* New York: Harper and Row.
Bemrose, Geoffrey
   1952   *Nineteenth century English pottery and porcelain.* London: Faber Monographs on Pottery and Porcelain.
Bennett, J. W.
   1969   *Northern plainsmen: Adaptive strategy and agrarian life.* Chicago: Aldine.
Berelson, B., and G. A. Steiner
   1964   *Human Behavior: An inventory of scientific findings.* New York: Harcourt, Brace and World.
Berreman, Gerald D.
   1962   Behind many masks: ethnography and impression management in a Himalayan village. *Society for Applied Anthropology, Monograph No. 4.*
Binford, Lewis R.
   1973   Interassemblage variability—The Mousterian and the "functional" argument. In *The explanation of culture change: Models in prehistory*, edited by Colin Renfrew. London: G. Duckworth. Pp. 227-253.
Binford, Sally R., and Lewis R. Binford
   1969   Stone tools and human behavior. *Scientific American 220*(4):70-84.
Blackman, A. W.
   1914   The rock tombs of Meir, Vol. 1. The tomb-chapel of Ukh-Hotp's Son Senbi. *Archaeological Survey of Egypt, Memoir 22.* London.
Blackman, A. W. and M. R. Apted
   1953   The rock tombs of Meir, Part V. *Archaeological Survey of Egypt, Memoir 28.* London.
Blalock, Hubert M.
   1960   *Social statistics.* New York: McGraw-Hill.

Blanc, A. C.
1938   Industria paleolitica e mesolitica del Moggio presso Addis Abeba (A.O.I.). *Rivista di Antropologia 32*:3-7.
Bloch, Maurice E. F.
1977   The past and the present in the present. *Man NS 12*(2):278-292.
1979   Knowing the world or hiding it. *Man NS 14*(1):165-167.
Bonnichsen, Robson
1973   Some operational aspects of human and animal bone alteration. In *Mammalian Osteo-Archaeology: North America*, edited by B. Miles Gilbert. Columbia: Missouri Archaeological Society, University of Missouri. Pp. 9-24.
1977   Models for deriving cultural information from stone tools. *National Museum of Man, Mercury Series, Archaeological Survey of Canada. Paper* No. 60.
Borchardt, L.
1907   *Das Grabdenkmal des Königs Ne-User-Rê.* Leipzig.
Bordes, F.
1969   Reflections on typology and techniques in the Paleolithic. *Arctic Anthropology 6*(1):1-29.
Bordes, François, and Maurice Bourgon
1951   Le complexe Mousterien, Levalloisien et Tayacien. *L'Anthropologie 55*(1-2):1-23.
Braidwood, Robert J.
1963   Themes and course progression. In *The teaching of anthropology*, edited by David G. Mandelbaum, Gabriel W. Lasker, and Ethel M. Albert. *American Anthropological Association, Memoir 94.* Pp. 239-246.
Broad, W. J.
1979   Science museums panned for pushing industry lii.?. *Science 204*:1180-1181.
Brose, David S.
1967   The Custer Road Dump site: An exercise in Victorian Archaeology. *The Michigan Archaeologist 13*(2).
1975   Functional analysis of stone tools: A cautionary note on the role of animal fats. *American Antiquity 40*:86-94.
Brown, Charles S. and Lane P. Johnson
1973   The secret use-life of a mayonnaise jar . . . or, how I learned to love lateral cycling. Manuscript on deposit, Arizona State Museum Library, Tucson.
Bryan, C. D. B.
1979   *The National Air and Space Museum.* New York: H. N. Abrams.
Burt, R. S.
1973   The differential impact of social integration on participation in the diffusion of innovations. *Social Science Research 2*(1):125-144.
Caldwell, J. A.
1967   Investigations at Tal-i Iblis. *Illinois State Museum Preliminary Reports* 9.
Caneva, I.
1970   I crescenti litici del Fayum. *Origini 4*:161-203.
Casson, S.
1933   *The technique of early Greek sculpture.* Oxford: Clarendon Press.
Caton-Thompson, G., and E. W. Gardner
1934   *The desert Fayum.* The Royal Anthropological Institute of Great Britain and Ireland.
Childe, V. G.
1954   Rotary motion. In *History of technology*, edited by C. Singer *et al.*, New York and London: Oxford University Press. Pp. 187-215.

Chilcott, John H., and James F. Deetz
1964 The construction and uses of a laboratory archaeological site. *American Antiquity 29*: 328-337.

Christaller, W.
1966 *Central places in southern Germany*. Translated by C. W. Baskin. Englewood Cliffs, N.J.: Prentice-Hall.

Claassen, Cheryl
1975 Antiques—objects of lateral cycling? *Arkansas Academy of Science, Proceedings*.

Clarke, David L., Editor
1977 *Spatial archaeology*. London: Academic Press.

Clarke, Rainbird
1935 The flint-knapping industry at Brandon. *Antiquity 9*(33):38-56.

Coles, John
1973 *Archaeology by experiment*. New York: Scribners.

Collier, John Jr.
1967 *Visual anthropology: Photography as a research method*. New York: Holt, Rinehart and Winston.

Collins, M.
1972 Statement of Michael Collins, Director, National Air and Space Museum, Smithsonian Institution, on appropriations requested for construction of the National Air and Space Museum. Hearings before the Subcommittee on Department of Interior and Related Agencies Appropriations, March 13, 1972.

Contenson, H. de
1959 Les fouilles à Axoum en 1957: Rapport préliminaire. *Annales d'Ethiopie 3*:25-42.

Cook, S.
1973 Stone tools for steel-age Mexicans? Aspects of production in a Zapotec stoneworking industry. *American Anthropologist 75*(5):1485-1503.

Cook, S. F., and R. F. Heizer
1965 The quantitative approach to the relation between population and settlement size. *Reports of the University of California Archaeological Survey*. No. 64. University of California Archaeological Research Facility.

Cooper, Clare
1967 Fenced back-yard, unfenced front yard, enclosed porch. *Journal of Housing 24*:268-273.

Copeland, Irene
1977 *The flea market and garage sale handbook*. New York: Popular Library.

Coser, Lewis
1964 *The functions of social conflict*. New York: The Free Press.

Cotter, John
1970 Colonial Williamsburg. *Technology and Culture 11*:417-427.

Darnay, Arsen, and William E. Franklin
1972 *Salvage markets for materials in solid wastes*. Washington, D.C.: U.S. Environmental Protection Agency.

Daumas, M., Editor
1962 *Les origines de la civilisation technique*. Vol. I. Paris: Presses Universitaires de France.

Davies, N. de G.
1902 The Rock tombs of Deir el Febrawi. Part I: Tomb of Aba and smaller tombs of the southern group. *Archaeological Survey of Egypt, Memoir* 11. London.

Deetz, J.
1967 *Invitation to archaeology*. New York: Doubleday.

1970   Archaeology as a social science. In *Current directions in anthropology*, edited by Ann Fischer. *Bulletin of the American Anthropological Association 3*(3, Part 2):115-125.

1977a   Material culture and archaeology—what's the difference? In *Historical archaeology and the importance of material things*, edited by L. Ferguson. *Society for Historical Archaeology, Special Publication Series*, No. 2:9-12.

1977b   *In small things forgotten: The archaeology of early American life.* Garden City, N.Y.: Anchor Doubleday.

de Lumley, Henry

1969   A paleolithic camp at Nice. *Scientific American 220*(5):42-50.

Dethlefsen, Edwin

1969   Colonial gravestones and demography. *American Journal of Physical Anthropology 31*:321-334. Reprinted, 1979, in *Studies in historical demography*, edited by Maris Vinovskis. New York: Academic Press.

1972   Life and death in colonial New England. Unpublished Ph.D. dissertation. Department of Anthropology, Harvard University.

Dethlefsen, Edwin, and James Deetz

1966   Death's heads, cherubs and willow trees: Experimental archaeology in colonial cemeteries. *American Antiquity 31*(4):502-510.

Dethlefsen, Edwin, and Kenneth Jensen

1977   Social commentary in the cemetery. *Natural History*, November:32-39.

Dickens, R. S., and W. R. Bowen

1978   Problems and promises in urban historical archaeology: The MARTA Project. Paper presented at the 43rd annual meeting of the Society for American Archaeology, Tucson.

DiMaggio, P., M. Useem, and P. Brown

1978   Audience studies of the performing arts and museums: A critical review. *Research Division Report*. No. 9. National Endowment for the Arts, Washington.

Donnan, C. B., and C. W. Clewlow, Jr.

1974   *Ethnoarchaeology*. University of California, Los Angeles, Institute of Archaeology, Monograph IV.

Dooling, D.

1976   History of the National Air and Space Museum. *Spaceflight 18*(7-8):249-262.

Douglas, M.

1966   *Purity and danger.* New York: Praeger.

Douglas, Mary

1973   *Natural symbols.* London: Tavistock.

Dundes, Alan

1966   Here I sit—A study of American latrinalia. *The Kroeber Society Anthropological Papers 34*:91-105.

Eggan, F.

1950   *Social organization of the western pueblos.* Chicago: University of Chicago Press.

Eighmy, J. L.

1977   Mennonite architecture: Diachronic evidence for rapid diffusion in rural communities. Unpublished Ph.D. dissertation, Department of Anthropology, University of Arizona, Tucson.

1979   Logistic trends in southwest population growth. In *Transformations: The mathematical study of social change*, edited by C. Renfrew and R. L. Cooke. New York: Academic Press.

Embree, John F.

1939   *Suye Mura.* Chicago: University of Chicago Press.

Emery, W. B.
1948   *Nubian treasure.* London.
1961   *Archaic Egypt.* Baltimore: Penguin.
Epstein, T. S.
1973   *South India: Yesterday, today, and tomorrow; Mysore villages revisited.* New York: Holmes and Meier.
Erasmus, C. J.
1961   *Man takes control.* Minneapolis: University of Minnesota Press.
Erman, A.
1894   *Life in ancient Egypt.* London: Macmillan and Co.
Evans, John
1872   *The ancient stone implements, weapons, and ornaments of Great Britain.* New York: D. Appleton and Company.
Fagan, Brian M.
1977   Canst thou draw out Leviathan with a Hook? (Job 41: 1)—an essay on the teaching of introductory archaeology. In *Teaching and training in American archaeology: A survey of programs and philosophies,* edited by William P. McHugh. *Southern Illinois University at Carbondale, University Museum Studies* 10. Pp. 196-208.
Feldman, C., and W. W. Hughes
1972   A brief study of seriation using functional and stylistic attributes of automobiles. Paper prepared for Anthropology 136. Manuscript on deposit. Arizona State Museum Library, University of Arizona, Tucson.
Ferguson, L.
1975   Historical archeology and the importance of material things. Paper delivered at the 1975 meetings of the Society for American Archaeology, January 5-11. Charleston, South Carolina.
1977   Historical archaeology and the importance of material things. In *Historical archaeology and the importance of material things,* edited by L. Ferguson. *Society for Historical Archaeology, Special Publication Series* No. 2:5-8.
Feuer, L. S.
1975   *Ideology and the ideologists.* New York: Harper and Row.
Firth, C. M.
1930   A datable flint tool. *Antiquity* 4:104-105.
Firth, C. M., J. E. Quibell, and J. P. Lauer
1935   *The step pyramid.* Vol. I, Text. Cairo: Imprimerie de l'Institut Français d'Archéologie Orientale.
Fitting, James E.
1968   Northern Lake Michigan lithic industries. *Anthropological Papers, Museum of Anthropology,* University of Michigan. No. 34.
Flannery, Kent V.
1972   The cultural evolution of civilizations. *Annual Review of Ecology and Systematics* 3:399-425.
1976   Two possible village subdivisions: the courtyard group and the residential ward. In *The early mesoamerican village,* edited by K. V. Flannery. New York: Academic Press. Pp. 72-75.
Flannery, Kent V., Editor
1976   *The early mesoamerican village.* New York: Academic.
Flannery, Kent V., and Marcus C. Winter
1976   Analyzing household activities. In *The early mesoamerican village,* edited by K. V. Flannery. New York: Academic Press. Pp. 34-47.

Fletcher, Roland
1977   Settlement studies (micro and semi-micro). In *Spatial archaeology*, edited by D. L. Clarke. London: Academic Press. Pp. 47-162.

Fontana, Bernard L.
1968   Review of: *The Custer Road Dump Site: An exercise in Victorian archaeology. The Michigan Archaeologist*, Vol. 13, No. 2, by David S. Brose. *Historical Archaeology* 2:125-127.
1970   In search of us. *Historical Archaeology* 4:1-2.

Ford, President G.
1976   The President's remarks at the dedication ceremonies for the National Air and Space Museum, July 1, 1976. *Weekly Compilation of Presidential Documents 12*(27): 1087-1135.

Foucault, M.
1970   *The order of things: An archaeology of the human sciences.* New York: Random House.

Francaviglia, Richard V.
1971   The Cemetery as an Evolving Cultural Landscape. *Annals, American Association of Geographers 61*:501-509.

Fraser, Douglas
1968   *Village planning in the primitive world.* New York: Braziller.

Fry, E. F.
1972   The dilemmas of the curator. In *Museums in crisis*, edited by B. O'Doherty. New York: Braziller.

Gallagher, J. P.
1977   Ethnoarchaeological and prehistoric investigations in the Ethiopian Central Rift Valley. Unpublished Ph.D. dissertation, Department of Anthropology, Southern Methodist University, Dallas.

Geertz, C.
1963   *Agricultural involution: The processes of ecological change in Indonesia.* Berkeley: University of California Press.
1972   Religion as a cultural system. In *Reader in comparative religion, an anthropological approach*, 3rd edition, edited by W. A. Lessa and E. Z. Vogt. New York: Harper & Row.

Glassie, H.
1968   *Pattern in the material folk culture of the eastern United States.* Philadelphia: University of Pennsylvania Press.
1975   *Folk housing in Middle Virginia: A structural analysis of historic artifacts.* Knoxville: University of Tennessee Press.
1977   Archaeology and folklore: Common anxieties, common hopes. In *Historical archaeology and the importance of material things*, edited by L. Ferguson. *Society for Historical Archaeology, Special Publication Series* No. 2:23-35.

Godden, Geoffrey A.
1963   *British pottery and porcelain 1780-1850.* A. S. Barnes Co.

Goffman, Erving
1959   *The presentation of self in everyday life.* Garden City, N.Y.: Doubleday.

Gonos, George, V. Mulkern, and N. Poushinsky
1976   Anonymous expression: A structural view of graffiti. *Journal of American Folklore 89*(351):40-48.

Gosse, A. B.
1915   *The civilization of the ancient Egyptians.* London: T. C. and E. C. Jack.

Gould, Richard A.
  1968   Living archaeology: The Ngatatjara of Western Australia. *Southwestern Journal of Anthropology 24*:101-122.
  1971   The archaeologist as ethnographer: A case from the Western Desert of Australia. *World Archaeology 3*:143-177.
  1974   Some current problems in ethnoarchaeology. In *Ethnoarchaeology*, edited by C. B. Donnan and C. W. Clewlow, Jr.. Los Angeles: UCLA Institute of Archaeology. Pp. 29-48.
Gould, R. A., Editor
  1978a   *Explorations in ethnoarchaeology*. Albuquerque: University of New Mexico Press.
Gould, Richard A.
  1978b   The anthropology of human residues. *American Anthropologist 80*(4):815-835.
Greenberg, J. H.
  1953   A new interpretation of the so-called "violence texts" based on the new discoveries from Upper Tell-El-New York III. Manuscript on deposit. Arizona State Museum Library, University of Arizona, Tucson.
Gregg, M. L.
  1975   A population estimate for Cahokia. *Perspectives in Cahokia Archaeology, Illinois Archaeological Survey Bulletin* 10. Illinois Archaeological Survey Inc., Urbana, Illinois.
Gregor, Thomas A.
  1974   Publicity, privacy and Mehinacu marriage. *Ethnology 13*:333-349.
Guimet, E.
  1909   Observations sur la fabrication des vases egyptiens de l'epoque prehistorique. *Societe Anthropologique de Lyon, Bulletin 28*:8-10.
Gumerman, G. J.
  1975   Alternative cultural models for demographic change: Southwestern examples. In *Population studies in archaeology and biological anthropology: A symposium, Memoir 30*, edited by A. C. Swedlund. Society for American Archaeology.
Hagen, E. E.
  1962   *On the theory of social change: How economic growth begins*. Homewood, Ill.: Dorsey Press.
Hall, A. J.
  1977   Dazzling legacy of an ancient quest. *National Geographic 151*(3):293-311.
Hamblin, R. L., R. B. Jacobson, and J. L. Miller
  1973   *A mathematical theory of social change*. New York: Wiley.
Handsman, R. G.
  1977   The Bushkill complex as an anomaly: unmasking the ideology of American archaeology. Ph.D. dissertation, American University. University Microfilms, Ann Arbor.
Harding, A.
  1971   Review of: *Minoan stone vases*, by Peter Warren. *Proceedings of the Prehistoric Society 37*(1):242-243.
Harrington, Faith
  1976   No title (Preliminary analysis of 1976 Reuse Project data). Manuscript on deposit, Arizona State Museum Library, Tucson.
Harris, E. C.
  1975   The stratigraphic sequence: A question of time. *World Archaeology 7*:109-121.
  1977   Units of archaeological stratification. *Norwegian Archaeological Review 10*:84-94.
Harris, J. R.
  1961   *Lexicographical studies in ancient Egyptian minerals*. Deutsche Akademie der Wissenschaften zu Berlin Institut für Orientforschung, 54.

Harris, M.
  1964   *The nature of cultural things.* New York: Random House.
  1968   *The rise of anthropological theory.* New York: Thomas Y. Crowell.
Harrison, G. G., W. L. Rathje, and W. W. Hughes
  1975   Food waste behavior in an urban population. *Journal of Nutrition Education* 7(1):13-16.
Hartenberg, R. S., and J. Schmidt, Jr.
  1969   The Egyptian drill and the origin of the crank. *Technology and Culture* 10(2):155-165.
Heizer, R. F.
  1966   Ancient heavy transport, methods and achievements. *Science 153*:821-830.
Heizer, R. F., F. H. Stross, T. R. Hester, Albee, Perlman, Asaro, and Bowman
  1973   The Colossi of Memnon revisited. *Science 182*:1219-1225.
Heizer, R. F., F. H. Stross, and T. R. Hester
  1973   New light on the Colossi of Memnon. *Southwest Museum Masterkey 47*(3):94-105.
Hester, T. R.
  1976   Functional analysis of ancient Egyptian stone tools: The potential for future research. *Journal of Field Archaeology 3*(3):346-351.
Hester, T. R., and R. F. Heizer
  1980   *Making stone vases: Ethnoarchaeological studies at an alabaster workshop in upper Egypt.* Malibu, Calif.: Undena Publications.
Hester, T. R., R. F. Heizer, and J. A. Graham
  1975   *Field methods in archaeology.* 6th Edition. Palo Alto: Mayfield.
Hill, James N.
  1968   Broken K Pueblo: Patterns of form and function. In *New perspectives in archeology,* edited by S. R. and L. R. Binford. Chicago: Aldine. Pp. 103-142.
  1970   *Broken K Pueblo: Prehistoric social organization in the American Southwest.* Anthropological Papers of the University of Arizona No. 18. Tucson: University of Arizona Press.
  1977   Individual variability in ceramics and the study of prehistoric social organization. In *The individual in prehistory: Studies of variability in style in prehistoric technologies,* edited by James N. Hill and Joel Gunn. New York: Academic Press. Pp. 55-108.
  1978   Individuals and their artifacts: an experimental study in archaeology. *American Antiquity 43*:245-257.
Hirst, P. Q.
  1976   Althusser and the theory of ideology. *Economy and Society 5*(4):385-412.
Hodder, I. R.
  1972   Locational models and the study of Romano-British settlement. In *Models in archaeology,* edited by D. L. Clarke. London: Methuer. Pp. 887-909.
Hodgen, M. T.
  1945   Glass and paper, an historical study of acculturation. *Southwestern Journal of Anthropology 1*:446-497.
  1950   Similarities and dated distributions. *American Anthropologist 52*(4):445-467.
  1974   *Anthropology, history, & cultural change.* Viking Fund Publications in Anthropology, 42, Tucson: University of Arizona Press.
Hodges, H.
  1964   *Artifacts.* London: John Baker.
  1970   *Technology in the ancient world.* New York: Knopf.
Hohman, J.
  1975   Road end behavior. Paper prepared for Anthropology 136. Manuscript on deposit, Arizona State Museum Library, University of Arizona, Tucson.

Hole, F., and R. F. Heizer
    1977   *Prehistoric archeology: A brief introduction.* Holt, Rinehart and Winston, New York.
Holton, Felicia
    1979   Death's heads, cherubs and shaded urns. *Early Man,* Autumn:5-9.
Homans, G. C.
    1961   *Social behavior: Its elementary forms.* Harcourt Brace, New York.
Hostetler, J. A.
    1968   *Amish Society.* Revised edition. Baltimore: Johns Hopkins University Press.
Hudson, K.
    1977   *Museums for the 1980's: A survey of world trends.* New York: Holmes and Meier.
Hutton, J. H.
    1944   The place of material culture in the study of anthropology. *Royal Anthropological Institute Journal 44:*1-6.
Ingersoll, Daniel W., Jr.
    1971a   Settlement archaeology at Puddle Dock. Doctoral dissertation, Department of Anthropology, Harvard University.
    1971b   Problems of urban historical archaeology. *Man in the Northeast 1*(2):66-74.
Irwin, Henry T., and H. M. Wormington
    1970   Paleo-Indian tool types in the Great Plains. *American Antiquity 35:*24-34.
Jacoby, Jacob, Carol K. Berning, and Thomas F. Dietvorst
    1977   What about disposition? *Journal of Marketing,* April:22-28.
Jeane, Donald G.
    1969   The traditional upland south cemetery. *Landscape 18:*39-41.
Jennings, Jesse D.
    1950   Table top archaeology. *Archaeology 3:*175-178.
    1963   Educational functions. In *The teaching of anthropology,* edited by David G. Mandelbaum, Gabriel W. Lasker, and Ethel M. Albert. *American Anthropological Association, Memoir* 94. Pp. 247-272.
Jelinek, Arthur L.
    1962   Use of the cumulative graph in temporal ordering. *American Antiquity 28:*241-243.
Johnson, G. A.
    1972   A test of the utility of Central Place Theory in archaeology. In *Man, settlement and urbanism,* edited by P. J. Ucko, R. Tringham, and G. W. Dimbleby, London: Duckworth. Pp. 769-785.
    1977   Aspects of regional analysis in archaeology. *Annual Review in Anthropology 6:*479-509.
Joussaume, H., and R. Joussaume
    1972   Anciennes villes dans le Tchercher (Hadror). *Annales d'Ethiopie 9:*21-43.
Judge, W. James
    1977   The field school: Training session or legitimate research? In *Teaching and training in American archaeology: A survey of programs and philosophies,* edited by William P. McHugh. *Southern Illinois University at Carbondale, University Museum Studies* 10. Pp. 122-135.
Kassander, Helen
    1973   Second Hand Rose, or lateral cycling: A study in behavioral archaeology. Manuscript on deposit, Arizona State Museum Library.
Kato, Gerald
    1979   Pair found guilty of manslaughter. *Honolulu Advertiser,* May 11, p. A-3.
Kavanaugh, J. V.
    1978   The artifact in American Culture: The development of an undergraduate program in American studies. In *Material culture and the study of American life,* edited by I. M. G. Quimby. New York: Norton. Pp. 65-74.

Keeley, L.
1977   An experimental study of microwear traces on selected British Palaeolithic implements. Unpublished Ph.D. dissertation, Oxford University.
Kelley, K. B.
1976   Dendritic central-place systems and the regional organization of Navajo trading posts. In *Regional analysis*, Vol. 1, edited by C. A. Smith. New York: Academic Press. Pp. 219-254.
Kerrich, J. E., and D. L. Clarke
1967   Notes on the possible misuse and errors of cumulative percentage frequency graphs for the comparison of prehistoric artifact assemblages. *Proceedings of the Prehistoric Society for 1967, NS 33*(4):57-69.
Kidder, Alfred II
1963   Course design. In *The teaching of anthropology*, edited by David G. Mandelbaum, Gabriel W. Lasker, and Ethel M. Albert. *American Anthropological Association, Memoir 94.* Pp. 233-238.
Kira, Alexander
1966   *The bathroom.* Ithaca, N.Y.: Cornell University Press.
Klebs, L.
1915   *Die Reliefs des alten Reiches* (2980-2475 v. Chr.). *Material zur agyptischen Kulturgeschichte.* Abhandlungen der Heidelberger Akademie der Wissenschaften, Philosophisch-historische Klasse 3.
Knowles, Francis H. S., and Alfred S. Barnes
1937   Manufacture of gunflints. *Antiquity 11*(42):201-207.
Kramer, Carol, Editor
1979   *Ethnoarchaeology: Implications of ethnography for archaeology.* New York: Columbia University Press.
Kroeber, A. L.
1919   On the principle of order in civilization as exemplified by changes of fashion. *American Anthropologist 21*:235-263.
1925   Handbook of the Indians of California. *Bulletin of the Bureau of American Ethnology 78.*
Lauer, J. P., and F. De Bono
1950   Technique de façonnage des croissants de silex utilisés dan l'enceinte de Zoser. *Annales du Service des Antiquités de l'Egypte 50*:1-18.
Leach, Edmund
1961   Two essays concerning the symbolic representation of time. In *Rethinking anthropology*. London: Athlone Press.
Leakey, L. S. B.
1931   *The stone age cultures of Kenya Colony.* London: Cambridge University Press.
Lee, R. B., and I. DeVore, Editors
1968   *Man the hunter.* Chicago: Aldine.
Leone, Mark P.
1973   Archaeology as the science of technology: Mormon town plans and fences. In *Research and theory in current archaeology*, edited by Charles L. Redman. New York: Wiley. Pp. 125-150.
1977   The new Mormon Temple in Washington, D.C. In *Historical archaeology and the importance of material things*, edited by L. Ferguson. *Society for Historical Archaeology, Special Publication Series* No. 2:43-61.
Levi-Strauss, C.
1964   *The raw and the cooked.* New York: Harper & Row.

Lewis, B.
   1975   *History: Remembered, recovered, invented.* Princeton, N.J.: Princeton University
           Press.
Lewis, Oscar
   1961   *The children of Sanchez.* New York: Random House.
Limbrey, Susan
   1975   *Soil science and archaeology.* London: Academic Press,
Linton, Cathy
   1977   Garage sales. Manuscript and 59 questionnaires. On deposit, Arizona State Museum
           Library, Tucson.
Loesch, A.
   1954   *The economics of location.* Translated by W. F. Stolper. New Haven: Yale Univer-
           sity Press.
Longacre, W. A.
   1968   Some aspects of prehistoric society in east-central Arizona. In *New perspectives in ar-
           cheology,* edited by S. R. and L. R. Binford. Chicago: Aldine. Pp. 89-102.
   1970   *Reconstructing prehistoric pueblo societies.* Albuquerque: University of New Mexico
           Press.
   1975   Population dynamics at Grasshopper Pueblo, Arizona. In *Population studies in
           archaeology and biological anthropology: A symposium, Memoir 30,* edited by A. C.
           Swedlund. Society for American Archaeology.
Longacre, William A., and J. Jefferson Reid
   1974   The university of Arizona archaeological field school at Grasshopper: Eleven years of
           multidisciplinary research and teaching. In *Behavioral archaeology at the Grass-
           hopper Ruin,* edited by J. Jefferson Reid. *The Kiva 40:3-38.*
Love, T. F.
   1977   Ecological niche theory in sociocultural anthropology: A conceptual framework and
           an application. *American Ethnologist 4*(1):27-41.
Lucas, A., and J. R. Harris
   1962   *Ancient Egyptian materials and industries.* London: Edward Arnold.
Mackie, J. L.
   1975   Ideological explanation. In *Explanation,* edited by S. Korner. New Haven: Yale Uni-
           versity Press. Pp. 185-197.
Martin, Paul S.
   1975   Philosophy of education at Vernon Field Station. *Fieldiana: Anthropology 65:3-11.*
   1977   An approach to training archaeologists as anthropologists: An education philosophy.
           In *Teaching and training in American archaeology: A survey of programs and phil-
           osophies,* edited by William P. McHugh. *Southern Illinois University at Carbondale,
           University Museum Studies 10.* Pp. 154-160.
Marx, K., and F. Engels
   1970   *The German ideology,* edited with an introduction by C. Arthur. New York: Interna-
           tional Publishers. (Originally published, 1846.)
Matson, R. G., and W. D. Lipe
   1976   Settlement patterns on Cedar Mesa: Boom and bust on the northern periphery.
           Museum of Northern Arizona, Bulletin No. 50. Flagstaff, Arizona.
MacCannell, D.
   1976   *The tourist: A new theory of the leisure class.* New York: Schocken Books.
McCarthy, K.
   1976   The household life cycle and housing choices. *Papers of the Regional Science Asso-
           ciation 37.*

McGlynn, Paul D.
1972   Graffiti and slogans: Flushing the Id. *Journal of Popular Culture* 6(2):351-356.

McHugh, William P.
1977   Prologue. In *Teaching and training in American archaeology: A survey of programs and philosophies*, edited by William P. McHugh. *Southern Illinois University at Carbondale, University Museum Studies* 10. Pp. iii-vi.

McNutt, Charles H.
1973   On the methodological validity of frequency seriation. *American Antiquity 38*: 45-60.

McVicker, D.
1972   The cemetery seminar: Exploring the research and learning potential of the "New Archaeology." Paper presented at the 37th annual meeting of the Society for American Archaeology, Miami.
1973   Pots—Past and present. Paper presented at the 38th annual meeting of the Society for American Archaeology, San Francisco.

Meighan, Clement W.
1977   Research versus pedagogy in archaeological field schools. In *Teaching and training in American archaeology: A survey of programs and philosophies*, edited by William P. McHugh. *Southern Illinois University at Carbondale, University Museum Studies* 10. Pp. 111-121.

Mendez, D. A.
1968   Social structure and the diffusion of innovation. *Human Organization 27*(3): 241-249.

Mendras, H.
1970   *The vanishing peasant: Innovation and change in French agriculture.* Cambridge: MIT Press.

Mindeleff, C.
1900   Localization of Tusayan clans. *Nineteenth Annual Report of the Bureau of American Ethnology*, Washington, D.C.: Smithsonian Institution.

Montet, P.
1925   *Les scénes de la vie privée dans les tombeaux Égyptiens de l'ancien empire.* Imprimerie Alsacienne, Strasbourg.

Montgomery, E.
1977   Human ecology and the population concept: The Yelnadu Reddi population of India. *American Ethnologist* 4(1):175-189.

Morenon, E. P.
1978   Garages, task groups and functional variability: Torque wrenching the present and side-scraping the past. Paper presented at the 77th annual meeting of the American Anthropological Association, Los Angeles.

Morgan, J. de
1896   *Recherches sur les origines de l'Egypte. L'Age de la pierre et les metaux.* Paris: Ernest Leroux.

Muhly, F., Jr.
1975   The quick and the dead: Thieves and tombs along the Nile. *New York Times*, Sunday, December 28:1,10.

Murphy, L.
1978   'Once is not enough,' say NASM visitors. *The Smithsonian Torch 78*(3):8.

Naroll, R.
1968   Some thoughts on comparative method in cultural anthropology. *Methodology in social research*, edited by H. M. Blalock and A. Blalock. New York: McGraw-Hill.

National Air and Space Museum
1976   *Celebrating the National Air and Space Museum.* CBS Publications.

National Endowment for the Arts.
1974   *Museums USA.* Washington, D.C.: United States Government Printing Office.

Needham, Rodney
1972   *Belief, language, and experience.* Chicago: University of Chicago Press.

Newsom, B., and A. Silver, Editors
1978   *The art museum as educator.* Berkeley: University of California Press.

New York Times
1979   Susan B. Anthony coin receives a poor rating (10 October).

Nie, Norman H., C. Hadlai Hull, Jean G. Jenkins, Karin Steinbrenner, and Dale H. Bent
1975   *Statistical package for the social sciences,* 2nd edition. New York: McGraw-Hill.

Nissen, K., and M. Dittemore
1974   Ethnographic data and wear pattern analysis: A study of socketted Eskimo scrapers. *Tebiwa* 17(1):67-88.

Nöel-Hume, I.
1974   *All the best rubbish.* New York: Harper & Row.
1976   *A guide to historic artifacts of colonial America.* New York: Knopf.

Norbeck, Edward
1959   *Pineapple town: Hawaii.* Berkeley: University of California Press.

Oakley, Kenneth P.
1967   *Man the tool-maker.* London: The British Museum (Natural History).

Ong, Vickie
1978   Kalani (school) takes a swing at violence. *Honolulu Advertiser,* February 2, p. A-1.

Oswalt, Wendell H.
1974   Ethnoarchaeology. In *Ethnoarchaeology,* edited by C. B. Donnan and C. W. Clewlow. U.C.L.A. Institute of Archaeology, Los Angeles. Pp. 3-11.

Packard, Vance
1959   *The status seekers.* New York: David McKay.
1960   *The waste makers.* New York: David McKay.

Petrie, W. M. F.
1901   *Diospolis Parva. The cemeteries of Abadiyeh and Hu, 1898-9.* London: Special Extra Publication of the Egypt Exploration Fund.
1902   *Abydos.* Part I. 1902. *The Egypt Exploration Fund, Memoir 22.*
1910   *Arts and crafts of ancient Egypt.* Chicago: A. C. McClure.
1917   *Tools and weapons.* British School of Archaeology in Egypt and Egyptian Research Account, Twenty-Second Year, 1916, Publication 30. London.
1937   *Stone and metal vases.* British School of Egyptian Archaeology, London.

Petrie, W. M. F., E. Mackay, and G. Wainwright
1910   *Meydum and Memphis (III).* British School of Archaeology in Egypt, London.

Phillips, Philip, J. A. Ford, and J. B. Griffin
1951   Archaeological survey in the lower Mississippi Alluvial Valley, 1940-47. *Papers of the Peabody Museum of American Archaeology and Ethnology, Harvard University,* Vol. 25.

Phillipson, D.
1977   The excavation of Gebedra Rock-shelter, Axum. *Azania* 12:53-82.

Piperno, M.
1973   The lithic industry of Tepe Yaha: A preliminary typological analysis. *East and West* 23(1-2):59-74.

Plog, F. T.
1974   *The study of prehistoric change.* New York: Academic Press.
1977   Explaining change. In J. N. Hill. *Explanation of prehistoric change,* edited by School of American Research Advanced Seminar Series. Albuquerque: University of New Mexico Press.

Plog, F. T., and D. G. Bates
1976   *Cultural anthropology.* New York: Knopf.

Polanyi, K., C. M. Arensberg, and H. W. Pearson, Editors
1957   *Trade and market in the early empires.* New York: Free Press.

Poor, Allen
1978   The antique car market and reuse processes—or—Have you seen my Huppmobile? Manuscript on deposit, Arizona State Museum Library, Tucson.

Popper, K. R.
1972   Epistemology without a knowing subject. In *Objective Knowledge: An evolutionary approach,* edited by K. R. Popper. Oxford: The Clarendon Press. Pp. 106-152.

Portnoy, Alice W.
1975   Some relationships between family behavior and the physical arrangement of the home. Unpublished M.A. thesis, Texas Tech University, Lubbock.
1979   An approach to the study of the effects of housing on people. Paper presented at the 78th annual meeting, American Anthropological Association, Cincinnati.

Prezeworski, A., and H. Teune
1970   *Logic of comparative social inquiry.* New York: Wiley-Interscience.

Puglisi, S. M.
1946   L'Industria niolitica di Axum. *Rassegna di Science Preistoriche* 2:284-290.

Quibell, J. E., and F. W. Green
1902   *Hierakonpolis.* Part II. Egyptian Research Account, Fifth Memoir, London.

Quibell, M.
1905   Archaic objects. *Catalogue General des Antiquités Egyptiennes du Mugee du Caire.* Cairo: Service des Antiquites de l'Egypte.
1935   Stone vessels from the step pyramid. *Annales du Service des Antiquités de l'Egypte* 35:76-80.

Quimby, Ian M. G.
1978   *Material culture and the study of American life.* New York: Norton.

Radcliffe-Brown, A. R.
1952   *Structure and function in primitive society.* Glencoe, Ill.: Free Press.

Rapoport, Amos
1977   *Human aspects of urban form.* Oxford: Pergamon Press.

Rathje, William L.
1974   The Garbage Project: A new way of looking at the problems of archaeology. *Archaeology* 27:236-241.
1978   Archaeological ethnography . . . because sometimes it is better to give than to receive. In *Explorations in ethnoarchaeology,* edited by R. A. Gould. Albuquerque: University of New Mexico Press. Pp. 49-76.
1979a   Trace measures. In *Unobtrusive measures today, new directions for methodology of behavioral science,* edited by L. Sechrest. San Francisco, Jossey-Bass. Pp. 75-91.
1979b   Modern material culture studies. In *Advances in archaeological method and theory.* Volume 2, edited by Michael B. Schiffer. New York: Academic Press. Pp. 1-37.

Rathje, W. L., and G. G. Harrison
1978   Monitoring trends in food utilization. *Proceedings, Federation of Experimental Biologists* 37:9-14.

Rathje, W. L., and M. McCarthy
1977 Regularity and variability in contemporary garbage. In *Research strategies in historical archaeology*, edited by S. South, New York: Academic Press. Pp. 261-286.

Read, H.
1945 *Education through art.* New York: Pantheon.

Redekop, C. W.
1969 *The old colony Mennonites: Dilemmas of ethnic minority life.* Baltimore: Johns Hopkins Press.

Redfield, R.
1950 *A village that chose progress: Chan Kom revisited.* Chicago: University of Chicago Press.

Reich, Wendy, R. Buss, E. Fein, and T. Kurtz
1977 Notes on women's graffiti. *Journal of American Folklore* 90(356):188-191.

Reid, J. J.
1973 Growth and response to stress at Grasshopper Pueblo, Arizona. Ph.D. dissertation, Tucson, University of Arizona. Ann Arbor, University Microfilms.

Reid, J. J., W. Rathje, and M. Schiffer
1974 Expanding archaeology. *American Antiquity 39*:125-126.

Reid, J. Jefferson, Michael B. Schiffer, and William L. Rathje
1975 Behavioral archaeology: Four strategies. *American Anthropologist 77*:864-869.

Renfrew, C.
1977 Models for exchange and spatial distribution. In *Exchange systems in prehistory*, edited by T. K. Earle and J. E. Ericson. New York: Academic Press. Pp. 71-90.

Rhind, A. H.
1862 *Thebes: Its tombs and their tenants, ancient and present.* London.

Richardson, J., and A. L. Kroeber
1940 Three centuries of women's dress fashions: A quantitative analysis. *University of California Anthropological Records* 5(2):111-153.

Richardson, Miles, Editor
1974 *The human mirror.* Baton Rouge: Louisiana State University Press.

Rickert, J. F.
1967 House facades of the northeastern United States: A tool for geographical analysis. *Annals of the Association of American Geographers* 57(2):211-238.

Ritter, L. S., and W. L. Silber
1970 *Money.* New York: Basic Books.

Roberts, R. L.
1977 Human population estimates. In *The Talking Crow site,* edited by C. S. Smith. Lawrence: *University of Kansas Publications in Anthropology 9.*

Robertson, B.
1972 The museum and the democratic fallacy. In *Museums in crisis,* edited by B. O'Doherty. New York: Braziller.

Robinson, C. R., and C. B. Young
1965 *A nation without coins.* New York: Vantage Press.

Rogers, E. M.
1962 *Diffusion of innovation.* New York: Free Press.

Rogers, E. M., and L. Svenning
1969 *Modernization among peasants: The impact of communication.* New York: Holt, Rinehart and Winston.

Rowe, A.
1931 The Eckley B. Coxe, Jr., expedition excavations at Meydûm, 1929-30. *The Museum Journal 22*(1).

Rowe, John H.
1962   Worsaae's law and the use of grave lots for archaeological dating. *American Antiquity 28*(2):129-137.
Rudwick, M. J.
1972   *The meaning of fossils: Episodes in the history of paleontology.* London: MacDonald and Company.
Sadek-Kooros, H.
1972   Primitive bone fracturing: A method of research. *American Antiquity 37*:369-382.
Salwen, Bert
1973   Archeology in megalopolis. In *Research and theory in current archeology,* edited by Charles L. Redman. New York: Wiley-Interscience. Pp. 151-163.
Sanders, William T.
1965   The cultural ecology of the Teotihuacan Valley. Department of Sociology and Anthropology, Pennsylvania State University.
Saraydar, Stephen C., and Izumi Shimada
1973   Experimental archeology: A new outlook. *American Antiquity 38*:344-350.
Sawatzky, H. L.
1971   *They sought a country: Mennonite Colonization in Mexico.* Berkeley: University of California Press.
Schiffer, Michael B.
1972   Archaeological context and systemic context. *American Antiquity 37*(2): 156-165.
1973a The relationship between access volume and content diversity of storage facilities. *American Antiquity 38*:114-116.
1973b Cultural formation processes of the archaeological record: Applications at the Joint Site, east-central Arizona. PhD. dissertation, University of Arizona. Ann Arbor: University Microfilms.
1975   Archaeology as behavioral science. *American Anthropologist 77*(4):836-848.
1976a *Behavioral archeology.* New York: Academic Press.
1976b Prospects for the archaeological study of reuse processes in modern America. Unpublished manuscript, on file, Arizona State Museum Library, Tucson.
1977   Toward a unified science of the cultural past. In *Research strategies in historical archaeology,* edited by Stanley South. New York: Academic Press. Pp. 13-50.
1978   Methodological issues in ethnoarchaeology. In *Explorations in ethnoarchaeology,* edited by R. Gould. Albuquerque: A School of American Research Book. University of New Mexico Press. Pp. 229-247.
Schiffer, Michael B., and Jerome Schaefer
n.d.   The ethnoarchaeology of periodic markets. Manuscript in preparation.
Schlereth, Thomas J.
1978   It wasn't that simple. *Museum News 56*(3):36-44.
Schuyler, Robert L.
1970   Review of: The Custer Road Dump site: An exercise in Victorian Archaeology. The Michigan Archaeologist, Vol. 13, No. 2, by David S. Brose. *American Anthropologist 72*:179-180.
Semenov, S. A.
1964   *Prehistoric technology.* London: Cory, Adams and Mackay.
Shack, W. A.
1966   *The Gurage: A people of the Ensete Culture.* London: Oxford University Press.
Shackley, Myra L.
1975   *Archaeological sediments: A survey of analytical methods.* New York: Halsted Press.

Schafer, Harry J., and Vaughn M. Bryant, Jr.
 1977   *Archaeological and botanical studies at Hinds Cave, Val Verde County, Texas.* Texas
          A & M University. Anthropology Laboratory Special Series No. 1.
Skertchly, Sydney B. J.
 1879   *On the manufacture of gunflints; The methods of excavating for flint; the connection
          between neolithic art and the gunflint trade.* London: District Memoir of the Geo-
          logical Survey of Great Britain and Ireland.
Smith, C. A.
 1976   Regional economic systems; Linking geographical models and socioeconomic prob-
          lems. In *Regional analysis,* Vol. 1, edited by C. A. Smith. New York: Academic
          Press. Pp. 3-63.
Smith, Samuel D., and Stephen T. Rogers
 1979   *A survey of historic pottery making in Tennessee.* Division of Archaeology, Tennes-
          see Department of Conservation.
South, Stanley, Editor
 1977   *Research strategies in historical archaeology.* New York: Academic Press.
Spargo, John
 1926   *Early American pottery and china.* The Century Company.
Spicer, E. H.
 1962   *Cycles of conquest: The impact of Spain, Mexico, and the United States on the In-
          dians of the Southwest, 1533-1960.* Tucson: The University of Arizona Press.
Spier, Robert F. G.
 1973   *Material culture and technology.* Minneapolis: Burgess.
Sprague, Mary Gay
 1979   The life cycle of a quern: An analysis of the grindstones from the Neolithic site of
          Selevac, Yugoslavia. Senior Honors Thesis, Department of Anthropology, Harvard
          University.
Stahl, N.
 1975   Jelly side down: Questions soon beyond a mother. Universal Press Syndicate.
St. Thomas, L.
 1977   NASM staff reminisces on first birthday. *The Smithsonian Torch* 77(7):8.
State of Hawaii (Department of Planning and Economic Development)
 1972   *Census tract data by race from the 1970 census of population.* Reproduced by
          Hawaii State Library System.
Steponaitis, V. P.
 1978   Location theory and complex chiefdoms. In *Mississippian settlement patterns,* edited
          by B. D. Smith. New York: Academic Press. Pp. 417-453.
St. John, B.
 1852   *Village life in Egypt with sketches of the Said.* Vol. I. London: Chapman and Hall.
Stiles, D.
 1977   Ethnoarchaeology: A discussion of methods and applications. *Man* 12:87-103.
Stocker, Terrance L., L. Dutcher, S. Hargrove, and E. Cook
 1972   Social analysis of graffiti. *Journal of American Folklore* 85(338):356-366.
Struever, Stuart, and Felicia A. Holton
 1979   *Koster: Americans in search of their prehistoric past.* Garden City, N.Y.: Anchor
          Press.
Thomas, David Hurst
 1971   On the use of cumulative curves and numerical taxonomy. *American Antiquity* 36:
          206-209.
 1976   A Diegueño Shaman's wand: An object lesson illustrating the "heirloom hypothesis"
          The Journal of California Anthropology 3(1):128-132.

Tixier, Jacques
1963   Typologie de l'épipaléolithique du Maghreb. *Memoires du Centre de Recherches Anthropologiques Prehistoriques et Ethnographiques 2*:163-168.
Trigger, B. G.
1968   The determinants of settlement patterns. In *Settlement archaeology*, edited by K. C. Chang. Palo Alto: National Press Books.
Tringham, Ruth
1978   Experimentation, ethnoarchaeology, and the leapfrogs in archaeological methodology. In *Explorations in ethnoarchaeology*, edited by Richard A. Gould. A School of American Research Advanced Seminar Book. Albuquerque: University of New Mexico Press.
Tringham, R., G. Cooper, G. Odell, B. Voytek, and A. Whitman
1974 ·   Experimentation in the formation of edge damage: A new approach to lithic analysis. *Journal of Field Archaeology 1*:171-196.
Tucson Newspaper, Inc.
1976   *Tucson 'trends 1976*. Valley National Bank and Tucson Daily Citizen, Tucson.
Turnbaugh, William A.
1976   An on-campus alternative to the archaeological field school. *American Antiquity 41*: 208-211.
Turner, C. G., and L. Lofgren
1966   Household size of prehistoric western Pueblo Indians. *Southwestern Journal of Anthropology 22*:117-132.
Turner, Victor W.
1969   *The ritual process: Structure and anti-structure.* Chicago: University of Chicago Press.
U.S. Bureau of the Census
1975   *Historical statistics of the United States from Colonial Times to 1970.* Washington, D.C.: U.S. Government Printing Office.
United States Department of Commerce
1978   *Statistical abstract of the United States.* 99th Annual Edition. Bureau of the Census. Washington, D.C.: U.S. Government Printing Office.
United States House of Representatives
1964   *A primer on money.* The sub-committee on domestic finances, Committee on Banking and Currency. Washington, D.C.: U.S. Government Printing Office.
United States Mint
1954, 1955, 1956, 1964, 1965, 1968, 1974, 1976   *Annual Report of the Director.* Washington, D.C.: U.S. Government Printing Office.
Van Gennep, Arnold
1961   *Rites of passage.* Translated by M. B. Vizedon and G. L. Caffee. Chicago: University of Chicago Press.
Vance, J. E.
1970   *The merchant's world.* Englewood Cliffs, N.J.: Prentice-Hall.
Vogt, E.
1960   On the concept of structure and process in cultural anthropology. *American Anthropologist 62*(1):18-33.
Wagner, P. T.
1972   *Environments and peoples.* Englewood Cliffs, N.J.: Prentice-Hall.
Warren, P.
1969   *Minoan stone vases.* Cambridge: Cambridge University Press.
Webb, Eugene J., Donald T. Campbell, Richard D. Schwartz, and Lee Sechrest
1966   *Unobtrusive measures: Nonreactive research in the social sciences.* New York: Rand McNally.

White, Marian E.
  1977 An archaeological field school in New York State. In *Teaching and training in American archaeology: A survey of programs and philosophies,* edited by William P. McHugh, *Southern Illinois University at Carbondale, University Museum Studies* 10. Pp. 144-152.

Wilcox, David R.
  1975 A strategy for perceiving social groups in puebloan sites. In *Chapters in the prehistory of Eastern Arizona, IV. Fieldiana: Anthropology* 65:120-159.

Wilk, Richard, and Michael B. Schiffer
  1979 The archaeology of vacant lots in Tucson, Arizona. *American Antiquity 44:* 530-536.

Willcox, W. F., Editor
  1969 *Demographic monographs.* Vol. 7, *International migrations, I, Statistics.* New York: Gordon and Breach.

Wilmsen, E. N.
  1968 Functional analysis of flaked stone artifacts. *American Antiquity 33:*156-161.

Wilson, J. A.
  1964 *Signs and wonders upon Pharoah.* Chicago: University of Chicago Press.

Winlock, H. S.
  1942 *Excavations at Deir el Bahari, 1911-1931.* New York.

Wobst, H. M.
  1977 Stylistic behavior and information exchange. In *For the Director: Research essays in honor of James B. Griffin.* Anthropological Papers 61. Ann Arbor: Museum of Anthropology, University of Michigan. Pp. 317-342.

Woo, Douglas
  1978 Tony and heckler discuss the merits of racial tolerance. *Honolulu Advertiser,* December 13, p. A-1

Wood, C. M.
  1975 *Culture change.* Dubuque, Iowa: Wm. C. Brown.

Wood, Patrick
  1973 Survey of artifact distributions at a swap meet through time. Manuscript on deposit, Arizona State Museum Library, Tucson.

Woodbury, Richard B.
  1963 Purposes and concepts. In *The teaching of anthropology,* edited by David B. Mandelbaum, Gabriel W. Lasker, and Ethel M. Albert. *American Anthropological Association, Memoir* 94. Pp. 223-243.

Yellen, J. E.
  1977 *Archaeological approaches to the present: Models for reconstructing the past.* New York: Academic Press.

Young, Ellen
  1973 Lateral cycling of clothing within the nuclear family unit. Manuscript on deposit, Arizona State Museum Library, Tucson.

Young, Jean, and Jim Young
  1973 *The garage sale manual: Alternate economics for the people.* New York: Praeger.

Ziontz, L. M.
  1979 The museum community: Social and ethnic diversity on museum boards and in the museum audience. Unpublished M.A. thesis, University of Washington.

Zisfein, M. B.
  1976 Introduction. In *Celebrating the National Air and Space Museum,* CBS Publications.

Subject Index

STUDIES IN ARCHAEOLOGY

Consulting Editor: Stuart Struever

Department of Anthropology
Northwestern University
Evanston, Illinois

Charles R. McGimsey III. **Public Archeology**

Lewis R. Binford. **An Archaeological Perspective**

Muriel Porter Weaver. **The Aztecs, Maya, and Their Predecessors: Archaeology of Mesoamerica**

Joseph W. Michels. **Dating Methods in Archaeology**

C. Garth Sampson. **The Stone Age Archaeology of Southern Africa**

Fred T. Plog. **The Study of Prehistoric Change**

Patty Jo Watson (Ed.). **Archeology of the Mammoth Cave Area**

George C. Frison (Ed.). **The Casper Site: A Hell Gap Bison Kill on the High Plains**

W. Raymond Wood and R. Bruce McMillan (Eds.). **Prehistoric Man and His Environments: A Case Study in the Ozark Highland**

Kent V. Flannery (Ed.). **The Early Mesoamerican Village**

Charles E. Cleland (Ed.). **Cultural Change and Continuity: Essays in Honor of James Bennett Griffin**

Michael B. Schiffer. **Behavioral Archeology**

Fred Wendorf and Romuald Schild. **Prehistory of the Nile Valley**

Michael A. Jochim. **Hunter-Gatherer Subsistence and Settlement: A Predictive Model**

Stanley South. **Method and Theory in Historical Archeology**

Timothy K. Earle and Jonathon E. Ericson (Eds.). **Exchange Systems in Prehistory**

Stanley South (Ed.). **Research Strategies in Historical Archeology**

John E. Yellen. **Archaeological Approaches to the Present: Models for Reconstructing the Past**

Lewis R. Binford (Ed.). **For Theory Building in Archaeology: Essays on Faunal Remains, Aquatic Resources, Spatial Analysis, and Systemic Modeling**

James N. Hill and Joel Gunn (Eds.). **The Individual in Prehistory: Studies of Variability in Style in Prehistoric Technologies**

Michael B. Schiffer and George J. Gumerman (Eds.). **Conservation Archaeology: A Guide for Cultural Resource Management Studies**

Thomas F. King, Patricia Parker Hickman, and Gary Berg. **Anthropology in Historic Preservation: Caring for Culture's Clutter**

Richard E. Blanton. **Monte Albán: Settlement Patterns at the Ancient Zapotec Capital**

R. E. Taylor and Clement W. Meighan. **Chronologies in New World Archaeology**

Bruce D. Smith. **Prehistoric Patterns of Human Behavior: A Case Study in the Mississippi Valley**

Barbara L. Stark and Barbara Voorhies (Eds.). **Prehistoric Coastal Adaptations: The Economy and Ecology of Maritime Middle America**

Charles L. Redman, Mary Jane Berman, Edward V. Curtin, William T. Langhorne, Nina M. Versaggi, and Jeffery C. Wanser (Eds.). **Social Archeology: Beyond Subsistence and Dating**

Bruce D. Smith (Ed.). **Mississippian Settlement Patterns**

Lewis R. Binford. **Nunamiut Ethnoarchaeology**

J. Barto Arnold III and Robert Weddle. **The Nautical Archeology of Padre Island: The Spanish Shipwrecks of 1554**

Sarunas Milisauskas. **European Prehistory**

Brian Hayden (Ed.). **Lithic Use-Wear Analysis**

William T. Sanders, Jeffrey R. Parsons, and Robert S. Santley. **The Basin of Mexico: Ecological Processes in the Evolution of a Civilization**

David L. Clarke. **Analytical Archaeologist: Collected Papers of David L. Clarke. Edited and Introduced by His Colleagues**

Arthur E. Spiess. **Reindeer and Caribou Hunters: An Archaeological Study**

Elizabeth S. Wing and Antoinette B. Brown. **Paleonutrition: Method and Theory in Prehistoric Foodways.**

John W. Rick. **Prehistoric Hunters of the High Andes**

Timothy K. Earle and Andrew L. Christenson (Eds.). **Modeling Change in Prehistoric Economics**

Thomas F. Lynch (Ed.). **Guitarrero Cave: Early Man in the Andes**

Fred Wendorf and Romuald Schild. **Prehistory of the Eastern Sahara**

Henri Laville, Jean-Philippe Rigaud, and James Sackett. **Rock Shelters of the Perigord: Stratigraphy and Archaeological Succession**

Duane C. Anderson and Holmes A. Semken, Jr. (Eds.). **The Cherokee Excavations: Holocene Ecology and Human Adaptations in Northwestern Iowa**

Anna Curtenius Roosevelt. **Parmana: Prehistoric Maize and Manioc Subsistence along the Amazon and Orinoco**

Fekri A. Hassan. **Demographic Archaeology**

G. Barker. **Landscape and Society: Prehistoric Central Italy**

Lewis R. Binford. **Bones: Ancient Men and Modern Myths**